INTERNATIONAL DIMENSIONS OF
HUMANITARIAN LAW

UNITED NATIONS
EDUCATIONAL, SCIENTIFIC AND CULTURAL
ORGANIZATION

International Dimensions
of Humanitarian Law

HENRY DUNANT INSTITUTE – GENEVA
UNESCO – PARIS
MARTINUS NIJHOFF PUBLISHERS
DORDRECHT/BOSTON/LONDON

Library of Congress Cataloging in Publication Data

International dimensions of humanitarian law / Henry Dunant Institute.
    p.   cm.
    Translated from the French.
    Bibliography: p.
    Includes index.
    ISBN 9231023713
    1. War victims--Legal status, laws, etc.   I. Institut Henry
-Dunant.
JX5136.I594 1988
341.6'7--dc19   88-25927
                                                                     CIP

ISBN 92-3-102371-3

Published in 1988 by

Unesco
7 Place de Fontenoy, 75700 Paris, France

Henri Dunant Institute
114 Rue de Lausanne, 1202 Geneva, Switzerland

and

Martinus Nijhoff Publishers
P.O. Box 163, 3300 AD Dordrecht, The Netherlands

Sold and distributed in the U.S.A. and Canada
by Kluwer Academic Publishers,
101 Philip Drive, Norwell, MA 02061, U.S.A.

In all other countries, sold and distributed
by Kluwer Academic Publishers Group,
P.O. Box 322, 3300 AH Dordrecht, The Netherlands

Also sold throughout the world by Unesco
through its sales agents

Printed in the Netherlands.

CONTENTS

PART II

THE DEVELOPMENT OF INTERNATIONAL HUMANITARIAN LAW

PART III

THE LAW OF ARMED CONFLICTS

Section 1: Conflicts of international character

Section 2: Conflicts of a non-international character

PART IV

APPLICATION OF INTERNATIONAL HUMANITARIAN LAW

FOREWORD

In 1978, Unesco took the initiative of commissioning the preparation of this publication from the Henry Dunant Institute. The General Conference of Unesco had expressed the wish that co-operation with the International Committee of the Red Cross, the Henry Dunant Institute and the International Institute of Humanitarian Law should lead to the development of an international programme for the teaching of international humanitarian law (20C/Resolutions 3/1.5 and 2.3/3).

The present collective work forms the basis of this international programme within the framework of Unesco's Plan for the Development of Human Rights Teaching.

Unesco wishes to thank the Henry Dunant Institute, without the help of which the initial project could never have become a reality, as well as all the contributing authors whose conviction and co-operation have made the book possible. Unesco wishes, in particular, to render homage to the memory of Richard R. Baxter and Claude Pilloud who both died before the original French edition was published: their devotion to the cause of humanitarian law survives them in this publication.

It is hoped that the publication of this volume, which, in its original French edition, coincided with the 40th anniversary of Unesco and the International Year of Peace proclaimed in 1986 by the United Nations General Assembly, will help to reinforce the determination of the international community to achieve the aim of the founders of Unesco, namely, to construct the defences of peace in the minds of men.

We dedicate this work to the millions of men, women and children who are, today, still victims of war.

UNESCO

PREFACE

All efforts in the sphere of international humanitarian law are meaningless if they do not help alleviate the untold suffering caused by armed conflicts. I am greatly pleased that this textbook has been published because I firmly believe that it satisfies this expectation.

International humanitarian law finds its origin in Henry Dunant's spontaneous gesture in helping the victims left unassisted after the bloody battle of Solferino. Reflection followed very closely upon this action. To make it possible to assist victims of conflicts and to make such assistance standard practice, medical personnel needed to have a status guaranteeing them protection during combat. He had for that reason to appeal to the States which, once won over, adopted the first Geneva Convention in 1864.

The development of international humanitarian law – a process entailing humanitarian action, careful consideration of the problems encountered and codification to facilitate further action – is an ongoing process; the latest attempt at codification led to the adoption by States in 1977 of the Protocols additional to the 1949 Geneva Conventions.

But humanitarian issues have become considerably more complex in the course of time and, correspondingly, so has international humanitarian law: ten articles in 1864, more than 600 since 1977. To ensure that this process evolves in the right direction and that humanitarian law does not remain a dead letter it has therefore become essential to explain the meaning of this law and the obligations it places on those who must comply with it.

Apart from considerable effort, dissemination of knowledge about humanitarian law involves the adaptation of objectives and methods to the numerous classes of people intended to be reached. Among these groups, academics do not seem to warrant priority over military personnel whose instruction in this sphere is clearly a necessity. However, one must understand that given the important rôle of universities in the dissemination of knowledge, this volume is addressed particularly to academics and students.

It is in universities that the future leaders of a country become aware of international humanitarian law, that training is given to people who will become specialized jurists attached to the armed forces, and it is there also that future teachers receive their education. I firmly believe that this textbook will be a very valuable instrument for imparting this teaching of international humanitarian law.

It is my convictior that all those who have collaborated on this textbook have contributed, like the doctor who performs operations on the war wounded, the relief worker who brings food to a starving population or the delegate of a neutral organization visiting prisoners and bringing them news of their families, to humanitarian action.

It is my hope that their diverse origins and their collective endeavour in this fine work of dissemination may also contribute to a better understanding between men and, thereby, to peace on earth.

ALEXANDRE HAY
Former President of the International Committee
of the Red Cross

CONTRIBUTORS

ABI-SAAB Georges: Professor of International Law at the Graduate Institute of International Studies, Geneva, Switzerland.

ADACHI Sumio: Professor at the National Defence Academy, Japan.

BAXTER Richard R.: Professor of Law at Harvard University, Cambridge, Massachussetts, USA. Judge at the International Court of Justice at the Hague. Deceased.

BLISHCHENKO Igor P.: Director of the Department of International Law at Patrice Lumumba People's Friendship University, Moscow, USSR.

BLIX Hans: Former Minister of Foreign Affairs of Sweden; Director-General of the International Atomic Energy Agency, Vienna, Austria.

DRAPER G.I.A.D.: Professor Emeritus of Law at the University of Sussex, United Kingdom.

EIDE Asbjörn: Director of the Norwegian Institute of Human Rights, Oslo, Norway.

HERCZEGH Géza: Dean of the Faculty of Law and Professor of International Law at the Janus Pannonius University of Pécs, Hungary.

NAHLIK Stanislaw E.: Professor Emeritus of Public International Law at the Jagiellonian University, Cracow, Poland.

NDAM NJOYA Adamou: Former Minister of Education of the Republic of Cameroon, Plenipotentiary Minister.

PARTSCH Karl Joseph: Professor Emeritus of Public Law at the University of Bonn, Federal Republic of Germany.

PICTET Jean S.: Honorary Vice President of the ICRC, Geneva, Switzerland; Former President and Director of the Henry-Dunant Institute, Geneva, Switzerland.

PILLOUD Claude: Former Legal Advisor and Director of the ICRC, Geneva, Switzerland. Deceased.

REZEK José Francisco: Professor of Constitutional Law at the University of Brazil; Judge at the Supreme Court of Brazil, Brazilia, Brazil.

RUDA José María: President of the International Court of Justice at the Hague; Professor of Public International Law at the University of Buenos Aires, Argentina.

SANDOZ Yves: Director, Principles, Law and Relations with the Movement, ICRC, Geneva, Switzerland.

SULTAN Hamed: Former Professor of Public Law at Cairo University. Member of the Institute of Egypt.

UMOZURIKE U. Oji: Professor at the Faculty of Law of the University of Nigeria, Nigeria.

VASAK Karel: Former Director of the Division of Human Rights and Peace and Former Legal Advisor of Unesco, Paris, France.

Translations from French and Spanish by the Translation Service of the International Committee of the Red Cross.

Revised and edited for the English edition by Jiri TOMAN.

ABBREVIATIONS

AFDI	*Annuaire Français de Droit International* (Paris)
AJIL	*American Journal of International Law* (Washington D.C.)
BYIL	*British Yearbook of International Law* (London)
CDDH	Diplomatic Conference on the Reaffirmation and Development of International Humanitarian Law Applicable in Armed Conflicts, Geneva 1974–1977 (abbreviation used in the Conference documents).
Commentary to the Geneva Conventions of 1949 I–IV	*The Geneva Conventions of 12 August 1949: Commentary published under the general editorship of Jean S. Pictet:* 4 vols.

I. Geneva Convention for the Amelioration of the Condition of the Wounded and Sick in Armed Forces in the Field, Geneva, ICRC, 1952, 446 p.

II. Geneva Convention for the Amelioration of the Condition of the Wounded, Sick and Shipwrecked Members of Armed Forces at Sea, Geneva, ICRC, 1960, 320 p.

III. Geneva Convention Relative to the Treatment of Prisoners of War, Geneva, ICRC, 1960, 764 p.

IV. Geneva Convention Relative to the Protection of Civilian Persons in Time of War, Geneva, ICRC, 1958, 660 p.

Conference of	Conference of Government Experts on the Re-

Government Experts (1971), *Report*	affirmation and Development of International Humanitarian Law Applicable in Armed Conflicts, Geneva, 24 May–12 June 1971, *Report on the Work of the Conference*, Geneva, ICRC, 1971, 121 p.
Conference of Government Experts (1972), *Report*	Conference of Government Experts on the Reaffirmation and Development of International Humanitarian Law Applicable in Armed Conflicts, Second Session, 3 May–3 June 1972, *Report on the Work of the Conference*, Geneva, ICRC, 1972, 2 vols. 209 p., 116 p.
Deltenre	Deltenre Marcel, *Recueil général des lois et coutumes de la guerre terrestre, maritime, sous-marine et aérienne, d'après les actes élaborés par les Conférences internationales depuis 1856.* Brussels, Wellen-Pay, 1943 LXXVI, 887 p.
1949 Geneva Convention I–IV	Geneva Conventions for the Protection of War Victims of 12 August 1949:
	Ist Geneva Convention for the Amelioration of the Condition of the Wounded and Sick in Armed Forces in the Field;
	IInd Geneva Convention for the Amelioration of the Condition of the Wounded, Sick and Shipwrecked Members of Armed Forces at Sea;
	IIIrd Geneva Convention Relative to the Treatment of Prisoners of War;
	IVth Geneva Convention Relative to the Protection of Civilian Persons in Time of War.
Geneva Diplomatic Conference of 1949	Diplomatic Conference convened by the Swiss Federal Council for the Establishment of International Conventions for the Protection of War Victims and Held at Geneva from 21 April to 12 August 1949.
Geneva Diplomatic Conference of 1974–1977	Diplomatic Conference on the Reaffirmation and Development of International Humanitarian Law Applicable in Armed Conflicts, Geneva, 1974–1977.
The Hague Convention IV	Convention No. IV respecting the Laws and Customs of War on Land, signed at The Hague on 18 October 1907.
The Hague	Convention for the Protection of Cultural Property in

Convention of 1954	the Event of Armed Conflict, signed at The Hague on 14 May 1954.
The Hague Protocol of 1954	Protocol for the Protection of Cultural Property in the Event of Armed Conflict, signed at The Hague on 14 May 1954.
The Hague Regulations of 1907	The Hague Regulations concerning the Laws and Customs of War on Land, annexed to The Hague Convention No. IV of 1907.
The Hague Regulations of 1954	Regulations for the Execution of the Convention for the Protection of Cultural Property in the Event of Armed Conflict, annexed to The Hague Convention of 14 May 1954.
ICRC	International Committee of the Red Cross.
IMT	International Military Tribunal.
International Red Cross Handbook	*International Red Cross Handbook*, 12th edition, Geneva, I.C.R.C., L.R.C.S. in collaboration with the Henry-Dunant Institute, 1983, 744 p.
IRRC	*International Review of the Red Cross* (Geneva).
LRCS	League of Red Cross and Red Crescent Societies.
Nahlik: *Protection internationale des biens culturels*	Nahlik, Stanislaw. "La protection internationale des biens culturels en cas de conflit armé". *Recueil des cours de l'Académie de droit international de La Haye*, Vol. 120–I, 1967, 00. 61–163.
Official Records of the Geneva Diplomatic Conference 1974–1977	*Official Records of the Diplomatic Conference on the Reaffirmation and Development of International Humanitarian Law Applicable in Armed Conflicts, Geneva (1974–1977)* 17 vols., Bern, Federal Political Department, 1978.
Protocol I	Protocol Additional to the Geneva Conventions of 12 August 1949, and Relating to the Protection of Victims of International Armed Conflicts (Protocol I), Geneva, 8 June 1977.
Protocol II	Protocol Additional to the Geneva Conventions of 12 August 1949, and Relating to the Protection of Victims of Non-International Armed Conflicts (Protocol II), Geneva, 8 June 1977.
Record of The Hague	Intergovernmental Conference on the Protection of

Conference of 1954 Cultural Property in the Event of Armed Conflict – The Hague, 1954: *Record of the Conference*. The Hague, Staatsdrukkerij- en uitgeverijbedrijf, 1960, 452 p.

Recueil des Cours *Recueil des cours de l'Académie de droit international de La Haye, Collected Courses of The Hague Academy of International Law* (Leyden)

UNTS *United Nations Treaty Series*, Treaties and international agreements registered or filed and recorded with the Secretariat of the United Nations, 1946–

INTERNATIONAL HUMANITARIAN LAW: DEFINITION

JEAN PICTET

1. The purpose of international humanitarian law is to regulate hostilities in order to attenuate hardship[1]

Humanitarian law constitutes that important part of international public law which finds its inspiration in humane ideals, and which focuses on the protection of the individual in time of war.

When the author of the present paper proposed this definition, it was criticized for bringing together two distinct notions, one of a legal nature and the other moral. This particular discipline, however, is based precisely on transposing moral – and more especially humanitarian – concerns into international law. Consequently, the definition would seem to be appropriate.

The fact that this law relates so closely to man enables it, moreover, to take on its true dimensions; it is on these legal provisions and no other that the life and freedom of countless human beings may depend if, by mischance, war casts its sinister shadow over the world.

The term "international humanitarian law", which soon gained the approval of most publicists has now become official.[2] Humanitarian law has two branches: the law of Geneva and the law of The Hague.

2. The law of Geneva or, by its correct name, humanitarian law tends to safeguard military personnel placed *hors de combat* and persons not taking part in hostilities

This law has been given form in the four Geneva Conventions of 1949, supplemented by their 1977 Protocols, the whole forming a monumental legal work of some six hundred articles and setting forth rules for the protection of the individual in the event of armed conflict. Being of a specifically humanitarian nature and a paramount factor of civilization and peace, the law of Geneva incarnates the very ideal of the Red Cross. Moreover, it was the International Committee of the

Red Cross which gave it its initial impulse and brought it into being. Now the ICRC, the neutral organization of the Red Cross in time of conflict, finds therein the necessary legal basis for its work of protection and assistance.

The Geneva texts were drawn up solely for the benefit of war victims; unlike the Hague texts, they do not grant States any rights to the individual's detriment. In Geneva an era was opened in which man and the principles of humanity come first.

Nowadays the distinction between the Geneva Conventions and those of The Hague is less accentuated than in the past, owing to the modern development of warfare and the adoption of the Protocols Additional to the Geneva Conventions. Protocol I contains an extremely important part on the protection of the civilian population against the effects of war, and another on the conduct of combatants, subjects already incorporated in The Hague Conventions. The recent efforts to ban or restrict the use of cruel or indiscriminate weapons may be considered to be a step further in regulating combat; they have resulted in the "Convention on Prohibitions or Restrictions on the Use of Certain Conventional Weapons Which May be Deemed to be Excessively Injurious or to have Indiscriminate Effects", which was concluded under the auspices of the United Nations at Geneva on 10 October 1980.

But although the traditional distinction between the law of Geneva and the law of The Hague has become less apparent, it must be maintained because it stems from an essential difference in kind.

3. The law of The Hague, or the law of warfare, determines the rights and duties of belligerents in the conduct of operations and limits the choice of warfare methods

The texts of The Hague are also unquestionably of humanitarian inspiration. It is their purpose however to regulate hostilities and they are accordingly based in part on military necessities and the preservation of the State.

The essence of all these texts originated from The Hague Conventions of 1899, revised in 1907. However, large sections of the Conventions passed within the scope of the law of Geneva in 1929 and 1949, where indeed they logically belonged, that is, the status of prisoners of war, of the wounded and shipwrecked in hostilities at sea, and of civilians in occupied territories. It might justifiably be said that, in the 1977 Protocol relating to the protection of the civilian population, the "Geneva point of view" has won the day, whereas the conduct of combatants tends to remain a subject within the moral realm of The Hague.

4. At this point, we should briefly examine some of the connections that exist between international humanitarian law and human rights legislation, the purpose of the latter being to guarantee at all times that individuals benefit from their basic rights and freedoms and that they are protected from social evils

The promoting institution in this case is the United Nations, as successor to the League of Nations. Within their own geographical boundaries, regional institutions such as the Council of Europe and the Organization of American States have also made their contributions.

In terms of written documents, international humanitarian law was first consecrated in the initial Geneva Convention of 1864, and human rights in the 1948 Universal Declaration. But in terms of ideas, both movements have the same historical and philosophical origins: both were the product of ancient times when it was necessary to protect human beings against the evil forces that threatened them. This conception nonetheless gave rise to two distinct efforts: limiting the evils of war and protecting man against despotism. Over the centuries, they have developed side by side.

Certainly, the principles of human rights are of a more general nature and application, whereas humanitarian law has a special and exceptional character, since it applies, in fact, when war prevents human rights from being exercised or limits their application.

Yet the two legal systems are different; while humanitarian law is only applicable in cases of armed conflict, human rights are operative above all in times of peace, since their instruments contain waiver clauses for cases of conflict. Furthermore, human rights essentially concern relationships between a State and its own subjects, whereas humanitarian law concerns those between a State and enemy subjects.

In conclusion, the two systems are related but distinct, and must remain so. They are complementary, and indeed complement each other admirably.

If we were to bring them together under one all-embracing title, we might think of the term "humane law", which would be defined as follows: humane law consists of all international legal provisions ensuring respect for and full development of the human being.

---

1. The United Nations prefer to use the synonymous expression "law of armed conflicts".
The International Committee of the Red Cross, for its part, has adopted the following as a full definition:
By "international humanitarian law applicable in armed conflicts" the International Committee of the Red Cross means international rules, established by treaties or custom, which are specifically intended to solve humanitarian problems directly arising from international or non-international armed conflicts and which, for humanitarian reasons, limit the right of parties to a conflict to use the methods and means of warfare of their choice or protect persons and property that are, or may be, affected by conflict.

2. The term is used in the title of the Geneva Diplomatic Conference, 1974–1977, on "the reaffirmation and development of international humanitarian law applicable in armed conflicts".

PART I

NATURE OF INTERNATIONAL
HUMANITARIAN LAW AND ITS PLACE IN
INTERNATIONAL LAW

INTRODUCTION

HUMANITARIAN IDEAS SHARED BY DIFFERENT SCHOOLS OF THOUGHT AND CULTURAL TRADITIONS

JEAN PICTET

The modern world has placed its hopes in internationalism and therein no doubt its future lies. Now, in an international environment, man's rights can only be on what is universal, on ideas capable of bringing together men of all races, cultures and creeds. Within this environment, therefore, one must guard against one's subjectivity and education, for an adult is often a prisoner of ideas received in childhood and upheld by his social milieu. In study and especially in legislation, simplicity and objectivity must be observed in respect of one's sources and a positive attitude adopted.

Similarity alone can be the basis for universality and, although men are different, human nature is the same the world over.

International humanitarian law in particular has this universal vocation, since it applies to all men and countries. In formulating and perfecting this law, to which it gave birth and of which it encourages the promotion and dissemination, the International Committee of the Red Cross has sought precisely this common ground and put forward rules acceptable to all because they are fully consistent with human nature. This is, moreover, what has ensured the strength and durability of these rules.

However, today the uniformity of human psychological make-up and the universality of standards governing the behaviour of nations are recognized, and no longer is there belief in the supremacy of any one civilization: indeed, the plurality of cultures and the need to take an interest in them and study them in depth is acknowledged.

This leads to an awareness that humanitarian principles are common to all human communities wherever they may be. When different customs, ethics and philosophies are gathered for comparison, and when they are melted down, their particularities eliminated and only what is general extracted, one is left with a pure substance which is the heritage of all mankind.

It is equally important to be familiar with the evolution of humanitarian thought through the ages and to see what circumstances have forged the law we are studying.

Finally, those who, in every country, work to disseminate knowledge of humanitarian law so that it may be applied and respected throughout the world, will find in local traditions and in the symbols peculiar to each race the form of expression and the imagery which will make it more readily understood and accepted.

For these reasons the editors of this manual decided to begin it with accounts by several authors of the development of humanitarian ideas in different schools of thought and cultural traditions.

By the very fact that each contribution has to describe a particular concept, they vary considerably both in form and content. We have retained their original colour, the better to achieve the desired aim, and even some ideological data which may appear unrelated to the subject on hand but which are bound up with, and therefore make clearer, the concept that the author is expressing.

CHAPTER I

THE AFRICAN CONCEPT

ADAMOU NDAM NJOYA

From what we now know, it would seem that Africa was the main place where man emerged and political society evolved. It is therefore not surprising that we turn to Africa to begin our research into the humanitarian principles which keep in check the violence that human communities have encountered since the very beginning of their existence. The human being has been respected in Africa in various degrees and situations at different periods of history. That respect, when studied at the stage of African independence, can be seen to have a special character. It was different during the period of foreign domination and colonialisation, that is, when Africa lost its national and international character in political, economic and social fields, not to mention the changes which occurred in ideas and thought. Now a new stage has succeeded those two periods; namely the independence which Africa began to rediscover in the sixties when Africans took over the management of their national and international affairs, keen to recover their national identities and cultural traditions.

A. Pre-Colonial Era: The Sacred Nature of the Human Being in Independent Africa

In the pre-colonial era Africa comprised independent cities and principalities, kingdoms and empires. Their relations were based on sovereignty, independence and cooperation. There was a real system of African states. That community of African states was characterized by the flexibility and permeability of the frontiers between the diverse units of which it was composed, making for the *rapprochement* of peoples.

In peacetime, relations between the authorities of the various states depended on the exchange of messages between sovereigns and on the establishment of diplomatic relations. As in all ancient civilizations, foreigners who passed through or stayed were hospitably treated. The Emperor of Mali, Kankan Moussa, had diplomatic relations with the Maghreb sultans and with Cairo.

After a pilgrimage to Mecca, he brought back architects, poets and Arab scientists, all captivated by the Mali sovereign's humanity as well as by his wealth. The Songhay emperor, Mamadou Touré, developed cultural relations with north Africa and the Arabs to the east by exchanges of teachers and Arab scientists. Several universities and cultural centres existed in his empire – Djenné, Timbuktu, Oualata. In these empires and the kingdoms which succeeded them, great importance was attached to human values.

The ease with which frontiers could be crossed was most notable in the border regions of kingdoms and principalities where the populations held the same values, making greater understanding between sovereigns easier and contributing to the elimination of conflicts.

In any state, the village and the family were the main constituents. Land counted for little and it was for that reason that, for African states, borders were something mobile and indefinite.[1]

The rights and obligations of the individual at that time must be seen in that collective context and in terms of the traditional obligations to the family and the village. Humanitarian questions, human rights and rights of the individual of that time cannot be understood out of the group context. They were always of a collective or "human rights at large" nature.[2]

The community comprised all the families which had a head. The unity of the community and the distribution of labour depended on the African family spirit. The head of the family, like the sovereign at a higher level, ensured the continuity of the human race, the family and the whole community with the basic concern to enlarge it. In the first place the members of the family had to be protected and in the second place those who were outside the family circle were to be brought in. As a result there was, in times of conflict and war, a humanitarian atmosphere intended to protect not only members of the family but also those who might increase it.

Private ownership developed within and on the basis of common property, hence the apparition of state authorities differing from those in Europe. They were a form of monarchy which was limited and decentralized, leaving the local communities a large measure of autonomy. Slavery was minor in scale. A prisoner of war who was not ritually sacrificed became a slave, often with some right to own property, and soon integrated into the family which owned him.[3]

A study of the conduct of conflicts in pre-colonial Africa shows that before the outbreak of conflict the parties tried to settle the dispute peacefully. In Togo such attempts were entrusted to nobles of the two adversary groups; in Burkina Faso to the imperial guards; in Burundi and Rwanda to notables; and in Uganda and Kenya to the elders. Only when all efforts to achieve conciliation had come to nought did the parties resort to force.

There were rules also governing the start of hostilities. It was announced by the beating of drums or the blowing of horns, or by a warning volley of arrows.[4] In theory, hostilities did not start until the adversary was aware of the intention to attack and of the reasons for it. Thus, as in most ancient civilizations, war was preceded by a declaration delivered by messengers: the *griots* (witchdoctors-cum-minstrels) in Senegal and Burkina Faso, the notables in Mali. War and the defence of the realm were the privilege of nobles, the highest social class. A veritable ethical conduct in war was taught to the young nobles before they took part in the fighting. The conduct of war was considered as noble, conforming to rules and principles. Some of these rules of honour applied to the conduct of war and the behaviour of the warriors; others were concerned with the treatment of non-combatants and their belongings. Tradition forbade the use of weapons considered to be too dangerous. A traditional Bantu saying in East Africa is "you hit but you do not kill". This brings to mind the definition of superfluous injury, drafted in 1973 by a group of experts: "... if a combatant can be put out of action by injury, he should not be killed...".[5] The prohibition against weapons likely to cause unnecessary suffering included the ban on poisoned arrows or spearheads in war.[6] There were also restrictions on methods of combat. A fallen enemy should not be killed, a disarmed enemy should not be struck, the fight should always be face to face. Elsewhere, in forest countries for instance, there was no tradition of clemency. The enemy was slaughtered. Fighting was interrupted by truces during harvest and sowing times. Any person who sought refuge during wartime in a place of asylum became sacrosanct.

However, these regulations were often limited to fighting between adversaries of the same ethnic group. They applied only within the same branch since the African mentality has a need for the feeling of solidarity with one's group, family, tribe or race.[7]

So far as the treatment of non-combatants was concerned, the ethical code of war ensured respect and protection for women, children and old people. Respect for women was imperative: they represented the "origin", the "source" of life. The child represented innocence, while the elderly were considered to be close to the spirits of ancestors.[8]

In Burkina Faso custom forbade the killing of persons taking no part in the fighting. The wounded of both sides had to be cared for. The dead had to be respected and were entitled to a decent burial.

In other tribes, civilians – the non-combatants – were left with no protection and they were treated like prisoners of war. Some tribes promoted the assimilation of civilians from the adversary by encouraging marriage between young warriors and women of the enemy camp.[9]

It is interesting to consider the role played by the Tallensi women who participated in conflicts by bringing water to the warriors, removing the wounded and the dead from the battlefield and shouting encouragement to the combatants. They took an active part in fighting even though they did not carry weapons. As they had often originated from the adverse party, they could sometimes be impartial or at least not too enthusiastic in their support for either side.[10]

The treatment meted out to prisoners of war depended on their social status and their functions in the group. Depending on regions and tribes, prisoners of war were reduced to slavery, ransomed or killed.[11] Others, as already mentioned, were assimilated into the population.

Such assimilation of the prisoner is a manifestation of the respect for the human being, for man, the image of his creator who transcends everything: the dignity of man as the basis of the family, the community and of society was recognized. His position had to be consolidated, safeguarded at all times, in peacetime and in war.

In traditional Africa there were innumerable sacred places (trees, ancestral huts, shrines in which fetiches were kept, places where initiation ceremonies were held, and so on). There was therefore respect for places of a religious nature, of culture and art.

In Africa as elsewhere, conflict entailed destruction of civilian property. E. Bello mentions the destruction of old records and books in conquered villages merely because the inhabitants did not hold the same beliefs as the victors. So it was with works of art. For the Tallensi, looting for personal gain and taking home objects stolen from an enemy was forbidden, but that did not prevent them from eating an enemy's food or destroying his property.[12]

As in other ancient civilizations, the question of reparations arose with the end of a war. It was usual for the two chiefs to meet, in the presence of a member of a neutral community, to balance reparations in cash or in kind against the damage suffered.[13]

As in every war, slaughter and breaches of humanitarian rules were inevitable, but these were exceptions confirming the rule that human beings must be protected. Humanity included, and was understood to mean, solidarity and the recognition of common traits in the human species which longed for happiness and justice.

Of course, the rules were not the same or applied uniformly throughout the continent. They varied with the region, civilization, ethnic group and religion. The lack of source material does not permit definite conclusions. The history of Africa is being written and future research will reveal more details of our picture of humanitarian law in Africa.

The widely varying application of humanitarian rules and the many examples of their violation have led some writers to take an unfavourable view of African tradition in that field.[14] Yet humanitarian rules for the conduct of war in all ancient civilizations – Egyptian, Greek, Roman, Assyrian, European – were also marred by as many, if not more, breaches. The humanization of war is a process. Its ideal is to eliminate war and the use of force from human society. If that ideal cannot be achieved, efforts to eliminate the worst consequences of recourse to force must be continued. We subscribe to Yoland Diallo's conclusion that "many principles expressed in the Geneva Conventions are to be found in the law of war in pre-colonial Africa. It was only after the introduction of slavery and the inroads of colonialism into Africa south of the Sahara that traditional societies began to disintegrate, causing the code of honour to fall into disuse in war. However, the memory of this code of honour is kept alive in the narratives of the storytellers, and the code perhaps could be revived as a means of humanizing present-day conflicts. Perhaps Africa will remember, now that it is reviving its own cultural values, that this sense of humanity is one of its permanent values and that it must accept the obligation not to let those values be forgotten."[15]

B. Impact of Foreign Domination and Influence: Desecration of Human Life

Colonialization broke up the historical pattern and cut the geographic, economic, legal and human ties with the empires which preceded it. One consequence of this break was that Africans did not look upon international law as a product of their own tradition but as retrograde colonial interference. It is therefore important to study more thoroughly the history of Africa and to demonstrate that inter-state law was peculiar to Africans, to their traditions and to their history.

The colonization of Africa reduced to nought the continent's participation in international life, preventing the development of political ideas, concepts and principles. This stagnation prevailed from the end of the 18th century until the 1960s. It was a period of colonial aggression which relegated humane feelings to the background. The traditional concept that human life was sacred was derided. The new state system showed a different face, keeping its distance from the individual and the family spirit. It was there for no other purpose than to crush, dominate and destroy the African. Respect for human dignity meant respect for the white man. The dominating values were western. Another form of aggression was developed: members of a community and even of a family were often in opposing camps fighting, without knowing it, to consolidate the foreign power. In such circumstances societies and families were disorganized. It was the end of a belief in human values, sowing doubt in the mind by profaning man and destroying the natural order.

In every civilization religion is important to humanitarian ideas. Christianity, although pure in essence, appeared during the colonial era to be the religion of the dominator, a prop to a policy of inequality, and representative of the political power. Islam was different. Those who had brought it had left and the African converts to it interpreted it in their own way, while maintaining their traditional values.

Jomo Kenyatta stressed the demoralizing impact of European aggression and colonization in Africa. While tribal wars had affected relatively few people, war waged by Europeans with little or no regard for law and human suffering, resulted in the loss of many innocent human lives. That had unsettled the harmony and stability of the African way of life.[16] Bello gives many examples of such devastating effects of colonization: the Nuer people, the Arusha society in the face of German colonization, the encouraging of inter-tribal fighting for causes quite alien to the African people and which destroyed their solidarity (arms deliveries, attacks on civilian populations).[17] It was in that way that the French colonialists, wishing to obtain slaves, gave the Moors weapons and encouraged them to cross the Senegal river to attack the tribes, capture slaves and slaughter those who resisted. The British and the Germans fought whoever would not submit to their domination. That is why, like Kenyatta, we must ask whether it would not have been better to leave the Africans to their tribal warfare instead of imposing on them "the so-called civilizing missions which meant the subjugation of the African races to a perpetual state of serfdom".[18]

C. The Road to Independence

One century of foreign domination, however, was not enough to destroy the bases of African values. From the first decade of political independence, the fundamental idea which emerged and spread throughout Africa was to return to traditional values and to African institutions, the sole foundation for the future of African society.

Africa will recover its unity only in the restitution and rediscovery of its moral and cultural values, and in the return to that humanism which is an inalienable trait of the African personality.

With few exceptions (e.g. Egypt and Ethiopia), African countries took no part in drawing up the rules of the law of war. Their voice was heard resoundingly for the first time during the procedure leading to the reaffirmation and development of international humanitarian law applicable in armed conflicts, beginning at the International Human Rights Conference in Teheran from 22 April to 13 May 1968.[19] The Geneva Diplomatic Conference which met in the years 1974–77 became the forum at which the states of the "Third World", and hence of Africa, were able to express their fundamental concern for the development of humanitarian law.[20]

Uppermost in the minds of the African states represented at that conference were wars of national liberation, civil wars and the employment of mercenaries.

The states of the "Third World" called for wars of liberation to be recognized as international armed conflicts. Their demand was met: at the first session of the Diplomatic Conference, Committee I approved Article 1 (paragraph 4) which says that "armed conflicts in which peoples are fighting against colonial domination and alien occupation and against racist regimes in the exercise of their right of self-determination, as enshrined in the Charter of the United Nations and the Declaration of Principles of International Law concerning Friendly Relations and Co-operation among States" are included in the situations referred to in Article 2 common to the Geneva Conventions which defines armed international conflicts. This had unquestionably been a fundamental problem and it was raised at the beginning of the Conference in the opening address by the President of Mauritania, in which he expressed the hope of the "Third World" countries that the Conference would take their lawful rights into account.

Concerned to protect the victims of non-international conflicts while safeguarding their recently acquired national sovereignty and the principle of non-interference in internal affairs, the African states supported the simplified draft of Protocol II.[21] In that way it was possible to reach a compromise and avert the danger that a protocol on internal conflicts might not be adopted.

Taking recent conflicts into account, the African states were concerned by the phenomenon of mercenaries – representing colonialist regimes and racial repression. In the Organization of African Unity efforts had resulted in the adoption of a convention in 1972. In the United Nations several resolutions have condemned as a crime the employment of mercenaries by colonial and racist regimes against liberation movements struggling for their freedom and their independence of the colonial yoke and foreign domination.[22]

On the initiative of Nigeria the 1974–77 Diplomatic Conference adopted Article 47 of the Additional Protocol I. This defines the mercenary and denies him combatant or prisoner-of-war status.[23]

African states actively participated in the drafting of the new humanitarian law. They approved it and several have since ratified these new instruments, the 1977 Protocols additional to the Geneva Conventions. Other states will undoubtedly soon follow suit.

International humanitarian law as it stands today is not a law which is alien to Africans. It is in line with their most ancient humanitarian traditions. It reflects the concerns which Africans shared and the constructive efforts to which they contributed.

Many African notables, however, are disturbed by the breaches of humanitarian rules committed in the conflicts which ravage the continent. The modern soldier is trained to kill, in both international and internal conflicts. The only way to avoid breaches is to apply the fundamental principles of international humanitarian law. To be applied they must be known.

> But in order to attain this end it is not sufficient for sovereigns to promulgate new laws. It is essential, too, that they make these laws known among all people, so that when a war is declared, the men called upon to take up arms to defend the causes of the belligerent States, may be thoroughly impregnated with the special rights and duties attached to the execution of such a command.[24]

Notes

1. Westermann, D. H., *The African To-day and To-morrow*, 3rd ed., London and New York, 1949, pp. 28 ff. and 129 ff.
2. Mazrui, Ali A., *Towards a Pax Africana. A Study of Ideology and Ambition: Essays on Independant Africa*, Chicago, The University of Chicago Press, 1967, pp. 118 ff. and pp. 135 ff.
3. *General History of Africa, I. Methodology and African Prehistory*, Ki-Zerbo, J. (ed.), Paris, Unesco, Berkley, The University of California Press, London, Heinemann, 1981, pp. 740–741.
4. Diallo, Y., *African Traditions and Humanitarian Law*, Geneva, ICRC, 1978, pp. 2–3.
5. International Committee of the Red Cross: *Weapons that may cause Unnecessary Suffering or have Indiscriminate Effects*. Report on the work of a group of experts, Geneva, ICRC, 1973, para. 23, p. 13.

6. Diallo, Y., *op. cit.*, pp. 16–17.

Bello, E., *African Customary Humanitarian Law*, Geneva, ICRC, Oyez Publishing Ltd., 1980, pp. 20–21.

7. Diallo, Y., *op. cit.*, p. 17.

8. Diallo, Y., *op. cit.*, pp. 5–7.

9. Bello, E., *op. cit.*, pp. 34 ff.

10. *Ibid.*, pp. 35–36.

11. *Ibid.*, pp. 28–33.

12. *Ibid.*, pp. 36–37.

13. *Ibid.*, pp. 33 ff.

Meek, C. K., *Law and Authority in a Nigerian Tribe*, London, Oxford University Press, pp. 242–244, 1951.

14. Bello, E., *op. cit.*, p. 50.

See also Adda B. Bozzeman: Death is inflicted without regard either for human suffering or for such demographic effects as depopulation. Practices of war that are condemned elsewhere as needless atrocities, such as the razing of villages, the killing or mutilation of prisoners and the slaughter of women and children, are condoned here as natural sequential corollaries of an original military thrust, and as integral aspects of a sacerdotal code in which the shedding and use of human blood have profound symbolic importance. (Bozzeman, Adda B., *Conflict in Africa, Concepts and Realities*, Princeton, Princeton University Press, 1976, p. 207).

15. Diallo, Y., *African Traditions and Humanitarian Law: Similarities and Differences*, Geneva, ICRC, 1976, p. 16.

16. Kenyatta Jomo, *Facing Mount Kenya*, London, Secker and Warburg, 1956, pp. 212 ff.

17. Bello, E., *op. cit.*, pp. 24–27.

18. Kenyatta Jomo, *op. cit.*, p. 212. "The so-called civilizing missions which meant the subjugation of the African races to a perpetual state of serfdom".

19. *Final Act of the International Conference on Human Rights*, Teheran, 22 April to 13 May 1968, New York, United Nations, 1968 (doc. A/Conf. 32/41), particularly resolution IV on the treatment of persons who oppose racist regimes and resolution XXIII concerning the respect of the human rights in armed conflicts.

20. *Official record of the Geneva Diplomatic Conference on the Reaffirmation and Development of International Humanitarian Law Applicable in Armed Conflicts, Geneva, 1974–77*, 17 vols., Berne, Federal Department of Foreign Affairs, 1978

21. The draft was submitted by Pakistan to the 49th plenary meeting of the Conference (doc. CDDH/427 and Corr. 1).

22. Resolution 2395 (XXIII) of 29 November 1968; 2465 (XXIII) of 20 December 1968; 2548 (XXIV) of 11 November 1969 and 3103 (XXVIII) of 12 December 1973.

23. At its 35th session, the UN General Assembly adopted on 4 December 1980 resolution 35/48 on the drafting of an international convention against the recruitment, use, financing and training of mercenaries. A 35-member ad hoc drafting committee was appointed.

24. *The Laws of War on Land*. Manual published by the Institute of International Law at Oxford, 9 September 1880. *Resolutions of the Institute of International Law*, Scott, J. B. (Ed.), New York, Oxford University Press, 1915, p. 26. *The Laws of Armed Conflicts: A Collection of Conventions, Resolutions and Other Documents*, Edited by D. Schindler and J. Toman, 3rd revised and completed edition; Dordrecht, Martinus Nijhoff Publishers, Geneva, Henry Dunant Institute, 1988, p. 37.

CHAPTER II

THE ASIAN CONCEPT

SUMIO ADACHI

1. Introduction

History always reveals barbarous conduct in the course of war. Even the Old Testament refers to such conduct by Nebuchadnezzar II, the King of the neo-Babylonian Kingdom, who fought the Egyptians in Syria-Palestine, captured Jerusalem, destroyed the Temple, looted the city and deported the King of Jerusalem, after hollowing out his eyes, to Babylon together with thousands of Jews. European countries gradually developed humane conduct towards war victims and this became established practice during the latter half of the eighteenth century. The Asian concept is considered substantially different from these European practices in spirit and philosophy.

Sun Tzu, in "The Art of War"[1] – the foremost classic of Chinese literature on military strategy, written about 500 B.C. – expressed some important requirements implied by humanity during combat; these in part may be understood as follows: a commander must show intelligence, sincerity, humanity, courage and dignity; he may utilize captured enemy equipment but must respect prisoners of war; a commander should endeavour to win the victory without harming enemy military and civilian personnel and should avoid using needless violence; a commander should not seek the total annihilation of an enemy.

The Code of Manu (Mañava-dharma-sāstra),[2] the basis for the laws, morals and customs of the people of India developed between 200 B.C. and 200 A.D., also referred to protection of war victims. In its Chapter Seven on the duty of a king, there are many detailed regulations which in part read as follows: a king must protect his people when an enemy declares war on them on the battlefield, a soldier must not kill an enemy by using a hidden weapon, hook-shaped weapon, poisonous weapon or fire weapon; a soldier must not attack an enemy who has surrendered; a soldier must not attack an enemy who is not ready for combat, who is severely wounded, is giving up the fighting, or is fleeing.

However, Asian countries being so divergent in their culture, religion, philoso-phy, geology and social condition, it is hardly possible to show the common denominators of their ideals in a short article. As the Japanese people over the past thousand years assimilated religions, cultures and philosophies from India and China into their own heritage, their philosophy and some practices are quoted below as an example of Asian views.

2. Origin of Humanitarian Ideas

Although humanitarian ideas may be universal, as an attribute of the human soul, the mode and degree of intensity of their expression differ considerably because the mental traits of people tend to acquire a special colouring through the natural and human influences of geography, topography, geology, climate, fauna and flora of their lands. The Japanese people worshipped the goddess Amaterasu-Omikami as their common ancestress. The innermost belief that a person with a pure mind free from external distractions could find the images of ancestors reflected within himself led to the cult called *Shinto*. This presents the mind of man as innately good, and maintains that virtues of humanity and tolerance accompany man as a matter of course, resulting in respect for ancestor worship, tolerance, mercy, purity and cleanness.

Confucianism was first introduced to Japan about 285 A.D. Its ideals were so realistic, sensible and social that it was incorporated into the Japanese heritage and in the Middle Ages it was adopted as the basis of education of the people. Confucian terminology for the qualities of loyalty, filial piety, benevolence, righteousness, propriety, wisdom and sincerity clarified traditional Japanese moral concepts which had existed since antiquity.

Buddhism was introduced about 560 A.D. and its early stage was the cause of bitter disputes in society. However, by the end of the sixth century it had been gradually incorporated into the traditional ethos and made great impact on the people. As the original doctrine of Buddhism aimed at release from bondage to the material world, it did not necessarily conflict with the traditional belief in a common ancestor and so became fused with the ancestor cult and loyalty to the State. Moreover, Buddhist practice of the virtues of mercy, patience, asceticism and courage greatly contributed to the development and refinement of the Japanese heritage of humanity, dedication, self-sacrifice and tranquility.

The above-mentioned thoughts had a profound influence on the mind and philosophies of the ruling class, and on the development of the spirit of *Bushido*.

3. Bushido as a Moral Code

The spirit of Bushido which dictates the duties of the noblemen known as Bushi (warriors) – a special class with greater honour and privileges – significantly developed from the early feudal age (12th century onwards). It was the unwritten law, a code of precepts governing the way of life of the Bushi for several hundred years. It had much broader implications than western chivalry because the Bushi acknowledged greater responsibility toward the whole society and thus the need of a code of conduct not only for war disciplines but also for all aspects of daily life.

It was derived mainly from Shinto, Buddhism and Confucianism. Shinto stressed loyalty to the lord, regard for ancestor worship and filial devotion; Bushido added the concept of a higher order and thus accelerated a national rather than a private moral sense. The doctrine of Buddhism armed the mind of the Bushi that the peace which arises from acceptance of fate. Confucianism gave a clear-cut moral doctrine.

The spirit of Bushido counts seven essential doctrines. The first is righteousness, which means a rationale of justice and duty and it gives special importance to a moral code. The second is courage, which means moral rather than physical courage. This notion is deeply rooted in honour. The third is humanity which is derived from love, tolerance, affection, sympathy and compassion. These characteristics are attributed to the lord and king, and well-harmonized with their absolute authority. Love is never a blind impulse but gives due consideration to justice. Therefore in battle, human conduct towards the weak and the defeated was highly praised the Bushi. Annihilation of an enemy had never been the sole object of combat. With this sense of humanity, the people could easily accept the western movement of the Red Cross in later times. The people had already learned the well-established custom of giving medical aid to enemy wounded through the famous novel by Bakin Takizawa which appeared more than sixty years before Henry Dunant wrote his famous "A Memory of Solferino". In this regard music and literature played an important role in engendering the spirit of *inter arma caritas*. The fourth is propriety which means paying due regard to social position and spiritual discipline. Strict propriety can be obtained through moral training. The fifth is sincerity. The Bushi kept their – generally oral – promises very faithfully. Honesty was considered the best policy and cultivated within the philosophical rather than the economic or political environment. Bushido eliminates the notion of reward. The sixth is honour which includes awareness of true values. Honour does not arise from man's social position but from the discharge of his duty. In order to acquire a true sense of honour, the Bushi from childhood had to endure harsh trials of both physical and spiritual pain. The seventh is loyalty which means obedience and loyalty to one's superior. Bushido considers that an individual is always part of the nation, and that the nation precedes the individual. This political notion produced the ethics of loyalty. However, Bushido never claimed that individual conscience should be a slave to the will of the lord. Therefore to sacrifice conscience to satisfy the whim of a superior merits but low esteem.

The spirit of Bushido was instilled through strict and hard education and training, with the aim, among others, of cultivating character rather than the intellectual talent, which is acquired through the study of literature and through philosophical discussion. It is not only the backbone of this special class but also, as it spread rapidly among the people, the ideal of all the population. It became a moral standard for all, and the driving power of the Japanese spirit.

4. Military Philosophies

The above-mentioned philosophies had a profound influence on the development of military science and strategy. Japanese thought had always been closely related to historical and ideological factors. The military art was the only one that had been practiced since antiquity. The people adopted the military tactics of the Orient and later of the West and put them to use in a field already well-ploughed.

As a State composed of a single culture, language and nationality Japan was considered, unlike the European artificial nation-state, to have originated spontaneously. Therefore there had been no need to discuss war problems in order to analyse national and social composition as had Thomas Hobbes, Immanuel Kant, Hippolyte Taine, Charles Montesquieu and Jean-Jacques Rousseau. The people considered war justifiable for the safeguard of national polity but not if it was a private war for political power. The Emperor Jinmu, founder of the nation, when engaged in his expedition to repress rebellion, resorted to violence solely against the rebels and afforded favourable treatment to those who surrendered. Strategy was based on the concept of passiveness which meant that peace should be kept as far as possible by avoiding violence. About 200 A.D. when the Empress Jingu engaged in conflict with Silla in the Korean Peninsula, she issued orders that violence should be avoided and that captives should not be slain. The Emperor Godalgo in 1339, when dispatching his army to suppress a rebellion, instructed his commander-in-chief that the army was to exterminate only rebels but none of the innocent who were to be given merciful protection and were not to be looted; that lower ranks were to be promptly released when captured and higher ranks detained pending punishment. He prohibited the killing of innocent inhabitants, who should always be free from any requisition or pillage. On the conduct of war, he gave instructions that to set fire to shrines and temples was strictly forbidden and that when billeting by the army was needed, compensation should be paid to those who supplied accommodation.

In the Middle Ages prisoners of war were generally soon released and allowed to settle in appropriate localities; their living costs were paid by the State; calling them prisoners was prohibited and the use of name or rank was encouraged; graves and temples for war victims were erected; priests were dispatched to collect the wounded, to bury the dead and pray for friend or enemy. Thus many foreign prisoners became naturalized subjects and contributed to the development of Japanese culture, art and technology.

From about the 16th century military theory and strategy made rapid progress under the influence of many strategists. Among them, Soko Yamaga (1622–1685), the founder of modern strategy in Japan, advocated as the basic object of strategy the attainment of justice, humanity, peace and order, and avoiding unnecessary killing. Ogyu Sorai (1666–1728) wrote in his treatise on military tactics that humanity was the key to military operations, that without humanity the troops would not be united and that without unity there would never be victory. Further, he stressed the just treatment of prisoners of war as an essential rule which in part reads as follows: "Every soldier must report to the commander about prisoners of war, must not interrogate them privately to secure information concerning enemy situations. He shall be guilty of manslaughter if he kills them with his own hands. Prisoners of war shall not be executed wantonly regardless of whether they laid down arms or fought to the last arrow." He maintained as a rule of attack that, since attacking the wrong and relieving the innocent was the basic military law, unjust violence in the enemy's land, harming the aged and infants, desecrating tombs, burning houses and warehouses, destroying forest-land and dykes and poisoning wells and kitchens were strictly forbidden. Another strategist, Nobuhiro Sato (1769–1850), also expressed as a clear rule that killing prisoners of war was inhuman, and developed detailed rules of treatment of the surrendered enemy. He concluded that all of these were the law as handed down from antiquity to the generation of his time and as taught by all military strategists. Further he stated that, in enemy land, coercing inhabitants and plundering their food was inhuman and that violent action was dishonourable. He mentioned detailed rules about methods of requisition.

The literature of military science and strategy was made known through well-established educational and training systems: instructors were carefully selected and appointed; degree systems were introduced for graduates according to their qualifications; an age limit was prescribed; and an educational degree according to ability for senior, middle or junior was established. These systems contributed to correct promulgation of strategy and discipline among people and stressed the sense of humanism with due regard to man's honour.

5. Modern Practices

At the beginning of the Meiji Era (1868), Japan abandoned its national policy of isolation which had lasted almost three hundred years, and rapidly developed a policy of internationalization. At the time of the Civil War of 1877, two senators proposed to the Government the setting up of a Society of Humanity modelled on the European Red Cross. This proposal was approved and in 1886 the Society was renamed the Red Cross Society of Japan and admitted to the family of Red Cross Societies.

During the Sino-Japanese War of 1894–1895, there were no written laws of war except the Geneva Convention of 1864. Then the Japanese Government and the military command, while engaged in operations according to well-tried practices of combat, adopted measures for the treatment of war victims. In the Battle of the Yellow Sea of 1895, the Japanese Fleet commanded by Admiral Ito defeated the Chinese Northern Fleet commanded by Admiral Ting who surrendered and soon after committed suicide. Admiral Ito had admired Admiral Ting as the foremost naval officer in the Orient, and expressed deep regret over his death. Admiral Ito returned Admiral Ting's remains to China with full military honours on board a large Chinese vessel which had been captured but which was released for the purpose of that repatriation.

In the Russo-Japanese War of 1904–1905, full consideration was given to carrying out the provisions of the Geneva Convention and the Hague Convention respecting the Laws and Customs of War on Land. Moreover, the Government and the Army paid close attention to the fact that the campaign was carried out in the territory of a neutral state. Above all, arrangements were made for the treatment of war victims, for that war was the first opportunity of applying the Hague Convention and the Russian Czar Alexander II had sponsored the Convention. For these reasons, Japan enacted a number of laws and regulations for the treatment of prisoners of war. At that time, the Convention afforded prisoners of war favourable treatment. However, Japan considered such treatment inadequate because the customs and social standards of western people were so different from those of the Japanese. Japan therefore adopted more favourable treatment according to traditional philosophies and past experiences. The Imperial Expeditionary Armies established prisoner-of-war committees within their headquarters and drew up field regulations in order to ensure fair treatment. There being no international law for victims of maritime warfare, the Imperial Navy applied *mutatis mutandis* the Geneva Convention on land warfare. Japan also reviewed the western statistics concerning the wounded and their death ratio and reduced the death rate of both friendly and enemy personnel by almost 800 percent compared with the past 200 years of European experiences. For the dead on the battlefield, there was no written international law. Japan spontaneously adopted regulations for disposal of the dead, including collection, burial, identification of possessions left behind and prohibition of looting. This all goes to show that Japan tried to assimilate fully the western methods and practices prescribed in the Conventions, while maintaining her fundamental spirit and philosophy which usefully supplemented the Conventions concerned and remedied some of their shortcomings.

After the First World War, the conscience of humanity was gradually blunted by the fearful magnitude and development of war, military strategies, tactics and destructive power of weapons. There might be many reasons for this. One might be that science and technology ignore the spiritually and humanely important. Arbitrary ideologies backed by political aims have swept human feelings aside. The military strategists see survival as depending on annihilation of the opponent. However great these influences may be, the humanitarian idea fostered and handed down from generation to generation for thousands of years will ever guide coming generations.

Notes

1. Sun Tzu/Siun Tseu/. *The Art of War*. Translated and with an introduction by Samuel B. Griffith. With a foreword by B.H. Liddell Hart. Oxford, Clarendon Press, 1965. XVIII, 198 p.
2. *The Laws of Manu*. Oxford, Clarendon Press, 1886.

CHAPTER III

THE CONCEPT OF THE SOCIALIST STATES

GÉZA HERCZEGH

The term "Socialist State" used in this study requires some explanation. A State is called socialist if its economic structure is based on public ownership of the means of production, a decisive factor for the entire juridical, political and intellectual superstructure. Such a State was built for the first time in the history of mankind on Russian soil, after the October Revolution; later, after the Second World War, a large number of countries in Europe and various other parts of the world opted for socialism. There are, however, several states which have not established public ownership òf the means of production but which call themselves socialist and consider that socialism provides the solution to their social and national problems. Because of the differences existing in their economic and social systems, a comparative study of their professed political and juridical ideas reveals a variety of divergencies which also affect humanitarian concepts. A comprehensive survey of these ideas would be too arduous a task in the present context and would be further restricted by linguistic and technical difficulties. This brief outline will therefore focus on the most salient features of the concept which has been expressed and developed by jurists in the socialist states of Europe.[1]

Science and culture in the socialist states have been influenced throughout their development by Marxism-Leninism, and the distinguishing features of socialist humanitarian ideas and concepts are enlightened by reference to Marxist-Leninist theory. Marxism established itself as a criticism of the capitalist society engendered by the bourgeois revolution. When the bourgeoisie seized power in the State, it proclaimed the freedom and equality in law of all citizens but it did not put a stop to man's exploitation of man. "Modern bourgeois society, built on the ruins of feudal society, has not abolished class antagonisms. It has merely replaced the old classes by new classes, new conditions of oppression and new forms of struggle."[2] By applying dialectical materialism to the study of social phenomena, Marx and Engels used historical materialism to demonstrate that juridical relations and political structures are shaped by the economic structure of society, i.e. the relations of production. While private ownership of the means of production subsists, the vast majority of society – the working masses – will be exploited and oppressed. Man's place in society, his rights and freedoms, are therefore central to Marxist theory. Under the traditional bourgeois concept, immunity from State intervention, freedom to control the means of production and the inviolability of private ownership of these means were the very essence of human rights, whereas the existence of genuine guarantees that conditions would be such as to make life fit to be lived was of crucial importance for each and every member of the exploited classes. The creation of such conditions is the historical role of the proletariat, which cannot break free from the class which exploits and oppresses it without, at the same time, freeing society from exploitation once and for all. "In the place of the old bourgeois society with its classes and its class antagonism, there will be an association in which the free development of each is the condition for the free development of all".[3]

However, our task is not to sketch a general outline of the humanitarian ideas professed by society in the socialist states but to present in concise form those ideas which have a direct bearing on international humanitarian law. Humanitarian law in the broad or narrow sense of the term? Socialist doctrine has produced writers who hold that the concept of international humanitarian law encompasses both the rules of international law relating to the protection of the human person and the respect of human rights in peacetime as well as in armed conflicts. "International humanitarian law" – as I.P. Blishchenko says – "includes two parts: the body of international legal norms regulating human rights and freedoms in time of peace and the body of international norms protecting basic human rights and freedoms in time of armed conflicts".[4] Others place emphasis on the close interrelationship between the law of The Hague and the Geneva Conventions and consider the traditional distinction between the so called Geneva law and The Hague law as no longer valid and superfluous. "The whole constitutes a pyramid of legal norms composed of different grades", concludes S.E. Nahlik.[5] Yet others use the term in its narrow sense.[6] The scope of international humanitarian law and its relation to other branches of international law raise many theoretical and practical issues which we do not intend to try to settle here. In our presentation of the socialist states' concept, we shall confine ourselves to the rules of international law relating to the protection of victims of armed conflicts or, to use an abridged but familiar term, the law of Geneva.

The eminent jurist Max Huber, who was President of the International Committee of the Red Cross for seventeen years, stressed the importance of new democratic and social ideas in his analysis of the factors which contributed to the success of Henry Dunant's undertaking. "Democratic and pre-socialistic ideas, beginning to gain a foothold in Europe, helped to put a higher price upon human life...".[7] Marxism played a significant role in this development. The workers' movement became a major political force during the nineteenth century. Although it was not able at that time to exert a direct influence on the formulation of the rules of international law, the ideas expressed by its representatives gradually began to transform mental attitudes, despite the denials and heated debates which the process occasioned. Indisputably these ideas also helped to place the safety and protection of the members of society at the very centre of political thought.

No society which attaches importance to the welfare and safety of its members and endeavours to provide living conditions fit for human beings can remain indifferent to the number of lives lost in war. Thus the protection of the victims of armed conflicts, a task which used to be left to individual charity, became first a social task and then a legal and even international obligation for states engaged in conflicts.

The importance of this task and of the related juridical rules has been greatly enhanced as a result of the new conflicts engendered by imperialism, the highest stage of capitalism; the catastrophic First World War exemplifies this type of conflict in its most acute form. Vladimir Ilich Lenin's historical merit is to have subjected the inherent contradictions of imperialist society to scientific analysis as well as to have led the revolution of the working masses and the construction of the first socialist state. Not only did the October Revolution overthrow the exploiting classes in Russia it also took a firm stand against the international imperialist system that triggered off the Great War and then proved incapable of putting an end to the killing and restoring peace. Characteristically, one of the victorious revolution's very first deeds was the Decree on Peace which proposed to all the belligerents of the time the immediate conclusion of a peace treaty with no annexations or war contributions.[8] The maintenance of peace has always been the main objective of foreign policy in the socialist states. This policy of peace is not to be equated with the sort of pacifism that denies legitimacy to all forms of constraint; rather, it should be seen as condemning unjust wars aimed at the conquest and oppression of other peoples and nations: "It would be simply foolish to repudiate 'defence of the fatherland' on the part of the oppressed nations in their wars against the imperialist Great Powers, or on the part of a victorious proletariat in its war against some Galliffet of a bourgeois state".[9]

Without embarking on the detailed history of the *bellum justum* theory, suffice it to note that the Marxist-Leninist approach to different types of war is fully consistent with the principles of contemporary international law. The Charter of the United Nations expressly prohibits recourse to the threat or use of force against the territorial integrity or political independence of any state, or in any other manner inconsistent with the purposes of the United Nations. At the same time, the Charter recognizes the inherent right of individual or collective self-defence in the event of armed aggression; it explicitly recognizes the equality in law of peoples and their right to self-determination, and it condemns all discrimination based on race, sex, language, etc.

The 1949 Geneva Conventions and the Additional Protocols of 1977 are part of the new body of international law aimed essentially at the maintenance of peace. Although their provisions are to be fully applied in all circumstances to all protected persons, without any adverse distinction based on the nature or origin of the armed conflict or on the causes espoused by the parties to the conflict, the Preamble to Protocol I of 1977 expressly stipulates that none of its provisions can be construed as legitimizing or authorizing any act of aggression or any other use of force inconsistent with the Charter of the United Nations. The law of Geneva is therefore fully consistent with the provisions of the Charter, which it supplements. The very fact that it highlights the dangers threatening persons and their objects in an armed conflict as well as the physical and moral suffering against which it endeavours to afford effective legal protection, provides us with a cogent argument in the struggle for peace and against warmongers. The dissemination of humanitarian ideas and the relief afforded to victims will increase mutual understanding among peoples and thus promote peaceful coexistence. Furthermore, by prohibiting the use of certain methods and means of warfare and forbidding attacks against protected persons and objects, the law of Geneva can help to lessen the advantages which today's armed aggressor has over the victim of the aggression, who is weaker from both the military and the technical standpoints.[10] International humanitarian law is thus a factor of peace, and the motto of the international Red Cross movement, *"Per humanitatem ad pacem"*, accurately expresses the goal and essence of the system as a whole.

What are the salient features of international humanitarian law as conceived by the socialist states? First, it is an international. It constitutes an integral part of contemporary international law. The basic principles of contemporary international law, which include the sovereignty and equality in law of states, non-interference in domestic matters and the right of peoples and nations to self-determination, are also among the principles of international humanitarian law, which cannot develop otherwise than in full consonance with the democratic and progressive principles mentioned earlier. The Geneva Convention of 1864 was the first international instrument to be open for accession by all States, and international humanitarian law has from the outset shown a marked tendency towards universality. Today it must respond to the humanitarian aspirations of all the states which go to make up the world community. The community of states has changed and grown radically in recent decades. Any adverse distinction between States or nations as to their economic and social system, stage of development or any other factor is inconsistent with the law of Geneva. It is therefore essential that the related provisions should take account of new world realities and of the situations which may arise in new forms of struggle, such as national liberation and anti-colonialist wars, and afford protection to the victims of such conflicts. The armed organizations of resistance or liberation become Parties to the conflict and subjects of international law without being recognized as such by the adversary. The rules of the law of Geneva must be fully applied in armed conflicts in which peoples are fighting against colonial domination and alien occupation and against racist regimes in the exercise of their right to self-determination. At the same time the law of Geneva must afford protection to the victims of non-international armed conflicts, especially since they subject the civilian population to great hardships and often expand into international armed conflicts. The protection of victims is based on humanitarian principles that are valid in all types of armed conflict, but the related legal provisions must take account of the peculiarities which differentiate civil wars from international armed conflicts.[11]

For the socialist states, the adjective "humanitarian" is just as important as the adjective "international". Humanism has evolved over the centuries and, thanks to new ideas, its content is far richer today than in the past. We have already endeavoured to show very briefly how Marxism-Leninism has contributed to modern humanism.

Regarding international humanitarian law, it must be borne in mind that today's armed conflicts and weapons, with greater and more effective powers of destruction, are an ever-increasing threat to an ever larger number of human beings. Effective protection is no longer required only for the combatants who take a direct part in hostilities, but also for many broad social classes, such as the entire civilian populations, women, children, the aged, the handicapped, etc. The socialist states' concept, while recognizing the importance of protecting individuals, places emphasis on the protection of social classes and protects the individual as part of a community. Protection must be preventive. It cannot be limited to easing the condition of people who are wounded, ill or in enemy hands and therefore already victims of the armed conflict; it must also prevent the number of victims from increasing and keep that number as low as possible by means of provisions that are both realistic and stringent.[12]

It also emerges very clearly from the socialist states' concept that the respect and protection of the human person are dependent upon the existence of material conditions which make life fit to be lived. That is why it is prohibited to attack or destroy not only objects indispensable to the survival of the civilian population but also civilian objects in general, cultural objects and – very important today – the natural environment, which must be protected against widespread, long-term and severe damage prejudicial to the health or survival of the population.[13]

Lastly, the socialist concept places very strong emphasis on the fact that international humanitarian law comprises a set of compulsory rules of conduct and a juridical system which penalizes their infringement. This law is applied in time of armed conflict, when chaotic situations offer many opportunities for abuse, and it is therefore of crucial importance to provide safeguards for its enhancement and respect. In this connection, it should be emphasized that reprisals, which certain proponents of the doctrine still consider to be sanctioned by international law, have no place in humanitarian law. The fundamental injustice of reprisals resides in the fact that they affect the innocent[14] rather than the guilty. The 1929 Prisoner of War code prohibited all reprisals against prisoners of war, and several articles of the four Conventions signed at Geneva on 12 August 1949 prohibit reprisals against protected persons and objects. Additional Protocol I of 1977 has made many additions to the list of such prohibitions, and the restrictions in question correspond perfectly to the socialist states' concept which gives pride of place, among the sanctions of international humanitarian law, to the penal repression of grave breaches;[15]. Nobody who is sentenced for committing a war crime is entitled to the protection afforded by the Conventions and the Protocol while he is under sentence. It would be an obvious and unjustifiable contradiction to place the innocent victims of violations of the rules applicable in armed conflicts on the same level as those who have deliberately added to the number of victims. Protection cannot be extended alike to the martyr and his tormentor, the war criminal. It follows that mercenaries do not have the right to be combatants or prisoners of war, for to participate in hostilities and to take human life essentially for private gain and material compensation is quite clearly an absolute denial of the humanitarian spirit which prevails throughout the provisions of the law of Geneva.[16]

The socialist states are Parties to the Geneva Conventions for the protection of the victims of armed conflicts, and their representatives were among the first to sign the Additional Protocols of 1977. International humanitarian law is also their law, and they have contributed actively to its progress and development. Although, in a spirit of compromise and conciliation, the socialist states abandoned their efforts to secure the inclusion of a number of rules aimed at providing even greater protection for the victims of armed conflicts, the recently reaffirmed and enlarged body of international humanitarian law adequately reflects their humanitarian concept, which they respect and endeavour to enforce, ever conscious that their principal aim is peace the world over.

Notes

1. The limited size of the chapter gives no possibility to present the publications on the theoretical and practical aspects of international humanitarian law in the socialist countries. The rare references which will be found in the footnotes are only few examples as random choice. For the more complete collection of materials see: *Bibliography of International Humanitarian Law Applicable in Armed Conflicts*. Second edition revised and updated. Geneva, ICRC & Henry Dunant Institute, 1987, xxix + 605 p.

2. Marx-Engels: Manifesto of the Communist Party in Marx, K. & Engels, F., *Collected Works*, London, Lawrence & Wishart, 1976, p. 485.

3. Marx-Engels: *op cit.*, p. 506.

4. Blishchenko, I. P.: Die Definierung des humanitaren Völkerrechts. *Festschrift für Friedrich Berber*, München, C. H., Back, 1973, p. 78. Khlestov, O. N.- Blishchenko, I. P.: *Krasnyi Krest i mezhdunarodnoe gumanitarnoe pravo* (Red Cross and international humanitarian law), Moskva, Medicina, 1977, p. 8.

5. Nahlik, S. E.: 'Droit dit "de Genève" et droit dit "de La Haye": unicité ou dualité', *Annuaire Français de Droit International* (Paris), Vol. XXIV, 1978, pp. 1–27. Poltorak, A., Savinskii, L.: *Vooruzhennyi konflikt i mezhdunarodnoe pravo*, (Armed conflict and international law), Moskva, Nauka, 1976, 416 p.

6. Herczegh, G.: 'Recent problems of international humanitarian law', in *Questions of International Law*, Haraszti, G. (ed.), Budapest, Akadémiai Kiadé, 1977, pp. 77–93.

7. Huber, Max, *Genfer Konvention und Rotes Kreuz. Grundsätze und Probleme*, Zürich-Berlin, Atlantis Verlag, p. 144 *The Red Cross, Principles and Problems*, Geneva, A. Kundig Press, p. 110.

8. It is also worth mentioning that following the decree of 8 July 1918 signed by V. I. Lenin, which repealed the secret annexionist treaties and denounced the unequitable treaties concluded by the tsarist government, the Soviet state notified the ICRC and the governments of states having ratified

the Geneva Convention that the said Convention and all other conventions and international agreements concerning the Red Cross which had been recognized by Russia prior to August 1917 were recognized and would be observed by the Russian Soviet Government, which preserved all the rights and prerogatives attendant upon those conventions and agreements.

9. Lenin, V. I., 'The War Programme of the Proletarian Revolution', in *Selected Works*, Vol. 1, Moscow, Foreign Languages Publishing House, 1960, pp. 818–819.

10. Gozze-Gucetic, V., 'Dopunski protokol uz Zenevske Konvencije za zastitu zrtava rata', (Protocol Additional to the Geneva Conventions for the Protection of War Victims), *Jugoslovenska Revija za Medunarodno Pravo*, (Beograd), Vol. 24, No. 3, 1977, p. 324.

11. Khlestov, O. N., Blishchenko, I. P.: *op. cit.*, pp. 86–102 and Khlestov, O. N., Sabinov, M., 'Vklad v progressivnoe razvitie mezhdunarodnogo gumanitarnogo prava', (Contribution to the progressive development of international humanitairian law), *Sovetskoe gosudarstvo i pravo* (Moskva), No. 5, 1978, pp. 89–97.

12. Several authors contend that the rules of Additional Protocol I relating to methods and means of warfare and the conduct of combatants belong with the law of The Hague. However, the said rules substantially modify the law of The Hague. See Obradovic, K., 'La protection de la population civile dans les conflicts armés internationaux', *Revue Belge de Droit International* (Bruxelles), No. 1, 1976, p. 141. Others hold that this constitutes an extension and development of the law of Geneva.

13. Khlestov, O. N., Blishchenko, I. P., *op. cit.*, pp. 75–76.

14. Nahlik, S. E., 'Le problème des représailles à la lumière des travaux de la Conference Diplomatique sur le Droit Humanitaire', *Revue Générale de Droit International Public* (Paris), No. 1, 1978, p. 157.

15. See Graefrath, B., 'Verantwortlichkeit für Kriegsverbrechen-Weiterentwicklung der Strafsanktionen der Genfer Konvention', *Neue Justiz* (Berlin), No. 2, 1977, pp. 42–48.

16. Khlestov, O. N., Sabinov, M., *op. cit.*, pp. 94–95.

CHAPTER IV

THE ISLAMIC CONCEPT

HAMED SULTAN

The Islamic concept of international humanitarian law is an essential element and fundamental principle of the Islamic legal system – a deliberate, considered, sovereign and fascinating concept in that it is the fruit of strong, sincere and earnest reasoning.

To extract its essential values, this concept must be placed in its true context and seen in its proper historical perspective, for the course of Islam – which is essentially cosmic, a bridging of time and space – is based not only on the notion of armed conflict but also on the Muslim faith, on the nature of the Islamic legal system and its conception of relations between the Islamic world and the world outside itself. In order to elucidate that concept and make it comprehensible, therefore, we should examine its chief components while bearing in mind the factors necessary to any mature and orderly reflection.

Accordingly, let it be said at the outset that the Islamic legal system has two mainstays which are unlike those of any other contemporary legal system.

First, the Islamic system is by its very nature not a secular legal order but one of divine and sacred emanation. It constitutes a specific application of the Islamic faith to human relations: Islam is not only a religion but also a set of rules which governs the behaviour of the faithful and organizes their relations within society. Under Islam, faith and legal order form an inseparable whole, with faith as the source and the legal order as its necessary complement.

Second, the Islamic legal order is not broken down into separate branches of law like most contemporary legal systems, which include public and private law. On the contrary, its rules – drawn from the Koran[1] – form a whole addressed to everybody across both time and space: rules of divine origin intended for individuals as such and for collectivities and communities whatever their form, variety or structure. God, through his Messenger, is addressing Himself to man as a whole, without distinction, laying down principles for governing his behaviour within society and guiding him in his beliefs and in his faith. Within Islam, therefore, there is but one God and one Law. This law is addressed to all without distinction or discrimination. It comprises a set of rules which govern all our different relationships and all human relations. Whatever the nature of those relations, and however diverse the relationships, the basis of the rules is the same. Let it be noted, however, that within that Law the jurist of the day may always engage in scientific classification of the rules, ascribing to this or that rule the character of domestic or international law or private or public law, depending on its content or purpose. That is a matter for legal research and science. What cannot be done in the field of Islamic legal science, however, is to try to introduce such an entirely alien notion as monism or dualism or alter the sacrosant features of the legal system itself, i.e. unity of foundation, equality of the binding obligation of its rules and generality of their scope of application.

Another point worth noting is that any really thoughtful examination of the Islamic concept of international humanitarian law must take account of the historical context. To be fair, any comparison must take into account two necessary dimensions, namely, the criteria of time and environment: Islam emerged in the seventh century, whereas the modern concept of international humanitarian law did not crystallize until the second half of the twentieth. There are therefore thirteen centuries between the birth of these two concepts. And if we compare, with 13 centuries of hindsight, the state of the world and society then with conditions today, we are bound to conclude that the change which has occurred in all walks of life has been so great as to represent a genuine upheaval. It is not, of course, a part of this study to paint a sombre picture of the world and society in the seventh century and compare it with the world and society of today. Let us simply draw attention to this basic factor, for we must confuse neither the problem nor the age but place the comparison in its true framework.

Islam entered upon the scene in the seventh century in a world where warfare, domination, servitude, slavery and ignorance reigned. Power was asserting itself in all walks of life and was absolute. The societies of the day had little or no social or economic structure. Any notion of State, territory, frontier, nationality, organized relations, information or communications was either lacking or unknown. The purpose of Islam was to fill that sombre vacuum; the aim of its fundamentally religious and civilizing mission was to achieve and assert the will to cohesion and action of a new community which thereafter was to become master of its own destiny. The new community was endowed with a new monotheistic religion and a new legal order which sprang from three sources: the Koran, the Sunna and the Ijtihad.

The Koran is the uncreated word of God, the "Lord of Worlds", as revealed to his chosen Messenger for communication to all peoples. It was revealed in fragments over 23 years (610–632), each revelation being made when and where required, usually to solve a specific problem. The Koran is given as a guide to man, in the totality of his temporal, spiritual, individual and collective life, and to all classes of individual and community throughout time and space. The central theme of the Koran is, of course, pure and simple monotheism – belief in the oneness of God, although it also deals with all aspects of life. It is divided into 114 chapters (Sura) which are highly varied in their dimensions. Each chapter contains a number of verses (Ayats) of which the Koran as a whole has 6,600. Some 200 of these make up the body of Islamic law which governs legal relations. The rules of this *corpus* are imperative and must always be applied to the specific relations they govern. It is worth mentioning that all the rules in these 200 verses have their *raison d'être* in five basic principles which constitute the foundation of the Islamic legal system as a whole; these are;

Justice;

Equality;

Democratic consultation;

Respect for commitments;

Reciprocity.

The last-mentioned principle is limited in its application by moral ethics. Together, the five principles are the central values of the Islamic legal system, because the Revelation came to an end with the death of the Messenger and nothing more could be added to the Koran. This is where the Ijtihad found its role, which was to deduce from the five basic principles all the rules and new solutions needed for the normal conduct of human life. It must be stressed that any new rule or solution which does not conform to those basic principles cannot be regarded as an Islamic one.

The Sunna, or tradition of the Prophet, is the second source of the Islamic legal order. The Messenger's behaviour and conduct in his missionary life, his words, his deeds and his reactions to the deeds of others, constitute a source of rules which have legal force under the Islamic system. These rules are complementary to those of the Koran in that they simply reaffirm or interpret them or specify how they should be applied.

As mentioned earlier, the Koran and the Sunna are deeply rooted in the life of the Messenger, and after his death they ceased to produce new rules. Since life is constantly evolving, however, and Islam by its very nature has a continuing field of application, a new living source was needed, one capable of producing all the new rules needed for continuing application, through time and space, to all the new relationships of dynamic societies. This third source of the Islamic legal order is the Ijtihad, or reasoned deduction, a source expressly mentioned in both the Koran and the Sunna. It deduces by reasoning all the new rules essential to the changing conditions of life of constantly developing societies. As already indicated, however, this reasoned deduction can be made only within the framework of the five basic principles of Islam.

It was this third source which gave Islam all its spiritual and temporal strength during the first three centuries of its existence. Unfortunately, under the Abbasids, the authorities – who sought to wield absolute power – deemed it expedient to suppress the Ijtihad by decreeing a "closing of doors" to the deductive approach. Islam and its legal system have ever since remained static in an increasingly dynamic world. The consequences of the decision have harmed both Islam and its civilizing mission. Only during the past few decades have new generations of Islamic jurists resorted again to the Ijtihad in an effort to deal with the problems of the world today. So far, however, their efforts of deduction have been hesitant and timid, for their role has already been circumscribed by the legislative power of the modern State.

It is within this sketchily brushed framework that the Islamic concept of international humanitarian law must be approached. The concept is founded above all on the verses of the Koran (particularly Ayats 190–194 of the second Sura and Ayats 102–105 and 107–110 of the third Sura), on the words and deeds of the Messenger during the hostilities imposed upon him and, lastly, on the rules deduced from the five fundamental principles of the Islamic legal system, which forged the instructions given to the armies of Islam.

Perhaps the best way to make this concept clearer and more readily comprehensible to those not initiated in Islamic doctrine is to explain it briefly in the contemporary context of the Geneva Conventions of 1949 and the Protocols additional thereto. In so doing, we shall follow the order already adopted in the First Protocol, namely: the basic rules, methods and means of combat, protection of the civilian population and protection of civilian objects.

I. The Islamic concept of international humanitarian law includes certain rules which are regarded as fundamental and which colour the whole of the Islamic system of humanitarian law.

To begin with, the Islamic concept draws no distinction between the various types of war or armed conflict. Whether a war be waged to propagate the Islamic faith or inform people about it, or whether it be a defensive war or one directed against apostates, schismatics or rebels, the rules governing it are the same because they were laid down by the same divine Authority to be observed by all and applied without distinction or discrimination. Those rules therefore cover all armed conflicts regardless of their nature. So far as application of the humanitarian rules is concerned, under Islam there can be no distinction between international and non-international armed conflicts. The very notion of the State was non-existent in the seventh century, and the same applies to struggles against colonial domination, foreign occupation and racist régimes by peoples exercising their right to self-determination. Although all these are modern notions inconceivable to the societies living in the seventh century, Islam covers them all without drawing any distinction. The same rules apply to war at sea, in the air and even nuclear warfare, to name some modern forms of combat. Although all of Islam's rules of war are based on mercy, clemency and compassion and draw their binding force from divine Authority, their field of application extends through time and space to armed conflict of all sorts and denominations. Any contrary doctrine is alien to Islam.

Then again, one of the basic rules of the Islamic concept of humanitarian law enjoins the faithful, fighting in the path of God against those waging war against them, never to transgress, let alone exceed, the limits of justice and equity and fall into the ways of tyranny and oppression (Ayats 109 *et seq.* of the second Sura of the Koran, and the Prophet's instructions to his troops). Expressed in modern parlance, is not this rule more demanding than the Martens clause embodied in The Hague Regulations of 1907 and in Article 35[1] of the First Protocol Additional to the Geneva Conventions of 1949, which states that the right of Parties to the conflict to choose the methods or means of warfare is not unlimited? Yet thirteen centuries lie between the formulation of these two fundamental rules of conduct in armed conflict.

The third fundamental rule of the Islamic concept of humanitarian law concerns the dignity and integrity of the human person: it formally prohibits mutilation, torture and any other degrading treatment of enemies in armed conflict. At the time, of course, it was common practice to inflict phallotomy and other savage forms of mutilation on enemies killed in battle. But Islam has formally forbidden to believers any similar practices. The verses of the Koran, the rules of the Sunna and the reasoned deductions of Islam's leading jurists are explicit in that respect. For instance, when it was decided to mutilate captives as a measure of reciprocity, the Messenger, whose uncle had just been mutilated, gave the following express order to the faithful: "Never mutilate even a dog". That order has always been mentioned among the instructions given to soldiers of Islam by their commanding officers. From this fundamental rule, laid down thirteen centuries ago to combat a practice which was common at the time and long after, can be deduced all the fundamental guarantees to the Geneva Conventions of 1949. This deduction, a logical one from our point of view, is fully justified within the framework of the five basic principles of the Koran, namely, the principle of justice, equality, democratic consultation, reciprocity in morality and respect for prior commitments. It should be added that this deduction is bound up with respect for human rights, which the Islamic legal system was the first to recognize and enshrine.

II. Part III of the First Protocol of 1977 Additional to the Geneva Conventions of 1949 contains rules relating to methods and means of warfare and to combatant and prisoners-of-war status. These rules were debated at length in Committee III of the Diplomatic Conference on the Reaffirmation and Development of International Humanitarian Law Applicable in Armed Conflicts, and the Conference's acceptance of the provisions was regarded as a genuine success for the cause of humanitarian law. It should be noted that these provisions were negotiated in a time of peace when war had lost its entire *raison d'être* in that it was no longer regarded as a necessary or valid means for solving disputes or as a means acceptable to world opinion. Yet it took four years to work them out and the Final Act giving them legal force was not signed until 10 June 1977, i.e. thirteen centuries after the birth of Islam.

Most of the provisions of Parts III and IV of the First Additional Protocol can be seen on careful examination to fall explicitly within the Islamic concept of humanitarian law. Other provisions of the same Parts are not directly mentioned in that system, and the reason for this is simple: they are details relating to notions of the life of modern society, notions which were therefore unthinkable in the seventh century. Yet the very essence of all these provisions is enshrined in the general principles of the Islamic concept. And the rules relating to new facts of life of present and future societies must be considered within the framework of the five basic principles of the Islamic legal system. By reasoned deduction those new facts must be accepted or rejected depending on whether they conform to or contradict the essence of the five basic principles. In other words, any new legal provision of today or the future which is reconcilable with the basic principles of Islam is automatically incorporated in the Islamic legal system and becomes an integral part of the Islamic concept of humanitarian law.

Having said that, let us consider in particular the notions enshrined in the Islamic concept of humanitarian law in the order adopted in Part III of the First Protocol of 1977 Additional to the Geneva Conventions.

According to Article 35 (paragraph 1) of this Protocol, "In any armed conflict, the right of the Parties to the conflict to choose methods and means of warfare is not unlimited." As demonstrated earlier, this fundamental rule was preceded by the fundamental rule of the Islamic concept, which is far more demanding and specific. Indeed, Article 35 (paragraph 1) seems timid and passive in that it contains no explicit ban and lays down no precise limits on Parties to armed conflict as regards the choice of means and methods of warfare; it simply states that the right of choice 'is not unlimited". On the other hand, the fundamental rule under the Islamic concept contains a specific and positive ban and lays down precisely defined limits in stating that one must never transgress, let alone exceed, the limits of justice and equity and fall into the ways of tyranny and oppression.

Since neither Article 35 (paragraphs (2) and (3)) nor Article 36 of Protocol I were expressly contemplated under the Islamic humanitarian concept, we must examine them by reasoned deduction and apply to them the criterion mentioned above; in other words, we must consider them within the framework of the five basic principles of the Islamic legal system to determine whether or not they can be incorporated in the Islamic humanitarian concept. Careful examination shows that these provisions are in perfect harmony with the basic principles and in conflict with none of them.

The provisions of Article 37 of the First Protocol Additional to the Geneva Conventions refer to the prohibition of perfidy and the admissibility of ruses of war. Under the Islamic humanitarian concept, ruse is a lawful means of warfare. As the Messenger himself said, "warfare is a stratagem". Yet ruses cannot simply mean lying. The use of camouflage, decoys, mock operations and misinformation are permitted forms of ruse. As is well known, on the eve of the Ramadan War of 1973, Egypt – whose official religion is Islam – made intensive use of ruses of war, ruses being admissible under the Islamic concept.

Conversely, perfidy and treason are strictly prohibited, "for God loveth not the treacherous" (Sura VIII, Ayat 58). Every believer must therefore scrupulously abstain from perfidy and from any act equated or equatable with it, for Islam requires absolute loyalty in every action. Islam's leading jurists are unanimous in condemning perfidy, because "if stratagems are always permitted, perfidy always deserves anathema". As God's Messenger often said, "Give back trust to he who has trusted in you and betray not he who betrays you"; and he added: "Good faith in exchange for perfidy is better than perfidy for perfidy".

The Islamic humanitarian concept makes no direct allowance for the provisions of Articles 38 and 39 of the First Additional Protocol, on the use of recognized emblems and symbols of nationality, because the societies of the seventh century had no notion of such concepts. Since those provisions are in complete harmony with the five basic principles of Islam, however, we must conclude that they form part of the Islamic humanitarian concept by way of reasoned deduction (Ijtihad).

The provisions of Articles 40 and 41 on quarter and the safeguard of an enemy *hors de combat* are either explicitly or implicitly covered by the Islamic humanitarian concept or form part thereof by dint of reasoned deduction, as in the case of the provisions relating to the occupants of aircraft in distress (Article 42). Since the aim of armed conflict is to break hostile resistance, no enemy – the chief instrument of the resistance – once he is *hors de combat* as a result of surrender or capture, should be put to death or subjected to torture. This principle is fully in line with the Islamic humanitarian concept. To order that there should be no survivors and conduct hostilities in consequence would be contrary to all the principles of the Islamic faith and to all the foundations of the Islamic legal system. All forms of torture and mutilation of prisoners of war are forbidden. But ransoming and the exchange of prisoners are permitted and, in practice, both God's Messenger and the officers commanding the Islamic armies have unconditionally freed prisoners of war. As to the treatment of prisoners of war, suffice it to recall the words of God in the Koran:

"...The Righteous shall drink from a Fountain where the Devotees of God do drink, making it flow in unstinted abundance... they perform their vows, and they fear a Day Whose evil flies far and wide. And they feed, for the love of God, the indigent, the orphan and the captive." (Koran, Sura LXXVI, Ayats 6, 7 and 8). Moreover, God's Messenger often said: "Always look after captives".

Section II of Part III of the First Protocol Additional to the Geneva Conventions of 1949 contains provisions relating to the membership, formation and organization of armed forces (Article 43), combatants and prisoners of war (Article 44), the protection of persons who have taken part in hostilities (Article 45), spies (Article 46) and, lastly, mercenaries (Article 47). Obviously, the question of the membership, formation and organization of armed forces is closely bound up with the notion of the State, and no such notion existed when Islam was born in the seventh century. Moreover, armed forces are constantly developing in all those respects, which vary from State to State, from war to war and according to the new weapons introduced. In this respect, however, the command responsible for leading the combatants, the disciplinary system to which the latter are subject, and respect for the rules applicable in armed conflict are constant factors, and these essential and permanent features of military life have always been uppermost in the membership, formation and organization of the armed forces of Islam. Under the Islamic concept, responsible leadership, strict discipline and absolute respect for Islamic law together constitute the criterion for drawing the essential distinction between combatants and civilians. And that distinction is a basic rule of warfare according to Islam. We thus consider the new provisions of Articles 44 and 45 to be compatible with the Islamic humanitarian concept because they respect the fundamental rule concerning the need to distinguish in armed conflict between combatants and civilians.

Article 46 of the First Additional Protocol contains rules relating to spies. Under Islam, whenever anybody suspected of having committed espionage is arrested, the penalties to which he is exposed differ according to his religion, age and the circumstances of his confession. If the accused is a Moslem and makes a full confession of his offence, he is usually given a correctional sentence because he has presumably acted not from any lack of faith but through cupidity. This treatment is based on a precedent from the times of the Messenger, who pardoned a Moslem who had written a compromising letter to the Quaraishites. If the accused, although not a Moslem, is a Moslem subject (Zimmi) and voluntarily confesses, he is treated as a Moslem and incurs the same penalty. If the spy belongs to the enemy and is arrested on Moslem territory, however, he incurs the death sentence. If the crime is not proved and no confession is forthcoming, the suspect may not lawfully be killed. Confessions made under threat or torture cannot be regarded as valid by the judge, who must have a voluntary confession or statements from two witnesses in order to find the accused guilty. In any event, under the Islamic concept, no spy is entitled to the treatment accorded to prisoners of war.

Lastly, it goes without saying that Islam does not recognize the notion of mercenaries, a repugnant one which is totally rejected whatever the circumstances. This is in conformity with the very essence of the provisions of Article 47 of the First Protocol Additional to the Geneva Conventions of 1949.

III. As is well known, the conditions of life for people living in the fourth and fifth centuries were among the darkest and saddest in the history of mankind, particulary in the field of armed conflicts: devastation, cruelty and the mutilation of corpses were common practice. No distinction was drawn between combatants and non-combatants, nor was any protection afforded to women, children, the aged or the sick. There was nothing to restrict the destruction of objects of any sort. Laws went unheeded, for the world had fallen into a sort of moral and material decay. It was in those times that Islam was born. Its civilizing mission was to remedy the terrible conditions of life of the societies of the time and to fill the moral and legal vacuum in which they dwelt. Its humanitarian approach made a heavy impact in matters of armed conflict and played a decisive role in the formation and formulation of the laws of modern warfare. "Necessity" was tempered by "humanism" and "chivalry": "necessity" was for the first time subjected to wide and far-reaching restrictions. Islam's civilizing mission was accomplished in a remarkable way and its influence was a powerful stimulus to the rebirth of civilization in the world.

The general principles of the Islamic humanitarian concept as regards the protection of the civilian population and civilian objects, are enshrined in the Koran, the Sunna and in reasoned deduction. And those principles are binding and constantly applicable through time and space, whatever the nature of the armed conflict in progress. They were clearly conceived and precisely expressed at a time when the maxim was "necessity knows no law".

The following writings exemplify the general principles of the Islamic humanitarian concept:

(a) "Fight in the cause of God those who fight you..." (Koran, Sura II, Ayat 190);

(b) "But if they cease, God is Oft-forgiving, most Merciful" (Sura II, Ayat 192);

(c) "And fight them on until there is no more tumult or oppression and there prevail justice and faith in God; but if they cease, let there be no hostility except to those who practise oppression (Sura II, Ayat 193);

(d) "If then anyone transgresses the prohibition against you, transgress ye likewise against him" (Sura II, Ayat 194);

(e) Whenever the Messenger of God sent out a battalion or an army, he recommended the officers to remember their devotion to God, saying: "Fight in the name of God, fight those who deny God; kill not children and do not betray, mutilate or commit perfidy."

Omar, the second caliph, was repeating the same instructions when he said: "Oppress nobody, for God loves not oppressors. Be not cowardly in combat, cruel in strength nor abusive in victory. Kill not the aged, women or children and be mindful not to kill them during skirmishes or cavalry incursions."

From the above may be deduced the following general principles governing the protection of the civilian population and civilian objects.

First, according to the Islamic humanitarian concept, it is a duty to distinguish between two categories of persons in cases of armed conflict whatever its nature: combatants and non-combatants. Hostilities are permitted only between combatants. This is a basic binding rule of the Islamic system. God said: "Fight those who fight you". In contemporary terms, this means that acts of war may be committed only by combatants. Islamic jurists unanimously recognize the obligation to distinguish between combatants and non-combatants. Non-combatants are those who take no active part in hostilities. The definitions of civilian population and civilian objects given in the three sections of Article 50 of the First Additional Protocol of 1977 merely endorse and implement a basic rule of the Islamic concept. And the basic rule in Article 48 of the same Protocol simply reflects the instructions given by the caliphs Abu Bakr and Omar to their armies thirteen centuries earlier. The provisions of Article 49, on the definition of attacks and scope of application, constitute rules which are implicitly admitted under the Islamic concept because they merely specify certain details of application.

Second, under the Islamic concept, non-combatants – in other words, civilians and the civilian population – enjoy general protection from the dangers of hostilities and military operations provided they do not directly participate in them. Should they take part, their non-combatant status is forfeit and replaced by combatant status. The general protection accorded to non-combatants naturally implies that they are not subjected to attack or to threats of violence. All indiscriminate attacks, threats for the purpose of spreading terror and reprisals against civilians or the civilian population are expressly prohibited in the Islamic concept of humanitarian law.

Third, the Islamic concept provides special protection for certain categories of civilians: children, women, the elderly, the sick and monks. All the instructions given by God's Messenger and the caliphs explicitly stated that such persons should be specially protected against all hostile acts. It goes without saying that the provisions of Article 51 of the First Protocol Additional to the Geneva Conventions of 1949 apply to such people, as do those of Articles 76, 77 and 78.

Fourth, under the Islamic concept of humanitarian law, the obligation to distinguish between civilian and military objects is clearly imperative and permits no exception. Caliph Abu Bakr gave orders never to destroy palm trees, burn dwellings or cornfields, cut down fruit trees, kill livestock unless constrained by hunger, and never to lay hands on monasteries. Attacks should therefore be strictly confined to military targets, i.e. to objects which by their nature or use are intended for the pursuit of hostilities. The nature, use and intended purpose of the objects are the criteria for distinguishing between military and civilian objects. The Islamic concept presumes all objects to be civilian unless proved otherwise. This is obvious from the instructions and orders given by Abu Bakr. It is worth adding that under this concept all destruction is "ugly and blameworthy" and can be tolerated only in exceptional circumstances. The scope of application of the protection of civilian goods is wider under the Islamic concept than in the provisions of Chapters III *et seq.* of Part IV of the First Protocol Additional to the Geneva Conventions of 1949, for it is more precise, more general and more humanitarian; however, the stipulations, criteria and details enunciated in the provisions of Articles 52–69 and 60–65 of the First Additional Protocol are, of course, in perfect harmony with the very essence of the Islamic concept and can therefore be regarded as forming an integral part of it.

In conclusion, the Islamic concept of humanitarian law has, by its generous and religious nature, a field of application covering any new provisions which might be necessary or favourable to the protection of victims of armed conflict in this turbulent world. To all the scourges of war it opposes protection and counsels clemency, compassion and mercy. Where need be, it automatically embraces all new provisions relating to new situations, provided they are in keeping with the five basic principles of the Islamic legal system. It is in this framework that all the other provisions of the First Protocol Additional to the Geneva Conventions of 12 August 1949 must be considered and examined. For the believer, such consideration and examination must always take place with the following words of God in mind:

> "Let there arise from out of you a band of people inviting to all that is good, enjoining what is right and forbidding what is wrong: they are the ones to attain felicity."
>
> (Sura III, Ayat 104)

Notes

1. *The Holy Qur'an*. Arabic text and English translation by the late Maulawi Sher'ali.
Published under the auspices of Harzat Mirza Bashir-Uddin Mahmud Ahmad. Rabwah, West Pakistan, The Oriental and Religious Publishing Corporation, 1955, 643 p.
The Glorious Qur'an. Translation and commentary by Abdullah Yusuf Ali. Published by the Muslim Students' Association of the United States and Canada, 1975, 1862 p.

CHAPTER V

THE LATIN AMERICAN CONCEPT OF HUMANITARIAN LAW

JOSÉ MARIA RUDA

1. Independence

Concern for the suffering of combatants and of the civilian population was present among those who led the struggle for independence of the Spanish-American colonies. In 1820, for instance, following the battle of Boyacá, Bolivar and the Spanish commanders came to an agreement containing humanitarian rules for the conduct of hostilities as regards the treatment due to prisoners of war and the civilian population in territory occupied by the belligerents. This instrument contains provisions of the procedure to be followed for exchanging prisoners and the duty of the victor to bury any corpses found on the battle-field. As the Colombian jurist, José María Yepes, says, "The two contracting nations undertook to make war subject to the most liberal, humanitarian and Christian practices that could be expected of a civilized nation".[1]

2. Nineteenth Century Doctrine

Principios de Derecho International,[2] a work published for the first time in 1832 at Santiago de Chile from the pen of Andrés Bello, a Venezuelan jurist who spent much of his life in Chile, is generally regarded in Latin America as being the first modern book on the subject ever published in the region. It was widely read and had a major impact on the thinking of the time. Until then, Vattel's work had had considerable influence in the universities as well as on the public figures who had achieved American independence; after the revolutionary period, however, it proved to be too outdated to deal with some of the problems arising from emancipation. Bello filled the gap with his own masterly book, which is still being republished in Latin America.

Basing himself on the theory of natural law, in which he was a firm believer, Bello held notions inspired by humanitarian law. His basic idea was that in war we are entitled to use the most effective means for weakening the enemy "provid-ed they are not unlawful or contrary to natural law".[3] From that, he added, the rules relating to hostilities against persons should be deduced. Let us recall some of Bello's particular concepts.

For instance, after justifying the use of force to repel an aggressor, he claimed that it was unlawful to take the life of a surrendered enemy except in cases where he had been guilty of serious violations of *jus gentium*.[4]

With reference to the civilian population, Bello said that nobody had the right to take the life of women, children, the elderly, the wounded or the sick, because "they offered no resistance nor of ministers of religion or practitioners of peaceful professions.[5]

As for persons wounded in battle, Bello asserted that it was for the victor to aid them and that the laws of humanity and honour prohibited killing or despoil-ing them.[6]

Bello devoted a large section of his work to prisoners of war. Among civilized nations, he said, the practice of taking prisoners of war was exercised only between individuals who carried arms, adding that it was not lawful to kill them except in exceptional cases of resistance, the appearance of an enemy force or in circumstances of the most dire need.

Referring to the treatment due to prisoners, Bello reminds us that they should not be killed unless they have committed some crime; that officers, on their word of honour, could neither take up arms nor serve under flags inimical to the country of the prisoner or of third powers but could reside in a given area. Bello contended that the State had a duty to maintain prisoners, although not in luxury or comfort; that their maintenance costs should be borne by the sovereign of the prisoner and that any delay in paying them, once peace was restored, was no reason for holding on to prisoners "since the latter are not responsible for their sovereign's debts".[7]

Another important book, one more widely read than Bello's because it was written in French and translated into several languages is *Le droit international théorique et pratique*, by the Argentinian jurist Carlos Calvo.[8] Section V of the part devoted to the state of war refers to the laws and duties of warfare in relation to the enemy's person. In it, among other general concepts, Calvo says that as a result of improved standards of conduct and higher principles of natural law, persons falling into enemy hands benefited from special protection.

Calvo says that prisoners of war are not punishable because of their capacity as enemies and that, accordingly, they should not be maltreated; at most they may be detained or interned to prevent their escape. Their treatment, he adds, consists principally, if not exclusively, in effective and temporary deprivation of liberty.[9]

Calvo's humanitarian leanings are patent when he refers to the acceptance, based on a doctrine of his time, of the right to refuse quarter to the vanquish-ed. Taking the life of a conquered enemy, he says, is a crime no law can explain, adding that an enemy who in combat violates the laws of warfare commits an offence under ordinary law, subject to ordinary penal law, and that there should be no vengeance or reprisal of a general nature.

Another manifestation of Calvo's humanitarian sentiment is his criticism of the stand taken by those who justify the killing of prisoners in cases of dire necessity. War, he maintains, should not silence Christian sentiment or conscience; a disarmed enemy, vanquished and taken prisoner, "is sacred as a man" and "to state as doctrine that one may attempt to take his life to save one's own means looking for arguments to justify a crime against humanity – it is putting the clock back".[10]

Calvo considers that prisoners should be maintained by whichever belligerent has them in its power. Such an obligation is imposed by "the laws of humanity and universally accepted usage"; any State which disregards them will find itself outside the international community. He maintains that there is nothing against prisoners working, for a wage, on public works or in ordinary industry adding that the right to require prisoners to work for their upkeep is a thing of the past: "no such law springs from any international principle, nor from any law of modern warfare". Prisoners should be engaged in work that is not dishonourable; it must be voluntary and in keeping with the military rank and "social status" of the prisoner, "not a punishment but a reward for good conduct, a way of keeping captives occupied and healthy".[11]

Calvo takes the view that a prisoner who escapes may be shot at; if he is captured, however, he must not be punished for his attempted escape because the laws of warfare do not hold such an act to be an offence except in conspiracies to make a mass escape, in which case the death penalty is applicable.

The exchange of prisoners is, for Calvo, a genuine sign of progress, although he recognizes its voluntary character. With regard to the wounded in battle and the neutralization of hospitals and ambulances, Calvo refers to the Geneva Convention of 1864 which, he says "has rendered tremendous service to mankind". Unfortunately, however, its application has not matched the hopes of its signatories and has even given rise to abuses; and he quotes various examples from the Franco-Prussian war of 1870. According to him, such problems demonstrate the need to revise the Convention and to take the necessary action to ensure that stricter control is applied. Such are his comments about the ICRC project of 1872, drafted by Gustave Moynier, to set up an international legal institution to prevent and repress offences against the Geneva Convention; but he evokes a comment from the *Journal de Genève* of 21 February 1872, to the effect that the proposed court had no power to enforce its decisions – a problem we still see today in contemporary international tribunals.

Calvo praises the work of local societies in helping the wounded and their preparatory work in times of peace.

In 1866, during the cruel war which pitted Argentina, Brazil and Uruguay against Paraguay, the second volume of *Curso Elemental de Derecho de Gentes*, by Gregorio Pérez Gomar, was published in Montevideo at whose university the author had until a short time earlier held a chair in international law. Pérez

Gomar upholds the idea that private individuals of belligerent States are enemies only when they represent those States, i.e. soldiers, or when they join in with a view to harming another State: "so the belligerents have no right to inflict personal harm upon ordinary local people or peaceful citizens".[12] He goes on to say that, during the Dano-German dispute over Schleswig-Holstein, an attempt was made to neutralize hospitals and ambulances and he heralds this as an advance to be consolidated. He makes no mention of the 1864 Convention.

Pérez Gomar takes the view that there exists no right to kill, offend or enslave prisoners, who should simply be looked after or detained if necessary.

As to the occupation of enemy territory, this Uruguayan author maintains that the occupier has only "eminent domain" and must therefore respect private property; expropriation is permitted by lawful means only, for the dual reason that one should not be deprived of what one is entitled to own and should not get rich by blameworthy methods.[13]

Other works such as *Nociones de Derecho Internacional* by Ángel Tremosa y Nadal[14], published in Havana in 1896, and *El Derecho Internacional Público*, by O. Rodríguez Saráchaga[15], published in Buenos Aires in 1895, contain comments and observations similar to those of the authors mentioned earlier.

Tremosa y Nadal, a law graduate and soldier, quotes numerous provisions of the Spanish Army's Campaign Service Regulations of 1882, the French Regulations of 1859, the *Manuel de l'Institut* of 1880, the Brussels Declaration of 1874 and the Geneva Convention of 1864. Rodríguez Saráchaga sums up his thinking with the reflection that modern law has made great progress in revealing the juridical element of warfare, humanizing the use of war and reducing the horrors of battle by developing the principles of international law;[16] his book, intended for students, refers in detail to prisoners of war and to the sick and wounded in battle and under military occupation. He proposes that the 1864 Convention should be applied by all States and disseminated among national armies.[17]

An analysis of Latin-American legal doctrine in the nineteenth century reveals great interest in the development of humanitarian law on the part of writers imbued with the doctrine of natural law, who sought to influence the leaders of the times by disseminating still recent humanitarian rules. Moreover, some political thinkers, like the Argentinian Juan Batiste Alberdi, went further and got to the bottom of the problem by opposing the existence of any laws of warfare, which Alberdi called a crime in a historical work which influenced Latin-American thinking for several decades. His thought is synthesized at the beginning of his book *El Crimen de la Guerra*, where he says:

> "*The crime of war*. This word surprises us only because we are so used to warfare, which is really incomprehensible and monstrous: *the law of warfare*, i.e. the law of murder, pillage, arson and devastation on the largest possible scale...".[18]

3. Humanitarian Conferences in the Nineteenth Century

It took the Latin American States several decades following their independence to find their place in the organized international community; this was largely because of the long war of emancipation waged by the Spanish colonies – which lasted over a decade in South America – and because most of the colonies were caught up in endless civil wars. In fact, not until the early twentieth century were these countries invited to take part in conferences and meetings to approve legal standards and policies of a universal scope.

For instance, no Latin American country participated in the Geneva Conference of August 1864, which approved the Convention for the amelioration of the condition of the wounded in armies in the field. The invitation to attend was addressed "to all civilized powers[19] and no Latin American country was included. Nor had they taken part in the previous conference held in October 1863.[20] Nonetheless, many Latin American States subsequently acceded to the 1864 Convention.[21]

The same applied to the conferences held at Geneva and St. Petersburg in 1868 and to the Brussels Conference of 1874.

The only meeting attended by representatives of several Latin American States[22] was the Spanish-Portuguese-American Military Congress held in Madrid in 1892, which prepared a draft codification of the laws and usages of continental and maritime warfare.[23]

It should be remembered, however, that Mexico was the only Latin American participant in the Hague Conference of 1899; although its delegation endorsed conventions and declarations, it took no active part in the discussions.

4. International Conferences in the Early Twentieth Century

The Geneva Conference of 1906, convened by the Swiss Government to review the 1864 Convention, was attended by several Latin-American countries: Argentina, Brazil, Guatemala, Honduras, Mexico, Nicaragua, Peru and Uruguay.[24]

Their delegations said and did little, and that only sporadically, although some of their statements are worth recalling.

For instance, Mr. Lemgruber-Kropf, the representative of Brazil, accepted the principle that the wounded and sick are subject to the laws of warfare and will be regarded as prisoners if they fall into enemy hands; this principle, he said, had been applied by his country during the wars against Uruguay (1864) and Paraguay (1864-1870).[25] His delegation also opposed the deletion of Article 5 of the Convention of 1864 – concerning respect for civilians helping the wounded – contending that such aid was to be encouraged.[26]

Mr. Edwards, the Chilean representative, proposed that protection and respect should be extended to mobile sanitary formations even when not carrying wounded or sick persons[27], and that voluntary aid societies should be declared inviolable.[28]

Mr. de la Fuente, representing Peru, asked whether it would be possible, during the period of capture of a protected establishment, to fly only the Red Cross flag;[29] this idea was subsequently adopted in Article 21(2) of the Draft Convention.[30]

The Argentinian[31] and Chilean[32] delegations upheld the traditional emblem of the Red Cross, although the latter deemed it inappropriate to propose that parliaments should ban the use of red crosses as trade marks.[33]

Several Latin American delegations (Peru[34], Argentina[35] and Brazil)[36] supported the idea of arbitration as a method for resolving conflicts. Chile rejected the idea of compulsory arbitration.[37]

The Hague Peace Conference of 1907[38] marked the debut at the world level, of the South American States in international political life. For most of them, this was their first meeting of that sort.

The Conference's discussions centred on two topics fundamental to national interests, namely, the peaceful solution of disputes – particularly through arbitration – and the compulsory collection of international public debts. Eminent Latin American figures such as the Argentinian Luis María Drago – already known for his famous doctrine – Ruy Barboza of Brazil and José Battle y Ordóñez of Uruguay took an active part in the discussions. On subjects relating to humanitarian law, however, their contribution was minimal to the extent of being almost non-existent.

The Tenth Convention, regarding the application of the Geneva Convention to war at sea, was discussed at the first two meetings of Sub-Commission II of Commission III[39], in the first two meetings of Commission III itself[40], and at the third plenary meeting; there were no Latin American statements during the discussions, nor were any proposals forthcoming.

Regulations concerning the laws and customs of war on land, annexed to the Fourth Convention, were discussed at the first four meetings of Sub-Commission I of Commission II.[41] Cuba proposed[42] the insertion in Article 5 of words to the effect that the internment of prisoners of war should last only as long as the circumstances which made that measure necessary and, in Article 14, that the offices dealing with matters relating to prisoners of war should report on any prisoners who had been freed on parole or exchanged or who had escaped. These amendments were adopted unanimously.[43] There were no Latin American interventions when the Regulations were debated at the fourth plenary meeting.[44]

Nor were there any Latin American statements or proposed amendments when the other instrument involving humanitarian law (Chapter II, Articles 11–15 of the Fifth Convention respecting the Rights and Duties of Neutral Powers and Persons in Case of War on Land) which concerned the status of belligerent soldiers on neutral territory – was discussed at the fourth meeting of Sub-Commission II of Commission II,[45] the third meeting of Commission [46] and at the nineth plenary meeting.[47]

5. Early Twentieth Century Doctrine

The approval of the Geneva and Hague Conventions brought about a radical change in the approach of writers to matters of humanitarian law. Given the lack of any positive rules, they stopped putting forward considerations of a general nature and concentrated instead on analysing and commenting upon the existing conventions. Latin American doctrine was no exception. It must also be remembered that international conflicts were dying out on the American continent, so that State action gave rise to neither precedent nor to appeals to the rules in force.

There was a considerable increase in works on international law at this stage, so let us refer to just a few of the more widely-read authors.

In the opening pages of the section "On War" of the book *Nociones de Derecho Internacional*, published in 1902, the Chilean jurist, Miguel Cruchaga Tocornal, refers to Christian influence for mitigating the cruelties of war and says that "the laws of warfare are at present dominated by the principles of necessity and humanity", adding that, although everything necessary may be done to reduce the enemy to impotence, "it is not lawful to exceed oneself in the exercise of such rights to cause unnecessary or gratuitous suffering or to harass peaceful persons".[48] The sections entitled "On Combatants and Non-Combatants", "On Mutual Obligations after Battle; Wounded and Prisoners" and "On Military Occupation" contain a detailed analysis of the rules and practices of States, with some innovation such as regarding airmen as messengers who may be captured and held as prisoners.

In 1910, the Brazilian jurist, Epitacio Pessoa, published a *Projecto Código de Dereito Internacional Publico*[49] which he prepared as his country's representative to the Legal Advisory Commission. In 1906, the Third Inter-American Conference had asked the Commission to draft such a code. Two consecutive chapters of his work are devoted to "The Dead, Wounded, Suffering and Shipwrecked" and "Prisoners of War" (51 articles in all), while the ten articles of an earlier chapter deal with "The Rights and Duties of the Occupier Regarding the Person and Property of the Inhabitants". The Draft Code is a highly detailed account of standards, based on the Conventions of Geneva and The Hague. The articles contain no innovation, possibly because of their codifying intent, but are written in tremendous detail.

In 1911, another well-known Brazilian jurist, Clovis Bevilaqua, published his *Direito Público Internacional* which also contains chapters on subjects of humanitarian law. Its greatest interest is the fact that it refers to Brazil's practices of the time, particularly the treatment of Paraguayan prisoners of war, who, according to instructions by the Argentinian General, Bartolomé Mitre, should be treated "not only with humanity, but also with benevolence".[50] Generally speaking, the book makes no reference to other texts of the day.

In 1916, the Venezuelan, Simón Planas Suárez, published the second volume of his Treatise on International Law in time of war. As he says at the beginning of the book, the impact of the First World War and the ignorance manifested therein of many of the humanitarian rules which he himself recognized did not warrant him altering anything he had written because his work was based "on the healthiest legal reasoning"; he adds, however, that ignorance of the rules does not diminish the work done, which, on the contrary, "will re-emerge, perhaps stronger and better projected, and will follow its course towards perfection, gaining greater practical efficacy".[51]

Planas Suárez repeatedly stresses that reasons of humanity and civilization have imposed rules for avoiding unnecessary suffering in war.[52] As in the case of the authors mentioned earlier, he spares no pains to explain the Conventions of Geneva and The Hague.

Another writer who had great influence in Latin America was Antonio Sanchez de Bustamante y Sirven, the Cuban professor who worked in the fields of both international public and private law. His treatise, in several volumes, is in the style of Calvo's treatise and refers repeatedly to the doctrine and practice of States. Published in 1937, it contains references to the Geneva Conventions of 1929, on the commentary of which the chapters relating to prisoners of war and to the wounded and sick in battle are based. Bustamante regards these instruments as a step forward for law and says he is carefully analysing their provisions because he believes it essential that they be known as widely as possible in order to secure the support of public opinion and bring about an increase in the number of countries ratifying them.[53]

Latin American doctrine at that time continued supporting the movement of ideas for endorsing rules of humanitarian laws but, unlike during the previous period, it gradually set aside the natural law basis and gave itself over to commenting on the conventions in force. Nonetheless the sentiments which moved earlier writers predominate in many of the new pages.

6. The Geneva Conference of 1929

Participation in this Conference by Latin American States was none too wide, although the Swiss Government had invited them all to attend as Parties to the Geneva Conventions of 1864 and 1906.[54]

The most active delegations, amid a very moderate showing, were those of Mexico, Uruguay and Venezuela. Let us recall their statements on the main topics in which they showed interest.

Mr. Castillo y Nájera, representing Mexico, was in favour of including in the Convention on the wounded and the sick special provisions relating to medical aircraft and covering both crew members and wounded or sick persons transported by air.[55] He also spoke of the need to mark medical airships with the Red Cross emblem[56] and said that medical aircraft flying over defended areas should comply with any orders transmitted to them[57] after being warned that they are in a prohibited area, and that the markings on aircraft should be visible.[58]

The same Mexican representative[59] and Mr. Parra Pérez,[60] representing Venezuela, said that war-gas victims should be specifically included among the wounded and sick protected under the Convention.

Venezuela advocated that temporary medical personnel should enjoy the same status as permanent medical staff members when, for example, they were employed as stretcher bearers and fell into enemy hands;[61] Mr. Parra Pérez submitted a text on the subject[62] which he subsequently defended and eventually got accepted.[63] Mr Castillo y Nájera supported a United States proposal that any veterinary personnel serving in medical units should not be deprived of immunity.[64]

Perhaps the most interesting Latin American statement during the Conference came from Mr. de Castro,[65] the Uruguayan representative, when, during the discussion of Article 2, he supported the Italian delegation's idea that the principle whereby wounded and sick persons who fall into enemy hands should be regarded as prisoners should be changed, because the capture of prisoners was based on the right to weaken the enemy and, if such people were already captured, wounded or sick, it meant that the enemy was already weakened.[66] The Conference later rejected the idea.[67]

As to the so-called "Prisoner-of-War Code", the only statement worth mentioning came from Mr. de Castro of Uruguay in support of general solutions for prohibiting all forms of propaganda relating to prisoners.[68]

As will be appreciated, Latin America's contribution to the Geneva Conference of 1929 was not a great one.

7. Humanitarian Law in the Inter-American System

A concern for humanitarian law took root very quickly within the Inter-American system, for its second Conference, held in Mexico City in 1901–1902, approved a Protocol of Accession to the Hague Conventions which recognized the Conventions of 1899 as part of American international public law.[69]

After the First World War, Inter-American Conferences approved a series of resolutions recommending encouragement and aid for founding National Societies of the Red Cross[70] and calling attention to the importance of their services.[71]

Shortly before the Second World War, resolutions on the humanization of warfare were passed. The 1936 Inter-American Conference for the Maintenance of Peace adopted Resolution XXXIV on the "Humanization of Warfare", which repudiates war as a means of settling disputes, prohibits the use of chemicals that cause unnecessary suffering, excludes the civilian population wherever possible from the effects of conflict and recommends that arms limitation agreements should include humanitarian provisions.[72] The Eighth Inter-American Conference, held in 1938, approved Resolution XVI, on "Defence of Human Rights", which calls for respect in time of war for human beings who do not directly participate in the conflict, for humanitarian sentiments and the heritage of civilization.[73] It also adopted a resolution on the development of Red Cross Societies in the Americas.[74]

When war broke out, the First Consultative Meeting of Foreign Ministers took place in Panama (September 1939). Among other things, it adopted Resolution VI on the "Humanization of Warfare", calling on the European countries in conflict to refrain from certain itemized methods of warfare and condemning the limited use of measures which cause unnecessary or inhuman suffering to the enemy; lastly, the resolution expresses the hope that National Societies of the Red Cross will assist war victims.[75] Resolution IX of the same Meeting, entitled "Maintenance of international activities in accordance with Christian morality", reaffirms, *inter alia*, faith in the principles of Christian civilization and condemns attempts to set international relations and the conduct of war outside the scope of morality.[76]

The Second and Third Meetings of Foreign Ministers, held in 1940 and 1942, simply approved resolutions supporting National Societies of the Red Cross.[77] The Nineth Conference, in 1948, adopted a resolution passed by the U.N. General Assembly on 19 November 1946.[78] In 1954, the Tenth Conference recommended in a resolution that Governments should guarantee the autonomy of and cooperation with National Red Cross Societies.[79]

Since then, no resolution of any importance relating to humanitarian law has been taken.

8. The Geneva Conference of 1949

A vast majority of the Latin American countries attended this conference.[80]

Committee I considered the review of the 1929 Convention to improve the lot of military personnel sick or wounded in battle and of the Hague Convention of 1907 to apply to war at sea the principles of the Geneva Convention of 1906. Mr. Rocha Schloss, representing Colombia, proposed an amendment[81] to extend protection to hospital ships in rivers and on lakes, but he later withdraw it.[82] Other Latin Americans, including Mr. de Rueda of Mexico and Mr. Falcón Briceño of Venezuela, spoke in favour of using only the traditional emblem of the Red Cross.[83]

In plenary meeting, Mr. Orozco, the Mexican delegate, proposed that neutral vessels carrying wounded or shipwrecked persons should be recognized as having the right to enter blockaded ports while flying the flag of the Convention;[84] but the idea was rejected.

Committee II was given the task of reviewing the 1929 Convention on the treatment of prisoners-of-war. Mr. Moll of Venezuela played an active part and his delegation spoke in favour of encouraging religious activities among prisoners.[85] "He stressed the principle that responsibility should lie with Governments rather than with camp commanders;[86] he spoke in favour of the idea that only prisoners of war with experience should be used for removing mines;[87] he maintained that climatic conditions should be taken into account when detailing prisoners for work;[88] he expressed the view that prisoners should be allowed to purchase goods and services outside the camp and to receive money through the Protecting Power to pay for them;[89] he considered it necessary to facilitate Red Cross correspondence and particularly messages from prisoners;[90] he asserted that a reference should be included to the right of visit of representatives of religious organizations;[91] and lastly, for reasons related to his country's Constitution, he opposed the possible application of the death penalty.[92] Together with Mexico, his delegation submitted an amendment concerning the disposal of mines,[93] which the Brazilian delegation also supported at the plenary meeting.[94]

Committee III was entrusted with preparing a Convention on the protection of civilians in time of war. Mexico took an active part in the discussions and its representative, Mr. de Alba, supported the following ideas: that the purpose of applying the Convention should be the signing of a peace treaty;[95] that children orphaned or separated from their families by reason of war should wear insignia of identification;[96] that there should be no discrimination on grounds of nationality in the treatment of protected persons;[97] that mothers of children of 7–14 years and not only up to 5 years – should receive preferential treatment;[98] that medical experimentation on civilians should be considered a crime;[99] that there should be no repatriation without the consent of the person concerned;[100] that the Occupying Power should seek the cooperation of specialized agencies in matters relating to child welfare;[101] that the Occupying Power may amend the laws of the territory occupied only if they contravene the Universal Declaration of Human Rights;[102] that the legislation on labour and other laws of the occupied State must be respected by the occupier;[103] that salary cuts may not be imposed to punish internees;[104] and that the preamble to the Convention should contain a pressing call for peace.[105] Mr. Moll of Venezuela maintained that internees could not be compared to common criminals[106] and proposed that religious organizations should be allowed to visit protected persons and distribute aid.[107]

As to the amendments to this Convention, Argentina, Uruguay and Venezuela joined other countries[108] in proposing that civilian hospitals should be marked with the emblem of the Red Cross, as is prescribed in Article 18 of the Convention in force. Uruguay and Venezuela also submitted an amendment, together with other countries, calling for a specific mention of the Universal Postal Union's current agreements concerning the waiving of postage stamp duties;[109] this now appears as Article 110 of the Convention.

The Joint Committee examined the articles common to the four Conventions approved. Mr. de Alba of Mexico supported the inclusion of "armed conflicts not of an international character". He pointed out that emancipating movements of a genuine moral character sometimes emerged and said that under no circumstances should the rights of the State come before humanitarian considerations.[110] In such cases, therefore, the humanitarian organizations could replace the Protecting Power;[111] civil wars were often even more cruel than international conflicts and the voice of the suffering could not go unheard. Mr. Blanco, the representative of Uruguay, recalled that, in Latin America, the protection afforded to the victims of both parties in civil war had often been the fruit of Red Cross initiative.[112] In plenary meeting, Mr. Falcón Briceño of Venezuela stated that the expression "armed conflicts not of an international character" did not include skirmishes by bandits or riots of any sort.[113]

At the close of the Conference, the Mexican delegation submitted a draft resolution, which was partially accepted,[114] recalling that peace should always prevail.[115]

Although few Latin American delegations played an active part, their contribution to the discussions was substantially greater than at the previous Conferences at Geneva and The Hague.

9. Doctrine since the Second World War

Doctrine since the Second World War has brought nothing new to the concepts held before the conflict.

In his book *Derecho Internacional Público*, the Argentinian jurist, Luis Podestá Costa, recalls that since the end of the Middle Ages hostilities have been restricted by moral standards derived from the sentiment of humanity preached by Christianity, and from "standards of honour peculiar to chivalry", which found their expression in kinder treatment for prisoners, relief for the wounded, respect for non-combatants, care of the elderly, women and children, and the non-use of barbaric or unfair means of warfare. Later, these "usages of war" became customary as well as positive law. Podestá Costa does not regard this legal system as either complete or perfect; but even if the texts of the Conventions approved have not achieved universal force, they cannot be disregarded "insofar as they lay down and clarify rules established by international custom"; accordingly, he recalls that on entering the last war some countries which had not ratified the Hague Conventions, in particular, stated that they would abide by their rules if the enemy did likewise.[116] The author considers that the conventions on prisoners, the wounded and the sick were applied during both world conflicts, and he mentions the work of the Red Cross in that respect.[117]

Similar concern is expressed by the Uruguayan jurist, Eduardo Jiménez de Aréchaga, who says that one of the disadvantages of the Hague Conventions is that they are subject to a general participation clause and some States had not ratified them; but, he adds, "many of the conventions were respected and none of the ones establishing clear unequivocal duties was disregarded on grounds of lack of legal efficacy or compulsion".[118]

At greater or lesser length, most authors confine themselves to analyzing the Conventions of Geneva and The Hague.[119]

10. The Geneva Conference of 1974–1977

Latin-American participation at the Conference on the Reaffirmation and Development of International Humanitarian Law Applicable in Armed Conflicts was greater and more active than at previous meetings.[120] Let us refer to just a few of the main subjects dealt with and recall that Protocol II on victims of armed conflicts of a non-international nature was accepted with a minimum of discussion following the submission of amendments by Pakistan, representing a gentleman's agreement between the various groups of the Conference; the work of the previous three years was changed in two weeks.[121]

Article 1 of Protocol I on the protection of victims of international armed conflicts, which lays down the scope of application, is of special importance. At the first session, Latin-American delegations sponsored, along with others, an amendment, subsequently approved by an ample majority, which, besides the situations contemplated in Article 2 common to the Conventions of 1949, includes armed conflicts "in which peoples are fighting against colonial and alien occupation and racist régimes in the exercise of their right of self-determination".[122]

Among other basic rules, Article 35 of Protocol I stipulates that the right of the Parties to an armed conflict "to choose methods or means of warfare is not unlimited" and prohibits the use of weapons which cause unnecessary suffering and methods which cause extensive and lasting damage to the environment. This article was approved by consensus. Nonetheless, Argentina stated that, had a vote been taken, it would have abstained. It also stated that the provision had no connection with the work of the Committee on Disarmament, which culminated in the approval of the Convention on the Prohibition of Military or Any Other Hostile Use of Environmental Modification Techniques[123] Venezuela, on the other hand, gave its approval which, it said, would not prejudice its position on the above-mentioned Convention.[124]

Paragraphs 3 and 4 of Article 44 on combatants and prisoners of war lay down that a combatant will preserve his status so long as he carries his arms openly during each military engagement and during the period prior to attack, and that if he falls into the hands of the adversary without meeting those requirements he will not be regarded as a prisoner of war but will receive equivalent protection. This article gave rise to detailed discussion.[125] Latin American voting at the plenary meeting was divided: Cuba, Ecuador, Panama, Peru and Venezuela voted for, while Argentina, Brazil, Chile, Colombia, Guatemala, Honduras and Nicaragua abstained.[126] There were several explanations of the vote. Mr. Cerda, the Argentinian representative, recalled that his country had co-sponsored the amendment to Article 1 to extend the notion of conflict to situations in which peoples were struggling against colonial domination, foreign occupation and racist régimes, but that paragraph 3 of the approved article did not guarantee the protection due to the civilian populations.[127] This position was shared by Mr. Hernández of Uruguay.[128] Mr. Román, representing Chile, said he understood that in dealing with "equivalent protections," paragraph 4 was referring to "the penal and procedural guarantees of a regular trial for an offence against the Protocol".[129] Mr. Icaza of Mexico, who voted in favour, said that, in struggles against colonial domination, the whole of the population took part in the struggle; it was therefore important to grant prisoner-of-war status "to those who were participating directly in a struggle undertaken by the whole population".[130]

The Mexican and other Latin-American delegations proposed the setting up of a Committee of States Parties to submit, having regard to Article 35, recommendations giving expression to the principles whereby the Parties in conflict had no unlimited right as regards the choice of means of warfare.[131] The proposal was not accepted.

The Mexican delegation was also extremely active in the *Ad Hoc* Committee on Conventional Weapons, where it submitted a draft Additional Protocol on the prohibition of the use of incendiary weapons;[132] among other initiatives, it also co-sponsored, with Switzerland, a draft article on anti-tank and anti-personnel mines.[133] Venezuela submitted a draft article on booby-traps.[134] The Conference transmitted all these proposals to Governments and to the Secretary-General of the United Nations.[135]

Several Latin-American delegations tried to limit the scope of Protocol II – and not only of the original but also of the Pakistani draft; while approving the conditions prescribed in Article 1, Brazil wanted the Protocol applied only if the established government agreed to its application.[136] At the plenary meeting, Colombia upheld the same view and gained some support, although it was finally decided not to submit any amendment on the matter.[137]

Generally speaking, Latin-American participation in this conference on such delicate topics was based on support for the traditional and generous values of Humanitarian Law, but at the same time with an eye to the defence of national sovereignty.

Notes

1. Yepes José Maria, 'La contribution de l'Amerique Latine au développement du droit international public et privé', *Recueil des Cours*, Académie de Droit International, La Haye, 1930, Vol. 32-II, pp. 740–741.
2. Bello Andrés, *Principios de Derecho Internacional*. (Estudio Preliminar de Rafael Caldera), Buenos Aires, Editorial Atalaya, 1946, 397 p.
3. *Ibid.*, p. 263.
4. *Ibid.*, p. 263.
5. *Ibid.*, p. 264.
6. *Ibid.*, p. 265.
7. *Ibid.*, p. 266.
8. Calvo Carlos, *Le droit international théorique et pratique*, 5 th. ed., Paris, A. Rousseau, 1896, 6 Vols.
9. *Ibid.*, Vol. IV, p. 191.
10. *Ibid.*, Vol. IV, p. 197.

11. *Ibid.*, Vol. IV, pp. 198–199.
12. Pérez Gomar Gregorio, *Curso Elemental de Derecho de Gentes*, Montevideo, Imprimerie de el Pueblo, 1967, Vol. II, p. 35, [Colleccion Clasicos Uruguayos].
13. *Ibid.*, p. 67.
14. Tremosa y Nadal Angel, *Nociones de Derecho Internacional*, Havana, La Australia, 1896, 222 p.
15. Rodriquez Sarachaga, O., *El Derecho Internacional Publico*, Buenos Aires, T. Real y Prado, 1895, 692 p.
16. *Ibid.*, p. 319.
17. *Ibid.*, p. 415.
18. Alberdi Juan Bautista, *El Crimen de la Guerra*, Buenos Aires, Editorial El Tonel, 1915, p. 11. [English version: Mac-Connel, C. J. (trans. and ed.), *The Crime of War*, London and Toronto, Dent, J. M. & Sons, 1913].
19. *Le Congrès de Genève d'août 1864*, 2nd ed., Genève, Imprimerie Ramboz et Schuchardt, 1864, p. 56.
20. *Ibid.*, p. 14.
21. Argentina (1879), Bolivia (1879), Brazil (1906), Colombia (1906), Cuba (1907), Chile (1879), Dominican Republic (1907), Ecuador (1907), El Salvador (1874), Guatemala (1903), Haiti (1907), Honduras and Nicaragua (1898), Mexico (1905), Panama (1907), Paraguay (1907), Uruguay (1900) and Venezuela (1894).
22. *The Proceedings of the Hague Peace Conferences: The Conference of 1907*. Translation of the Official Texts. James Brown Scott (ed.), Vol. III, New York, Oxford University Press, 1921, pp. 97, 168 [Carnegie Endowment for International Peace. Publication of the Division of International Law].
23. Tremosa y Nadal, A., *Nociones de Derecho Internacional*, Havana, La Australia, 1896, pp. 183–92.
24. *Actes de la Conférence de Révision réunie à Genève du 11 juin au 6 juillet 1906*, Genève, Imprimerie Henry Jarrys, 1906, 310 p.
25. *Ibid.*, p. 80.
26. *Ibid.*, p. 182.
27. *Ibid.*, p. 132.
28. *Ibid.*, p. 111.
29. *Ibid.*, p. 189.
30. *Ibid.*, p. 287.
31. *Ibid.*, p. 175.
32. *Ibid.*, p. 175.
33. *Ibid.*, p. 180.
34. *Ibid.*, p. 230.
35. *Ibid.*, p. 240.
36. *Ibid.*, p. 240.
37. *Ibid.*, pp. 230–31.
38. *The Proceedings of the Hague Peace Conferences: The Conference of 1907*. Translation of the Official Texts. James Brown Scott (ed.), New York, Oxford University Press, 1920–1921, 4 vols., [Carnegie Endowment for International Peace, Publication of the Division of International Law].
39. *Ibid.*, Vol. III, pp. 557–572.
40. *Ibid.*, pp. 289–304.
41. *Ibid.*, pp. 97–144.
42. *Ibid.*, pp. 241.
43. *Ibid.*, pp. 103, 106.
44. *Ibid.*, Vol. I, pp. 83–85.
45. *Ibid.*, Vol. III, pp. 179–180.
46. *Ibid.*, pp. 35–70.
47. *Ibid.*, Vol. I, p. 339.
48. Cruchaga Tocornal, M., *Nociones de Derecho Internacional*, 2nd. ed., Santiago de Chile, Impr. litog. y encuadernación, Barcelona, 1902, 529 p.

49. Pessoa Epitacio, *Projecto de Código de Direito Internacional Público*, Rio de Janeiro, Imprensa Nacional, 1911, 335 p.

50. Bevilaqua Clovis, *Direito Público International*, Rio de Janeiro, Freitas Bastos, 1911, Vol. II, p. 337.

51. Planas Suarez Simon, *Tratado de Derecho Internacional Público*, 2nd ed., Madrid, Hijos de Reus, 1916, p. 1.

52. *Ibid.*, pp. 5, 7, 9, 15, 18, 62, 76.

53. Bustamente y Sirven Antonio Sanchez (De), *Derecho Internacional Público*, Havana, Carasa y Cia., 1937, Vol. IV, p. 261.

54. Of the nineteen Latin American States, the following nine did not attend: Argentina, Costa Rica, Ecuador, El Salvador, Guatemala, Haiti, Honduras, Panama, Peru.

55. *Actes de la Conférence Diplomatic de Genève du 1929*, Genève, Imprimerie du Journal de Genève, 1930, p. 84.

56. *Ibid.*, p. 222.

57. *Ibid.*, p. 226.

58. *Ibid.*, p. 228.

59. *Ibid.*, pp. 88, 93, 94 and 95.

60. *Ibid.*, p. 87.

61. *Ibid.*, p. 172.

62. *Ibid.*, p. 175.

63. *Ibid.*, p. 187.

64. *Ibid.*, p. 189.

65. *Ibid.*, p. 123.

66. *Ibid.*, pp. 108–109.

67. *Ibid.*, p. 142.

68. *Ibid.*, pp. 465 and 533.

69. *International Conferences of American States, 1889–1928*, Washington, Carnegie Endowment for International Peace, New York, Oxford University Press, 1931, p. 61.

70. See resolutions of the Fifth and Sixth Inter-American Conferences (1923 and 1928) on Red Cross Socities and of the Pan-American Conferences of the Red Cross, *International Conferences of American States, 1889–1928*, Washington, Carnegie Endowment for International Peace, New York, Oxford University Press, 1931, pp. 229 and 311.

71. See Resolution XXXII of the Seventh Inter-American Conference, 1933, *International Conference of American States, First Supplement, 1933–1940*, Washington, Carnegie Endowment for International Peace, 1940, p. 49.

72. *Ibid.*, pp. 164–65.

73. *Ibid.*, pp. 245–46.

74. *Ibid.*, pp. 291–92.

75. *Ibid.*, pp. 329–30.

76. *Ibid.*, p. 332.

77. *Ibid.*, p. 352 and *International Conference of American States, Second Supplement 1942–54*, Washington D.C., Pan American Union, 1958, p. 39.

78. *Ibid.*, p. 253.

79. *Ibid.*, pp. 446–47.

80. Haiti, Honduras, Panama and Paraguay did not attend; the Dominican Republic sent an observer.

81. *Final Record of the Diplomatic Conference of Geneva of 1949*, Berne, Federal Political Department, s.d., Vol II, sect. A., p. 64.

82. *Ibid.*, Vol. II, Sect. A, p. 64.

83. *Ibid.*, pp. 93, 136, 151, 173. This idea was also upheld at the plenary meeting by Mr. Speroni, the Argentinian representative. Sect. B. p. 230.

84. *Ibid.*, Vol. II, Sec. B, pp. 262–63.

85. *Ibid.*, Vol. II, Sec. A, p. 261.

86. *Ibid.*, p. 264.

87. *Ibid.*, p. 273.

88. *Ibid.*, p. 274.

89. *Ibid.*, p. 278.

90. *Ibid.*, p. 288.

91. *Ibid.*, p. 301.

92. *Ibid.*, pp. 311, 327.

93. *Ibid.*, Vol. III., p. 71.

94. *Ibid.*, Vol. II., Sect. B, p. 296.

95. *Ibid.*, Sect. A., p. 624.

96. *Ibid.*, p. 637–638.

97. *Ibid.*, p. 641.

98. *Ibid.*, p. 643.

99. *Ibid.*, p. 646.

100. *Ibid.*, p. 655.

101. *Ibid.*, p. 664.

102. *Ibid.*, p. 671.

103. *Ibid.*, p. 679.

104. *Ibid.*, p. 685.

105. *Ibid.*, p. 691.

106. *Ibid.*, p. 686.

107. *Ibid.*, p. 690.

108. *Ibid.*, Vol. III, p. 108.

109. *Ibid.*, p. 154.

110. *Ibid.*, Vol. II, Sect. B, p. 11. The same position was upheld by Mexico at the plenary meetings. *Ibid*, p. 333.

111. *Ibid.*, p. 22.

112. *Ibid.*, p. 42.

113. *Ibid.*, p. 333.

114. *Ibid.*, pp. 509–12.

115. *Ibid.*, Vol. III, p. 177.

116. Podesta Costa, Luis, *Derecho Internacional Público*, 3rd ed., Buenos Aires, Tipográfica Ediora Argentina, 1955, pp. 60–65.

117. *Ibid.*, pp. 94–95.

118. Jiménez de Aréchaga, Eduardo, *Curso de Derecho Internacional Público*, Mimeographed, Montevideo, Centro Internacional Público, 1960, Vol. III.

119. See for example Sierra, Manuel, *Tratado de Derecho Internacional Publico*, Mexico, Editorial Porrua, 1955, pp. 475–77;

Cock Arango Alfredo, *Derecho Internacional Público Contemporáneo*, Medellin, Imprimeria de la Universidad de Antioquia, 1955, Vol. II, pp. 61–485;

Accioly, Hidelbrando, *Tratado de Direito Internacional Publico*, 2nd. ed., Rio de Janeiro, Ministry of Foreign Relations, 1957, Vol. III, p. 144.

120. Only El Salvador, Haiti and Paraguay were absent.

121. Forsythe, David, P., 'Legal Managment of International Wars', *American Journal of International Law*, (Washington D.C.), Vol. 72, April 1978, p. 278.

122. *Official Records of the Diplomatic Conference on the Reaffirmation and Development of International Humanitarian Law Applicable in Armed Conflicts, Geneva (1974–1977)*, Berne, Federal Political Department, 1978, CDDH/I/71, Vol. III, P. 8–9.

123. *Ibid.*, Vol. VI, CDDH/SR.39/Add.1., p. 113.

124. *Ibid.*, p. 118.

125. *Document of the Diplomatic Conference*, Committee III, Draft Report of 12 May 1977, CDDH/III/408, pp. 6–8.

126. *Official Records of the Diplomatic Conference on the Reaffirmation and Development of International Humanitarian Law applicable in Armed Conflicts*, Geneva (1974–1977), Berne, Federal Political Department, 1978, Vol. VI, CDDH/SR.40, par. 15, pp. 120–121.

127. *Ibid.*, Vol. VI, CDDH/SR.40, Par. 29–34, pp. 124–125.

128. *Ibid.*, CDDH/SR.41, Par. 18, p. 144.

129. *Ibid.*, CDDH/SR.41, Par. 22, p. 145.

130. *Ibid.*, CDDH/SR.41, Par. 41, p. 149.

131. *Ibid.*, Vol. III, CDDH/I/340, pp. 360–61. The other co-sponsors were Bolivia, Ecuador, Guatemala, Honduras, Peru, Nicaragua, Panama and Venezuela.

132. *Ibid.*, Vol. XVI, CDDH/IV/226, pp. 555–579; CDDH/IV/SR.10, Par. 25, pp. 38–39; CDDH/IV/SR.36, par. 37, p. 380.

133. *Ibid.*, CDDH/IV/211, pp. 585–586.

134. *Ibid.*, CDDH/IV/212, p. 587.

135. See Resolution 22 (IV) of the Conference on the continuation of work on the "follow-up regarding prohibition or restriction of use of certain conventional weapons", *Diplomatic Conference on the Reaffirmation and Development of International Humanitarian Law Applicable in Armed Conflicts*, Final Act, Vol. I, pp. 52–53. *The Laws of Armed Conflicts: A Collection of Conventions, Resolutions and Other Documents*. Edited by D. Schindler and J. Toman, 3rd revised and completed edition; Dordrecht, Martinus Nijhoff Publishers, Geneva, Henry Dunant Institute, 1988, pp. 729–730.

136. *Official Records of the Diplomatic Conference on the Reaffirmation and Development of International Humanitarian Law Applicable in Armed Conflicts, Geneva (1974–1977)*, Berne, Federal Political Department, 1978, Vol. VIII, CDDH/I/SR.29, Par. 7, p. 286.

137. *Ibid.*, Vol. VII, CDDH/SR.49, Par. 39, p. 66.

CHAPTER VI

THE WESTERN CONCEPT

KARL JOSEPH PARTSCH

Humanitarian ideas have certainly been developed by various schools of thought in the western world. Is it really possible, however, to speak of a "western concept"? Can this concept be clearly distinguished from those of three continents which for a long time were strongly influenced by European culture, civilization and legal thought?

"Western civilization or culture" is a political term originating only a few decades ago and applying to certain highly industrialized countries with an economic system based on private enterprise, and a political system based on respect for individual rights and the rule of law. The greater part of that civilization originates in Greek and Roman philosophies and in the Christian faith. Viewed from outside, this civilization or culture is largely identified with those states which in the nineteenth century ruled over other parts of the world, mainly as colonial powers. Only from this point of view can the term "western" be justified. The "western" concept of things has no geographical or regional basis and should not be related to periods of history. When the Czar of Russia joined the Holy Alliance in 1815 or when he proposed the Hague Peace Conference in 1899, he clearly followed "western ideas". The same was the case when, in 1856, Turkey, though an Islamic State, joined the alliance of European powers.

On the other hand, not all countries which are at present regarded as "western" have always identified themselves with this qualification. Significant, for instance, are the words of the German writer, Thomas Mann.[1] When speaking about the concept of freedom, he emphasized the spiritual nature of this concept as developed in the German tradition in contrast to its more concrete meaning in the "political west". The world of ideas and culture, because of its very nature, cannot be identified with certain political groups. It knows other frontiers and other regions. In examining the development of international humanitarian law, two main schools of thought have to be taken into consideration: on the one hand, Christianity in all its different forms, with its doctrines of charity and brotherhood; on the other hand secular humanism based on the revival and development, at the time of the enlightenment, of classical thought. Its main element is the recognition of each human being as such, irrespective of his relation to supernatural powers or to the State to which he belongs.

Besides the difficulty of defining "western" concepts, there is the reality that humanitarian endeavours, by their very nature, tend to be universal. In order not to discredit the universal character of their mission, those who developed the ideas of humanitarian law were very often reluctant to disclose the source of their motives. Although, in the following pages, some testimonies of the founders of the humanitarian movement, closely connected with the Red Cross, are cited, this does not imply that the humanitarian movement as a whole is considered to belong to the "west". Such references only help to show which schools of thought were influential.

Among the various elements included in the term a "western concept of humanitarian law", the oldest is certainly the Christian doctrine of charity and brotherhood. The practical charity of Christian orders in giving care to the sick and the wounded is well known.[2] In the sixteenth century, for instance, a congregation of Camillians known as "Fathers of the Good Cross" wore a Red Cross as their badge. During the 17th and 18th centuries, there were numerous agreements among Christian princes regarding the exchange of prisoners, the protection of the sick and wounded, respect for hospital sites and for medical personnel who were not to be made prisoners of war.[3] In the middle of the 18th century an English committee assisting French prisoners of war wrote: "To come to the aid of one's enemy, what else is this but to act humanely by uniting in brotherly affection, thus banishing the hatred which nations have for one another and preparing them to build a world of friendship and peace".[4] One has real cause to doubt whether what is expressed here is still exclusively a Christian feeling of brotherhood or a new concept of humanity based on modern concepts, similar to the words of Jean-Jacques Rousseau: "Since the aim of war is to subdue a hostile State, a combatant has the right to kill the defenders of that State while they are armed; but as soon as they lay down their arms and surrender, they cease to be either enemies or instruments of the enemy; they become simply men once more, and no one has any longer the right to take their lives". He added: "«These principles» are derived from the nature of things; they are based on reason".[5]

This new doctrine inspired by reason and not religion – and even opposed to the Church – had political effects. "The law of nature places limits on the rules of war" declared the "Encyclopédie" (1751 to 1775) and a "cosmopolitan humanitarian aspect" largely determined the "Declaration of the Rights of Men and Citizens" (1789) modelled on the Constitution of Virginia with the close co-operation of Thomas Jefferson.[6]

At the time when the great struggle between Christianity and the new doctrines of national humanism seemed to favour the former, the founders of the Holy Alliance declared their firm determination to apply exclusively the precepts of the Christian religion as their rule of conduct. In one of the rare instruments of a humanitarian character created at that time – the Declaration of the Abolition of the Slave Trade of 8 February 1815[7] – the same States declared that the trade of Negroes from Africa «was considered by just and enlightened men throughout time to be repugnant to the principles of humanity and universal morals», thus using the terminology of secular humanism instead of speaking of Christian brotherhood or charity.

A further similarity between secular humanism and the idea of Christian brotherhood is to be found in the work of J. Henry Dunant, "A Memory of Solferino".[8] It is well known that his family members were Seventh Day Adventists, a reform sect founded by the Methodists, and that he was brought up by a deeply religious mother. When still a young man he was one of the founders of the YMCA.[9]

The Christian faith had a strong influence on the formation of his personality. Even as an old man and after a deep cleft with Church and society he confessed: "I have never wanted to be anything but a disciple of Jesus Christ".[10] His report on the battle of Solferino is limited strictly to facts and very rarely mentions the motives and intentions which led him to publish it. Only towards the end, when he explains his plan of founding voluntary relief societies, do occasional sentences that explain his programme appear. Such societies would be of importance both from the point of view of humanism and of Christianity.[11] In the following pages, however, expressions taken from the ideology of the enlightenment or secular humanism appear more frequently than those from the Christian world: "humanity" and "philanthropy"[12], "civilization"[13] and "progress".[14]

Max Huber[15] even suggests that Dunant and the Committee of Five intentionally abstained from referring to Christian brotherhood or from giving their plans a Christian character, in order not to jeopardize the chances of their endeavours achieving universal success. Their programme of humanitarian work was to appear as an expression of humanism absolutely neutral towards both Christian ideologies and secular ethics.[16]

The only lawyer on the Committee of Five was Gustave Moynier, the first President of the ICRC, who held this position for no less than 47 years (1863 to 1910). It was certainly thanks to him that only the politically acceptable ideas of Dunant were given prominence. He also undoubtedly played a considerable part in drafting the first Convention of 1864. In his "Essai sur les caractères généraux des lois de la guerre"[17], however, his standpoint regarding the influence of Christian or secular ideas on the development of humanitarian law and of the Red Cross remains ambiguous. On the one hand, the new law of war is for him a "direct fruit of Christianity"[18], when he deals with the influence of moral ideas on the law of war. He admits that other religions such as Islam also contributed to the triumph of fraternity and justice.[19] He denies, however, any influence of the secular doctrine of fraternity propagated by the French Revolution. On the other hand, when speaking about the laws of war and the history of philosophies, he develops a spiritualist concept of progress which he identified originally with the solidarity of generations, calling the Law of War a result of the idea of progress[20], without explaining clearly the relationship between these two ideas. He is certainly right in saying that during the nineteenth century both ideas had an influence on the development of humanitarian law as well as on the Red Cross movement. It remains only to define the relationship of these influences. The third President of the ICRC, following Gustave Moynier (1864–1910) and Gustave Ador (1910–1928), was an eminent lawyer, Max Huber, whom Erich Kaufmann even called one of the very few great lawyers of his generation.[21] A former judge of the International Court of Justice whom important world powers chose on various occasions as individual arbitrator, he gave up his high office in order to serve the Red Cross during the difficult years from 1928 to 1944. For him, the conflict between the religious motives of the founders of the Red Cross movement and their neutral position towards any religious doctrine was a personal problem. He was not only a Christian believer but an active Christian thinker. His faith determined his attitude to problems of State, politics and the social order.[22] In his writings, however, he was able to draw a clear line between his personal convictions and the official position of the Red Cross which should correspond to the position of the States parties to the Geneva Conventions. In 1943 he wrote that, from different ideas of philosophical and religious thinking and also from different human experiences, one should be able to find an approach to the ideas of the Red Cross, to its ethical principles and also to its activities.[23] Nevertheless, he never tried to introduce his personal position into the ethics of the Red Cross, which he referred to as an incorporation of the idea of humanity and practical humanism with perfect neutrality towards any religious doctrine or intellectual ideology. He denied that the cosmopolitan and secular ethic of the Red Cross could be incompatible with religious neutrality. Religious or ideological orientation should be each individual's personal responsibility. Everyone – irrespective of his individual viewpoint – should have access to this absolutely neutral world of humanitarian work. He even formulated a new word for the collaboration of men of different ethics: they should work not only on an international but also on an "inter-ethical" neutral basis.[24]

It is not astonishing that it was a Swiss lawyer who developed and formulated in such a clear way the principles of neutrality which not only determine the work of the Red Cross but also play a decisive role in humanitarian law. The concept of "protecting powers"[25] is based upon the concept of neutrality. No doubt the Swiss Federation's tradition of permanent neutrality has had a great influence on the introduction of this idea into humanitarian law. Likewise the special protection accorded to all kinds of medical services is also based on this concept.

The extension of humanitarian law to territories and States outside Europe reflects the history of decolonization. The fact that nearly all of the new States ratified the Conventions only a short time after they gained independence, clearly demonstrates that they did not regard international humanitarian law as a domain of the former colonial powers but as a universal task. The idea of international humanitarian law was founded by individuals in Europe and in the United States of America. The States which initially took up this idea have certainly used their influence in other parts of the world in order to extend this idea to other continents. They have never regarded it as exclusively their own and it is remarkable that their idea has met with such universal approval.

Notes

1. Mann Thomas, *Betrachtungen eines Unpolitischen.* Berlin, S. Fischer, 1918, p. 264 ff.
2. Coursier Henri, *The International Red Cross*, Geneva, ICRC, 1961, p. 7.
Pictet Jean, 'La Croix Rouge et les Conventions de Genève', *Recueil des Cours*, Academie du Droit International, La Haye, 1950, p. 27 ff.
3. Pictet, Jean, *loc. cit.*, Chapter I, note 2, p. 27.
4. Coursier, Henri, *op. cit.*, Chapter I, note 2, p. 10.
5. Rousseau Jean-Jacques, *Du Contrat Social*, 1762, Livre I, Chapter IV. English text from Jean-Jacques Rousseau, *The Social Contract*. Translated by Maurice Cranston. Harmondsworth, Penguin Books, 1968, p. 57.
6. Coursier, Henri, *op. cit.*, Chapter I, note 2, p. 12.
7. De Martens, G.F., *Nouveau Recueil des Traités*, Tome II, 1814–1815, Goettingue, Dietrich, 1817, p. 432.
8. Dunant, Henry, *A Memory of Solférino.* (English version, American Red Cross, 1939, 1959), Geneva, International Committee of the Red Cross, 1986, 147 p.
9. Coursier, Henri, *op. cit.*, Chapter I, note 2, p. 15 ff.
10. Huber, Max, *The Good Samaritan: Reflections on the Gospel and Work in the Red Cross*, London, Gollancz, Ltd., 1945, p. 32.
Original version in German: *Der barmherzige Samariter: Betrachtungen über Evangelicum und Rotkreuzarbeit*, Dritte Auflage, Zürich, Schulthess and Co., 1944, p. 10. Cf. Also *Vermischte Schriften*, Band II, 1948.
11. Dunant, Henry, *op. cit.*, p. 116.
12. *Ibid.*, pp. 117, 120, 124–127.
13. *Ibid.*, pp. 126–127.
14. *Ibid.*, p. 127.
15. Huber, M., *The Good Samaritan: Reflections on the Gospel and Work in the Red Cross*, London, Gollancz, Ltd., 1945, p. 31.
16. *Ibid.*, pp. 31, 33, 35, 36.
17. Moynier, Gustave, *Essai sur les caractères generaux des lois de la guerre*, Genève, Eggiman, C. & Cie, 1895, 120 p.
18. *Ibid.*, p. 85.
19. *Ibid.*, p. 89.
20. *Ibid.*, p. 95 ff.
21. Memorial speech before the Knights of Order "Pour le Mérite" in Kaufmann Erich, *Gesammelte Schriften*, Göttingen, Schwartz, O., 1960, vol. III, p. 379 ff.
22. See also his other essays Huber, Max, *The Red Cross: Principles and Problems*, Geneva, ICRC, n.d., 191 p. and *Glaube und Kirche*, in *Vermischte Schriften*, Band II, Zürich, Atlantis Verlag, 1948, 371 p.
23. Huber, Max, *Glaube und Kirche*, in *Vermischte Schriften*, Band II, Zürich, Atlantis Verlag, 1948, p. 37. See also his essays 'The Red Cross Idea at the Present Time', 1934, in *The Red Cross: Principles and Problems*, Zürich, 1941, and 'Völkerrechtliche Grundsätze, Aufgaben und Probleme des Roten Kreuzes', *in Jahrbuch für internationales Recht*, Vol. I, 1944, pp. 1–47.
24. Huber, Max, *Glaube und Kirche*, in *Vermischte Schriften*, Band II, Zürich, Atlantis Verlag, 1948, p. 38.

25. Neutral states which are entrusted with the defence of a belligerent's interests on the territory of its enemies. Under the Geneva Conventions, it is a function of the Protecting Powers to operate in and scrutinize the application of the Conventions.

PART II

THE DEVELOPMENT OF INTERNATIONAL HUMANITARIAN LAW

CHAPTER VII

THE DEVELOPMENT OF INTERNATIONAL HUMANITARIAN LAW

G.I.A.D. DRAPER

A. The Origin and Emergence of Humanitarian Law

In one sense the tracing of the humanitarian law of armed conflicts embraces the history of the law of war, one of the oldest collective activities of mankind. More precisely, the emergence of that law is traceable from that period in the history of the law of war when the principle of humanity became the predominant element in restraint, as opposed to the older sources of restraint such as honour, religion and commercial profit. This principle of humanity lies at the root of our contemporary regimes of human rights. However, it began to take over and inform much of the content of the rules of the law of war at an earlier date. Opinions differ as to when the ascendancy of the principle of humanity in the law of war began. The unfolding of law follows broader movements of the moral, political, social and economic climate, which is part of the unfolding history of the civilization of the human race.

Contemporary jurists distinguish between the international law governing the recourse to war and the law governing conduct in war. This has been the position since the effective demise of the doctrine of the "just war" in its classical form.[1] Some modern recrudescences or modifications of the "just war" doctrine have not been lacking, but its practical dominance was in decline by the 17th century. Until the classical doctrine of the "just war" ended, the binding force of the rules of war governing the belligerents was weakened.[2] It was part of the seminal contribution of Grotius to the law of war that enunciated the doctrine that the "justness" or otherwise of the cause for which one or other belligerent had resorted to war was irrelevant to the duty of observing the rules of warfare by those belligerents.[3] This was innovatory thinking at a time considerably before that doctrine was accepted as a firm principle of international law. The second great contribution of Grotius to the law of war was the famous *temperamenta belli* which he appended to his great work on "The Law of War and Peace" published in 1625.[4] In the preface thereto he explains the reason for this part of his work which highlighted his Christian shame and horror at the current excesses in warfare. The war then in progress was the Thirty Years War concluded at the "Peace of Westphalia" in 1648. In words that perhaps augur the humanitarian approach to the law of war of the latter 19th century and of our own time, Grotius wrote:

> "Throughout the Christian world I observed a lack of restraint in relation to war such as even barbarous races would be ashamed of. I observed that men rush to arms for slight causes, or no cause at all, and that when arms have once been taken up, there is no longer any respect for law, divine or human; it is as if, in accordance with a general decree, frenzy had openly been let loose for the committing of all crimes".[5]

Although Grotius's approach to the current excesses in warfare is marked by a certain ambivalence between the actual practice of States in war and what he thought ought to be the law, Grotius's *temperamenta belli* came to be the basis and content of much of the 17th and 18th century customary law of war. Primarily Grotius's sense of outrage is rooted in his Christianity, and its traditional aversion from that lust for killing and destruction [6] which were the normal systems of warfare. This aversion inspired his writing on the law of war. Inherent in it are the Christian ideals of justice, love and mercy, and their nexus and harmony with the natural law. In those Christian values, shared by other religions, lies the basis of the contemporary compassion for all human suffering, the desire to reduce it, which is in its turn, the core of our secular humanitarianism of today.

Rousseau, in his influential work, "Le Contrat Social" (1752), which was promptly condemned and burnt in Geneva, propounded some new and revolutionary ideas about warfare. First, he advanced the theory that: "War, then, is not a relation between men, but between states, in war individuals are enemies wholly by chance, not as men, not even as citizens, but only as soldiers, not as members of their country, but only as its defenders".[7] This doctrine was born of his own era of the "cabinet wars" but it also had considerable influence upon the political and legal thinking about war in the 19th century. Its relevance to our modern warfare is open to doubt. Second, Rousseau argued that:

> "Since the aim of war is to subdue a hostile State, a combatant has the right to kill the defenders of that state while they are armed; but as soon as they lay down their arms and surrender, they cease to be either enemies or instruments of the enemy; they become simply men once more, and no one has any longer the right to take their lives. It is sometimes possible to destroy a state without killing a single one of its members, and war gives no right to inflict any more destruction than is necessary for victory. These principles were not invented by

Grotius, nor are they founded on the authority of the poets; they are derived from the nature of things; they are based on reason."[8]

As one writer has put it: -

"by raising the idea of war to the level of inter-State relations he (Rousseau) opened the way for an improvement in man-to-man relationships in time of war...Rousseau prepared the way for humanitarian ideas through his philosophy of rationalism and common sense. Along that route have gone the series of Geneva Conventions and other law-making instruments designed to establish the limits of violence in war and to impose humanitarian standards of conduct at all points beyond those limits".[9]

This thinking does not bring us to the complexity of modern humanitarian ideals. Rousseau is primarily concerned to advocate restraint in warfare, particularly in the treatment of surrendered or wounded enemy individuals who fall into the hands of their adversary. He proceeds on the basis of reason, rather than compassion and the mitigation of suffering as a value in its own right worthy of universal observance in warfare. With Rousseau's theories, we approach, and even enter, the ideal of humanitarianism, but we do not reach its core.

In the second half of the 19th century a number of factors combined to accelerate and augment the humanitarian approach to the law of war to an extent that it became an influential consideration in the formulation of the various international law instruments that sought to codify the existing customary law of war. Humanitarian thinking is manifest in the series of Hague Conventions of 1899 and 1907, the preceding Declaration of St. Petersburg of 1868 concerning small inflammatory projectiles, and the two Hague Declarations of 1899 dealing respectively with asphyxiating gases and expanding bullets.[10] The latter half of the 19th century, in terms of international law theory, marked the high tide of legal positivism exemplified in the urge for written texts as opposed to the supposed vagueness of customary rules. Positivism also emphasized Conventions to mark the crucial consent of states to the rules formulated therein.

In the history of international law, the law of war was the first part of it to receive codification.[11] As a result it has become, by our day, one of the most out of date parts of international law. Such is the price of precocity in codification. Legal positivism was allied with other contemporary developments of a non-legal nature. First, there was the enormous increase in the size of land armies through resort to conscription. That tendency detracted from the relevance of Rousseau's theory that war was primarily an affair between States and not between individuals. Second, there was the relatively major advance in the technology of weapons, primarily, artillery. Third, there was failure of the older tactics of mass infantry formations to hold their own with the new artillery capacity. At the battle of Gettysburg, 1862, the "flower" of the Virginian infantry of the Southern forces perished under the murderous artillery fire, at point-blank range, of the Northern

(Federalist) artillery.[12] Fourth, there was the inadequacy of the military medical services and skills available to meet promptly the needs of the wounded in large armies equipped with such destructive weaponry. This failure was marked for posterity by the appalling loss of life from failing to tend the wounded at and after the battle of Solferino in 1859. This battle is often considered to have been the beginning of the modern humanitarian movement creating law. At that battle about 38,000 were killed or wounded in fifteen hours. Of these wounded many died from lack of medical care and attention, aggravated by the heat of the day and the lack of water and medicaments for wounded men.[13] At this battle there was present a Swiss citizen, Henry Dunant, not as a soldier but as a civilian for purposes unrelated to the war then in progress between Austria and France. Dunant saw the full horrors of the battle. He organised on his own initiative, with civilian assistance, a rudimentary system for giving such medical aid and care to the countless wounded men in their agony as his limited and improvised resources permitted. That experience led him to write his famous pamphlet, "A Memory of Solferino", published in 1862 and again in 1863. This work, and the experience set out in it by Dunant from first hand knowledge, had a wide distribution and did as much as anything to initiate and expand the humanitarian climate of the period.

Dunant's first proposal was that each State should establish in time of peace a relief society to aid the army medical services in time of war. His second proposal was that the States of the world, primarily European, should conclude an international Convention acknowledging the status and function of such relief societies. Dunant, a citizen of Geneva, is generally recognized today as the founder of the Red Cross movement.[14] The International Committee of the Red Cross (ICRC), with its seat at Geneva and its membership confined to Swiss nationals,[15] has become the promoter and custodian of the humanitarian ideal and the primary initiator for its translation into international humanitarian law, as seen today in the series of Geneva Conventions designed for the protection of victims of war, 1864 to 1949, and of the Additional Protocols of 1977. This was and is a remarkable achievement which the world owes to the memory of Henry Dunant, and to other prominent Swiss citizens of his day such as General Dufour. The first and pioneering Geneva Convention in this development of humanitarian law was the Geneva Convention for the Amelioration of the Condition of the Wounded in Armies in the Field, of 1864.[16] By 1867 the Great Powers of the day had ratified this first modest step in the establishment of the modern international humanitarian law of war.

There had been, among the military classes from mediaeval times, a certain climate of mutual respect on the battlefield. The enemy belonged to the same class of military men governed by the same law, the law of arms. The older ideas of chivalry, honour and mutual respect complemented each other, so far as the military calling was concerned, but such ideas were confined to that calling only.[17] The humanitarian ideal has inherited those ideas, transformed them and expanded them with a new content. The older ideas of mutual respect and honour, in the process of time, become respect for and protection of the wounded, the sick and the prisoners of war. Such ideas expand into compassion for the suffering victims of warfare and into the attempt to reduce that suffering which is inherent in warfare.

The new 19th century humanitarian law has its remote parentage in religious and chivalric ideas. On these were superimposed 18th century nationalism and sensibility. They were, in their turn, followed by the 19th century acceptance of secular compassion and the resultant desire to reduce suffering in war, to protect and respect those who were, by definition, defenceless in the hands of the enemy as prisoners or wounded or sick, or as civilians. Such is the route of humanitarianism exemplified in the humanitarian law of our century.

This movement, in so far as it was translated into International Law for the regulation of warfare, had a triple base, which can be traced to three outstanding figures. The first was Henry Dunant, the man of compassion for the wounded in battle.[18] The second was the refugee professor who settled and made his career in the U.S.A., Francis Lieber,[19] a jurist with an extensive knowledge of the customary law of warfare acquired in Europe. In 1863, there was issued by President Lincoln "Army Order No. 100", entitled *Instructions for the Government of the United States Armies in the Field*. This work was prepared to meet the needs of the large numbers of commanders and staff officers in the Federal Forces, whose experience in the field was limited. These *Instructions* had been prepared, substantially, by Professor Lieber. He had reduced into written military instruction the customary law of land warfare, a considerable tribute to his legal ability and knowledge. These *Instructions* were accepted by the committee of Generals and others with whom he had worked and in due course promulgated by President Lincoln as *Army Order No. 100*. In effect, this work was a one-man codification of the customary law of land warfare, a considerable feat.

The third element was the initiative of Imperial Russia through the Tsars Alexander II and Nicolas II. In 1874 a Conference was convened at Brussels by Tsar Alexander II at which the *Instructions* drafted by Professor Lieber was a preparatory text. This Conference was abortive, but the proposals were brought forward to the First Hague Peace Conference of 1899 convened by Tsar Nicolas II. At this Conference, four Conventions were established. At the second Hague Peace Conference held in 1907, for which the U.S.A. shared the initiative with Tsar Nicolas II, 13 Conventions were established including those which had failed to secure adoption in Brussels in 1874. Of these adopted in 1907 the most important for the development of international humanitarian law was Hague Convention No. IV of 1907 concerning the Laws of Customs of War on Land. Throughout this precocious codification of the law of war on land and at sea, extending to 12 Conventions, the Russian jurist, Frederic de Martens,[20] played a prominent role. He held the chair of international law at the University of St. Petersburg and had written extensively on the subject. He was also the adviser to the Imperial Foreign Ministry at the two Hague Peace Conferences of 1899 and 1907. Critics have accused him of making expediency a principle of international law, but his place in the unfolding of humanitarian law is assured. He was the author of the "de Martens Preamble" to Hague Convention No. IV of 1907. He was, without doubt, the catalyzing figure at both Hague Peace Conferences. The importance of this Preamble is not limited to providing the principles underlying Convention No. IV. In more recent times, it has been the starting point and the avenue through which some of the most recent extensions and additions to humanitarian law have been made in the two "Additional Protocols" of 1977.

The de Martens preamble of 1907 [21] is expressive of the late 19th century humanitarianism which informed and guided the Hague Regulations annexed to Convention No. IV. Therein we find the classical attempt to accommodate military requirements to the principle of humanity in war. Frederic de Martens thought that this could best be done, on the one hand, by defining the laws of war with greater precision and, on the other hand, by confining them in such a way as to mitigate their severity as much as possible. This was a bold undertaking that reflected the contemporary humanitarian approach to the law of war and the positivist theory of the need for written texts of the law. It is perhaps not too much to say that the F. de Martens Preamble to the 1907 Hague Convention on the Laws and Customs of War on Land crystallized and summarized the 19th century development of the humanitarian law of war. The redactors of the modern law of war, whether of the Geneva Conventions of 1949 or of the Protocols Additional thereto of 1977, have exploited the ideas in the Martens' famous preamble. Developments in the law since 1945 have been based upon his thesis. The clauses in his preamble which have inspired and directed the ICRC in its 20th century endeavours to develop the humanitarian law of war are:

> "...Being animated also by the desire to serve, even in this extreme case (where war could not be prevented), the interest of humanity and the ever progressive needs of civilization;
> "...these provisions the drafting of which has been inspired by the desire to diminish the evils of war, so far as military requirements permit, are intended to serve as a general rule of conduct for the belligerents in their mutual relations, and in their relations with the inhabitants,...
> Until a more complete code of the laws can be drawn up, the High Contracting Parties deem it expedient to declare that, in cases not covered by the rules adopted by them, the inhabitants and the belligerents remain under the protection and governance of the principles of the law of nations, derived from the usages established among civilized peoples, from the laws of humanity, and from the dictates of the public conscience...

If there be any one place in the extensive codification of the law of war completed at the turn of the 19th century which proclaims the essence of the ideas which guided its redactors, it may be found in this preamble. It would be a mistake to regard it as no more than an oratorial flight of fine words. It reflects, on the contrary, with precision of language, the ideas of the positive jurists and of the essential nexus between military requirements, the dictates of humanity, the standards of civilization, and the value of codification of international law. This is the culmination of the work of Dunant, Lieber and de Martens during the second half of the 19th century, in establishing the inspiration, the theory, and the content of humanitarian law of war inherited by our century. The work of jurists and others in this century has been to explore and exploit this theory and to build upon the body of humanitarian rules of war which we have inherited from them. This process is still under way.

B. The Development of Humanitarian Law in the 20th Century

The extensive codification of the law of war at the start of the 20th century was the outcome of its approach to the central question of how to accommodate military needs to the dictates of humanity in time of war. In one sense, that has been the perennial endeavour of those concerned with the progressive development of the law of war. Lying behind these ideas were fundamental questions about the proper treatment of man by man in warfare, maintenance of the standards of civilization, and the need to answer such questions by the use of reason.

It is a curious paradox that the humanitarian approach was, in point of time, coincident with the high-tide of nationalism and the legal conception of State sovereignty. Thus, whilst the dictates of humanity, rationalism, and the standards of civilization, were informing and colouring much of the content of the law of war (*jus in bello*) as codified at the two Hague Peace Conferences of 1899 and 1907, respectively, the extensive claims for state sovereignty, under the impulse of nationalism, had no less success. Thus at that period, the opening of the 20th century, jurists of repute contended that, under international law, States had the right to resort to war as an instrument of national policy,[22] i.e., as an inherent part of their sovereignty which could be validly curtailed only by treaties, normally bilateral, of friendship or alliance, which inhibited the exercise of that right, and were concluded according to the policy of the day. Apart from such consensual legal restraints upon the resort to war by a State, there were two minor restraints imposed at the Hague 2nd Peace Conference of 1907, namely, Convention No. II on the Limitation on the Employment of Force for the Recovery of Contract Debts, and Convention No. III, relating to the Opening of Hostilities.[23] In relation to the law governing resort to war, *jus ad bellum*, the latter was of considerably more importance than the former. Convention No. II was a legal restraint upon certain aspects of "gunboat diplomacy" aimed at recovering the public debts owing to States which had lent money to the then developing countries, mainly in South America.

A more serious intrusion of the doctrine of sovereignty was contained in the Hague Conventions of 1907 relating to land and sea warfare. Thus in Convention No. IV on Land Warfare one finds the "General Participation Clause" (the clause *si omnes*)[24], the effect of which was to impair to a serious degree the application of the rules in the Convention designed to impose humanitarian standards on the conduct of belligerents. Thus, in Article 2 of that Convention we find:

> "The provisions contained in the Regulations (annexed) as well as in the present Convention, do not apply except as between Contracting Powers, and then only if all the belligerents are parties to the Convention".

This intrusion of sovereignty is something far more powerful than compelling military demands, the so-called doctrine of military necessity.[25] Unless all States engaged in the war are bound by the Convention in question, none is bound. It must also be recalled that the treaty tradition was bilateral rather than multilateral. To codify the existing customary law of war, and certainly to make new law, a multilateral Convention was needed. States thus reflected their reliance upon sovereignty and their lack of confidence at that time in international legislation about warfare.

At the same time another aspect of nationalism led to a new and interesting development in the regulations annexed to Hague Convention No. IV. Certain new States, such as Belgium, had to struggle for their accession and independence. Other States had been subjected to invasion and occupation in the course of the 19th century, such as Russia, Spain, Poland and the Netherlands. The smaller States were no less moved by nationalism, but were more vulnerable to invasion by a neighbouring State with large armed forces. In the Hague Peace Conferences such smaller States sought, and were opposed by more powerful States in their attempt, to include within the new codified rules of warfare an extended classification of those fighters who should be entitled to belligerent status.[26] Traditionally, the law of war had been jealous in its attribution of the privilege of belligerency and the consequential right to claim prisoner – of – war (POW) status upon capture. That status was at that time becoming more important with the codification of the customary rules governing their treatment. POW rights were being given precision through codification in the Regulations annexed to Convention No. IV. Smaller and weaker states, under the claim of nationalism, secured an extension of the class of fighters upon whom the benefit of "the laws, rights and duties of war were conferred". This entitlement expressly included the right to be treated as prisoners upon capture. As a result, Article 1 of the Regulations annexed to the Convention, provided:

> The laws, rights and duties of war apply not only to the army, but also to militia and volunteer corps fulfilling all the following conditions:
> 1. They must be commanded by a person responsible for his subordinates;
> 2. They must have a fixed distinctive sign recognizable at a distance;
> 3. They must carry arms openly; and
> 4. They must conduct their operations in accordance with the laws and customs of war.[27]

This was a considerable gain for States with small or no regular forces. It legitimated the franc-tireur and partisan group if its members met the requirements of the four conditions enumerated. This, however, was not enough, in the light of the adverse military experiences sustained by some States at the hands of a powerful invading force. To meet this situation Article 2 was included in the Hague Regulations. This provision was designed to meet the predicament of a State the territory of which had been invaded so swiftly that its defenders could not meet the requirements needed to come within the expanded class of belligerent armed forces specified in Article 1 above. Article 2, therefore, legitimizes in the utmost limit, the lawful belligerency of the irregular fighter. That limit was justified, in the minds of the redactors, by the lack of time within which to organize armed forces by a State confronted with a swift invasion. Its humanitarian value is open to doubt. Article 2 has rarely been applied since 1907. It has, however, provided a precedent for later developments of the law to meet the position of guerrilla fighters. It will be noted that it does not apply to resistance movements within occupied territory.

Article 2 of the Hague Regulations, 1907 is in these terms:

> "The inhabitants of a territory not under occupation, who, on the approach of the enemy, spontaneously take up arms to resist the invading troops without having had time to organize themselves in accordance with Article 1 (above), shall be regarded as belligerents if they carry arms openly and if they respect the laws and customs of war.[28]

Article 3 confers upon such inhabitants the right to be treated as POWs. This is an interesting provision from the viewpoint of the historian of the law of war. Older rules about the "openness" of the conduct of warfare, the avoidance of stealth or trickery, born of the ideals of chivalry and honour, and the practical and humanitarian need to recognize the adversary, meet, in this provision, the claims of nationalism and military needs. Humanitarian needs have been substantially ignored.

The Hague Regulations of 1907 have been seen, perhaps erroneously, as an instrument governing the conduct of hostilities on land. In fact, they also dealt with the protection of prisoners of war, spies, pacific relations between belligerents and military authority in occupied territory. Thus the isolation of Hague

Convention No. IV from the main stream of the development of humanitarian law is erroneous. Later developments, namely, the conclusion of the Geneva Conventions of 1929 and 1949, and the Protocols additional thereto of 1977 have in large part superseded Hague Convention No. IV for States which are Parties to these latter instruments. That part of the Regulations annexed to the Convention No. IV which dealt exclusively with the conduct of hostilities[29] is not entirely superseded today.

Between the codification of the law of war in 1907 and the outbreak of war in 1914, there was no significant augmentation to that law. The experiences of warfare during the years 1914–1918 revealed the inadequacy of the law of war, not so much in the breaches of it, as in the gaps in the content. Much of the content of the Hague Convention of 1907 was substantially a codification of the customary law up to that date. It was a backwards-looking instrument that had little relation to the scale and type of warfare conducted in World War I. That war witnessed the initiation of serial warfare and of limited serial bombing of land targets, an activity that had been envisaged in Hague Regulations, Article 25.[30] The impression of World War I, so far as the law of war was concerned, was threefold. First, the Geneva Sick and Wounded Convention of 1906 was not adequate for the scale and nature of casualties inflicted. Second, the rules for the proper treatment of POWs were likewise inadequate. The belligerents had found it necessary to conclude agreements during the course of the war to meet the deficiencies in the Hague Regulations. In particular, the Berne Agreements of 1917 and 1918 were concluded to resolve disputed matters which the Hague Regulations did not resolve.[31] Third, and more shocking to public opinion, was the use of poison gas by Germany, which caused that "unnecessary suffering" expressly condemned by Article 23(e) of the Hague Regulations of 1907. This was the first time that gas had been used in warfare. Chemical warfare had begun.[32]

All three experiences were countered with a legal response. The ICRC secured the establishment of the Geneva Convention for the Amelioration of the Condition of the Wounded and Sick in Armies in the Field and the Convention relative to the Treatment of Prisoners of War, of 1929. Both instruments were the outcome of a Diplomatic Conference convened by the Swiss Government, the preparatory work for which had been done by the ICRC with the assistance of experts.[33] The Geneva POW Convention of 1929 did not supersede the Hague Convention No. IV of 1907. The Geneva Sick and Wounded Conventions of 1864 and 1906, however, were replaced by the Sick and Wounded Convention of 1929 for those States which were Parties to the latter instrument. Both Geneva Conventions of 1929 expressly excluded the "general participation clause", which had been included in the Geneva Sick and Wounded Convention of 1906 and in Article 2 of the Hague Convention of 1907. Thus Article 25 of the Geneva Sick and Wounded Convention, 1929 provided:

"If, in time of war, a belligerent is not a Party to the Convention, its provisions shall, nevertheless, be binding as between all the belligerents who are parties thereto".[34]

A like provision was included in Article 82 of the Geneva POW Convention of 1929.[35] Thus, the paralyzing effects of the general participation clause were annulled in the humanitarian instruments of 1929 designed for the better and more humane protection of the sick and wounded and of POW war victims, the primary concern of the humanitarian law of war.

A traditional device for the enforcement of the law of war, inherited from the customary law, but not excluded by conventional law, was the resort to reprisals, i.e., an act of warfare otherwise illegal which is deprived of the taint of illegality when used as a final resort to stop previous illegalities committed by the enemy.[36] From a very early time reprisals had been used as a crude but sometimes effective method of enforcing the law of war, based on the pragmatic principle of reciprocity. In the law of sea warfare a number of accepted customary rules had emerged from reprisal practices. This had not proved to be an avenue for the establishment of humanitarian law. In practice, reprisals had led to increasingly grave violations of the law of war.

Reprisals are, in general, inimical to the implementation of humanitarian law. The ICRC of Geneva is entitled to much credit in its move to restrict the legality of the resort to reprisals in warfare, starting with the 1929 Geneva Conventions. The law relating to POWs did not fall within the ambit of the Geneva Conventions until 1929. As we have seen, respect for, and proper treatment of, the wounded and sick in the armed forces had been the subject of the Geneva Conventions from their inception in 1864. The Hague Convention No. IV of 1907 made no mention of reprisals; neither did the two Geneva Sick and Wounded Conventions of 1864 and 1906. In 1929 the development of humanitarian law took a major step forward. The law governing POWs and the sick and wounded in the armed forces was then referred to the same Diplomatic Conference working on texts prepared by the ICRC and experts. Article 2 of the Geneva POW Convention of 1929 provides:

"Measures of reprisal against them (POWs) are forbidden."[37]

This rule was then applicable to the treatment of sick and wounded in the Armed Forces in enemy hands by providing in Article 2 of the Sick and Wounded Convention of 1929:

"... the wounded and sick of an army who fall into the hands of the enemy shall be prisoners of war, and the general provisions of international law concerning prisoners of war shall be applied to them".[38]

Thus, by these two provisions the systems of resort to reprisals directed against members of the armed forces defenceless in the hands of the enemy was removed from the law of war. This was a notable gain in the development of humanitarian law which has had powerful repercussions on the most recent developments of humanitarian law in the Additional Protocols of 1977.[39]

The two Geneva Conventions of 1929 were notable additions to the corpus of humanitarian law. They established detailed rules for the better protection and humane treatment of those members of armed forces who were defenceless in the hands of an enemy and they prohibited reprisals against them. After 1907 little was attempted to revise the law of war governing hostilities. The use of poison gases in World War I led to the conclusion, in 1925, of the Geneva Gas Protocol,[40] under the auspices of the League of Nations and with the encouragement of the ICRC. The Gas Protocol reinforced the earlier prohibition in the Hague Declaration Respecting Asphyxiating Gases of 1899.[41] The Protocol of 1925 both consolidated that prohibition and extended it to "bacteriological methods of warfare". The reason and purpose of the instrument is stated in the preamble thus:

> "Whereas the use in war of asphyxiating, poisonous or other gases, and of all analogous liquids, materials or devices, has been justly condemned by the general opinion of the civilized world..."

It is observed that, as late as 1925, the evolution of civilization is a concomitant of the humanitarian endeavour. The modern idea of humanitarian law is that it is universal.

Between the World Wars humanitarian law development was confined to the two Geneva Conventions of 1929, the Geneva Gas Protocol of 1925 and to the Protocol to the London Naval Agreement of 1936.[42] This Protocol became necessary as a result of the increasing use of submarines and the effects of that use upon the customary law of sea warfare wherein the ship was considered the prime object of hostile action, rather than the crew. This Protocol was all that was salvaged from the London Naval Treaty of 1930 which lapsed, under its own terms, in 1936. The Protocol provided that, in their action in relation to merchant ships, submarines must conform to the established rules of international law to which surface vessels are subject; in particular, "except in cases of persistent refusals to stop on being duly summoned, or of active resistance to visit or search, a warship, whether surface vessel or submarine, may not sink... a merchant vessel without having first placed passengers, crew and the ship's papers in a place of safety". This prohibition was the subject of persistent violation by belligerents in World War II.[43]

The great failures in the development of humanitarian law in the inter-war period were first the abortive Treaty of Washington of 1922 [44] designed to protect neutrals and non-combatants at sea in time of war; and, second, the Hague draft Air Warfare Rules of 1923 [45] which were never ratified but which have not been without their value. They have had an impact upon later developments of humanitarian law. The Hague draft Rules dealt with aerial bombardment of civilians and attempted to confine lawful bombardment to defined military objectives.[46] These endeavours of 1923 were systematically disregarded in World

War II and thereafter. However, they can be seen as an endeavour to further the development of humanitarian law and as valuable precedent material which the ICRC brought forward in the latest humanitarian law, namely, the additional Protocols of 1977.[47]

Such was the stage of development of humanitarian law by the opening of World War II in 1939. At that moment in time it may be said that the knowledge of the law of war by statesmen, service commanders, staff officers, troops and other State agencies was minimal if not non-existent. Some States had published official manuals on the law of war on land to meet their obligations under Article 1 of the Hague Convention No. IV of 1907. Regular instruction in that law for the armed forces and others was conspicuous by its absence. Detailed knowledge of the subject was confined to the ICRC and to a few jurists and academics. The law itself was fragmentary, anachronistic, uncertain and inadequate. The legal devices to secure its implementation and its enforcement were few and fragile. The experiences of World War II exposed all these weaknesses to the world. The tide of inhumanity by man to man reached a level more shocking than the world had ever had the misfortune to witness. The behaviour of para-military agencies of the State far away from battlefields eclipsed even the scale of loss of innocent life by military action, prominent in which was the systematic bombardment of civilians in towns and countryside, as a deliberate form of "terror". The latter was not confined to any one belligerent. The former reached its climax of inhumanity in the deliberate and systematic extermination of Jews and certain ethnic groups in concentration camps by the use of gas chambers, mass shootings and grossly inhuman treatment.

The full scale of war criminality was not, and could not be, narrated at the "great assize", the International Military Tribunal Trial at Nuremburg in 1945–46.[48] For the first time in history, the surviving leaders of a major belligerent State were indicted as a group of war criminals. They were charged under three main heads of criminality, namely, crimes against peace, i.e., the planning and waging of aggressive war, a violation of the *jus ad bellum;* war crimes in the strict or classical sense, i.e., violations of the *jus in bello;* and crimes against humanity, a novel conception designed to include grossly inhuman acts directed against any civilian population and not merely the enemy population. This heading of war criminality thus went considerably beyond war crimes in the strict sense. This new conception of war criminality marked a new departure for the development of the humanitarian law of war. That law had been mainly concerned, as would be expected from the identity of its authors, the ICRC, with establishing positive substantive rules requiring humanitarian conduct or prohibiting the reverse. It had also involved devices for monitoring that law, mainly the Protecting Power system. The massive infringement of that law by inhumanity on a scale never experienced before exposed the poverty of its enforcement mechanisms. War crimes trials, which had proved a failure, if not a farce, after World War I, were, in 1945–1948, launched against the defeated enemy in Europe,[49] and activity made possible by its "unconditional surrender", the complete occupation of its territory and the full assumption of governmental power by the four victorious allied powers. The idea of crimes against humanity brought a new and penal perspective to the humanitarian law of war. Its arrival has been of doubtful value to the law of war criminality. However, it was an important stage in the emergence of the post-1945 human rights regime. The latter may owe in fact, its appearance to the international penal law of war. The prosecution of enemy war criminals at all levels evoked new legal questions that were the direct concern of those entrusted with the development of humanitarian law, e.g., affording proper judicial safeguards of fair trial to those accused of war criminality, proper treatment in custody before and after trial, and substantive matters of law such as the limits of a defence of superior orders in considering the guilt or sentence, or both, of the accused war criminal. The resort to mass war criminality by the organs and agents of a State which characterized World War II inevitably brought such a defence to the forefront of legal considerations. Humanitarian Law was forced to consider its own penal enforcement.

The total experience of inhumanity in World War II and its significance has not yet been fully digested by our generation. After the recoil from the exposures in the war crimes trials at Nuremburg, Tokyo and in other national jurisdictions, the first humanitarian instrument in response was the Genocide Convention of 1948. This was established by the UN General Assembly moved by a one-man campaign.[50] The Convention isolated the crime of genocide whether committed in peace or war, as an international crime which the Parties undertook to prevent and punish. Genocide was seen as a crime aimed at members of specified groups as such. It extended beyond the crime against humanity in that genocide need have no relation to warfare, but narrowed it by requiring the specific mental element of "intent to destroy, in whole or in part, a national, ethnical, radical, or religious group, as such".

The second and more substantial response to the inhumanity committed in World War II was the adoption of the four Geneva Conventions for the Protection of War Victims of 1949,[51] prepared by the ICRC with the help of experts. The first three Conventions were expansions of then existing areas of humanitarian law, namely, the protection of the sick and wounded in the armed forces, persons in like condition at sea, the shipwrecked and POWs. These instruments were the First and the Second Geneva Conventions respectively; the Third Convention extended the status and protection of POWs. These three instruments made a very substantial addition to the substantive body of humanitarian law both in the extent and calibre of protection afforded and in improved devices for their implementation and enforcement. The Fourth Convention broke new ground. It was devoted exclusively to the protection of civilians in the domestic territory of the enemy, and, more substantially, in occupied territory. It was in those areas that the experience of World War II had shown the more massive violations of the laws of humanity to have occurred. A limited part of the (Civilians) Convention applied to the whole civilian population of the belligerents. The greater part of this Convention established a detailed system of humanitarian protection for the civilians in occupied territory, expanding considerably and supplementing the more limited protection afforded by the relevant Section III of the Hague Regulations of 1907.

Improved monitoring provisions were inserted in all four Conventions, for securing the services of the Protecting Power and, in default, of substitute organizations [52] such as the ICRC, limited to humanitarian functions and excluding the political ones. A new device for enforcement introduced in all four Conventions was a system of mandatory penal repression of "grave breaches", as therein defined, of each of the four Conventions.[53], An obligation was imposed upon States, Parties to these instruments, to bring to trial in their own courts those responsible, irrespective of nationality, and, upon conviction to punish them, or, alternatively to hand them over for trial to other Parties who held the evidence of their criminality. To close the system, the Conventions made mandatory the giving of instruction in these Conventions to members of state armed forces and ancillary State agencies, and, if possible, to civilians.[54]

A remarkable innovative provision, common to all four Conventions, was contained in Article 3 which established specified minimum prohibitions of a fundamental humanitarian character which were to be observed by the parties to armed conflicts "not of an international character occurring in the territory of a State Party". Article 3 lacked any monitoring device in deference to state sovereignty. The basic humanitarian prohibitions therein were a "microcosm" of the remainder of the humanitarian prohibitions in each Convention.

These instruments were humanitarian throughout and are considered today as the core of the contemporary humanitarian law of war in force. These four Conventions, comprising some 317 Articles, conferred extensive humanitarian protection, with great particularity, upon those war victims "protected" by each of them. They did not purport to regulate or restrict the conduct of armed hostilities, beyond a limited restriction ancillary to the humanitarian protection of the "war victims", e.g., in the Fourth (Civilians) Convention attacks upon civilian hospitals were prohibited.[55] Analogous provisions in the First, Second and Third Conventions prohibited attacks upon the wounded and sick and shipwrecked in the armed forces and upon POW camps. Thus a certain element of imbalance was apparent in the law of war of 1949. The Hague Regulations of 1907 was a codifying instrument governing hostilities on land, while the Geneva Conventions of 1949 established a considerable body of humanitarian law protection for war victims, but did not touch, except marginally, the conduct of hostilities.

The post-1949 armed conflicts displayed only limited respect for the Geneva Conventions of 1949. In particular, the initial question of their applicability was often controversial, having regard to the types of armed conflict which marked a world divided by ideologies. Disputed state and government recognition frustrated the applicability of the Convention. Article 3 did not prove an unqualified success in the case of frequent internal conflicts. Modern weaponry, ground and aerial, negatived much that the Geneva Conventions sought to attain. Penal enforcement of the Conventions has not occurred to date.

The ICRC in 1956 sought to remedy this gaping hole in the humanitarian law system by drafting a body of rules designed to limit the dangers to the civilian population from the effects of the hostilities. This was the humanitarian ideal aiming at the very centre of the activity which is most inimical to it and the most difficult on which to impose any regime of law based upon that ideal. Nevertheless, the ICRC made the endeavour. These "Draft Rules"[56] proved unacceptable to governments at a Red Cross Conference in 1957, were politely welcomed, but subsequently ignored by governments.[57] The fear that such Rules might touch upon the use of nuclear weaponry alarmed the nuclear powers. Without their support the project was stillborn.

C. The Present Stage of Development

A number of factors combined to promote the next and latest humanitarian law endeavour. First, the post-1945 use of modern ground and aerial weaponry caused heavy losses of civilian life and destruction of the means of existence. Technology produced new weapons capable of causing great loss of life and suffering as well as massive destruction. Certain weaponry could not be limited to military targets and inflicted superfluous suffering. Huge areas necessary to support civilian life could be reduced to arid wastes in which nothing moved or grew. Such weaponry capability was independent of the nuclear armoury. Second, the intensity and scale of the fighting in internal armed conflicts was exceeded only by the loss of life, sufferings and destruction experienced by the civilian populations. Third, the monitoring system was defective and rarely used in international conflicts and did not exist in internal conflicts. Fourth, it was apparent that the civilian population required a system of protection and medical treatment of the sick and wounded at least as extensive as that enjoyed by the sick and wounded in the armed forces. Likewise, civilians detained for war purposes needed their protection to be strengthened to an extent beyond that afforded by the Geneva (Civilians) Convention of 1949. Fifth, the prevalent resort to guerrilla warfare led to a call for an extension to guerrilla fighters of the POW status under the Geneva POW (Third) Convention of 1949. Sixth, and probably the most important factor, was the urgent need to shut off the non-participant civilian from the effects of hostilities. This was the most urgent and the most difficult of the demands made of humanitarian law.

A powerful support to this development of humanitarian law came from contemporary developments in the law of human rights. This movement in International Law had been launched by the provisions of the UN Charter of 1945, and the UN Universal Declaration of Human Rights of 1948.[58] At the UN Conference on Human Rights at Teheran in 1968, a resolution requested the General Assembly to invite the Secretary-General to study the feasibility of new Conventions whereby better protection of civilians and other war victims might be secured.[59] The General Assembly then requested him to embark upon the necessary study, together with the ICRC. In effect, from 1968, close links have been established between the advance of human rights and of the humanitarian law of armed conflict. This movement was certain, but the legal theories in play were uncertain. The links are reflected in a series of General Assembly resolutions since 1968 adopted under the rubric – "Respect for Human Rights in Armed Conflicts", culminating in the latest one dated 8 December 1977.[60]

Jurists have been engaged in debating the juridical implications of this relationship between human rights and the humanitarian law of armed conflicts. However, the close affinity claimed has had considerable practical impact upon the latest contribution to the edifice of humanitarian law, namely, the two Protocols additional to the Geneva Conventions of 1949, established in 1977.[61] These two instruments required three years of preparatory work by the ICRC and government experts from 1971 to 1973, followed by four annual sessions of the Diplomatic Conference convened by Switzerland in Geneva from 1974 to 1977.

Protocol I is concerned with international armed conflicts, and Protocol II, somewhat debilitated in its final form, is limited to internal conflicts. Protocol I is also additional to the Section of the Hague Regulations of 1907 [62] concerned with the conduct of hostilities. Protocol I is probably the most forward point yet reached in formulating rules of humanitarian law. It has imposed severe limitations upon the conduct of hostilities by belligerents. In summary form, the principles which underlie Protocol I, are the following:

> (i) the close containment of lawful military targetry so as to exclude civilians, the civilian habitat and means of survival, the environment, dangerous installations, and cultural property;[63]
>
> (ii) where such absolute exclusion is not feasible, then the principle of proportionality in relation to the threat to civilians and military advantage is paramount;[64]
>
> (iii) the absolute prohibition of reprisals in combat conduct so far as the protection of civilians, the civilian habitat, the environment, dangerous installations and cultural property is concerned;[65]
>
> (iv) extended protection of civilian sick and wounded, medical installations and transport by land, sea and air; [66]
>
> (v) the extension of belligerent and POW status to organized groups of fighters dependent upon a Party to the conflict, and a lowering of the criteria for "openness" in combat, required by Article I of the Hague Regulations of 1907, to the minimum of carrying arms openly in military engagement;[67]
>
> (vi) an extension of the protection of civilians in enemy hands;[68]
>
> (vii) the "grave breaches" category of war criminality should include battle misconduct directed at civilians and civilian objects, both punishable by domestic penal law;[69]

(viii) the inclusion in the scope of Protocol I of armed conflicts "in which peoples are fighting against colonial domination and alien occupation, and against racist regimes in the exercise of their right to self-determination...";[70]

(ix) the requirement to have legal advisers in armed forces;[71]

(x) the extension of the provisions governing the protection of civilians from the effects of hostilities by air or sea operations which may affect civilians or civilian objects on land.[72]

Protocol II is the first international instrument exclusively concerned with regulating internal conflicts. It marks a limited lodgment of human rights ideas in the humanitarian law of armed conflicts. It leaves undisturbed Article 3 common to the four Geneva Conventions of 1949. With all its uncertainties, limitations and defeats, Article 3 was established in 1949 after considerable difficulty.[73] Protocol II applies to internal armed conflicts, and only to those conflicts which have reached the scale and intensity of the classical civil war situation, i.e. where two or more political authorities, with virtually *de facto* governmental authority in their respective territorial areas of control are engaged in armed conflict with organized armed forces under effective command.[74] This high level of application was framed at a time when Protocol II contained a substantial number of provisions echoing those in Protocol I. In the last phases of the Diplomatic Conference a considerable number of provisions were excluded. This exclusion resulted from the apprehension of a number of new States of the international community concerning their fragility. Moreover, "wars of national liberation" having found their juridical position in Protocol I, Protocol II lost some of its importance. However, there is much that remains in Protocol II that is undoubtedly progress in the development of humanitarian law, not least in the series of fundamental guarantees provided for those who do not take part in the hostilities, and the standards of humanitarian treatment guaranteed to those whose liberty is restricted by reason of the armed conflict.

Both instruments represent the most up-to-date achievement of the forward movement of humanitarian law, and must be read with, and as part of, the Geneva Conventions of 1949.

As we have seen, the ICRC sought in 1956–7 to bring about the adoption of draft regulations limiting the risks run by the civilian population in time of war and, particularly, to prohibit the use of weapons with potentially uncontrollable injurious effects. The weapons question was re-opened at the Twentieth International Red Cross Conference in Vienna, and at the International Conference on Human Rights in Teheran in 1968. During the first session of the Conference of Government Experts on the Reaffirmation and Development of International Humanitarian Law Applicable in Armed Conflicts, held in 1971, three tendencies emerged. The first group of experts considered that the weapons problem should not be discussed at the Conference. The second stressed the necessity of prohibiting weapons of mass destruction (nuclear, biological and chemical) since better protection of the civilian population ultimately depended on that prohibition. The third held that weapons of mass destruction should not be discussed at that forum since they were already under study by the Conference of the Committee on Disarmament, but suggested that attention be focused instead on other particularly cruel weapons not under discussion by any international bodies.[75] This third tendency prevailed at the second session of the Conference of Government Experts in 1972. The experts of the 19 participating countries then asked the ICRC to arrange a special meeting for the consultation of experts on the question of prohibitions or specific restrictions on the use of conventional weapons that may cause unnecessary suffering or have indiscriminate effects.[76] This meeting was held in Geneva in 1973.[77] The Draft Additional Protocols, submitted at the first session of the Diplomatic Conference of Geneva in 1974, included general principles concerning weapons, but no particular provisions covering the use of certain weapons.[78] The Conference established an *ad hoc* commission on conventional weapons. Moreover, during the same period, a Conference of Government Experts was convened by the ICRC. Two sessions took place, one in Lucerne in 1974 and one in Lugano in 1976.[79] The Diplomatic Conference of Geneva adopted no articles concerning particular weapons. However it recommended, in its resolution 22 adopted on 9 June 1977, that a Conference of Governments should be convened not later than 1979 with a view to reaching:

> "a) agreements on prohibitions or restrictions on the use of specific conventional weapons including those which may be deemed to be excessively injurious or have indiscriminate effects, taking into account humanitarian and military considerations; and
> b) agreements on a mechanism for the review of any such agreements and for the consideration of proposals for furthering such agreements."[80]

The United Nations General Assembly approved that recommendation.[81] A preparatory conference took place from August to September 1978 and March to April 1979, followed by a Conference on Prohibitions or Restrictions on the Use of Certain Conventional Weapons held in Geneva from 10 to 28 September 1979 and from 15 September to 10 October 1980. That Conference adopted the Convention on Prohibitions or Restrictions on the Use of Certain Conventional Weapons which may be deemed to be Excessively Injurious or to have Indiscriminate Effects. Three Protocols were added to the Convention as annexes: the Protocol on Non-Detectable Fragments (Protocol I), the Protocol on Other Devices (Protocol II) and the Protocol on Prohibitions or Restrictions on the Use of Incendiary Weapons (Protocol III).[82] The Conference had adopted, during its first session in 1979, the Resolution on Small-Calibre Weapons Systems. The Convention and its three Protocols came into force on 2 December 1983, six months after the deposit of the twentieth instrument of ratification, acceptance, approval or accession. The adoption and entry into force of the Convention and its three Protocols mark the accomplishment of an important step forward in the development of international humanitarian and disarmament law as well as a contribution to the humanization of armed conflict. The legal protection of the civilian population has been strengthened by the development of the principles governing the conduct of hostilities and by the prohibitions and restrictions imposed upon the use against civilians and combatants of excessively cruel weapons. This is also true as regards non-detectable fragments, mines, booby-traps and other devices, as well as incendiary weapons. The Convention and its three Protocols are a major complement to the Additional Protocols of 1977, particularly to articles 35, 36 and 51 of Protocol I. The Convention, like the Protocols additional to the Geneva Conventions, has made a substantial contribution towards advancing humanitarian principles and mitigating the cruellest aspects of war.

Notes

1. Cf. Lauterpacht H., The Grotius Tradition in International Law, in: *International Law being the collected papers of Hersch Lauterpacht, systematically arranged and edited by E. Lauterpacht*, Vol.2: The Law of Peace, part 1 – International Law in General. Cambridge, Cambridge University Press, 1975, pp. 346–350.

2. Draper, G.I.A.D., 'The Christian and War', *International Relations* (London), Vol.II, No. 6, October 1962, p. 397.

3. Grotius H., *De Jure Belli Ac Pacis Libri Tres*, Vol.2, English translation: *The Law of War and Peace*, Book III, by Francis W. Kelsey, Oxford, Clarendon Press, 1925, Book III, Chap. IV, Para. 18, pp. 653–656 [Carnegie Endowment for International Peace – The Classics of International Law].

4. Brierly, J.L., *The Law of Nations. An Introduction to the International Law of Peace*. 5th ed., Oxford, Clarendon Press, 1955, p. 32.

5. *Ibid.*, p. 29.

6. Draper, G.I.A.D., 'The Christian and War', *International Relations* (London), Vol.II, No 6, October 1962, p. 13.

7. Rousseau Jean-Jacques, *Du Contrat Social*, 1762, Livre I, chapter IV. English text from Jean-Jacques Rousseau, *The Social Contract*. Translated by Maurice Cranston. Harmondsworth, Penguin Books, 1968, p. 56. Cf. also Nussbaum, A., *A Concise History of the Law of Nations*, Rev. ed., New York, MacMillan, 1958, p. 139.

8. Rousseau Jean-Jacques, *Du Contrat Social*, 1762, Livre I, chapter IV. English text from Jean-Jacques Rousseau, *The Social Contract*. Translated by Maurice Cranston. Harmondsworth, Penguin Books, 1968, p. 56.

9. Draper, G.I.A.D., The Geneva Conventions of 1949. *Recueil des cours*, Vol.I, 1965, p. 64.

10. Carnegie Endowment for International Peace, *The Hague Conventions and Declarations of 1899 and 1907*, Edited by James Brown Scott, 2nd edition, New York, Oxford University Press, 1915, pp. 100–132, 225–228. *The Laws of Armed Conflicts. A Collection of Conventions, Resolutions and Other Documents.* Edited by D. Schindler and J. Toman, 3rd edition, Dordrecht, Martinus Nijhoff Publishers, Geneva, Henry Dunant Institute, 1988, pp. 101–111.

11. Nussbaum, A., *op.cit.*, pp. 236–237.

12. Draper, G.I.A.D., The Geneva Conventions of 1949, *Recueil des cours*, Vol.I, 1965, p. 64.

13. *Ibid.*

14. Cf. Note in Draper, G.I.A.D., *The Red Cross Conventions*, London, Stevens, 1958, p. 233.

15. Cf. *International Red Cross Handbook*, 12th edition, Geneva, ICRC, League of Red Cross Societies, 1983, pp. 421–424 (Statutes of the International Committee of the Red Cross).

16. Cf. *International Red Cross Handbook*, 12th edition, Geneva, ICRC, League of Red Cross Societies, 1983, pp. 19–20.

17. Keen, M.H., *The Laws of War in the Late Middle Ages*. Toronto, Routledge and Kegan Paul, 1965, chap. IV, pp. 45–62.

18. Nussbaum, A., *op.cit.*, pp. 224–227.

19. *Ibid.*, p. 227.

20. *Ibid.*, pp. 248–249.

21. Carnegie Endowment for International Peace, *The Hague Conventions and Declarations of 1899 and 1907*, James Brown Scott (ed.), 2nd edition, New York, Oxford University Press, 1915, p. 100. *The Laws of Armed Conflicts. A Collection of Conventions, Resolutions and Other Documents.* Edited by D. Schindler and J. Toman, 3rd edition, Dordrecht, Martinus Nijhoff Publishers, Geneva, Henry Dunant Institute, 1988, p. 70.

22. Hall, W.E., *A Treatise of International Law*; 8th edition, Oxford, Clarendon Press, 1924, p. 82.

23. Carnegie Endowment for International Peace, *The Hague Conventions and Declarations of 1899 and 1907*, James Brown Scott (ed.), 2nd edition, New York, Oxford University Press, 1915, pp. 89–100.

24. Cf. Oppenheim, L., *International Law – A Treatise*. Vol.II, Disputes, War and Neutrality, 7th edition, H. Lauterpacht (ed.), London, Longmans, 1952, pp. 234–236.

25. *Ibid.*, pp. 232–233.

26. Draper, G.I.A.D., The Status of Combatants and the Question of Guerrilla Warfare, *British Yearbook of International Law* (London), Vol. 44, 1971, pp. 180–181.

27. These requirements were repeated substantially in Art. 4(A)2 of the Geneva Convention Relative to the Treatment of Prisoners of War, of 12 August 1949. *UNTS*, vol. 75 (1950), p. 138; *The Laws of Armed Conflicts. A Collection of Conventions, Resolutions and Other Documents.* Edited by D. Schindler and J. Toman, 3rd edition, Dordrecht, Martinus Nijhoff Publishers, Geneva, Henry Dunant Institute, 1988, pp. 430–431; *International Red Cross Handbook.* 12th edition. Geneva, ICRC, League of Red Cross Societies, 1983, p. 68.

28. These requirements were repeated substantially in Art. 4(A)2 of the Geneva Convention Relative to the Treatment of Prisoners of War, of 12 August 1949. *UNTS*, vol. 75 (1950), p. 140; *The Laws of Armed Conflicts. A Collection of Conventions, Resolutions and Other Documents.* Edited by D. Schindler and J. Toman, 3rd edition, Dordrecht, Martinus Nijhoff Publishers, Geneva, Henry Dunant Institute, 1988, p. 431; *International Red Cross Handbook*, 12th edition, Geneva, ICRC, League of Red Cross Societies, 1983, p. 69.

29. Section II, Chapter 1 of the Hague Regulations. Cf. Carnegie Endowment for International Peace. *The Hague Conventions and Declarations of 1899 and 1907.* Edited by James Brown Scott, 2nd edition, New York, Oxford University Press, 1915, pp. 116–118; *The Laws of Armed Conflicts. A Collection of Conventions, Resolutions and other Documents.* Edited by D. Schindler and J. Toman, 3rd edition, Dordrecht, Geneva, Martinus Nijhoff Publishers, Henry Dunant Institute, 1988, pp. (à compléter); *International Red Cross Handbook*, 12th edition, Geneva, ICRC, League of Red Cross Societies, 1983, pp. 327–328.

30. Art. 25: "The attack or bombardment, by whatever means, of towns, villages, dwellings, or buildings which are undefended, is prohibited".

31. The Geneva Conventions of 12 August 1949: *Commentary*, published under the general editorship of Jean S. Pictet, Vol. III, Third Geneva Convention Relative to the Treatment of Prisoners of War, Geneva, ICRC, 1960, p. 5.

32. Art. 23: "... it is especially forbidden... (e) to employ arms, projectiles, or material calculated to cause unnecessary suffering". The Greek fire had been used in medieval warfare.

33. *League of Nations Treaty Series*, Vol. CXVIII, No. 2733, 2734, pp. 303–341 and 343–411; *The Laws of Armed Conflicts. A Collection of Conventions, Resolutions and Other Documents.* Edited by D. Schindler and J. Toman, 3rd edition, Dordrecht, Martinus Nijhoff Publishers, Geneva, Henry Dunant Institute, 1988, pp. 325–366.

34. The Geneva Conventions of 12 August 1949: *Commentary*, published under the general editorship of Jean S. Pictet, vol.I, First Geneva Convention for the Amelioration of the Condition of the Wounded and Sick in Armed Forces in the Field, Geneva, ICRC, 1952, p. 436; *The Laws of Armed Conflicts. A collection of Conventions, Resolutions and Other Documents*. D. Schindler and J. Toman (eds., 3rd edition, Dordrecht, Martinus Nijhoff Publishers, Geneva, Henry Dunant Institute, 1988, p. 332.

35. The Geneva Conventions of 12 August 1949: *Commentary*, published under the general editorship of Jean S. Pictet, Vol.III, Third Geneva Convention relative to the Treatment of Prisoners of War, Geneva, ICRC, 1960, p. 681. *The Laws of Armed Conflicts. A Collection of Conventions, Resolutions and Other Documents*. D. Schindler and J. Toman (eds.), 3rd edition, Dordrecht, Martinus Nijhoff Publishers, Geneva, Henry Dunant Institute, 1988, p. 358.

36. Cf. Oppenheim, L., *International Law – A Treatise*. Vol. II, 'Disputes, War and Neutrality', 7th edition, H. Lauterpacht (ed.), London, Longmans, 1952, pp. 136–141.

37. The Geneva Conventions of 12 August 1949: *Commentary*, published under the general editorship of Jean S. Pictet, Vol.III, Third Geneva Convention relative to the treatment of prisoners of war, Geneva, ICRC, 1960, p. 689. *The Laws of Armed Conflicts. A Collection of Conventions, Resolutions and Other Documents*. Edited by D. Schindler and J. Toman, 3rd edition, Dordrecht, Martinus Nijhoff Publishers, Geneva, Henry Dunant Institute, 1988, p. 342.

38. The Geneva Conventions of 12 August 1949: *Commentary*, published under the general editorship of Jean S. Pictet, Vol.I, First Geneva Convention for the Amelioration of the Condition of the Wounded and Sick in Armed Forces in the Field, Geneva, ICRC, 1952, p. 443; *The Laws of Armed Conflicts. A Collection of Conventions, Resolutions and Other Documents*. Edited by D. Schindler and J. Toman, 3rd edition, Dordrecht, Martinus Nijhoff Publishers, Geneva, Henry Dunant Institute, 1988, p. 326.

39. Cf. Additional Protocol I of 1977: Art. 51 (6), 52 (1), 53 (c), 54 (4), 55 (2) and 56 (4).

40. *League of Nations Treaty Series*, Vol. XCIV, pp. 65–74; *The Laws of Armed Conflicts. A Collection of Conventions, Resolutions and Other Documents*, Edited by D. Schindler and J. Toman, 3rd edition, Dordrecht, Martinus Nijhoff Publishers, Geneva, Henry Dunant Institute, 1988, pp. 115–127.

41. Carnegie Endowment for International Peace, *The Hague Conventions and Declarations of 1899 and 1907*, Edited by James Brown Scott, 2nd edition, New York, Oxford University Press, 1915, pp. 225–226. *The Laws of Armed Conflicts. A Collection of Conventions, Resolutions and Other Documents*, Edited by D. Schindler and J. Toman, 3rd edition, Dordrecht, Martinus Nijhoff Publishers, Geneva, Henry Dunant Institute, 1988, pp. 105–107.

42. Cf. Oppenheim, L., *International Law – A Treatise*, Vol.II, 'Disputes, War and Neutrality', 7th edition, Edited by H. Lauterpacht, London, Longmans, 1952, pp. 490–491. For the text of the Protocol, cf. *League of Nations Treaty Series*, Vol. 173, 1936, pp. 353–357; *The Laws of Armed Conflicts. A Collection of Conventions, Resolutions and Other Documents*, Edited by D. Schindler and J. Toman, 3rd edition, Dordrecht, Martinus Nijhoff Publishers, Geneva, Henry Dunant Institute, 1988, pp. 883–885.

43. Oppenheim, L., *International Law – A Treatise*, Vol.II, 'Disputes, War and Neutrality', 7th edition, H. Lauterpacht (ed.), London, Longmans, 1952, pp. 491–493.

44. Ibid., p. 490. *The Laws of Armed Conflicts. A Collection of Conventions, Resolutions and Other Documents*, Edited by D. Schindler and J. Toman, 3rd edition, Dordrecht, Martinus Nijhoff Publishers, Geneva, Henry Dunant Institute, 1988, pp. 877–879.

45. Ibid., pp. 518–523. *The Laws of Armed Conflicts. A Collection of Conventions, Resolutions and Other Documents*, Edited by D. Schindler and J. Toman, 3rd edition, Dordrecht, Martinus Nijhoff Publishers, Geneva, Henry Dunant Institute, 1988, pp. 207–217.

46. Art. 24 (2). Cf. Oppenheim, L., *International Law – A Treatise*. Vol.II, 'Disputes, War and Neutrality', 7th edition, H. Lauterpacht (ed.), London, Longmans, 1952, p. 522.

47. Additional Protocol I of 1977, Art. 52.

48. *Annual Digest and Reports of Public International Law Cases*. Year 1946, H. Lauterpacht (ed.), London, Butterworth and Co., Case No 92: *In re* Goering and others, pp. 203–222.

49. *History of the U.N. War Crime Commission*. London, HMSO, 1948, 592 p., as a general account of war crimes trials after World Wars I and II.

50. Oppenheim, L., *International Law – A Treatise*, Vol.II, 'Disputes, War and Neutrality', 7th edition, Edited by H. Lauterpacht, London, Longmans, 1952, p. 585, note 4. The man was R. Lemkin. For the text of the Convention on the Prevention and Punishment of the Crime of Genocide, of 9 December 1948, cf. *UNTS*, Vol. 78, p. 277 ff. and *The Laws of Armed Conflicts. A Collection of Conventions, Resolutions and Other Documents*, Edited by D. Schindler and J. Toman, 3rd edition, Dordrecht, Martinus Nijhoff Publishers, Geneva, Henry Dunant Institute, 1988, pp. 231–249.

51. The most informative writing on these Conventions is the Commentary in 4 volumes, published by the ICRC, Geneva, in 1952, 1958 and 1960, respectively, one volume for each of the four Conventions. The texts are published in *UNTS*, Vol. 75, 1950, pp. 31–417, *International Red Cross Handbook*, 12th edition, Geneva, ICRC, League of Red Cross Societies, 1983, pp. 23–212, and in *The Laws of Armed Conflicts. A Collection of Conventions, Resolutions and other Documents*, Edited by D. Schindler and J. Toman, 3rd edition, Dordrecht, Martinus Nijhoff Publishers, Geneva, Henry Dunant Institute, 1988, pp. 373–594.

52. Articles 8, 9, 10 and 11, common to the four Conventions.

53. Articles 49, 50, 129 and 146, common to the four Conventions.

54. Articles 47, 48, 127 and 144, common to the four Conventions.

55. Article 18 of the IVth Geneva Convention.

56. XIXth International Conference of the Red Cross (New Delhi, October–November 1957). *Draft Rules for the Limitation of the Dangers incurred by the Civilian Population in Time of War*. 2nd edition. 1958, 170 p. and *The Laws of Armed Conflicts. A Collection of Conventions, Resolutions and Other Documents*. Edited by D. Schindler and J. Toman. 3rd edition, Dordrecht, Martinus Nijhoff Publishers, Geneva, Henry Dunant Institute, 1988, pp. 251–257.

57. Resolution XIII of the XIXth International Conference of the Red Cross (New Delhi, October–November 1957). Cf. *International Red Cross Handbook*, 11th edition, Geneva, ICRC, League of Red Cross Societies, 1971, p. 451.

58. UN document A/811, 10 December 1948.

59. Resolution XXIII. *Final Act of the International Conference on Human Rights*, Teheran, 22 April to 13 May 1968, UN document A/CONF.32/41, p. 18.

60. United Nations General Assembly resolution 32/44 of 8 December 1977.

61. UN document A/32/144, annex I and II.

62. Section II, Chapter 1 of the Hague Regulations. Cf. Carnegie Endowment for International Peace. *The Hague Conventions and Declarations of 1899 and 1907*, Edited by James Brown Scott, 2nd edition, New York, Oxford University Press, 1915, pp. 116–118; *The Laws of Armed Conflicts. A Collection of Conventions, Resolutions and Other Documents*, Edited by D. Schindler and J. Toman, 3rd edition, Dordrecht, Martinus Nijhoff Publishers, Geneva, Henry Dunant Institute, 1988, pp. 82–85; *International Red Cross Handbook*, 12th edition, Geneva, ICRC, League of Red Cross Societies, 1983, pp. 327–328.

63. Protocol Additional to the Geneva Conventions of 12 August 1949, and relating to the Protection of Victims of International Armed Conflicts (Protocol I), of 8 June 1977. Articles 48–60. (The text of the Protocols is published in the *International Red Cross Handbook*, 12th edition, Geneva, ICRC, League of Red Cross Societies, 1983, pp. 216–296; *The Laws of Armed Conflicts. A Collection of Conventions, Resolutions and Other Documents*, Edited by D. Schindler and J. Toman, 3rd edition, Dordrecht, Martinus Nijhoff Publishers, Geneva, Henry Dunant Institute, 1988, pp. 621–718). The most informative writings on these Protocols are the two commentaries: *Commentary on the Additional Protocols of 8 June 1977 to the Geneva Conventions of 12 August 1949*. Yves Sandoz, Christophe Swinarski, Bruno Zimmermann (eds.), Geneva, International Committee of the Red Cross, Martinus Nijhoff Publishers, 1987, 1625 p. and *New Rules for Victims of Armed Conflicts. Commentary on the Two 1977 Protocols Additional to the Geneva Conventions of 1949* (Michael Bothe, Karl Josef Partsch, Waldemar A. Solf), The Hague, Boston, London, Martinus Nijhoff Publishers, 1982, 746 p.

64. *Ibid.*, Articles 57 and 58.

65. *Ibid.*, Articles 51 (6), 52 (1), 53 (c), 54 (4), 55 (2) and 56 (4).

66. *Ibid.*, Articles 8–31.

67. *Ibid.*, Articles 43–45.

68. *Ibid.*, Articles 72–73.

69. *Ibid.*, Articles 85–91.

70. *Ibid.*, Articles 1 (4) and 96 (3).

71. *Ibid.*, Article 82, with which must be read Article 83, relating to dissemination and instruction, and Resolution 21 adopted at the Diplomatic Conference on the signing of the Final Act on 7 June 1977.

72. *Ibid.*, Article 49 (3).

73. The Geneva Conventions of 12 August 1949: *Commentary*, published under the general editorship of Jean S. Pictet, Vol. IV, Fourth Geneva Convention relative to the Protection of Civilian Persons in Time of War, Geneva, ICRC, 1958, pp. 25–34.

74. Protocol Additional to the Geneva Conventions of 12 August 1949, and Relating to the Protection of Victims of Non-International Armed Conflicts (Protocol II), of 8 June 1977, Article 1. This Protocol consists, in its final form, of 28 Articles. As it came before the Diplomatic Conference in 1974 it had 46 Articles adopting in general the pattern of the content of Protocol I. (The text of the Protocol is published in *International Red Cross Handbook*, 12th edition, Geneva, ICRC, League of Red Cross Societies, 1983, pp. 286–296; *The Laws of Armed Conflicts. A Collection of Conventions, Resolutions and Other Documents*, Edited by D. Schindler and J. Toman, 3rd edition, Dordrecht, Martinus Nijhoff Publishers, Geneva, Henry Dunant Institute, 1988, pp. 689–700).

75. Conference of Government Experts on the Reaffirmation and Development of International Humanitarian Law Applicable in Armed Conflicts (1971), *Report*, Para. 477, p. 84.

76. Conference of Government Experts (1972), *Report*, Vol. I, Paras 5.8–5.11.

77. Weapons That May Cause Unnecessary Suffering or Have Indiscriminate Effects. *Report on the Work of Experts*, Geneva, ICRC, 1973, 72 p.

78. *Draft Additional Protocols to the Geneva Conventions of August 12, 1949. Commentary*, Geneva, ICRC, 1973, p. 41 ff.

79. Conference of Government Experts on the Use of Certain Conventional Weapons (Lucerne, 24 Sep.–18 Oct. 1974), *Report*. Geneva, ICRC, 1975, 106 p. – Conference of Government Experts on the Use of Certain Conventional Weapons. Second Session, Lugano, 28 Jan. – 26 Feb. 1976, *Report*, Geneva, ICRC, 1976, 231 p.

80. *International Red Cross Handbook*, Geneva, 1983, pp. 314–316.

81. Resolutions of the United Nations General Assembly: 32/152 of 19 Dec. 1977; 33/70 of 28 Sept. 1978 and 34/82 of 11 Dec. 1979.

82. *International Red Cross Handbook*, pp. 380–394; – United Nations document A/CONF/95/15 and Corr. 1–5; I.R.R.C., Vol. 21, No. 220, Jan. – Feb. 1981, pp. 41–55; *The Laws of Armed Conflicts. A Collection of Conventions, Resolutions and Other Documents*, Edited by D. Schindler and J. Toman, 3rd edition, Dordrecht, Martinus Nijhoff Publishers, Geneva, Henry Dunant Institute, 1988, pp. 179–196.

PART III

THE LAW OF ARMED CONFLICT

SECTION 1

CONFLICTS OF INTERNATIONAL CHARACTER

CHAPTER VIII

THE DUTIES OF COMBATANTS AND THE CONDUCT OF HOSTILITIES (LAW OF THE HAGUE)

RICHARD R. BAXTER*

A. The Types of Armed Conflict to which the Humanitarian Law of War Applies

a. The Varied Forms of Armed Conflict

The state of affairs in which the humanitarian law governing armed conflicts has traditionally been held to apply is "war". The core of the concept of war is that it is the use of force by one state in order to impose its will upon another state. However, in recent years, the term "war" has taken on a multiplicity of meanings, depending on the context and the legal purpose for which it is used. "War" may be variously defined for the purpose of private law (such as the interpretation of charter parties or insurance contracts), neutrality, the conduct of economic warfare (under trading with the enemy legislation), the functions of the General Assembly and the Security Council, relations with the "enemy," the powers of a government under national law, international humanitarian law, and the law relating to the conduct of hostilities.[1] At the same time, there has been a revulsion against the idea of war itself, so that there is a widespread, but by no means universal, prejudice against use of the term.

But the wider development which has made the use of the concept of war somewhat inapposite is the emergence of types of armed conflict, such as internal armed conflict and wars of national liberation and international armed conflicts which the parties do not identify as war, to which humanitarian law is applicable. If the term "humanitarian law of war" is today employed, the reference is to a much wider category of armed conflicts, going beyond the use of force by one state against another.

Notwithstanding these developments, the term "law of war" has acquired a firm place, especially in so far as international law regulates the conduct of warfare – for example, through restraints on the use of certain weapons. Because the term "war," especially at the initiation of conflict, has taken on such a variety of meanings, it is not always easy to give a precise answer to the question when a particular legal rule, especially one found in customary international law or one of the older treaties, becomes applicable. Before turning to the types of armed conflicts which give rise to questions about the applicability of international humanitarian law, it will be necessary to allude briefly to the relationship of the concept of war to the legality of resort to the use of armed force.

The existence of a state of "war" or of "armed conflict" for the purposes of the application of humanitarian law does not in any way turn on the legality of the initial resort to the use of force. There is no necessary correlation between the existence of a "threat to the peace, breach of the peace, or act of aggression," within the meaning of Article 39 of the United Nations Charter, and the existence of a "war" or "armed conflict" calling for the application of the law of war or international humanitarian law. While an "act of aggression" will normally bring into play the law of armed conflict, certain forms of "act of aggression" which are set forth in the Definition of Aggression adopted by the General Assembly in 1974[2] do not necessarily involve either war or armed conflict on the part of the state responsible for the act of aggression. For example, a state's allowing its territory to be used by another state to perpetrate an act of aggression is an act of aggression by the first state but does not necessarily make it a party to a war or an armed conflict.[3]

In addition, the fact that the humanitarian law of war imposes duties on, and accords rights to, both parties to the conflict without regard to the legality or the illegality of the inception of the conflict makes irrelevant, for the operation of *this* body of law, any determination whether one party or the other was responsible for a threat to the peace, breach of the peace, or act of aggression or is acting in the exercise of the inherent right of individual or collective self-defence under Article 51 of the United Nations Charter.[4] The law of the conduct of hostilities and on the protection of war victims applies equally to all parties to the conflict. It must operate in this way if it is to perform its proper function of limiting the scope of hostilities, of protecting the victims of war, and of making possible the restoration of peace after the termination of hostilities.

The question of the existence of a "war" or "armed conflict" is intimately related to the questions of the beginning and end of the operation of the various forms of law governing the conduct of armed conflict. It will therefore be necessary to consider the time of initiation of "war" or "armed conflict" together with the question of whether such a state of affairs exists.

The declaration of war at the beginning of an armed conflict is now a comparatively rare phenomenon. As the scope for neutral rights and duties has been severely curtailed by the United Nations Charter, the need for a declaration to give notice to neutral states has diminished to the vanishing point. The state initiating hostilities will be reluctant to promulgate a legal instrument in which it acknowledges responsibility for starting the conflict, and the state acting in self-defence will consider it superrogatory to "declare" a war which it did not initiate. Moreover, from a military perspective, surprise may be advantageous, and an aggressor may rule out any advance notice of the initiation of hostilities.

Article I of Convention No. III of The Hague of 1907 Relative to the Opening of Hostilities[5] provides:

> "The Contracting Powers recognize that hostilities between themselves must not commence without previous and explicit warning, in the form either of a reasoned declaration of war or of an ultimatum with conditional declaration of war."

The International Military Tribunal at Nuremberg found it unnecessary to consider whether what were already characterized as aggressive wars were also "wars in violation of international treaties, agreements, or assurances," including Convention No. III of The Hague, to which Germany was a party.[6] The same position was taken by the International Military Tribunal for the Far East, which did not base any of its convictions of the defendants on the terms of Convention No. III of The Hague.[7] In those instances in which declarations of war were promulgated in the Second World War, they often took the form of reciting a preexisting state of war resulting from an act of aggression by the enemy which antedated the declaration itself.[8] The declaration thus provided no guidance as to the time when the conflict had actually begun, that question being decided on the basis of the outbreak of hostilities rather than on that of the issuance of declarations. Declarations have simply passed out of use since the Second World War. With their virtual disappearance, the instrument can no longer be relied upon as an indication of the existence of a war or a state of armed conflict.

Even before the Second World War, there had been instances in which the parties to an international conflict of major proportions had not only refrained from declaring war but had also been unwilling to characterize the conflict as war. In the Manchurian affair of 1931–32 (Japan and China), the Italo-Ethiopian conflict of 1935, and in the conflict between China and Japan from 1937 to 1941, one or both of the belligerents refused to characterize the conflict as war.[9] And yet these were undoubtedly conflicts in which the international law of war, as it then existed, should have been applied.

In cases in which a technical state of war exists, the parties may refrain from active hostilities, as in the early months of the war between the German Reich and the United Kingdom in 1939. And at the end of a conflict, hostilities may cease as the result of the conclusion of an armistice or an instrument of surrender, and the scope for the operation of the law will thus be reduced, although under contemporary international law the protection of the law of war nevertheless continues as regards the victims of war, such as prisoners of war.

The overwhelming use of force by an aggressor may also create a situation in which the aggressor and the victim of aggression do not actually engage in armed combat. When the German Reich invaded Czechoslovakia in 1939, the latter country simply capitulated without putting up resistance. And yet the International Military Tribunal at Nuremberg held that the law of war applied to the resulting occupation by the German forces.[10]

To this list of situations in which the applicability of the law of war has been questioned must be added the case of "intervention by invitation," in which what may or may not be an act of aggression is characterized as a response to an invitation from the authorities of the state into which the armed forces are sent. The situation is still further complicated when there are two contending factions within the state, and one of these, whether the authorities in power or not, requests the aid of the armed forces of the foreign state. The setting up of a puppet government subservient to the will of the foreign state sending in its armed forces can thus be used to obscure the existence of a hostile invasion of a state by foreign forces.

All of these types of conflict which have been referred to normally involve widespread use of violence, or at least the threat of overwhelming force, in what is an attempt by one party to the conflict, to impose its will upon the other. But below these instances of armed conflict on a major scale are many forms of low-level and small-scale use of violence.[11] Small detachments of troops from the armed forces of two states may engage in conflict over a boundary.

The armed forces of one state may be sent into the territory of another state for a short time, with limited use of force, and for a specific purpose, which, once accomplished, will lead to the timely withdrawal of the forces. These could run the gamut from "punitive expeditions" to instances of so-called "humanitarian intervention.' Even the capture of a few soldiers who may have wandered across an international boundary can give rise to the question whether the law governing the treatment of prisoners of war applies. To characterize these situations as "war" may raise the level of tension between the two countries concerned, and the application of the humanitarian law of war might have the same effect, as well as complicating the restoration of the *status quo ante*. Even under the treaties currently in force, including Protocol I of 1977 Additional to the Geneva Conventions of 1949, it is unclear whether the application of international humanitarian law for the protection of war victims is called for under conditions of small-scale or low-level violence between the armed forces of two states.

In addition to these traditional types of armed conflict or use of force involving the armed forces of one or more states, the establishment of United Nations forces and the emergence of wars of national liberation have created new forms of armed conflict which were not contemplated when the Geneva Conventions of 1949 for the Protection of War Victims were drawn up and for which those and earlier treaties accordingly do not make adequate provision. It will be necessary to return to these uses of force and the law applicable thereto in the context of the application of the humanitarian law of war to various types of armed struggle.

b. The Application of Treaty Law to Various Types of Armed Conflict

The customary international law of war, which has in any event been very largely superseded by the conventional law of war, never defined with precision the circumstances under which it would be applicable. It was simply assumed that the law would apply to war in the traditional sense between two or more states and correspondingly that it did not regulate the conduct of hostilities in civil wars or non-international armed conflicts, except to the extent that either or both parties might choose to apply part or all of the customary law of war in such circumstances.[12]

Convention No. IV of the Hague Respecting the Laws and Customs of War on Land, as originally adopted in 1899 and revised in 1907,[13] likewise did not specify the material or temporal conditions under which this revision of "the general laws and customs of war"[14] would become applicable. The use, throughout, of the term "war" in the preamble and the articles of the Convention and in the provisions of the annexed Regulations, indicates that the scope of application of this treaty was to be no less wide and no wider than that of customary international law. The treaty would govern armed conflict between states, unless the parties to a civil war or other form of internal armed conflict should elect to put the treaties in operation. As the Regulations annexed to Convention No. IV have, in the view of the Nuremberg Tribunal, passed into customary international law,[15] there can, in any event, be no doubt that customary international law and the Hague Regulations both apply to the same form of international armed conflict, that is to say war in the traditional sense.

The unwillingness of states to "declare" war or even to recognize the existence of a state of war, as well as the intense but unresisted use of force by one state against another during the Second World War called for greater precision in defining the circumstances under which the Geneva Conventions of 1949 for the Protection of War Victims would become operative. Article 2, common to the four Conventions, provides that:

> "In addition to the provisions which shall be implemented in peacetime, the present Convention shall apply to all cases of declared war or of any other armed conflict which may arise between two or more of the High Contracting Parties, even if the state of war is not recognized by one of them.
>
> The Convention shall also apply to all cases of partial or total occupation of the territory of a High Contracting Party, even if the said occupation meets with no armed resistance."[16]

The first paragraph makes references both, to declared war and to the type of armed conflict unaccompanied by a declaration of war, of which the conflicts between China and Japan were such striking instances. The reference to "any other armed conflict which may arise between two or more of the High Contracting Parties, even if the state of war is not recognized by one of them" presents a problem. If the state of war is recognized by one party but not the other, there can be no question about the effect of this provision, but what if the state of war is not recognized by both parties to the conflict? While the non-recognition of the state of war by both parties may pose certain practical impediments to the full operation of the law of war, it is much in the interest of the victims of war that in principle, in large-scale hostilities between states, the law of the treaties be applied without regard to the unwillingness or indifference of the parties as regards the operation of the Geneva Conventions of 1949.[17]

Small-scale and low-intensity conflicts between the armed forces of two states give rise to further questions. If the hostilities do not lead to a declaration of war and are not on the scale of traditional war between states, the automatic operation of the Geneva Conventions of 1949 may not be at all times in the interests of the war victims.

In the event of a local clash between small elements of the armed forces of two states, the characterization of any prisoners taken as prisoners of war may not only escalate the level of hostilities but might also delay the release and repatriation of prisoners, who might otherwise be released or returned, as if they were civilians, once events had taken a calmer course. On the other hand, the protection extended to the victims of conflict and to medical personnel under the Geneva Convention of 1949 on the Wounded and Sick is highly beneficial, however low may be the scale of hostilities. The proper view would seem to be that "any other armed conflict which may arise between two or more of the High Contracting Parties" should be taken as referring to any outbreak of violence between the armed forces of two states, regardless of the geographical extent and intensity of the force employed, except when characterization of the conflict as falling within Common Article 2 and the resulting application of one or more of the Geneva Conventions of 1949 would be prejudicial to the interests of war victims or might heighten tensions between the two countries.

The second paragraph of Common Article 2 of the Geneva Conventions of 1949, having reference to "all cases of partial or total occupation of the territory of a High Contracting Party, even if the said occupation meets with no armed resistance", is responsive to the situation of Czechoslovakia during the Second World War. There may be no declaration of war and no armed conflict between the forces of two states, and yet the threat of overwhelming force can lead to the subjugation of a state and its armed forces without the firing of a shot. If territory is occupied or prisoners of war are taken, the civilian personnel and military forces now benefit from the safeguards of the Geneva Conventions of 1949.

As further dealt with elsewhere in this volume,[18] neither the Hague Regulations of 1907 nor the Geneva Conventions of 1949 (except Article 3) have any application to civil wars or any other forms of non-international armed conflict, unless the parties to the conflict agree, in conformity with the third paragraph of Common Article 3, "to bring into force, by means of special agreements, all or part of the other provisions of the present Convention."

One of the major innovations introduced by Protocol I of 1977 to the Geneva Conventions of 1949[19] was the addition of wars of national liberation[20] to the categories of conflict covered by Article 2 of the Conventions of 1949. After stating in paragraph 3 of Article 1 that the Protocol "which supplements the Geneva Conventions of 12 August 1949 for the protection of war victims, shall apply in the situations referred to in Article 2 common to those Conventions," the Article goes on to say in paragraph 4:

> "The situations referred to in the preceding paragraph include armed conflicts in which peoples are fighting against colonial domination and alien occupation and against racist regimes in the exercise of their right of self-determination, as enshrined in the Charter of the United Nations and the Declaration on Principles of International Law Concerning Friendly Relations and Co-operation among States in Accordance with the Charter of the United Nations."

The application of the totality of the Geneva Conventions of 1949 and of Protocol I to wars of national liberation had been foreshadowed in resolutions of the United Nations General Assembly. For example, as early as 1972 General Assembly Resolution 2852 (XXVI) on Respect for Human Rights in Armed Conflict[21] had reaffirmed that:

> "persons participating in resistance movements and freedom fighters in southern Africa and in territories under colonial and alien domination and foreign occupation who are struggling for their liberation and self-determination should, in case of arrest, be treated as prisoners of war in accordance with the principles of the Hague Convention of 1907 and the Geneva Conventions of 1949."

It must first be observed that the parties to the conflict no longer need be "States"; Protocol I and the Conventions of 1949 are now to be applicable to an armed conflict between a "State" and a "people" under the circumstances described.

There are three sub-types of such conflicts. The first is an armed conflict against "colonial domination". By this is meant a conflict between a colonial power and the people of a dependent territory who have been denied their right to self-determination, as enshrined in Article 1, paragraph 2, of the United Nations Charter. Even before the drawing up of Protocol I, such a conflict could have been regarded as an international one, on the theory that a dependent territory, denied its independence in the exercise of the right of self-determination, should be treated as a separate and dependent state in the eyes of the law.[22] With the process of decolonization nearing an end, it is probable that there will be fewer conflicts of this sub-type than in the past.

The second type of conflict is one fought against "alien occupation." As the belligerent occupation by one state of the territory of another is already covered by provisions of the Hague Regulations of 1907 and of the Geneva Conventions of 1949, such conflicts were already international ones under the law prevailing prior to 1977. The term "alien occupation" must thus be taken as having identifiably wider scope, applying *inter alia* to situations in which territory sovereignty over which it is in doubt is occupied by the forces of a state alien to that territory, without regard to the fact that the conflict might otherwise be thought of as international or internal.

The third subtype of armed conflicts against "racist régimes" applies to such situations as those in Zimbabwe-Rhodesia (during the period of that entity's claimed independence) and in South Africa, wherein predominantly black populations were or are ruled by minority white régimes in the exercise of policies of apartheid or of white supremacy.

Protocol I to the Geneva Conventions of 1949 thus makes both its own terms and those of the Conventions of 1949 applicable to many conflicts which had previously been widely, if not universally, regarded as internal armed conflicts, regulated solely by the law operative in such conflicts.

Protocols I and II of 1977 to the Geneva Conventions of 1949 leave unresolved the troublesome question of the law to be applied to armed conflicts in which there are both international and non-international elements. If two factions within a state are in conflict, the situation may be such as to call for the application of Article 3 of the Geneva Conventions of 1949 or of Protocol II of 1977 to the Geneva Conventions of 1949. But if one or more foreign states participate in the conflict in order to render assistance to one faction or the other, it is not clear whether the relations between such a foreign state and an opposing faction are to be governed by the law concerning international or non-international armed conflicts.[23] However, in the event of direct confrontation between the forces of the two foreign states, it would appear that the conflict should be treated as an international one. It is thus possible that some aspects of the conflict will be regulated by the law applicable to international armed conflicts and others by the law applicable to non-international armed conflicts. Much the preferable solution is to bring as much as possible of the humanitarian law applicable to international armed conflicts into operation.

The applicability of the totality of the Conventions of 1949 and of Protocol I may also be called into question when one party to the conflict is a state party to the Conventions but there is a disagreement between the two belligerents whether the adversary is a group of rebels or a state, if that adversary has either acceded to the Conventions[24] or has attempted to bring them into force through the operation of the third paragraph of Article 2 of the Conventions. The recognition given to the international status of wars of national liberation has the potential for reducing the incidence of such problems, although not of eliminating them entirely.

No treaty concerning the protection of war victims contains a provision concerning its applicability to operations in which United Nations forces participate. While forces operating under the aegis of the United Nations would not be expected to take prisoners of war or to "occupy" territory, there are certain stipulations of the conventions on international humanitarian law, such as those on the protection of the wounded and sick, which are relevant to the operations of United Nations forces. It is for this reason that the regulations for such forces provide that the forces are to follow the general principles of humanitarian law. The Regulations for the United Nations Emergency Force in Egypt typically provided that "The Force shall observe the principles and spirit of the general international conventions applicable to the conduct of military personnel."[25]

The treaties setting forth the international humanitarian law of war are, like other treaties, applicable only in the event that both parties to the conflict are parties to the treaty in question.

Convention No. IV of The Hague contains a further qualification which is now of merely historical interest. Article 2 of the Convention provides:

> "The provisions contained in the Regulations referred to in Article 1, as well as the present Convention, do not apply except between Contracting Powers, and then only if all the belligerents are parties to the Convention."[26]

This article has lost its force by reason of the fact that The Hague Regulations of 1907, annexed to the Convention, have been held by the Nuremberg Tribunal to have passed into customary international law and are thus binding on all states.[27]

Under Common Article 2 of the Geneva Conventions of 1949, the Conventions apply only to cases of war and armed conflict which "may arise between two or more of the High Contracting Parties," However, provision is made for the bringing into force of the Conventions in the event that only one "Power in conflict" is a party to the Conventions. Article 2 further provides that:

> "Although one of the Powers in conflict may not be a party to the present Convention, the Powers who are parties thereto shall remain bound by it in their mutual relations. They shall furthermore be bound by the Convention in relation to the said Power, if the latter accepts and applies the provisions thereof."

The first sentence is an express rejection of the *si omnes* provision of Convention No. IV of The Hague, referred to above.[28] The second allows a non-party to be bound by and to secure the benefits of the Conventions if it both accepts and applies their provisions. It must be emphasized that this is a two-fold requirement. The non-party must agree to apply the Conventions and in fact do so; if its forces violate the Conventions, it loses the benefits thereof, and moreover ceases to be bound by them. The Conventions do not make clear how much application of the Conventions is sufficient to satisfy the requirements of Article 2 or the extent of deviation from their terms which will render the Conventions inapplicable.

The "acceptance" by a non-party might take the form of a unilateral declaration, a communication to the opposing belligerent, or a communication to the International Committee of the Red Cross or the Swiss Government.

The fact that Article 1 of Protocol I of 1977 would make the Protocol and the Geneva Conventions of 1949 applicable to wars of national liberation fought between a "people" and a "state" made it necessary to include a provision in Protocol I on the manner in which a "people" might accept the terms of the Convention and Protocol. Article 96, paragraph 3, provides:

> "The authority representing a people engaged against a High Contracting Party in an armed conflict of the type referred to in Article 1, paragraph 4, may undertake to apply the Conventions and this Protocol in relation to the conflict by means of a unilateral declaration addressed to the depositary [the Swiss Federal Council – author's note]. Such declaration shall, upon its receipt by the depositary, have in relation to that conflict the following effects:
>
> (a) the Conventions and this Protocol are brought into force for the said authority as a Party to the conflict with immediate effect;
>
> (b) the said authority assumes the same rights and obligations as those which have been assumed by a High Contracting Party to the Conventions and this Protocol; and
>
> (c) the Conventions and this Protocol are equally binding upon all Parties to the conflict."

The Protocol and the Conventions of 1949 may thus be brought into force only if the "state" which is the adversary in a war of national liberation has become a party to Protocol I. A state that is a party to the Geneva Conventions of 1949 alone is thus under no conventional obligation to apply the Conventions to a war of national liberation in which it is a belligerent.

What has been said about the types of conflict to which the treaties on the humanitarian law of war are applicable is naturally relevant to the time at which the treaties start to operate in a war or armed conflict. Of equal importance is when the conventions cease to be operative. As the Hague Regulations of 1907 apply to war in the traditional sense, they would cease to apply at the termination of war, which would normally be effected by the entry into force of a treaty of peace.

A general armistice or a general surrender of forces was generally considered to effect only a suspension of hostilities and not a termination of war.[29] Such an event would of course, leave no scope for the operation of those provisions that govern the actual conduct of warfare. At the time of the general surrender of Germany and Japan in 1945, the question arose whether the two countries should continue to benefit from the provisions of the Hague Regulations of 1907, notably those relating to the belligerent occupation of enemy territory. The position was taken by the occupying powers in Germany that that country, having surrendered unconditionally, being without a government, and lacking the means of resuming hostilities, should no longer be governed by provisions of law which looked to a situation in which control of territory was essentially tentative.[30] The Hague Regulations were accordingly not regarded as legally binding, although a number of their provisions were applied by the occupying powers as a matter of grace.[31]

Motivated in part at least by the problems to which the Hague Regulations had given rise, the Geneva Conference of 1949 took a more sophisticated approach to the duration of applicability of the treaties. Prisoners of war, were, for example, to benefit from the provisions of the Geneva Prisoners of War Convention until "their final release and repatriation," which was to be effected "after the cessation of active hostilities," except in the case of those who were serving sentences.[32] Under the Geneva Civilians Convention, the application of the treaty was to terminate in the territory of parties to the conflict "on the general close of military operations."[33]

The application of the treaty terminates in occupied areas one year after the general close of military operations, with the exception of certain specified articles which were to remain in operation for the duration of the occupation. And those individuals who are not released or repatriated until a date later than that continue to benefit from the Convention. Article 3 of Protocol I provides in more general terms:

> "the application of the Conventions and of this Protocol shall cease, in the territory of Parties to the conflict, on the general close of military operations and, in the case of occupied territories, on the termination of the occupation, except, in either circumstance, for those persons whose final release, repatriation or re-establishment takes place thereafter. These persons shall continue to benefit from the relevant provisions of the Conventions and of this Protocol until their final release, repatriation or re-establishment."

The duration of operation of the Conventions of 1949 will thus differ in certain respects according to whether a state is a party only to the Conventions or to the Conventions and Protocol I.

B. Combatants

a) Combatants and Non-combatants Distinguished

The whole humanitarian law of war is grounded on the principle that force may be employed only against those persons who themselves use or threaten to use force. In general, those who use or have the immediate capacity to employ force are characterized as combatants or belligerents. Those who are not combatants are in so far as possible to be spared from attack or violence. These limitations on the use of violence in war seek to achieve a reasonable balance between the necessary destruction of the military resources of the enemy in time of war and the equally compelling need not to cause the unnecessary suffering, destruction, and loss of life which confer no clear military advantage. It is for this reason that only combatants are to be made the object of attack and non-combatants are to be spared. Non-combatants are therefore the largest category of persons who fall under the safeguards of international humanitarian law. It is for their protection that prohibitions and limitations are placed on the use of violence against the civilian population.

Non-combatant personnel, who are not to be made the objects of attack, consist of two basic categories. Within the armed forces, medical personnel and chaplains are regarded as non-combatants. Within the civilian population, non-combatants consist of all those persons who do not take up arms and do not engage in, or actively assist in the use of force against the adversary:

In the past the term "combatant" has not been used as a technical term in the treaties relating to the conduct of warfare and the protection of war victims. In the doctrine, the term has been used in a general sense to describe any member of the "fighting" armed forces, (other than medical personnel and chaplains and service and support personnel),[34] or any civilian who engages in combat. Thus, until the adoption of Protocol I to the Geneva Conventions of 1949, the characterization of an individual as "combatant" or "non-combatant" of itself entailed no legal consequences.

Article 1 of the Hague Regulations of 1907[35] did define the qualifications of what were identified as "belligerents":

> "The laws, rights, and duties of war apply not only to armies, but also to militia and volunteer corps fulfilling the following conditions:
> 1. To be commanded by a person responsible for his subordinates;
> 2. To have a fixed distinctive emblem recognizable at a distance;
> 3. To carry arms openly; and
> 4. To conduct their operations in accordance with the laws and customs of war."

Members of a *levée en masse*, the mass uprising of the civilian population in the face of the enemy without their having had a chance to organize themselves in conformity with the foregoing article were likewise to be recognized as "belligerents" if they carried arms openly and respected the law of war.[36] And "combatants" and "non-combatants" were briefly referred to in Article 3, but without making a distinction between the two:

> "The armed forces of the belligerent parties may consist of combatants and non-combatants. In the case of capture by the enemy, both have a right to be treated as prisoners of war."

The determination of who constituted a "belligerent" thus dictated whether a person under arms would be treated as a prisoner of war,[37] but some non-combatant military personnel were also treated as prisoners of war. In Article 4 of the Geneva Prisoners of War Convention of 1949, the four criteria laid down in the Hague Regulations became simply the criteria for entitlement to prisoner of war status:

> "Prisoners of war, in the sense of the present Convention, are persons belonging to one of the following categories, who have fallen into the power of the enemy:
> (1) Members of the armed forces of a Party to the conflict, as well as members of militias or volunteer corps forming part of such armed forces.
> (2) Members of other militias and members of other volunteer corps, including those of organized resistance movements, belonging to a Party to the conflict and operating in or outside their own territory, even if this territory is occupied, provided that such militias or volunteer corps, including such organized resistance movements, fulfil the following conditions:
>   (a) that of being commanded by a person responsible for his subordinates;
>   (b) that of having a fixed distinctive sign recognizable at a distance;
>   (c) that of carrying arms openly;
>   (d) that of conducting their operations in accordance with the laws and customs of war."

The requirements thus established for the status of prisoners of war are more fully dealt with in Chapter V, section (b) of this study. The terms "combatant and non-combatant" and "belligerent" (as referring to individuals rather than states) were infrequently used in the Geneva Conventions of 1949, and rights and duties do not turn on such classifications. Under Article 19 of the Civilians Convention, for example, the presence of arms and ammunition taken from "combatants" and not yet handed in to the proper service do not deprive a civilian hospital of the protection to which it is entitled. And neutralized zones may house "wounded and sick combatants or non-combatants."

In the customary international law that coexisted with the Hague Regulations and the Geneva Conventions of 1949, the concept of "unlawful" or "unprivileged" belligerency continued to play a role.[38]

In resistance movements and in guerrilla warfare and more recently in wars of national liberation, individuals have taken part in hostilities without fulfilling the qualifications laid down for prisoners of war in Article 4 of the Geneva Prisoners of War Convention of 1949 and earlier treaties dealing with the protection of prisoners of war.[39] The treaties did not, except as to occupied areas, give any clear guidance about the treatment to be accorded to individuals who did not identify themselves as members of the armed forces and yet engaged in acts of hostility. They did not qualify as prisoners of war and they might likewise fail to come within the ambit of the Geneva Civilians Convention of 1949, which for the most part confined its protection to those civilians who lived in areas occupied by the adversary or who were within the domestic territory of the adversary.[40] Such individuals who upon capture were not entitled to be treated either as prisoners of war or as peaceful civilians fell outside the protected categories and, subject to the requirement of a fair trial, were therefore at the mercy of the Detaining Power. That Power might try them for a violation of its domestic law or of international law and sentence them to the extreme penalty of death.[41] There was some controversy about whether individuals who carried on hostilities in arms without being eligible for prisoner of war treatment simply suffered deprivation of protection under any existing body of law or actually violated the international law of war.[42]

If civilians became combatants or belligerents in occupied areas, they did benefit from the protection of Article 64 of the Geneva Civilians Convention of 1949.

The Convention first stipulated in the second paragraph of that article that:

> "The Occupying Power may, however, subject the population of the occupied territory to provisions which are essential to enable the Occupying Power to fulfil its obligations under the present Convention, to maintain the orderly government of the territory, and to ensure the security of the Occupying Power, of the members and property of the occupying forces or administration, and likewise of the establishments and lines of communication used by them."

The Convention then lays down the duties of the Detaining Power with respect to such persons.[43] Those who take up arms against the occupying power or likewise engage in conduct prejudicial to its security are accordingly protected by the Convention, but these provisions relate only to hostile acts committed in occupied areas.

A markedly different approach to the legal status of combatants is taken in Protocol I to the Geneva Conventions of 1949. "Combatants" are defined as "members of the armed forces of a Party to a conflict (other than medical personnel and chaplains covered by Article 33 of the Third Convention)." And, as stipulated in Article 1 of the Hague Regulations, combatants "have the *right* to participate directly in hostilities" [emphasis supplied]. The idea of a right to take part in conflict had disappeared from the treaties between 1907 and 1977 and does not sit well with the humanitarian law of war in so far as it implies that international law confers a right on individuals to employ violence. Its inclusion in Protocol I was an outgrowth of the demand for recognition of prisoner of war status for all or most of those who engage in combat.

The "armed forces of a Party to a conflict" are further defined in paragraph 1 of Article 43 to consist of:

> "...all organized armed forces, groups and units which are under a command responsible to that Party for the conduct of its subordi-

nates, even if that Party is represented by a government or an authority not recognized by an adverse Party. Such armed forces shall be subject to an internal disciplinary system which, *inter alia*, shall enforce compliance with the rules of international law applicable in armed conflict."

It will be observed that the origins of this provision are to be found in Article 1 of the Hague Regulations of 1907 and in the list of qualifications for prisoner of war treatment in Article 4 of the Geneva Prisoners of War Convention of 1949. "All organized armed forces, groups and units" have been substituted for the more cumbersome formula of Article 4 of the Geneva Prisoners of War Convention, referring to members of the "armed forces," "other militias and... other volunteer corps, including those of organized resistance movements," provided the latter category met the four requirements of the Hague Regulations and of Article 4, paragraph A(2)(a)–(d). Only one of those four requirements, "that of being commanded by a person responsible for his subordinates," survives in modified form as a requirement that forces, groups and units be "under a command responsible to that Party for the conduct of its subordinates." The extension of prisoner of war status to "Members of regular armed forces who profess allegiance to a government or an authority not recognized by the Detaining Power," as provided in paragraph A(3) of Article 4 of the 1949 Convention has now become a stipulation that armed forces of a Party include those of a Party "represented by a government or an authority not recognized by an adverse Party." The previous condition "that of conducting their operations in accordance with the laws and customs of war" has ceased to be part of the definition and is a separate duty – "shall be subject to an internal disciplinary system," as further elaborated in the text quoted above. Thus, the failure of forces to conduct their operations in accordance with the law of war will no longer be the cause for denial of prisoner of war status to the totality of militias and volunteer corps because of violations of the law by individuals. War crimes by individuals will still be subject to prosecution, but they will no longer cost whole units their right to claim combatant and prisoner of war status.

Paragraph 3 of Article 43 adds that:

> "Whenever a Party to a conflict incorporates a paramilitary or armed law enforcement agency into its armed forces it will so notify the other Parties to the conflict."

So much difficulty was experienced in determining whether *gendarmerie*, border guards, and other paramilitary forces, as they exist under the laws of various countries, are to be regarded as members of the armed forces that it was left to the Parties to the conflict to notify each other of the inclusion of such agencies into its armed forces. If a state has a law providing for the automatic incorporation of such forces into armed forces in time of war, the requirement of this paragraph can be satisfied by notification to all parties to the Protocol through the depositary.[44]

b) Special Categories of Persons Who May or May Not Qualify as Combatants

1. Persons of Doubtful Status

If the only combatants captured were those who clearly qualified for prisoner of war status under Article 4 of the Geneva Prisoners of War Convention of 1949 or Article 44 of Protocol I of 1977, the Detaining Power would be faced with no problems of classification of prisoners. The reality is that those who are taken prisoner may include such diverse categories of persons as (1) members of the Detaining Power's own forces who have willingly or unwillingly served in the armed forces of the enemy; (2) nationals of the Detaining Power; (3) persons in civilian dress who have engaged in hostilities but appear not to meet the requirements laid down for prisoner of war status under the treaties; (4) members of the enemy armed forces in civilian clothes, who might be either saboteurs, spies, persons evading capture, escaping prisoners of war, or other persons seeking to profit from the use of civilian disguise; (5) civilian spies or saboteurs; (6) civilians in occupied areas engaging in acts prejudicial to the security of the occupying power; or mercenaries (7). Classification of such persons can entail important consequences – either release, treatment as a prisoner of war, or punishment, including the ultimate penalty of death.

During the Second World War, determinations of this character were often made summarily by very junior personnel. An aviator who had been captured while attempting to make his way back to his own lines might be denied prisoner of war status by a non-commissioned officer and taken out and shot. To deal with this problem, the Geneva Conference of 1949 included in the Prisoners of War Convention a new provision to the following effect:

> "Should any doubt arise as to whether persons, having committed a belligerent act and having fallen into the hands of the enemy, belong to any of the categories enumerated in Article 4, such persons shall enjoy the protection of the present Convention until such time as their status has been determined by a competent tribunal."[45]

The "competent tribunal" could be a civil court[46] or a court-martial or a specially constituted tribunal. If the tribunal is a military one, it should presumably be made up of officers and of more than one officer.[47]

The question of when "doubt" arises can be seen in two guises, depending on the number of categories involved. According to one possible interpretation of Article 5, there are three possible categories of persons: (1) those who are clearly entitled to prisoner of war status; (2) those who are clearly not entitled to prisoner of war status; and (3) doubtful cases. Another possible interpretation is that there are two categories: (1) those who are clearly entitled to prisoner of war status, and (2) all those captured persons who are not clearly entitled to prisoner of war status and whose cases are therefore to be taken as creating "doubt". The first theory would envisage a much smaller number of cases of legal "doubt" than the second. The placing of all persons who are captured and are not clearly entitled to prisoner of war status before a tribunal would be administratively extremely cumbersome, although it would avoid abuses of discretion in classifying prisoners as clearly not entitled to prisoner of war treatment. The first of these two interpretations – "three-category" theory – was adopted by the United States in connection with the establishment of "competent tribunals" during the war in Viet Nam[48] – the one conflict in which, it is believed, "competent tribunals" had been specially constituted to screen prisoners.[49]

Much more flesh was put on the bare bones of the second sentence of Article 5 of the Geneva Prisoners of War Convention when the principle of the article was incorporated in Protocol I of 1977. In Article 45, it is provided that a person taking part in hostilities and falling into the hands of the adverse party is presumed to be a prisoner of war falling under the protection of the 1949 Convention "if he claims the status of prisoner of war, or if he appears to be entitled to such status, or if the Party on which he depends claims such status on his behalf by notification to the Detaining Power or to the Protecting Power."[50] As before, if doubt arises, the prisoner is to continue to receive the protection of the Convention until his status has been determined by a "competent tribunal." Paragraph 2 of Article 45 responds to the practice (which finds no support in the law), of denying prisoner of war status to certain captured personnel, such as aviators, and of placing them before courts on charges of having committed war crimes. The paragraph accordingly provides:

> "If a person who has fallen into the power of an adverse Party is not held as a prisoner of war and is to be tried by that Party for an offence arising out of the hostilities, he shall have the right to assert his entitlement to prisoner of war status before a judicial tribunal and to have that question adjudicated. Whenever possible under the applicable procedure, this adjudication shall occur before the trial for the offence."

In this instance a "judicial tribunal" is specified because the prisoner is charged with an offence and the proceedings will therefore be before a court, whereas determination of status can be made either by a court or an administrative tribunal.

If an individual is found not entitled to prisoner of war status under Protocol I and does not benefit from more favorable treatment under the Geneva Civilians Convention of 1949,[51] he has the right to benefit from a substantial number of "fundamental guarantees" which are extended to any person who is in the power of a Party to the conflict and does not benefit from more favorable treatment from other provisions of the humanitarian treaties.[52]

2. Civilians in the Territory of a Party to the Conflict and Occupied Areas

The Geneva Civilians Convention of 1949 establishes a special régime for protected persons who engage in hostile activities in the *territory* of a party to the conflict. Protected persons are defined as those who "find themselves, in case of a conflict or occupation, in the hands of a Party to the conflict or occupying Power of which they are not nationals."[53] Those protected persons who are "definitely suspected of or engaged in activities hostile to the security of the State" in the territory of a party to the conflict are not entitled to those rights and privileges the exercise of which would be prejudicial to the security of the State.[54]

The hostile activities referred to presumably include espionage, sabotage, and prohibited relations with the enemy state and enemy nationals. The rights and privileges that are thus lost would include the right to receive and send correspondence, the right to receive relief, spiritual assistance, and visits from the Protecting Power and the International Committee of the Red Cross.[55]

If in an *occupied territory* an individual protected person is detained as a spy or saboteur or is definitely suspected of activity hostile to the Occupying Power, the detainee forfeits his right of communication when military security absolutely so requires.[56]

The right of communication is with the exterior, and, in the view of the International Committee of the Red Cross at least, such rights as notification to the Protecting Power in case of trial remain.[57]

In so far as these provisions deal with suspected persons, they overlap with Article 5 of the Geneva Prisoners of War Convention, discussed in the preceding paragraphs, and give rise to the question whether a person purporting to be a civilian who has engaged in hostile or belligerent acts is entitled to treatment as a prisoner of war or as a civilian until his status is definitely determined. Neither the texts of the treaties nor the *travaux préparatoires* give any indication of which provisional status was to be given priority.

The better view would appear to be that the screening process under Article 5 of the Prisoners of War Convention and under Article 45 of Protocol I, which has recently been given close consideration, should be given priority when there is some doubt about prisoner of war status. Article 5 of the Civilians Convention might then be brought into play if an individual has been determined not to be entitled to prisoner of war status.[58]

All the persons referred to above, whether in the territory of a party to the conflict or in occupied territory, are to be treated humanely and benefit from the right to a "fair and regular trial."[59] The Geneva Civilians Convention contains elaborate provisions concerning the prosecution and trial of civilian protected persons (Articles 64–77) and the internment of protected persons (Articles 78–135).

When, as noted above, Protocol I refers to the possibility of "more favourable treatment in accordance with the Fourth Convention" for a person who has taken part in hostilities but is not entitled to prisoner of war status,[60] Article 5 and the articles on trial, punishment, and internment assume particular importance for that individual.

3. Spies

Espionage in time of war is, in essence, the gathering or attempted gathering by clandestine means of military information about the enemy. It is the clandestine character of the activity and the spy's intention to deceive, that distinguish espionage from the reconnaissance, scouting, or surveillance performed by military forces and by individual members of the armed forces.[61] Article 29 of the Hague Regulations of 1907 defines a spy in the following terms:

> "A spy can only be considered a spy when, acting clandestinely or on false pretences, he obtains or endeavors to obtain information in the zone of operations of a belligerent, with the intention of communicating it to the hostile party.
>
> Thus soliders not wearing a disguise who have penetrated into the zone of operations of the hostile army, for the purpose of obtaining information, are not considered spies..."[62]

The next article goes on to provide that:

> "A spy taken in the act shall not be punished without previous trial."

Thus, international law (the foregoing provisions having passed into customary international law) defines the conduct, but its further definition of prosecution and punishment, is left to national law and national courts, including military tribunals. Thus, the spy is normally tried for a violation of domestic law under authority granted by international law. For this reason, no great importance need be attached to the fact that Article 29 refers exclusively to espionage committed "in the zone of operations of a belligerent" and may on that account be thought not to include espionage conducted in the home territory of a belligerent far from the scene of hostilities.

Indeed, espionage may be committed in time of peace as well as in times of war; as to espionage committed in peacetime, international law provides no generally accepted guiding principles. It is left to each state to determine what sort of information is protected, what sort of information gathering is permissible and impermissible, and what penalties are to imposed for violation of national law. In addition there are difficult problems, falling outside the scope of this study, about whether the gathering of information from satellites,[63] high-flying aircraft,[64] and by naval vessels which have entered the waters of a foreign state[65] constitutes espionage and whether the responsibility of the state instigating such measures is thereby engaged. It is moreover, not clear whether the gathering of information through electronic means constitutes an unlawful encroachment on the sovereignty of a foreign state.[66]

But be these problems as they may, it is generally accepted that espionage in time of war is not a violation of international law and accordingly not a "war crime." The spy is deprived of any right to prisoner of war treatment and is exposed to prosecution under national law in order to deter resort to these means of information-gathering. The sentence imposed, which may extend to the death penalty, is not a "punishment" for the violation of international law but a "penalty" to make the occupation of the spy as hazardous as possible.[67] Of course, from the perspective of national law, the spy may very well be punished for his commission of a crime under national law. Consistent with this view of the nature of espionage under international law:

> "A spy who, after rejoining the army to which he belongs, is subsequently captured by the enemy, is treated as a prisoner of war, and incurs no responsibility for his previous acts of espionage."[68]

The inclusion of wars of national liberation within the scope of the international law of war, the relaxation of requirements for the treatment of individuals as members of the armed forces, and renewed emphasis on the right of a civilian population to defend itself led the draftsmen of Protocol I of 1977 to incorporate new provisions on espionage. The particular contribution of the new treaty was the clarification of the status of the member of the armed forces who gathered information of military value but who might not be wearing uniform or a fixed distinctive sign or be carrying arms openly (as permitted by Article 3 of Protocol I). Article 46, paragraph 3, provides:

> "A member of the armed forces of a Party to the conflict who is a resident of territory occupied by an adverse Party and who, on behalf of the Party on which he depends, gathers or attempts to gather information of military value within that territory shall not be considered as engaging in espionage unless he does so through an act of false pretences or deliberately in a clandestine manner. Moreover, such a resident shall not lose his right to the status of prisoner of war and may not be treated as a spy unless he is captured while engaging in espionage."

The paragraph responded to the consideration that residents of occupied territories should not be treated as spies if, as routinely happens, they come across information of value to their armed forces. As the report of Committee III of the Diplomatic Conference put the matter:

> "For example, the resident who observed military movements while walking along the street or who took photographs from his residence would not be engaged in espionage; whereas the resident who used a forged pass to enter a military base or who, if lawfully on the base, illegally brought a camera with him, would be engaging in espionage".[69]

For the rest, Article 46 of Protocol I, which deals exclusively with spies who are members of the armed forces, is little more than an amplification of the existing law as laid down in the Hague Regulations of 1907. The member of the armed forces who is a spy is not entitled to the status of prisoner of war if captured while engaged in espionage.[70] He may not be treated as a spy if he gathered or attempted to gather information while in uniform or if, after engaging in espionage in the territory occupied by the adverse Party, he has rejoined the armed forces to which he belongs.[71]

4. Mercenaries

Mercenaries have fought in international and internal armed conflicts for centuries. In various periods their pursuit of private gain and violation of the laws and customs of war gained them an unenviable reputation. However, neither under the Hague Regulations of 1907 nor under the Geneva Conventions of 1949 nor under customary international law were they denied the rights of combatants or belligerents or, upon capture, prisoners of war, provided of course they otherwise met the requirements of the law for such status.[72] However, in the era of decolonization and of wars of national liberation, the excesses of mercenaries in the Congo, Biafra, Angola, Rhodesia, and elsewhere led many states to take the view that mercenaries are criminals and that a country employing them or even allowing their recruitment on its territory violates international law.[73] In 1973, the General Assembly adopted Resolution 3103 (XXVIII), declaring *inter alia* that:

> "The use of mercenaries by colonial and racist régimes against the national liberation movements struggling for their freedom and independence from the yoke of colonialism and alien domination is considered to be a criminal act and the mercenaries should accordingly be punished as criminals."[74]

At the Diplomatic Conference on International Humanitarian Law, there was widespread sentiment in favor of denying rights as combatants or prisoners of war to mercenaries, but the definition of mercenaries proved to be exceedingly difficult to formulate. If the criterion were to be the receipt of pay, mercenaries are indistinguishable in this respect from members of the regular armed forces who are likewise paid. If the foreign character of mercenaries were to be emphasized, there was the danger of sweeping into the definition military advisers from abroad, volunteers who had come to fight in a war of national liberation, foreign troops, and foreign technicians, whether civilian or military. Even motivation proved to be a misleading criterion because the regular soldier may, like the mercenary, be induced to fight because of the pay he has been offered. The text which emerged at the Diplomatic Conference contains the following definition:[75]

"A mercenary is any person who:

(a) is specially recruited locally or abroad in order to fight in an armed conflict;

(b) does, in fact, take a direct part in the hostilities;

(c) is motivated to take part in the hostilities essentially by the desire for private gain and, in fact, is promised, by or on behalf of a Party to the conflict, material compensation substantially in excess of that promised or paid to combatants of similar ranks and functions in the armed forces of that Party;

(d) is neither a national of a Party to the conflict nor a resident of territory controlled by a Party to the conflict;

(e) is not a member of the armed forces of a Party to the conflict; and

(f) has not been sent by a State which is not a Party to the conflict on official duty as a member of the armed forces."

It will be observed that an individual meet all six criteria before he may be treated as a mercenary. The definition is so restrictive that there will probably be relatively few individuals who will be classified as mercenaries.

Mercenaries, according to paragraph 1 of Article 47 of Protocol I, "shall not have the right to be a combatant or a prisoner of war." Such individuals should nevertheless, it would seem, benefit from the list of basic safeguards contained in Article 75 of the Protocol. In the view of some at the Diplomatic Conference on Humanitarian Law, Article 47 did not go far enough in that it did not make it mandatory to deny prisoner of war treatment to mercenaries.[76]

C. Civilians and Their Protection

a) The Law Prior to Protocol I of 1977

The treaty law prior to the conclusion of Protocol I of 1977 to the Geneva Conventions of 1949 did little to regulate the protection of the civilian population from attack, and even the expression "civilians" went undefined, the preferred term, as noted above,[77] being, "non-combatant." While the Hague Regulations of 1899 and 1907 laid down a number of rules for the protection of the civilian population in occupied areas,[78] the provisions on hostilities were more concerned with the protection of civilian property and places than with the lives and welfare of civilians themselves. Article 23(g) of the Regulations of 1907 forbade the destruction or seizure of enemy property unless that action was imperatively demanded by the necessities of war. Article 25 provided that:

"The attack or bombardment, by whatever means, of towns, villages, dwellings, or buildings which are undefended is prohibited."

And Article 27 called for the taking of all necessary steps in sieges and bombardments to spare as far as possible "buildings dedicated to religion, art, science, or charitable purposes, historic monuments, hospitals, and places where the sick and wounded are collected," provided they were not used for military purposes. The Hague Convention No. IX on Bombardment by Naval Forces in Time of War[79] likewise forbade the bombardment by naval forces of undefended ports, towns, villages, dwellings, or buildings (except to secure compliance with requisitions of provisions or supplies).[80] What the Hague Regulations and Hague Convention No. IX on Naval Bombardment clearly implied is that there was no conventional legal prohibition on the bombardment of civilians in defended places.

The Geneva Civilians Convention of 1949 concerned itself largely with the position of civilians in occupied areas and in the domestic territory of a belligerent (i.e., the protection of the enemy alien in a belligerent's territory). The few provisions concerning the civilian population in general[81] afforded them no protection against the violence of hostilities, except in so far as Articles 14 and 15 provided for the establishment of "hospital zones" and "safety zones."[82]

Several attempts, separated by more than three decades, were made to bring about the progressive development of the treaty law of aerial warfare, including the protection of the civilian population from the effect of aerial bombardment. These efforts were failures. In 1923, a Commission of Jurists, meeting at The Hague, drew up draft Rules of Air Warfare,[83] which would have forbidden aerial bombardment for the purpose of terrorizing the civilian population or of injuring non-combatants and would have required bombardment from the air to be confined to military objectives, as further defined in the Rules.[84] While these Rules were never put in treaty form, they nevertheless had a profound impact on the customary international law governing aerial bombardment. Again, after the Geneva Conference of 1949 for the Protection of War Victims, the International Committee of the Red Cross formulated "Draft Rules for the Limitation of the Dangers incurred by the Civilian Population in Time of War." The Rules would have forbidden attacks against the civilian population as such and required that attacks might be directed only against military objectives.[85] But the sweeping requirements of the Rules concerning precautions in attack and its prohibitions on target-area bombardment and on the use of weapons with uncontrollable effects militated[86] against their general acceptance, and they were referred to governments by the XIXth Conference of the Red Cross in 1957. This, under the circumstances, amounted to shelving them.

Despite this discouraging record of efforts to protect civilians and the civilian population from attack, notably from the air, through the drawing up of new treaties, some general principles of customary international law emerged from the practice and pronouncements of states and from the writings of learned publicists. The Hague Rules of 1923 and the I.C.R.C. Draft Rules played their part in the fashioning of these principles. There appeared to be an international consensus that the civilian population as such should not be the object of attack, that the incidental harm caused to civilians through the bombardment of military objectives should not be out of proportion to the military advantage to be gained, and that precautions should be taken to protect the lives and well-being of civilians in so far as possible.[87] These principles gained general acceptance despite deliberate attacks on the civilian populations of cities in Europe and in Japan, the use of target-area or carpet bombardment for the destruction of military objectives, and the first use of nuclear weapons, which, because of their cataclysmic effects, could make no distinctions between military personnel and civilians and between military objectives and civilian objects. The juridical conscience of the international community was not prepared to accept these practices as legitimate.

The highly visible impact of aerial bombardment in recent wars, such as that in Viet Nam, and heightened interest in the protection of human rights in armed conflict, combined with scepticism about the effectiveness of aerial bombardment against the civilian population and the development of technology which permitted much greater accuracy in the aiming of bombs and missiles, brought about renewed concern in the late 1960s and the 1970s with the legal control of attacks on the civilian population from the air and from the ground. In 1968, the General Assembly adopted a resolution in which it

> "*Affirms* resolution XXVIII of the XXth International Conference of the Red Cross held at Vienna in 1965, which laid down, *inter alia*, the following principles for observance by all governmental and other authorities responsible for action in armed conflicts:
>
> (*a*) That the right of the parties to a conflict to adopt means of injuring the enemy is not unlimited;
> (*b*) That it is prohibited to launch attacks against the civilian populations as such;
> (*c*) That distinction must be made at all times between persons taking part in the hostilities and members of the civilian population to the effect that the latter be spared as much as possible."[88]

The next year the General Assembly was able to lay down eight basic principles for the protection of civilian population in armed conflicts, which included the following principles bearing on bombardment or attack from the air or ground:

> "...2. In the conduct of military operations during armed conflicts, a distinction must be made at all times between persons actively taking part in the hostilities and civilian populations.
> 3. In the conduct of military operations, every effort should be made to spare civilian populations from the ravages of war, and all necessary precautions should be taken to avoid injury, loss or damage to civilian populations.
> 4. Civilian populations as such should not be the object of military operations.

5. Dwellings and other installations that are used only by civilian populations should not be the object of military operations.

6. Places or areas designated for the sole protection of civilians, such as hospital zones or similar refuges, should not be the object of military operations.[89]"

These resolutions provided the foundation for provisions on the protection of the civilian population which were made part of Protocol I to the Geneva Conventions of 1949. But the law which was to be incorporated in the Protocol had its origins in the Hague Air Warfare Rules of 1923 and in the I.C.R.C. Draft Rules of 1956, various provisions of which had found their way into the doctrine and into the state practice of a number of countries, as reflected in their military manuals and in their pronouncements on the law of aerial bombardment.[90]

b) The Law under Protocol I to the Geneva Conventions of 1949.

It was only with the adoption in 1977 by the Diplomatic Conference on International Humanitarian Law of Protocol I to the Geneva Conventions of 1949 that rules governing attacks and protecting the civilian population were at last incorporated in a treaty.

The rules of the Protocol are not confined to aerial bombardment but govern all attacks – meaning "acts of violence against the adversary, whether in offence or in defence."[91]

The Section of the Protocol protecting the civilian population applies to any land, air or sea warfare, including attacks from the sea or from the air against objectives on land, to the extent that such warfare "may affect the civilian population, individual civilians or civilian objects on land."[92]

1. Civilians Defined

Under Article 50 of Protocol I a civilian is any person who is not a member of the armed forces in the sense of Article 4 of the Geneva Prisoners of War Convention of 1949 or of Article 43 of Protocol I.[93] The members of the armed forces, as so defined, are legitimate objects of attack, except in so far as the law of war extends protection to them under various circumstances.

For example, the member of the armed forces who falls into the hands of the adversary is treated as a prisoner of war, and it is then forbidden to attack him further. If a civilian takes a direct part in hostilities, he loses his protection as a civilian for as long as he engages in hostilities.[94] And if there is doubt whether a person is a civilian, he is to be treated as a civilian.[95]

The totality of all civilians constitutes the "civilian population," as that term is used in the Protocol.[96] It is virtually inevitable that in time of armed conflict, individual members of the armed forces will be intermingled with the civilian population, and their presence does not deprive the civilian population of its character as such or of the protection to which it is entitled.[97] Thus the presence of soldiers on leave amidst a large number of civilians does not mean that the group of civilians may be attacked. Obviously, at the other extreme, the presence of organized bodies of soldiers amidst the civilian population does not give the soldiers any immunity from an attack directed against them.

2. General Protection of the Civilian Population

The basic rule is that a Party to a conflict must "at all times distinguish between the civilian population and combatants and between civilian objects and military objectives," and must accordingly direct its operations only against military objectives.[98] The civilian population and individual civilians, who are to enjoy general protection from the dangers arising from military operations, must not be made the object of attack.[99]

Aerial bombardment for the purpose of "terrorizing" the civilian population had over the years since the First World War been regarded by various and authorities as in violation of international law.[100]

Indeed, the Hague Air Warfare Rules[101] would have prohibited aerial bombardment for this purpose. The issue had been kept alive by the bombardment of European cities (such as Rotterdam and Dresden) in order to cow the civilian population, by the incendiary bombing of Tokyo, and by the first use of atomic weapons at Hiroshima and Nagasaki. The ICRC Draft Rules would likewise have forbidden attacks directed against the civilian population "with the object of terrorizing it or for any other reason"[102] – which essentially emptied "terror attacks" of any separate legal significance. In view of this line of authority, it was natural that the Diplomatic Conference on International Humanitarian Law should have framed the following rules for inclusion in Protocol I:

> "Acts or threats of violence the primary purpose of which is to spread terror among the civilian population are prohibited."[103]

It will be noted that it is the *primary* intent or motive of the attack, and not its effect, that counts. An attack that is primarily intended to cause terror is unlawful, even if terror is not caused. And if an attack causes terror but this was not the primary purpose of the attack, the requirements of the provision are not satisfied. These questions are probably of marginal concern because attacks intended to cause terror will normally already fall under the interdiction of attacks directed against the civilian population as such. So much had been made of "terror attacks" in the past that some reference to them had to be made in Protocol I.

The civilian population is further protected by a prohibition against indiscriminate attacks, which are defined to include target-area or carpet bombardment and attacks which may be expected to cause incidental death and injury to civilians or damage to civilian objects[104] which "would be excessive in relation to the concrete and direct military advantage anticipated." This latter provision incorporated the rule of proportionality, which recognizes that attacks against military objectives will in certain circumstances inevitably cause incidental harm to civilians (e.g. from bombs being inaccurately dropped or from their effects spreading from military objectives to civilian objectives) but that this incidental harm becomes unlawful if it is out of proportion to the military advantage being pursued.[105] The question of methods of attack is more fully dealt with in connection with methods and means of warfare.[106]

3. General Protection of Civilian Objects

There is a need in war not only to protect the lives and well-being of individual civilians and of the civilian population but also to safeguard those objects that are civilian in nature, for without housing, sustenance, services, and places of employment the survival and security for the civilian population cannot be assured. Protocol I accordingly has provisions on the protection of civilian objects that run parallel to provisions on the protection of individual civilians and the civilian population. Civilian objects are not to be made the object of attack (or of reprisals).[107] As civilians are defined as those who do not belong to the armed forces, civilian objects are those objects which are not "military objectives."

It would have been impossible to draw up a full and precise list of what constitute military objectives, and so Article 52, paragraph 2, provides only a general definition:

> "In so far as objects are concerned, military objectives are limited to those objects which by their nature, location, purpose or use make an effective contribution to military action and whose total or partial destruction, capture or neutralization, in the circumstances ruling at the time, offers a definite military advantage."

The definition has three elements: (1) the nature, location, purpose or use of the object; (2) whether it makes an effective contribution to military action; and (3) and whether its destruction, capture, or neutralization would offer a definite military advantage.[108] The variety of criteria listed in (1) is necessitated by the fact that some military objectives, such as fortifications, military radar installations, and munitions factories, have that character inherently, whereas a school building used as a barracks acquires that character only because of its location and temporary use. Part (2) of the definition envisages the possibility that a military objective need not necessarily be destroyed; it may be enough to capture or neutralize it. And finally, (3) requires not merely some military advantage but a *definite military* advantage in light of the circumstances at the time. The Hague Air Warfare Rules of 1923 had attempted to enumerate exhaustively what constitute military objectives,[109] but the list of categories of military objectives which was to be appended to the I.C.R.C. Draft Rules of 1956 was never drawn up.[110] Mindful of the need to give clear guidance to their armed forces, a number of countries have attempted in their military manuals to identify with some specificity what constitute military objectives.[111]

The doubtful case is taken care of by a provision that if there is a question about whether an object which is normally used for civilian purposes (such as a house or a school) is "being used to make an effective contribution to military action," it is presumed not to be so used.[112]

Under Protocol I, three types of civilian objects are put under special protection. Cultural property, provided for in Article 53, and objects indispensable to the survival of the civilian population, provided for in Article 54, are dealt with elsewhere in the volume.[113] It is sufficient to observe here that there is an express prohibition on the attack or destruction, or removal of "objects indispensable to the survival of the civilian population, such as foodstuffs, agricultural areas for the production of foodstuffs, crops, livestock, drinking water installations and supplies and irrigation works, for the specific purpose of denying them for their sustenance value to the civilian population," with exceptions made in the case of sustenance for the armed forces or in direct support of military action.[114] The special protection afforded to works and installations containing dangerous forces calls for somewhat more detailed consideration.

At the Diplomatic Conference on International Humanitarian Law and at the Conferences of Government Experts which preceded it, concern was expressed about the effect that the bombardment of dams, dykes, and nuclear electrical generating stations would have on the civilian population. Attacks designed to damage or destroy such installations could very well let loose forces such as water or radiation which would have profoundly harmful effects on the civilian population.[115] Under Article 56 of Protocol I, such works and installations are not to be made the object of attack, even if they constitute military objectives, if the attack would set loose dangerous forces and thereby cause severe losses to the civilian population. Even military objectives at or near such installations are not to be attacked if the attack might cause the release of dangerous forces. The situation that was thought of was that of the anti-aircraft gun on the dyke: the installation cannot be attacked if the result might be the destruction of the dyke with consequent flooding and severe losses among the civilian population. However, if any of these works or installations should be used in "regular, significant and direct support of military operations" and attack is the only way to bring an end to that support, then the works or installations may be attacked.[116] The Parties to Protocol I have also agreed to try to avoid placing any military objectives in the vicinity of works or installations containing dangerous forces.[117] A special symbol has been provided for the marking of the works and installations covered by Article 52.[118]

4. Precautionary Measures

That a commander should, if possible, give warning before a bombardment which may affect the civilian population has been a recognized principle since at least the turn of the century and the drawing up of the Hague Regulations.[119] The necessity of surprise in attacking military objectives may make such a warning impossible; and repeated warnings, which may or may not be followed by bombardment or other form of attack, may themselves be instruments of psychological warfare against the enemy. Nevertheless, the encouragement of such warnings is basically in the interests of the civilian populations, and Protocol I strengthens the obligation somewhat, but not to the extent of making it militarily unrealistic, by stating that:

> "effective advance warning shall be given of attacks which may affect the civilian population, unless circumstances do not permit."[120]

The range of precautions that must be taken by those who plan or decide upon an attack has been materially widened in the new Protocol. Persons with these responsibilities must do everything feasible to verify that the objectives to be attacked are military objectives and not civilian objectives protected under the treaty. They must minimize incidental loss of life and injuries among civilians and damage to civilian objects. They must not launch an attack which will cause incidental loss of civilian life and property which would be excessive in proportion to the military advantage to be gained. The attack is to be called off if it becomes apparent that one or more of these principles may be violated.[121] Overreaching these specific requirements laid on those who plan or decide on attacks is the basic norm that:

> "in the conduct of military operations, constant care must be taken to spare the civilian population, civilians and civilian objects".[122]

Corresponding to the duties of the Party or the commander planning or executing an attack are the precautions which the other Party to the conflict is to take "to the extent feasible" – the removal of civilians from the area of military objectives, the location of military objectives away from densely populated areas, and other necessary precautions to protect civilians.[123] The guiding principle is that not only should civilians not be used to shield military objectives and operations[124] but that active measures should be taken to avoid having civilians in the vicinity of military objectives.

5. Areas Under Special Protection

A further manner in which parts at least of the civilian population can be protected from attack by aerial bombardment or otherwise is the establishment of special zones which are immune from attack. On the basis of some limited success which the International Committee of the Red Cross had had in the establishment of neutralized zones for the reception of the wounded and sick and civilian victims of war in the 1930s and 1940s,[125] provisions for hospital and safety zones and localities and neutralized zones were incorporated in the Geneva Civilians Convention of 1949. Hospital and safety zones could be established on a Party's own territory and in occupied territory for the reception of the wounded and sick, children, aged persons, expectant mothers, and mothers of small children.[126] In areas where fighting might be taking place, neutralized zones could be established to receive the wounded and sick and civilians who would do no work of a military character.[127] The efficacy of both types of zones could not be assured without an agreement between the two belligerents. While there was not extensive use of these two types of institutions in the years after 1949, it was nevertheless thought desirable to include in Protocol I provisions for two new types of "localities and zones under special protection" which are much more ambitious in character than the zones contemplated by the Geneva Civilians Convention of 1949. The Geneva Civilians Convention of 1949 and Protocol I thus cumulatively establish four types of special zones.

The two new types of localities and zones under special protection differ from the zones under the Convention of 1949 in that they are reserved for the civilian population as a whole, instead of special categories of civilians, and they are established where the civilians are, thus precluding the necessity of moving them to another spot protected under Article 14 or Article 15 of the Geneva Civilians Convention.[128]

The first type of locality and zone is the "non-defended locality" – that is, "any inhabited place near or in a zone where armed forces are in contact which is open for occupation by an adverse Party," which has been so declared by the Party.[129] As undefended localities may not be attacked in any event, pursuant to Article 25 of the Hague Regulations and customary international law,[130] Article 59 of Protocol I simply provides a structure or machinery for an existing safeguard. The concept of a "non-defended locality" also owes something to the concept of an "open city," which is undefended and open to occupation by the adversary and may not on that account be attacked.[131] The second new type of zone is the "demilitarized zone." Once the zone is established, both Parties to the conflict are forbidden to extend their military operations to the area.[132]

Both types of zones must meet the following conditions:

(a) all combatants, as well as mobile weapons and mobile military equipment, must have been evacuated;
(b) no hostile use shall be made of fixed military installations or establishments;
(c) no acts of hostility shall be committed by the authorities or by the population; and
(d) no activities in support of military operations shall be undertaken.[133]

Two important differences between the types of areas must be noted. The first is that a "non-defended locality" may be established by unilateral declaration, while a "demilitarized zone" may be set up only pursuant to an agreement between the parties.[134] The second is that the status of a "non-defended locality" is essentially temporary, because its status ends when it is occupied by the adversary.[135] The agreement establishing a "demilitarized zone" will govern whether the area will remain demilitarized no matter which party controls it or whether the special protection will end if the area is occupied by the adverse party.[136] Of course, if either type of area should fail to fulfil the conditions set forth above, it will lose its protection under Protocol I.[137] Articles 59 and 60 lay down further particulars about the presence of police forces, the marking of the zone, and the documentation and procedures for the establishment of the zone.

D. Certain Problems of Contacts Between Combatants (Perfidy, Misuse of Emblems, Quarter, Persons *Hors de Combat*)

a. *Treachery and Perfidy*

Article 23(b) of the Hague Regulations states that it is forbidden "to kill or wound treacherously individuals belonging to the hostile nation or army" – a prohibition that must be looked upon as declaratory of the law then existing. The prohibition of making "improper use of a flag of truce, of the national flag or of the military insignia and uniform of the enemy, as well as the distinctive badges of the Geneva Convention," in Article 23(f) must be looked upon as, in part at least, a particularization of the more general prohibition of treachery. In international law, as it existed at the time, treachery was thought to include such acts as feigned surrender in order to put the adversary off guard and thereby to gain an advantage over him as fighting resumes, killing of *parlementaires*, and misuse of the flag of truce[138] – all of these instances in which "the offender assumes a false character by which he deceives his enemy and thereby is able to effect a hostile act which, had he come under his true colours, he could not have done."[139]

Protocol I gives much greater clarity and precision to these concepts than the terse words of the Hague Regulations permitted. The key concept in Article 37, paragraph 1, of Protocol I, is that "perfidy" (which is for the purpose of the law of war synonymous with "treachery") is an "act inviting the confidence of an adversary to lead him to believe that he is entitled to, or is obliged to accord, protection under the rules of international law applicable in armed conflict, with intent to betray that confidence." The specific prohibition is one against killing, injuring, or capturing an adversary by resort to perfidy. To feign death in order to save one's life is thus not perfidious.[140] The rather abstract and difficult, but juridically accurate, definition of the concept is spelled out in four specific acts:

> "(a) the feigning of an intent to negotiate under a flag of surrender or of a surrender,
> (b) the feigning of an incapacitation by wounds or sickness,
> (c) the feigning of civilian, non-combatant status, and
> (d) the feigning of protected status by the use of signs, emblems or uniforms of the United Nations or of neutral or other States not Parties to the conflict.[141]"

Because of the fear that the idea of perfidy might be used under (c) in order to punish persons otherwise entitled to prisoner of war status under the new definition in Article 44, it is expressly provided in the latter article that acts complying with the article are not perfidious.[142] On the other hand, ruses of war, such as the use of camouflage or decoys or misinformation, are not perfidy and are not prohibited.[143]

The misuse of emblems, even when perfidy is not involved, falls under the prohibitions of Protocol I. It is forbidden to make improper use of the emblems of the Red Cross (and equivalent emblems), signs or signals provided for in the Geneva Conventions or Protocol I, the flag of truce, the protective emblem of cultural property,[144] and the insignia or uniforms of neutral or other states not parties to the conflict.[145] Use of the United Nations emblem without the authorization of the organization is also forbidden.[146]

Is it permissible for a belligerent to make use of the uniforms and insignia of its adversary as a ruse of war? Article 23(f) of the Hague Regulations was not very helpful; it forbade "improper" use of the enemy uniform but it did not specify what was improper. The general view has been that it is unlawful to use the enemy uniform in attack or combat, but that no rule of international law precludes the use of enemy uniforms as a ruse at other times.[147] Article 39, paragraph I, widens somewhat the prohibition recognized in customary international law:

> "It is prohibited to make use of the flags or military emblems, insignia or uniforms of adverse Parties while engaging in attacks or in order to shield, favour, protect or impede military operations."

The rule is not intended to affect the law applicable to espionage.[148]

b) Persons Passing into the Power of the Adversary

The brief period, often amounting to no more than minutes or seconds, when a combatant is or might be passing into the power of his adversary is one in which he is extremely vulnerable. Perhaps no longer able to fight freely as a combatant, he has not yet become a prisoner of war or passed into some other sheltered status. One of the basic rules is that it is forbidden to deny quarter[149] – that is, "to order that there shall be no survivors, to threaten an adversary therewith or to conduct hostilities on this basis," as Article 40 of Protocol I puts it. For, when an individual is *hors de combat*, he may not be attacked. He is *hors de combat* if

(a) he is in the power of an adverse Party
(b) he clearly expresses an intention to surrender, or
(c) he has been rendered unconscious or is otherwise incapacitated by wounds or sickness, and therefore is incapable of defending himself,[150]

if he refrains from hostilities and does not try to escape. When he is physically in the power of the adversary, he immediately becomes a prisoner of war, if he is entitled to that status. In the other two instances, the individual may not yet be actually within the power of the forces that will take him into custody.

Several practical problems about hostilities by small units and about persons parachuting to earth had not been satisfactorily dealt with in the Geneva Conventions of 1949 and were the cause of some concern to military personnel. Under combat conditions, small units of armed forces fighting with guerrilla tactics, airborne troops, rapidly moving armoured troops, armed forces of national liberation movements have found that they lacked the facilities for taking, guarding, looking after, and evacuating prisoners of war.[151] The answer of Protocol I is that if "under unusual conditions of combat" prisoners cannot be evacuated, they are to be released and "all feasible" precautions taken to ensure their safety.[152] The latter obligation is imposed so that captured troops will not be set free, deliberately deprived of food or drink or clothing, if the capturing forces have the means of seeing that those left free do not perish.

The individual descending from an enemy plane by parachute is not, as he descends, in any position to fight. On the ground he may fight, he may attempt to escape, or he may surrender.[153] May he be attacked in the air or when he lands? Protocol I provides that airborne troops receive no protection,[154] but a person parachuting from a plane in distress may not be made the object of attack when he is descending.[155] Once on the ground, in territory controlled by his adversary, he is to be given an opportunity to surrender before he is attacked. If, on the other hand, it is clear that he is engaged in a hostile (including for this purpose attempting to escape)[156] act, he may be attacked.[157]

Notes

* Richard R. Baxter died on 26 september 1980 at Cambridge (Massachusetts). This chapter published here is one of the last contributions of Professor R. R. Baxter to the doctrine of international humanitarian law.
1. Baxter Richard, 'The Definition of War', *Revue égyptienne de droit international* (Le Caire), Vol. 16, 1960, p. 1.
2. Annexed to General Assembly Resolution 3314 (XXIX), 14 December 1974; *General Assembly Official Records: Twenty-nineth Session, Supplement No. 31*, p. 30, UN Doc. A/9631 (1975).
3. *Ibid.*, Art. 3 (f)
4. Meyrowitz Henri, *Le principe de l'égalité des belligérants devant le droit de la guerre*, Paris, Editions A. Pedone, 1970, pp. 141–242.
5. Carnegie Endowment for International Peace, *The Hague Conventions and Declarations of 1899 and 1907*, Edited by James Brown Scott, 2nd edition, New York, Oxford University Press, 1915, p. 96. *The Laws of Armed Conflicts. A Collection of Conventions, Resolutions and Other Documents*, Edited by D. Schindler and J. Toman, 3rd edition, Dordrecht, Martinus Nijhoff Publishers, Geneva, Henry Dunant Institute, 1988, pp. 57–61.
6. Office of United States Chief of Counsel for Prosecution of Axis Criminality, *Nazi Conspiracy and Aggression: Opinion and Judgment*, Washington, United States Government Printing Office, 1947, p. 46.
7. *The Tokyo Judgment. The International Military Tribunal for the Far East* (I.M.T.F.E.), 29 April 1946 – 12 November 1948. Edited by Dr. B.V.A. Röling and Dr. C.F. Rüter, Vol. I, Amsterdam, APA – University Press Amsterdam BV, 1977, pp. 441–442.
8. On 11 December 1941, the Congress of the United States declared "that the state of war between the United States and the Government of Germany which has been thrust upon the United States is hereby formally declared" (Joint Resolution of 11 December 1941, Public Law 331, 77th Congress,

1st session, chapter 564); *American Journal of International Law* (Washington), Vol. 36, Supplement, 1942, p. 2.

9. Stone Julius, *Legal Controls of International Conflict*, New York, Reinehart & Co., 1954, No. 70, p. 311.

10. Office of United States Chief of Counsel for Prosecution of Axis Criminality, *Nazi Conspiracy and Aggression: Opinion and Judgment*, Washington, United States Government Printing Office, 1947, pp. 24–27, 63, 83–84.

11. See Grob Fritz, *The Relativity of War and Peace: A Study in Law, History, and Politics*, New Haven, Yale University Press, 1949, especially at pp. 189–324.

12. As provided for in Common Article 3 of the Geneva Conventions of 1949.

13. Carnegie Endowment for International Peace, *The Hague Conventions and Declarations of 1899 and 1907*, Edited by James Brown Scott, 2nd edition, New York, Oxford University Press, 1915, p. 100. *The Laws of Armed Conflicts. A Collection of Conventions, Resolutions and Other Documents*. Edited by D. Schindler and J. Toman, 3rd edition, Dordrecht, Martinus Nijhoff Publishers, Geneva, Henry Dunant Institute, 1988, pp. 63–98.

14. Convention (II) with Respect to the Laws and Customs of War on Land of The Hague of 1899 and Convention (IV) of The Hague of 1907 Respecting the Laws and Customs of War on Land: Preambule, third paragraph.

15. Office of United States Chief of Counsel for Prosecution of Axis Criminality, *Nazi Conspiracy and Aggression: Opinion and Judgment*, Washington, United States Government Printing Office, 1947, p. 83.

16. Conventions signed at Geneva, 12 August 1949: Convention for the Amelioration of the Condition of the Wounded and Sick in Armed Forces in the Field [hereinafter Geneva Wounded and Sick Convention], *United Nations Treaty Series*, Vol. 75, pp. 31–32, Convention for the Amelioration of the Condition of Wounded, Sick and Shipwrecked Members of the Armed Forces at Sea [hereinafter Geneva Wounded, Sick, and Shipwrecked Convention], *United Nations Treaty Series*, Vol. 75, pp. 85–96; Convention Relative to the Treatment of Prisoners of War [hereinafter Geneva Prisoners of War Convention], *United Nations Treaty Series*, Vol. 75, pp. 135–136; and Convention Relative to the Protection of Civilian Persons in Time of War [hereinafter Geneva Civilians Convention], *United Nations Treaty Series*, Vol. 75, pp. 287–288. Also in: *The Laws of Armed Conflicts. A Collection of Conventions, Resolutions and Other Documents*, Edited by D. Schindler and J. Toman, 3rd edition, Dordrecht, Martinus Nijhoff Publishers, Geneva, Henry Dunant Institute, 1988, pp. 376, 404, 429, 501; *International Red Cross Handbook*, 12th edition, Geneva, ICRC, League of Red Cross Societies, 1983, pp. 23, 47, 67, 236.

   Article 18 of the Convention for the Protection of Cultural Property in the Event of Armed Conflict, signed at The Hague, 14 May 1954, *United Nations Treaty Series*, Vol. 249, pp. 240–245; *The Laws of Armed Conflicts. A Collection of Conventions, Resolutions and Other Documents*, Edited by D. Schindler and J. Toman, 3rd edition, Dordrecht, Martinus Nijhoff Publishers, Geneva, Henry Dunant Institute, 1988, p. 753; *International Red Cross Handbook*, 12th edition, Geneva, ICRC, League of Red Cross Societies, 1983, pp. 366 ff., provides for the scope of application of the Convention in terms substantially identical with those of Common Article 2 of the Geneva Conventions of 1949.

17. de Preux, Jean, in: The Geneva Conventions of 12 August 1949: *Commentary*, The Third Geneva Convention Relative to the Treatment of Prisoners of War, published under the general editorship of Jean S. Pictet, Vol. III, Geneva, ICRC, 1960, p. 22.
   The Hague Cultural Property Convention avoids this difficulty by stipulating that it applies to any armed conflict between two or more High Contracting Parties "even if the state of war is not recognized by one *or more* of them". [emphasis supplied]

18. See *infra*, p. 217 (Chapter XIV).

19. Protocol Additional to the Geneva Conventions of 12 August 1949, and Relating to the Protection of Victims of International Armed Conflicts (Protocol I), in *Official Records of the Diplomatic Conference on the Reaffirmation and Development of International Humanitarian Law applicable in Armed*

Conflicts, Geneva (1974–1977) [hereinafter CDDH Official Records], Bern, Federal Political Department, 1978, Vol.1, p. 115; *The Laws of Armed Conflicts. A Collection of Conventions, Resolutions and Other Documents*, Edited by D. Schindler and J. Toman, 3rd edition, Dordrecht, Martinus Nijhoff Publishers, Geneva, Henry Dunant Institute, 1988, p. 628 ff.; *International Red Cross Handbook*, 12th edition, Geneva, ICRC, League of Red Cross Societies, 1983, pp. 216 ff.

20. Abi-Saab Georges, "Wars of National Liberation and the Laws of War", *Annales d'études internationales* (Geneva), 1972, p. 93; – Salmon Jean J. A., 'La Conférence diplomatique sur la réaffirmation et le développement du droit international humanitaire et les guerres de libération nationale', *Revue belge de droit international* (Brussels), Vol. 12, 1976, p. 2; – Baxter Richard R., 'The Geneva Conventions of 1949 and the Wars of National Liberation', *Rivista di Diritto Internazionale* (Rome), Vol. 57, 1974, p. 193; – Bretton Philippe, 'L'incidence des guerres contemporaines sur la réaffirmation et le développement du droit international humanitaire applicable dans les conflicts armés internationaux et non internationaux', *Journal du droit international* (Paris), Vol. 105, 1978, p. 208 et pp. 214–220; – Salmon Jean, 'Les guerres de libération nationale', in Cassese Antonio, *The New Humanitarian Law of Armed Conflict*, Naples, Editoriale Scientifica, 1979, p. 53.

21. *General Assembly Official Records: Twenty-sixth Session, Supplement No. 29*, p. 29, UN Doc. A/8429 (1972).

22. See Abi-Saab Georges, 'Wars of National Liberation and the Laws of War', *Annales d'études internationales* (Geneva), 1972, p. 93 and pp. 98–102.

23. As in the conflict of Viet Nam.

24. Carnegie Endowment for International Peace, *The Hague Conventions and Declarations of 1899 and 1907*, Edited by James Brown Scott, 2nd edition, New York, Oxford University Press, 1915, p. 102; *The Laws of Armed Conflicts. A Collection of Conventions, Resolutions and Other Documents*, Edited by D. Schindler and J. Toman, 3rd edition, Dordrecht, Martinus Nijhoff Publishers, Geneva, Henry Dunant Institute, 1988, p. 70–71.

25. In 1960, the Provisional Government of the Algerian Republic, which had not yet been recognized by France, deposited an instrument of accession to the Geneva Conventions of 1949. – Bedjaoui Mohammed, *La révolution algérienne et le droit*, Brussels, Editions de l'Association internationale des juristes démocrates, 1961, pp. 186–201; Veuthey Michel, *Guérilla et droit international*, Genèea, Institut Henry-Dunant, 1976, p. 49.

26. United Nations, Secretary-General, *Regulations for the United Nations Emergency Force*, UN Doc. ST/SGB/UNEF 1, ch. VI, sec. 44; and see Bowett, D. W., *United Nations Forces: A Legal Study of United Nations Practice*, London, Stevens & Sons, 1964, p. 121 and pp. 484–516.

27. Office of United States Chief of Counsel for Prosecution of Axis Criminality, *Nazi Conspiracy and Aggression: Opinion and Judgment*, Washington, United States Government Printing Office, 1947, p. 83.

28. See Chapter VII, pp. 76–77.

29. Baxter R. R., 'Armistices and Other Forms of Suspension of Hostilities', *Recueil des cours*, Vol. 149, 1976, pp. 353–359 and p. 372.

30. Von Glahn Gerhard, *The Occupation of Enemy Territory*, Minneapolis, University of Minnesota Press, 1957, pp. 273–290.

31. Hague Regulations, Art. 5.

32. *Ibid.*, Art. 114.

33. *Ibid.*, Art. 6.

34. See Spaight, J. M., *War Rights on Land*, London, MacMillan and Co., 1911, p. 58.

35. Carnegie Endowment for International Peace, *The Hague Conventions and Declarations of 1899 and 1907*, Edited by James Brown Scott, 2nd edition, New York, Oxford University Press, 1915, p. 107; *The Laws of Armed Conflicts. A Collection of Conventions, Resolutions and Other Documents*, Edited by D. Schindler and J. Toman, 3rd edition, Dordrecht, Martinus Nijhoff Publishers, Geneva, Henry Dunant Institute, 1988, p. 75.

36. Hague Regulations, Art.2. A similar definition is found in Article 4, paragraph A(6), of the Geneva Prisoners of War Convention of 1949.

37. Hague Regulations, Art. 3.

38. Baxter, R. R., "So-called 'Unprivileged Belligerency': Spies, Guerrillas, and Saboteurs", *British Year Book of International Law* (London), Vol. 28, 1951, p. 323.

39. E.g., Convention relative to the Treatment of Prisoners of War, signed at Geneva, 27 July 1929; *The Laws of Armed Conflicts. A Collection of Conventions, Resolutions and other Documents*, Edited by D. Schindler and J. Toman, 3rd edition, Dordrecht, Martinus Nijhoff Publishers, Geneva, Henry Dunant Institute, 1988, p. 339 ff.

40. See Geneva Civilians Convention, Arts. 27–141.

41. *Osman Bin Haj Mohamed Ali and Another v. Public Prosecutor*, 1969, 1 A.C. 430 (P.C.), 1968, 3 All E.R. 488.

42. Baxter, R. R., "So-called 'Unprivileged Belligerency': Spies, Guerrillas, and Saboteurs", *British Yearbook of International Law* (London), Vol. 28, 1951, p. 323; and Fauchille Paul, *Traité de droit international public*, 8th ed., Bonfils, Henry (ed.), Paris, Rousseau & Cie., 1921, Vol. 2, p. 99.

43. Geneva Civilian Convention, Arts. 65–77.

44. Report of Committee III, para. 45, Doc. CDDH/236/Rev.1 (1976), *CDDH Official Records*, Vol. 15, p. 377 and p. 390.

45. Geneva Prisoners of War Convention, Art. 5, second sentence.

46. As in *Public Prosecutor v. Oie Hee Koi* (1968), A.C. 829 (P.C.), in which the Privy Council dealt with the status of a group of Chinese Malays who had been captured as members of forces of Indonesian paratroops in Malaysia. See Baxter, R. R., ' The Privy Council on the Qualifications of Belligerents', *American Journal of International Law* (Washington), Vol. 63, 1969, p. 290.

47. de Preux, Jean, in: The Geneva Conventions of 12 August 1949: *Commentary*, The Third Geneva Convention relative to the treatment of prisoners of war, published under the general editorship of Jean S. Pictet, Vol. III, Geneva, ICRC, 1960, p. 78.

48. Headquarters, United States Military Assistance Command, Vietnam, *Directive Number 20–5. Inspections and Investigation: Prisoners of War – Determination of Eligibility*, 15 March 1968, subparas. 5e and 5f.

49. Levie Howard S., 'Prisoners of War in International Armed Conflict', *in* U.S. Naval War College, *International Law Studies*, Vol. 59, Newport, Naval War College Press, 1977, pp. 56–57.

50. In *Public Prosecutor v. Oie Hee Koi* (1968), A.C. 829 (P.C.), the Privy Council (per Hodson J.) had held that "Until 'a doubt arises' article 5 does not operate and the court is not required to be satisfied whether or not this safeguard should be applied. Accordingly, where the accused did not raise a doubt no question of mistrial arises." (p. 855)

51. IVth Geneva Civilian Convention, Art. 45, para. 3.

52. The guarantees are listed in Article 75 of Protocol I.

53. IVth Geneva Civilian Convention, Art. 4, first para.

54. *ibid.*, Art. 5, first para.

55. Uhler Oscar M. and Coursier, Henri in: The Geneva Conventions of 12 August 1949: *Commentary*, published under the general editorship of Jean S. Pictet, Vol. IV, IVth Geneva Convention Relative to the Protection of Civilian Persons in Time of War, Geneva, ICRC, 1960, p. 55–56.

56. IVth Geneva Civilian Convention, Art. 5, second para.

57. Uhler Oscar M. and Coursier, Henri in: The Geneva Conventions of 12 August 1949: *Commentary*, published under the general editorship of Jean S. Pictet, Vol. IV, IVth Geneva Convention relative to the protection of civilian persons in time of war, Geneva, ICRC, 1960, p. 78–79.

58. Article 45, paragraph 3, of Protocol I of 1977 preserves for the individual not entitled to prisoner of war status treatment "the more favourable treatment in accordance with the Fourth Convention," provided, of course, that the person is otherwise qualified therefor.

59. IVth Geneva Civilian Convention, Art. 5, third para.

60. IVth Geneva Civilian Convention, Art. 45, third para.

61. Castrén Erik, *The Present Law of War and Neutrality*, Helsinki, Suomalaisen Tiedeakatemian Toimituksia, 1954, p. 152.

62. The rest of the article deals with carriers of despatches, who are not to be considered as spies.

63. Dauses Manfred A. and Wolf Dieter O. A., 'L'espionnage par satellites et l'ordre international', *Revue générale de l'air et de l'espace* (Paris), Vol. 36, 1973, p. 283.

64. Gelberg Ludwik, "Uwagi pawne na tle incydentu z amolotem" *Panstwo i prawo* (Warsaw), Vol.15 (II) (1960), p. 272; – Wright Quincy, "Legal Aspects of the U-2 Incident", *American Journal of International Law* (Washington), Vol. 54, 1960, p. 836.

65. Francioni Francesco, 'Il caso del "Pueblo" e le norme internazionali sullo spionaggio', *Diritto internazionale: Rivista Trimestrale di Dottrina e Documentazione* (Milan), Vol. 23 (I), 1969, p. 319.

66. Rubin Alfred P., 'Some Legal Implications of the "Pueblo" Incident', *International and Comparative Law Quarterly* (London), Vol. 18, 1969, pp. 960–968.

67. Baxter, R. R., 'So-called "Unpriviliged Belligerency": Spies, Guerillas, and Saboteurs', *British Year Book of International Law* (London), Vol. 28, 1951, pp. 322–329; – Mc Dougal Myres S. and Feliciano Florentino, *Law and Minimum World Public Order*, New Haven and London, Yale University Press, 1961, pp. 559–560.

68. Hague Regulations, Art. 31.

69. Report of the Committee III, para. 36, Doc. CDDH/236/Rev.1 (1976), *CDDH Official Records*, Vol. 15, pp. 377–388.

70. Protocol Additional to the Geneva Conventions of 12 August 1949, and Relating to the Protection of Victims of International Armed Conflicts (Protocol I), Art. 46, para. 1.

71. Ibid., Art. 46, paras. 2 and 4.

72. Van Deventer Henry W., 'Mercenaries at Geneva', *American Journal of International Law* (Washington), Vol. 70, 1976, p. 811.

73. Yusuf Abdulgawi, A., 'Mercenaries in the Law of Armed Conflicts', in Cassese Antonio (ed.) *The New Humanitarian Law of Armed Conflict*, Naples, Editoriale Scientifica, 1979, p. 113.

74. Para. 5 of the United Nations General Assembly resolution 3103 (XXVIII) of 12 December 1973: Basic principles of the legal status of the combatants struggling against colonial and alien domination and racist régimes, *General Assembly Official Records: Twenty-eighth Session, Supplement No.30*, Vol. 1, 18 September – 18 December 1973, pp. 142–143, UN Doc. A/9030 (1974).

75. Protocol Additional to the Geneva Conventions of 12 August 1949, and Relating to the Protection of Victims of International Armed Conflicts (Protocol I), Art. 47, para. 2. See Burmester H.C., 'The Recruitment and Use Of Mercenaries in Armed Conflict', *American Journal of International Law* (Washington), Vol. 72, 1978, p. 37.

76. Report of the Committee III, para. 105, Doc. CDDH/236/Rev. 1 (1976), *CCDH Official Records*, Vol. 15, pp. 377–407.

77. See Part B: Combattants, p. 106 ff.

78. Hague Regulations, Arts. 42–56; Carnegie Endowment for International Peace, *The Hague Conventions and Declarations of 1899 and 1907*, Edited by James Brown Scott, 2nd edition, New York, Oxford University Press, 1915, pp. 100–122. *The Laws of Armed Conflicts. A Collection of Conventions, Resolutions and Other Documents*, Edited by D. Schindler and J. Toman, 3rd edition, Dordrecht, Martinus Nijhoff Publishers, Geneva, Henry Dunant Institute, 1988, pp. 88–92.

79. Convention (IX) concerning Bombardment by Naval Forces in Time of War, signed at The Hague, 18 October 1907. – Carnegie Endowment for International Peace, *The Hague Conventions and Declarations of 1899 and 1907*, Edited by James Brown Scott, 2nd edition, New York, Oxford University Press, 1915, p. 157. *The Laws of Armed Conflicts. A Collection of Conventions, Resolutions and Other Documents*, Edited by D. Schindler and J. Toman, 3rd edition, Dordrecht, Martinus Nijhoff Publishers, Geneva, Henry Dunant Institute, 1988, pp. 811–817.

80. Convention (IX) concerning Bombardment by Naval Forces in Time of War, signed at The Hague, 18 Oct. 1907, Arts. 2–3; Carnegie Endowment for International Peace, *The Hague Conventions and Declarations of 1899 and 1907*, Edited by James Brown Scott, 2nd edition, New York, Oxford University Press, 1915, p. 157 ff. *The Laws of Armed Conflicts. A Collection of Conventions, Resolutions and other Documents*, Edited by D. Schindler and J. Toman, 3rd edition, Dordrecht, Martinus Nijhoff Publishers, Geneva, Henry Dunant Institute, 1988, pp. 812–813.

81. IVth Geneva Civilian Convention, Art. 5 and Arts. 13–26.

82. See p. 122 *infra*.

83. *The Laws of Armed Conflicts. A Collection of Conventions, Resolutions and Other Documents*, Edited by D. Schindler and J. Toman, 3rd edition, Dordrecht, Martinus Nijhoff Publishers, Geneva, Henry Dunant Institute, 1988, pp. 207–217. *American Journal of International Law* (Washington), Vol.17, Supplement, 1923, p. 245.

84. Rules of Air Warfare, drafted by a Commission of Jurists at The Hague, December 1922 – February 1923, Arts. 22 and 24.

85. Draft Rules for the Limitation of the Dangers Incurred by the Civilian Population in Time of War, Geneva, International Committee of the Red Cross, 2d ed., 1958, p. 166; *The Laws of Armed Conflicts. A Collection of Conventions, Resolutions and Other Documents*, Edited by D. Schindler and J. Toman, 3rd edition, Dordrecht, Martinus Nijhoff Publishers, Geneva, Henry Dunant Institute, 1988, pp. 251–257.

86. Arts. 8–10 and 14.

87. United Nations, *Respect for Human Rights in Armed Conflicts: Exisiting rules for international law concerning the prohibition or restriction of use of specific weapons: Survey prepared by the Secretariat*, Vol. I (1973), UN Doc. A/9215 (Vol. I) (1973), pp. 172–177.

88. Resolution 2444 (XXIII), 19 December 1968, Respect for human rights in armed conflict, *General Assembly Official Records: Twenty-third Session, Resolutions, Supplement No.18*, p. 50, UN Doc. A/7218 (1969).

89. Resolution 2675 (XXV), 9 December 1970, Basic Principles for the protection of civilian populations in armed conflicts, *General Assembly Official Records: Twenty-fifth Session, Resolutions, Supplement No. 28*, (1971), p. 76, UN Doc. A/ 8028 (1971).

90. United Nations, *Respect for Human Rights in Armed Conflicts: Exisiting rules for international law concerning the prohibition or restriction of use of specific weapons: Survey prepared by the Secretariat*, Vol. I (1973), UN Doc. A/9215 (Vol. I) (1973), pp. 165–185.

91. Protocol Additional to the Geneva Conventions of 12 August 1949, and Relating to the Protection of Victims of International Armed Conflicts (Protocol I), Art. 49, para. 1.

92. Part IV, Section I, Art. 49, para. 2, of the Protocol Additional to the Geneva Conventions of 12 August 1949, and Relating to the Protection of Victims of International Armed Conflicts (Protocol I), provides that "The provisions of this Protocol with respect to attacks apply to all attacks in whatever territory conducted, including the national territory belonging to a Party to the conflict but under the control of an adverse Party". The Protocol thus extends protection to a Party's own civilians and civilian population when such persons are in an area occupied by or otherwise controlled by its enemy.

93. Protocol Additional to the Geneva Conventions of 12 August 1949, and Relating to the Protection of Victims of International Armed Conflicts (Protocol I), Art. 1, para. 1.

94. *Ibid.*, Art. 51, para. 3.

95. *Ibid.*, Art. 50, para. 1.

96. *Ibid.*, Art. 50, para. 2.

97. *Ibid.*, Art. 50, para. 3.

98. *Ibid.*, Art. 48.

99. *Ibid.*, Art. 50, paras. 1 and 2

100. United Nations, *Respect for Human Rights in Armed Conflicts: Exisiting rules for international law concerning the prohibition or restriction of use of specific weapons: Survey prepared by the Secretariat*, Vol. I (1973), UN Doc. A/9215 (Vol. I) (1973), p. 170 and pp. 177–178. The *Institut de Droit International* in its resolution on "The distinction between military objectives and non-military objectives in general and particularly the problems associated with weapons of mass destruction" had declared that "Existing international law prohibits, irrespective of the type of weapon used, any action whatsoever designed to terrorize the civilian population." (para. 6), *Annuaire de l'Institut de Droit International*, Basel, Editions juridiques et sociologiques, Vol. 53 (II), 1969, p. 375.

101. Rules of Air Warfare, drafted by a Commission of Jurists at The Hague, December 1922 – February 1923, Art. 22.

102. Draft Rules for the Limitation of the Dangers Incurred by the Civilian Population in Time of War, Art. 6.

103. Protocol Additional to the Geneva Conventions of 12 August 1949, and Relating to the Protection of Victims of International Armed Conflicts (Protocol I), Art. 51, para. 2.

104. *Ibid.*, Art. 51, paras. 4 and 5.

105. This is the view taken by at least one major military power, the United States. See letter from the General Counsel of the Department of Defence to Senator Kennedy, 22 Sep. 1972, in *American Journal of International Law* (Washington), Vol. 67, 1973, pp. 124–125.

106. See p. 135 ff. (Chaper IX).

107. Protocol Additional to the Geneva Conventions of 12 August 1949, and Relating to the Protection of Victims of International Armed Conflicts (Protocol I), Art. 52, para. 1.

108. See the corresponding analysis of an earlier and somewhat different draft in International Committee of the Red Cross, *Draft Additional Protocols to the Geneva Conventions of August 12, 1949: Commentary*. Geneva, 1973, pp. 60–61.

109. Rules of Air Warfare, drafted by a Commission of Jurists at The Hague, December 1922 – February 1923, Art. 24 (1).

110. Draft Rules for the Limitation of the Dangers Incurred by the Civilian Population in Time of War, Art. 6, third para.; and see *The Laws of Armed Conflicts. A Collection of Conventions, Resolutions and Other Documents*, Edited by D. Schindler and J. Toman, 3rd edition, Dordrecht, Martinus Nijhoff Publishers, Geneva, Henry Dunant Institute, 1988, pp. 253.

111. Federal Republic of Germany, Switzerland and the United States. United Nations, *Respect for Human Rights in Armed Conflicts: Exisiting rules for international law concerning the prohibition or restriction of use of specific weapons: Survey prepared by the Secretariat*, Vol. I (1973), UN Doc. A/9215 (Vol. I) (1973), p. 168.

112. Protocol Additional to the Geneva Conventions of 12 August 1949, and Relating to the Protection of Victims of International Armed Conflicts (Protocol I), Art. 52, para. 3.

113. See p. 143–144 (Chapter IX), p. 203 ff. (Chapter XIII).

114. Protocol Additional to the Geneva Conventions of 12 August 1949, and Relating to the Protection of Victims of International Armed Conflicts (Protocol I), Art. 54, paras. 2 and 3.

115. International Committee of the Red Cross, *Draft Additional Protocols to the Geneva Conventions of August 12, 1949: Commentary*, Geneva, 1973, pp. 62–63.

116. Protocol Additional to the Geneva Conventions of 12 August 1949, and Relating to the Protection of Victims of International Armed Conflicts (Protocol I), Art. 56, para. 2.

117. *Ibid.*, Art. 56, para. 5.

118. A group of three bright orange circles placed on the same axis, pursuant to Art. 56, para. 7, and Art. 16 of Annex I to Protocol I.

119. Art. 26 of the Hague Regulations of 1907, providing that "The officer in command of an attacking force must, before commencing a bombardment, except in cases of assault, do all in his power to warn the authorities".

120. Protocol Additional to the Geneva Conventions of 12 August 1949, and Relating to the Protection of Victims of International Armed Conflicts (Protocol I), Art. 57, subpara. 2 (C).

121. *Ibid.*, Art. 57, subparas. 2 (a) and (b).

122. *Ibid.*, Art. 57, para. 1.

123. *Ibid.*, Art. 58.

124. As provided in Art. 51, para. 7 of the Protocol Additional to the Geneva Conventions of 12 August 1949, and Relating to the Protection of Victims of International Armed Conflicts (Protocol I).

125. Uhler, Oscar M. and Coursier Henry in: The Geneva Conventions of 12 August 1949: *Commentary*, published under the general editorship of Jean S. Pictet, Vol. IV, IVth Geneva Convention Relative to the Protection of Civilian Persons in Time of War, Geneva, ICRC, 1960, pp. 128 ff.

126. IVth Geneva Civilian Convention, Art. 14.

127. *Ibid.*, Art. 15.

128. International Committee of the Red Cross, *Draft Additional Protocols to the Geneva Conventions of August 12, 1949: Commentary*, Geneva, 1973, p. 68.

129. Protocol Additional to the Geneva Conventions of 12 August 1949, and Relating to the Protection of Victims of International Armed Conflicts (Protocol I), Art. 59.

130. See p. 115.

131. Jennings, R.Y., "Open Towns", *British Yearbook of International Law* (London), Vol. 22, 1945, p 258.

132. Protocol Additional to the Geneva Conventions of 12 August 1949, and Relating to the Protection of Victims of International Armed Conflicts (Protocol I), Art. 60.

133. *Ibid.*, Art. 59, para. 2, and Art. 60, para. 3. Subpara. 3(d) of Article 60 differs somewhat in wording: "any activity linked to the military effort must have ceased."

134. *Ibid.*, Art. 59, paras. 2 and 4; Art. 60, paras. 1 and 2.

135. International Committee of the Red Cross, *Draft Additional Protocols to the Geneva Conventions of August 12, 1949: Commentary*, Geneva, 1973, pp. 69.

136. Report of Committee III, para. 111, Doc. CDDH/215/Rev. 1 (1975), *CDDH Official Records*, Vol. 15, p. 259 at p. 287.

137. Protocol Additional to the Geneva Conventions of 12 August 1949, and Relating to the Protection of Victims of International Armed Conflicts (Protocol I), Art. 59, para. 7, as to non-defended localities: *Ibid.*, Art. 60, para. 7, which stipulates loss of protection in the event of a material breach of Paragraphs 3 or 6 of that Article.

138. Spaight, J.M., *War Rights on Land*, London, MacMillan and Co., 1911, pp. 86–88.

139. *Ibid.*, p. 87.

140. Report of Committee III, para. 16, Doc. CDDH/236/Rev.1 (1976), *CDDH Official Records*, Vol. 15, p. 382.

141. Protocol Additional to the Geneva Conventions of 12 August 1949, and Relating to the Protection of Victims of International Armed Conflicts (Protocol I), Art. 37, para. 1.

142. *Ibid.*, Art. 44, para. 3. See Report of Committee III, para. 18, Doc. CDDH/236/Rev. 1 (1976), *CDDH Official Records*, Vol. 15, p. 382.

143. Protocol Additional to the Geneva Conventions of 12 August 1949, and Relating to the Protection of Victims of International Armed Conflicts (Protocol I), Art. 37, para. 2.

144. *Ibid.*, Art. 38, para. 1.

145. *Ibid.*, Art. 39, para. 1.

146. *Ibid.*, Art. 38, para. 1.

147. Oppenheim, L., *International Law*, Vol. 2, 7th ed., Edited by Lauterpacht, H., London, Longmans Green & Co., 1951, p. 429, and see Trial of Otto Skorzeny and Others (General Military Government Court of the US Zone of Germany, 1947), United Nations War Crimes Commission, *Law Report of Trials of War Criminals*, London, H.M.S.O., Vol. IX (1949), p. 92. The defendants, who had used American uniforms and equipment, were acquitted of treacherous killings of United States forces, since it was apparently not clear that they had used US uniforms in connection with the killing of US personnel.

148. Protocol Additional to the Geneva Conventions of 12 August 1949, and Relating to the Protection of Victims of International Armed Conflicts (Protocol I), Art. 39, para. 3.

149. Hague Regulations, Art. 23 (d).

150. Protocol Additional to the Geneva Conventions of 12 August 1949, and Relating to the Protection of Victims of International Armed Conflicts (Protocol I), Art. 41, para. 2.

151. See, concerning "long distance patrols", Report of Committee III, para. 24, Doc. CDDH/236/Rev. 1 (1976), *CDDH Official Records*, Vol. 15, p. 384.

152. Protocol Additional to the Geneva Conventions of 12 August 1949, and Relating to the Protection of Victims of International Armed Conflicts (Protocol I), Art. 41, para. 3.

153. See, concerning the range of questions considered, Report of Committee III, para. 29, Doc. CDDH/236/Rev. 1 (1976), *CDDH Official Records*, Vol. 15, p. 386.

154. Protocol Additional to the Geneva Conventions of 12 August 1949, and Relating to the Protection of Victims of International Armed Conflicts (Protocol I), Art. 42, para. 3.

155. *Ibid.*, Art. 42, para. 1.

156. Report of Committee III, para. 30, Doc. CDDH/236/Rev. 1 (1976), *CDDH Official Records*, Vol. 15, p. 386.

157. Protocol Additional to the Geneva Conventions of 12 August 1949, and Relating to the Protection of Victims of International Armed Conflicts (Protocol I), Art. 42, para. 2.

CHAPTER IX

MEANS AND METHODS OF COMBAT

HANS BLIX

A. Scope of Discussion

The rules of international law imposing restraints upon the means and methods of combat are derived from custom and conventions, e.g., the Hague Conventions. The very principle of restraint is stated in Article 22 of the Hague Regulations annexed to the Hague Convention No. IV, to the effect that "the right of belligerents to adopt means of injuring the enemy is not unlimited".

The 1977 Protocols additional to the Geneva Conventions of 1949 contain the most recent rules of the law of armed conflicts. Protocol I does not contain any comprehensive regulation imposing restraints. Indeed, the preamble of the Protocol states the truth – but not the whole truth – when describing the Protocol as supplementing the 1949 Geneva Conventions. In fact Part III, covering methods and means of warfare, and Part IV covering civilian population, contain vitally important rules which may be said to supplement the Hague Conventions more than the Geneva Conventions.

That the scope of the "additional" protocols was broader than that of the Conventions to which they were added was a somewhat controversial point throughout the 1974–1977 Geneva Diplomatic Conference. There was a body of opinion – which gradually diminished – that the Conference should confine itself strictly to the protection of the victims: the wounded, the prisoners, and the civilians. Those who held this view considered articles regarding area bombardment, perfidy, starvation, weapons causing unnecessary suffering, etc., as outside the proper scope of humanitarian law.

Another widely held opinion was that the distinction was somewhat artificial. Is a rule protecting the victim of saturation bombing more "humanitarian" than a rule restricting the use of this method? Are not the rules of warfare, after all, humanitarian in purpose? To these reflections was added the view that rules on methods and means of combat, which had not been reviewed since the turn of the century, were in even greater need of up-dating than the rules protecting victims of war, which had been the subject of comprehensive revision in the 1949 Conventions. After World War II, and during the Indochina war particularly, the lack of rules on bombing from the air was felt to be absurd. (Draft rules were elaborated by the International Commission of Jurists in 1923, but were not put into effect).[1]

Efforts limited to the drafting of additional rules on the appointment of protecting powers, on the evacuation of wounded, on the protection of civil defence personnel, etc., – ignoring the question of restraints on methods and means of combat – would have been hard to justify to the public.

The opinion which favoured the broader approach prevailed in large measure but its adherents refrained from pressing a demand that agreement on prohibitions or restrictions of use of specific conventional weapons be reached at the conference. Only France demurred to the end and declared that Article 35, which states that "in any armed conflict the right of the parties to the conflict to choose methods and means of warfare is not unlimited", was the first of a series of articles which went beyond the strict confines of humanitarian law and in fact regulated the law of war. It had "direct implications for the defence and security of states". The comment is incontrovertible, but even the rules relating to the protection of POWs, civil defence, ambulances, aircraft, etc., have implications for the defence and security of states.

Although the rules on methods and means of combat contained in the 1977 Protocol are not comprehensive, they might serve as the basis for discussion in this chapter. It seems all the more justified to use the limited space of the present chapter for this purpose as there exist many authoritative commentaries on the older rules. Accordingly the discussion below will deal first with the general rationale for the restraints imposed by Article 35 of the 1977 Protocol and with the types of restraints which exist. Thereafter, the discussion will focus upon the concepts of "unnecessary suffering" and "superfluous injury" inflicted by weapons, upon the principle of distinction between civilians and combatants and upon various restraints on means and methods of combat designed to protect civilians, viz., rules against the use of terror, starvation, indiscriminate methods and means including area bombardment. In this context the rule of proportionality will be examined together with the rules on precautionary measures required to avoid incidental effects upon civilians. Lastly, the rules of restraint devised to protect the environment will be examined.

B. Rationale for Restraints

The basic rule in Article 35 paragraph 1 that the right of the Parties to armed conflict to choose methods or means of warfare is not unlimited, and the earlier similar rule in Article 2 of the Hague Regulations are a general reminder that violence is permitted only in so far as it serves the specific purpose of subduing the enemy. The rationalism and humanitarianism which pervaded the enlightenment and the teachings of Jean-Jacques Rousseau, one of the inspirers of the laws of war, required that no suffering be inflicted, no injury caused, and no destruction or damage brought about which was not necessary for the sole legitimate purpose of overcoming the enemy.

Suffering, injury, destruction or damage should not be inflicted for personal reasons or for punishment. It followed from this that, from among several available means of achieving a legitimate military aim, should be chosen those which inflicted least suffering, injury, destruction or damage. It is said, for example, that if an enemy soldier can be placed *hors de combat* by being taken prisoner he should not be injured; if he can be disabled, he should not be killed, and if he can be neutralized by light injury, he should not be severely wounded.

While this reasoning obviously cannot be so rigorously applied as to oblige a soldier in the heat of battle to aim only at non-vital parts of the enemy's body, important conclusions do follow from it and most existing restraints can in fact be said to have been derived from it. This is true notably of the prohibition of the use of means and methods likely to cause superfluous injury or unnecessary suffering. The requirement that a distinction should at all times be made between the civilian population and combatants, and between civilian objects and military objectives, and that military operations shall be directed only at the latter (Article 48 of the 1977 Protocol) is also derived from the notion that the enemy can be overcome by attacks on such objectives, and that it is therefore not necessary to direct military operations against the civilian population or against civilian objects.[2] With the increasing ability to attack targets anywhere by air and the increasing industrial and economic integration of states, the category of legitimate military objectives has grown, but the basic rule and reason remain.

The principle of distinction is listed not in Article 35, under the basic rules regarding methods and means of combat, but in Article 48, in Part IV on the protection of the civilian population. Another basic rule is introduced in Article 35 paragraph 3, namely, the protection of the natural environment. This rule, like the two discussed above, is based on the postulate that, for the achievement of the legitimate aim of overcoming the enemy, it is not necessary to use "methods or means... which... may be expected to cause widespread, long-term and severe damage to the natural environment".

It may be concluded that the three major categories of restraints – aiming at protection against unnecessary suffering and superfluous injury, and protection of the natural environment – and the detailed rules which emanate from them have all developed with full account being taken of the needs of belligerents to be free to use all the methods and means which are rationally required to overcome the enemy. The notion of "military necessity" cannot be invoked against rules which already make allowance for it. This will be evident in the closer scrutiny below.

C. "Superfluous Injury" and "Unnecessary Suffering"

It is to be hoped that the wording of Article 35 paragraph 2 of the 1977 Geneva Protocol to the effect that "it is prohibited to employ weapons, projectiles and material and methods of warfare of a nature to cause superfluous injury or unnecessary suffering" will straighten out some interpretative tangles which have resulted from the English version of the Hague Regulations which used the expression "calculated to cause unnecessary suffering" (Art. 23 paragraph e). While the French *propres à causer des maux superflus* has not raised problems, the expression "calculated to" has occasionally and erroneously been taken to mean that the "unnecessary suffering" would have to be proved intentional. The expression "of a nature to" avoids this subjective interpretation. The expression, "unnecessary suffering" has never fully covered the meaning of the French *maux superflus*, which more broadly signifies excessive harmful effects. It seemed justified, in view of the long use of the expression "unnecessary suffering" in various war manuals, to render the French formulation by the two English notions of "superfluous injury" and "unnecessary suffering".

In introducing "methods of warfare" in the same prohibition, Article 35 paragraph 2 extends the scope of the principle far beyond the letter – although perhaps not the spirit – of the 1907 formulation. Most discussions of this article have dealt with the guidance it may give as to the legality of particular weapons.

The main questions – and they are not minor – concerning this article are the meaning of the word "unnecessary" and how "suffering and injury" are measured. The latter problem is perhaps the least intractable. The "injuries" caused by a weapon may be measured. The suffering inflicted by a weapon depends on individual reactions which vary greatly. It is hard, if not impossible, to quantify, even though it seems evident that some weapons would unquestionably cause more suffering than others, e.g., a gas merely rendering a soldier unconscious for a short time, as compared to a gas causing cramps and paralysis for a prolonged period. At a conference of government experts from a wide variety of states, it was generally considered that "injury" and "suffering" comprised such factors as mortality, the pain or severity of wounds, permanent damage and disfigurement.[3]

This conclusion would seem to be consistent with that which may be drawn from the historical background to the rule. That background also helps in understanding the meaning of the term "unnecessary". The 1868 St. Petersburg Declaration banned the use of projectiles weighing less than 400 grammes and which are explosive or charged with fulminating or inflammable substances. The rationale of this prohibition and the preamble of the Declaration remain important:

> "(2) that the only legitimate object which states should endeavour to accomplish during war is to weaken the military forces of the enemy;

(3) that for this purpose it is sufficient to disable the greatest possible number of men;

(4) that this object would be exceeded by the employment of arms which uselessly aggravate the sufferings of disabled men, or render their death inevitable;

(5) that the employment of such arms would, therefore, be contrary to the laws of humanity".

The idea underlying these rules was no doubt that, if explosive or inflammable projectiles were to be effective against objects such as buildings, they would have to weigh more than 400 grammes. If they weighed less they would be effective only against human beings but would then cause injury in excess of what was necessary to disable and thereby "uselessly aggravate" suffering. The required result could be obtained by the use of projectiles which relied solely on their kinetic energy for effect. The reasoning starts from the premise that the enemy is hit, and assumes that any hit will place a man *hors de combat*. Accordingly, injuries by projectile hits should not be made worse by explosive, incendiary or, for that matter, any other additional effects. Such additional effects are even more inadmissible if they render death inevitable. A bullet contaminated with lethal poison or a lethal infectious substance would be a case in point.

The type of projectile banned in the St. Petersburg Declaration later became useful against aircraft, and to this extent the ban must be regarded as having lapsed into desuetude. The rationale of the ban, namely to protect men against this type of projectile, still holds good, however, and this being so it may well be maintained that the ban, too, holds good.

The Hague Declaration of 1899 on the dumdum-bullet prohibited the use of "bullets which expand or flatten easily in the human body, such as bullets with a hard envelope which does not entirely cover the core or is pierced with incisions". Here, again, it was felt that the kinetic energy of a merely piercing bullet had a sufficient disabling effect and that the more severe wound which would result from a mushrooming bullet was an additional effect that could not be justified. Although the British delegation protested that ordinary piercing bullets were inadequate to stop "savages" from further fighting, such bullets were generally considered sufficient to disable a man.

From these two bans the least conclusion to be drawn is that a weapon which disables must not be given additional effects, i.e., increase the injury. A somewhat broader conclusion seems fully justified and is often drawn, namely, that it is unlawful to use a weapon which causes more suffering or injury than another which offers the same or similar military advantages. A third conclusion is that, to judge the legality of any given weapon, its military value must be weighed against the suffering/injury it causes. This conclusion is akin to the second, since the "military value" of a weapon can hardly be appreciated except when related to others.

It follows that the assessment of the legality of a weapon must take a number of factors into consideration, such as: disabling effect, hit probability, weight, cost, degree of injury, suffering, killing power. To assess these properties does not raise insuperable difficulties. It is when they are weighed against each other that the subjective element becomes dominant. That element can only be significantly reduced when the weapon in question and its merits and demerits from the humanitarian and military viewpoints are related to an alternative weapon.

It has been suggested that the practice of states "represents the best evidence of what reasonable men believe to be lawful and necessary weapons in war".[4]

The same view is taken in the US Manual of Land Warfare:

> "What weapons cause unnecessary injury can only be determined in light of the practice of states in refraining from the use of a given weapon because it is believed to have that effect..."[5]

This test begs the question, however. It is not helpful to a state that is about to determine whether a particular new weapon is legal. It may only be of help inasmuch as a weapon which is widely in use is unlikely to have been regarded as illegal by the governments using it. Such a practice would certainly weigh heavily, if not conclusively, on the judgement of the matter by an independent tribunal. But, for a weapon employed by some and consistently proclaimed illegal by others, no such presumption of lawfulness would be possible: the question is no different from other practices of states which may or may not constitute custom, depending upon how widespread and how little contested they are.

D. National Determination of the Legality of Weapons

In Article 36 labelled "new weapons" the 1977 Geneva Protocol prescribes that:

> "in the study, development, acquisition or adoption of a new weapon, means or method of warfare, a High Contracting Party is under an obligation to determine whether its employment would, in some or all circumstances, be prohibited by this Protocol or any other rule of international law applicable to the High Contracting Party".

Evidently, even without an article of this kind, it is incumbent upon a state to determine whether the means or methods of warfare it might employ are legal. The article serves to underline this duty, and this emphasis has already found administrative expression in several states which have established special procedures or mechanisms for the determination described.[6] The new rule has been hailed as a practical means of heightening government attention to the problem of weighing the military merits against the humanitarian demerits of new weapons.[7] The Soviet delegate was particularly pleased that no "supranational control organization" was introduced.[8]

Authorities – whether national or international – whose task it is to determine the permissibility of use of a weapon which is not commonly employed without protests will have to rely upon analyses, such as those above, of the question of unnecessary suffering/injury. But this rule is not the only one which would be relevant, however. Such authorities would also have to examine whether a given weapon contravened the prohibition on the use of means of warfare having indiscriminate effects (Article 51 paragraph 4(b)). This rule will be discussed below in connection with the principle of distinction. Although "treacherous" – Hague Regulation Art. 23 paragraph b – or "perfidious" – Geneva Protocol Art. 37 – means of warfare are prohibited, it is often assumed that weapons which might be indicted on this ground would equally fall under the proscription of indiscriminate weapons.[9]

Such authorities would have to look also to existing specific bans on use, not all of which are necessarily based on the criteria of unnecessary suffering/injury, or indiscriminateness. The prohibitions on the use of chemical and bacteriological weapons and of poison are cases in point. They constitute rules of international law "applicable to the High Contracting Party", regardless of ratification or accession, since both conventional rules have acquired the status of customary law.

E. Intergovernmental Discussions of Bans on the Use of Conventional Weapons

International examinations of different categories of weapons have been few and far between. After the negotiation of the Geneva BC-protocol of 1925 and the discussions at the 1932–34 League of Nations Disarmament Conference on incendiary and other weapons, discussions on specific weapons have taken place only at the 1974–1977 Geneva Conference and, in particular within its *ad hoc* commission.

As a follow-up to the recommendation of the Conference, the United Nations General Assembly convened a Conference on Prohibitions or Restrictions on the Use of Certain Conventional Weapons, which was held in Geneva in 1979 and 1980. The Conference adopted the Convention on Prohibitions or Restrictions on the Use of Certain Conventional Weapons Which May be Deemed to be Excessively Injurious or to have Indiscriminate Effects. Three Protocols were annexed to this Convention: the Protocol on Non-Detectable Fragments (Protocol I), the Protocol on Prohibitions or Restrictions on the Use of Mines, Booby Traps and Other Devices (Protocol II), and the Protocol on Prohibitions or Restrictions on the Use of Incendiary Weapons (Protocol III). The Conference also adopted a Resolution on Small-Calibre Weapon Systems.[10]

Lack of space prevents us from examining the different categories of weapons whose use is subject, or might be subject, to prohibitions or restrictions. Hence we have confined ourselves to certain questions of principle. However, before studying such questions it would be desirable to consider a few points.

Apart from the review procedure which, in conformity with Article 8 of the Convention, is in the hands only of States Parties to the Convention and the Protocols, any High Contracting Party may on its own initiative call for a new Conference to be convened ten years after the entry into force of the Convention.

The Depositary is obliged to convene it accordingly. Thus the Convention acquired a lasting value thanks to the mechanism leaving the door open to other restrictions and "by urging all States to practice constant vigilance to ensure that conventional weapons conform with the principles laid down in Protocol I of 1977. The revision method also represents a valuable addition to Article 36 of Protocol I, which binds all Contracting Parties to examine all new weapons to make sure their use is not prohibited by international law".[11]

Another feature which might be mentioned is the following: Article 36 of the 1977 Geneva Protocol asks for a determination of whether a "new weapon, means or method" would "in some or all circumstances" be prohibited. Prohibition on the use of a weapon "in some circumstances", e.g., anti-personnel use or use in populated areas, would in fact constitute a restriction on the methods of using a particular weapon.

F. The Principle of Distinction

The principle of distinction is the premise of several important rules regarding means and methods of warfare. Most of them are found in Article 51 of the 1977 Geneva Protocol.

It should be noted that these rules are confined to warfare affecting civilians or civilian objects on land, lakes, rivers, canals and other waterways, but not territorial waters. After much discussion at the Geneva Conference it was decided that the rules should not apply to naval and air warfare, except as regards attacks from the air or the sea against objectives on land.[12]

For warfare at sea, for which a large body of law exists, this is an important limitation: civilians and civilian objects at sea will not be protected by the new rules, but only by the older laws. For air warfare, however, which is mostly directed against objectives on land and which, moreover, has so far been governed only by general principles, the rules in the 1977 Geneva Protocol are a major expansion of the law.

a. Terror

Article 51 paragraph 2 prohibits methods of war – "acts or threats of violence" – the primary purpose of which is to spread terror among the civilian population. The provision was adopted after considerable discussion, primarily on two points. One trend of opinion, which finally did not prevail, wished to outlaw "propaganda" as a means of spreading terror. A more important difference arose between those who wished the article to cover only acts "intended" to spread terror and those who wished it to cover all acts actually causing or capable of spreading terror. It was underlined that the effect of the Article would be limited if it only covered cases where intention could be proved. On the other hand it was said that many acts or threats of violence would, in fact, spread terror although this was not their purpose. The wording eventually adopted steers between these difficulties. The criterion of intent was discarded and the wording chosen does not cover the cases where terror is a – perhaps even foreseeable – incidental effect. Acts whose primary purpose must, on an objective assessment, be deemed to be the spreading of terror are prohibited.[13]

b. Starvation

The general protection of civilian objects and the injunction in Article 52 paragraph 2 that attacks shall be strictly limited to military objectives should suffice in many cases to protect the civilian population from losing its means of sustenance. A new Article on the subject has been introduced, however, emphasizing this protection, extending it even to various objects which might fall under the definition of military objectives, and giving more precise guidance.

Article 54 on the protection of objects indispensable to the survival of the civilian population was adopted by consensus. It lays down in its first subparagraph that "starvation" as a method of warfare is prohibited.[14] This is really an introductory statement of the aim of the Article. The precise legal injunctions which may help to achieve this aim are found in the following subparagraphs and also in Article 55, protecting the natural environment,[15] Articles 68–71 on relief, and the 1925 Geneva Protocol prohibiting the use of chemical and bacteriological weapons).

Article 54 paragraph 2 protects "objects indispensable to the survival of the civilian population" against attacks, destruction removal etc., even by way of reprisal action. It offers a number of examples of such objects: food, agricultural areas, crops, animals, drinking water, installations, supplies and irrigation works. Although the list is not exhaustive – "tools" could be added for instance – it is believed to offer very useful guidance.

There are some important limitations upon this new rule designed to give effect to the principle of distinction. The first is that objects used as "sustenance solely for the members of the armed forces" of the adversary are not protected. It is a restricted exception. A food supply needed by the civilian population does not lose its protection simply because it is also used by the armed forces and may technically qualify as a military objective. It has to be used exclusively by them to lose its immunity. An even more understandable exception is the case where the objects are used by the adversary "in direct support of military action", although not as sustenance. It is not prohibited to shell the enemy merely because he is in a food growing or a food supply area. Such areas may obviously also be fired upon so as to deny the enemy access to them.[16]

The third exception, expressed in Article 54 paragraph 5, is included to sanction the scorched earth tactic. It is confined to use on a party's national territory and, in that case, to areas under the party's own control. It gives a party whose national territory is subjected to an enemy invasion a degree of freedom of action which it does not give armed forces withdrawing from enemy territory. Since the exception will place the party's own remaining civilian population in jeopardy, it may be assumed that there are natural inhibitions in using this tactic. In any case, it may be used only "where required by imperative military necessity".

The new rule is not meant to affect the principles concerning naval blockades.[17]

c. Indiscriminate Means

Under Article 51 paragraph 4 an attack may not be launched by employment of a "means of combat which cannot be directed at a specific military objective" or a "means of combat, the effects of which cannot be limited as required by this Protocol".

There was some difference of opinion as to whether any weapons actually existed which could not be directed at a specific military objective or the effects of which could not be limited as required by the rule of proportionality.[18]

Some delegates denied the existence of any weapon which, under the article, would be prohibited in all circumstances. They took the article as a reminder that the lawful use of means of combat depended upon circumstances.

Possibly this position was prompted by a wish to guard against any implication that Article 51 paragraph 4 could be invoked in support of the view that the use of nuclear weapons is prohibited. If so, the positions would seem to have been taken *ex abundanta cautela*, since the drafts submitted by the ICRC were not intended to introduce rules governing atomic, bacteriological and chemical weapons.[19]

It is certainly unlikely that weapons which are incapable of being directed at military objectives will be widely used. Reasons of economy alone will speak against such weapons. But are they totally excluded? The Military Manual of the Federal Republic of Germany stated that "the use of flying bombs (e.g. rockets) is not permissible when they can only be so imprecisely directed that the whole effect of the weapon hits the civilian population".

Bacteriological weapons, the use of which is banned under the 1925 Geneva Protocol, would presumably be another category which is difficult or impossible to direct. The same would be true to many environmental means of warfare.

Although, accordingly, it may be queried whether it is justified to exclude the existence or possible emergence of means of warfare incapable of being directed at military objectives, it is certainly correct to say that the legality of the use of most weapons depends upon the manner in which they are employed. A rifle may be lawfully aimed at the enemy or it may be employed indiscriminately against civilians and soldiers alike. Bombs may be aimed at specific military targets or thrown at random. The indiscriminate use of the weapon will be prohibited, not the weapon as such.

The question as to whether there can be means – weapons – the effect of which cannot in any circumstances be limited as required by the rules of the Protocol, notably the rule of proportionality, is most likely to be answered in the negative. That rule requires that the incidental effects upon civilians and civilian objects must not be excessive in relation to the direct military advantage anticipated. If the means – weapons – are at all capable of being directed, one can always envisage the location of military targets so isolated that an infringement of the rule of proportionality is inconceivable. Hence, the legality of the use of such weapons would depend upon the circumstances.

The difference of opinion regarding the existence of indiscriminate means of combat does not extend to indiscriminate *methods* of combat. Even those who denied that there existed any weapon which was indiscriminate by nature, maintained that the question that could arise was whether a particular use or method of use of a weapon was indiscriminate. The laying of unanchored automatic contact sea mines – prohibited by The Hague Convention No. VIII – is a classical example of an indiscriminate – illegal – method of using a weapon. Innumerable other methods of combat may be imagined which do not permit direction at specific military targets or limitation in their effects, as required, notably by the rule of proportionality. One such method, much discussed, is area bombardment. Under Article 51 paragraph 5 (a) a ban is introduced upon attacks

> "by bombardment by any methods or means which treats as a single military objective a number of clearly separate and distinct military objectives located in a city, town, village or other area containing a similar concentration of civilians or civilian objects".

The authors of the article "considered it unnecessary to refer to 'massive' bombardment, 'target area' bombardment, or 'carpet bombing', since all are covered by this prohibition; and use of such expressions might be construed to restrict the protection of civilians from other types of bombardment".[20]

The adoption of this provision is seen as an important humanitarian gain. Bombardment of large urban areas containing scattered military objectives has certainly been one of the worst war methods from the viewpoint of civilian populations. It has been severely criticized from the humanitarian and legal viewpoints, and its military value has also been questioned. It may be assumed that this combination of circumstances made the adoption of the rule possible. It should be noted that the prohibition is confined to the situation where the humanitarian case is the strongest, namely in areas where there is a concentration of civilians or civilian objects. Area bombardment of countryside is not affected. Even with this limitation the provision was unacceptable to one country. The French delegation declared that "in a good many situations of armed conflict it would be very difficult, if not impossible, to determine precisely what constitutes a military objective especially in large towns or wooded areas, either of which might harbour indiscriminately enemy military forces and groups of civilians more or less closely mixed together".[21]

Despite its apparent straight-forwardness, the expression "clearly separate and distinct military objectives" which was adopted after much discussion, raises some questions. How far apart should the objectives be to require separate attacks? This question is not answered in the rule, nor is it answered in the only military manual containing a provision on the matter, that of the Federal Republic of Germany, which simply made it "forbidden to treat several military objectives and populated areas between them as a single objective and to attack or bombard this area indiscriminately in its entire extension".[22]

While the ICRC draft described the military objectives as being "at some distance from each other", one amendment sought to describe them as "so distant from one another that it is reasonably possible to attack them individually".[23] Another amendment would have placed them "at such distance from each other that they are capable of being attacked individually".[24]

The US representative stated, in explaining the positive vote of the United States, that in his view the expression adopted

"refers not only to a separation of two or more military objectives which can be observed or which are visually separated, but also includes the element of significant distance. Futhermore, that distance must be at least sufficient to permit individual military objectives to be attacked separately".

The problem is linked to weapons. Two objectives that are "clearly separate and distinct" if laser-guided "smart" bombs are used, may not be distinct if other bombs are used. Such difficulties of interpretation cannot, of course, serve as excuses for any relapses into some of the methods used in World War II, which the new rule is intended to preclude.

Another question raised by the new rule is what is meant by "military objectives". That term is defined in article 52 as follows:

"In so far as objects are concerned, military objectives are limited to those objects which by their nature, location, purpose or use make an effective contribution to military action and whose total or partial destruction, capture or neutralization, in the circumstances ruling at the time, offers a definite military advantage".

It must be noted that several representatives of Western governments went on record as interpreting the above definition of military objectives as also covering "a specific area of land... if, because of its location or for other reasons specified in the article, its total or partial destruction, capture or neutralization, in the circumstances ruling at the time, offers a definite military advantage".[25]

However, this interpretation was advanced under the discussion of Article 52 – draft Article 47 – not under the article on indiscriminate methods of combat, and the intention does not seem to have been to reduce the scope of the latter article. The interpretation seeks to point not to cases where there are several military objectives in an area, but to those where a specific area – the whole of it – is a genuine military objective. There might indeed be a legitimate military need to pound an area – rather than specific objects – before a ground attack or to deny that area to the enemy.

G. Precautions and Proportionality

Various modern means and methods of combat have contributed to the increasing toll of civilian victims in modern armed conflicts. The method of bombardment of urbanized areas has been discussed above. Two other threats to the principle of distinction are intended to be averted by article 57, namely that of inadequate identification of objectives as military before attack, and that of attacks of military objectives with excessive incidental effects upon civilians and civilian objects.

No precision in the attack of a target or precaution to avoid effects beyond the target is helpful if the target itself is wrongly identified as military, e.g., a civilian village identified as a guerrilla base. Various methods of automatic identification of targets, e.g., by electronic or infra-red devices, may endanger the civilian population, particularly in attacks on land. Electronic sensors which register vibrations of trucks and release air attacks may not be capable of distinguishing between ammunition transports and busses of school children. Infra-red sights will register civilians and soldiers without distinction. While no specific ban on devices such as these is introduced, Article 57, on precautions in attack, enjoins those who plan or decide upon an attack to

> "do everything feasible to verify that the objectives to be attacked are neither civilians nor civilian objects... and that it is not prohibited by the provisions of this Protocol to attack them".

It should be noted that the provision is directed to those who plan or decide upon the attack. Those who actually perform the attack will often, with modern methods and means of combat, be unable to see in advance what they attack. Where they do so, however, and discover that the target has been wrongly identified, they must refrain from attack. Article 57 (2b) requires that "an attack shall be cancelled or suspended if it becomes apparent that the objective is not a military one" or for any other reason should not be attacked. Even objects which may constitute military objectives under Article 52 may be immune from attack, e.g., because they contain dangerous forces, (Article 56) or are indispensible for the survival of the civilian population (Article 54), or where attack would result in excessive civilian losses.

Two other points should be noted. The parties are enjoined to give "effective advance warning" of attacks which may affect the civilian population, "unless circumstances do not permit". The term "feasible" which was preferred to "reasonable" was intended to mean "that which is practicable or practically possible".[26]

Although the rules of the Protocol do not apply to naval operations or air warfare which do not affect civilians or civilian objects on land (Art. 49), Article 57 paragraph 4 nevertheless contains a general injunction that even in such operations the parties shall take "all reasonable precautions to avoid losses of civilian lives and damage to civilians".[27]

While the first requirement for the protection of the civilian population is adequate identification of military objectives, the second is that attacks be made in such a way and with such means and methods that incidental effects upon the civilian population are avoided or minimized. (Art. 57 paragraph 2 (ii)). The so-called rule of proportionality is an amplification, albeit controversial, of this general requirement.

The rule of "proportionality", which appears in the military manuals of several states, is now included in Art. 57 paragraph 2 (iii). The Article as a whole deals with "precautions in attack" and the insertion of the principle in this context is intended to indicate that the principle is adopted for the purpose of urging restraint, not of legitimizing civilian losses. The provision requires a party to

> "refrain from deciding to launch any attack which may be expected
> to cause incidental loss of civilian life, injury to civilians, damage to
> civilian objects, or a combination thereof, which would be excessive
> in relation to the concrete and direct military advantage anticipated".

As noted above, an attack which is already under way shall be cancelled – where possible – if it becomes apparent that the rule would be infringed.

It has been frequently said that it is impossible to assess what civilian losses are "disproportionate" to a specific military advantage. The rule adopted has, indeed, discarded this commonly used term and speaks of losses, injury and damage "excessive" in relation to the military advantage. The notion of any quantifiable proportions is perhaps somewhat reduced, but basically the judgement which is to be exercised is the same. That judgement necessarily contains a large subjective element. How important is the military advantage gained by the attack? How serious are the civilian losses to be regarded? Only practice, world opinion and the judgement of tribunals will answer these questions.

Some representatives were of the opinion that it would have been better not to include the rule of proportionality, because it tended to blur the clear-cut principle of distinction and could be abused. Nobody will deny, however, that many attacks in armed conflicts, by whoever conducted, will result in losses, injury and damage to civilians and civilian objects. The view prevailed that it was preferable that the law should reflect this reality and be used to enjoin restraint, rather than be silent on the matter and leave it entirely to the practice of belligerents.

H. Protection of the Environment

Article 35 paragraph 3 lays down as one basic rule regarding methods and means of warfare, i.e., that

> "it is prohibited to employ methods or means of warfare which are intended, or may be expected, to cause widespread, long-term and severe damage to the natural environment".

In Article 55, coming within the chapter on protection of civilian objects, the general rule is elaborated and adapted to the particular context.

> "Care shall be taken in warfare to protect the natural environment against widespread, long-term and severe damage. This protection includes a prohibition of the use of methods or means of warfare which are intended or may be expected to cause such damage to the natural environment and thereby to prejudice the health or survival of the civilian population".

The background to these provisions was the widespread environmental destruction which was brought about during the Indochina war through the use of herbicides, bulldozers and extensive bombardment. In the public debate some of these means and methods of warfare were denounced as producing "ecocide", and a ban on "environmental" warfare was urged. Although the ICRC had not tabled any proposal on this matter, amendments were submitted to fill the gap and a special working group submitted two texts which were subsequently amended and accepted as the provisions quoted above.[28]

It is evident that armed action will usually harm the natural environment. Forests and fields may be "cratered", oil may leak into the water table, etc. Many such effects will inevitably be incidental to attacks on military objectives. Quite another thing is action purposely designed to damage the natural environment of the enemy. The Convention on the Prohibition of Military or Any Other Hostile Use of Environmental Modification Techniques, signed in Geneva in 1977 was drawn up to guard against such intentional use of non-conventional methods damaging the environment.

The Articles in the Geneva Protocol are devised primarily to protect against conventional means and methods of action affecting the environment. But they are not limited to actions which are intended to damage the environment. The articles also cover means and methods which "may be expected" to cause such damage. Hence, if the foreseeable environmental damage is of the kind described in the articles, the means or method will stand condemned, even though the damage may have been incidental to attacks upon legitimate military objectives.

Since most armed action will cause some environmental damage, it was evidently necessary to find a wording limiting the scope of the ban. The working group proposed that the decisive criterion be "the stability of the ecosystems". This phrase, which was possibly deemed not altogether explicit by a conference of legal and military experts, was discarded and replaced by the expression "wide-spread, long-term and severe damage". All three criteria must be present for the ban to be applicable to a means or method of warfare. In Article 35 paragraph 3 such means and methods are banned generally. In Article 55 this ban is related to the harm which might be caused to the health or survival of the population.

This is not, however, an additional condition for application of the prohibition, but rather an illustration of the seriousness of the damage contemplated by the article.

Notes

1. Rules Concerning the Control of Wireless Telegraphy in Time of War and Air Warfare fixed by the Commission of Jurists entrusted with studying and reporting on this revision of the laws of war, assembled at The Hague on December 11, 1922, Cf. *Recueil général des lois et coutumes de la guerre terrestre, maritime, sous-marine et aérienne*, Documents recueillis et annotés par Deltenre M. Marcel, Bruxelles, Les Editions Fred Wellens-Pay, 1943, pp. 818–848; *The Laws of Armed Conflicts. A Collection of Conventions, Resolutions and Other Documents*, Edited by D. Schindler and J. Toman, 3rd edition, Dordrecht, Martinus Nijhoff Publishers, Geneva, Henry Dunant Institute, 1988, pp. 207–217.

2. Kalshoven Frits, *The Law of Warfare. A summary of its recent history and trends in development*, Leiden, A.W. Sijthoff, 1973, p. 28.

3. Conference of Government Experts on the Use of Certain Conventional Weapons. Lucerne, 24.9 – 18.10.1974. *Report*, Geneva, ICRC, 1975, pp. 8–9.

4. Roblee Paul A., 'The legitimacy of modern conventional weaponry', *Military Law Review* (Charlottesville), Vol. 71, Winter 1976, p. 148.

5. Department of the Army Field Manual FM 27–10, *The Law of Land Warfare*, Washington D.C., Department of the Army, July 1956, Par. 34, p. 18.

6. Canada, Sweden, United Kingdom, United States.

7. See the statements at the 39th Plenary session of the Geneva Diplomatic Conference on the Reaffirmation and Development of International Humanitarian Law Applicable in Armed Conflicts of 1977, Doc. CDDH/SR. 39.

8. See also Roblee Paul, *loc. cit.*, pp. 108–109.

9. Conference of Government Experts on the Use of Certain Conventional Weapons. Lucerne, 24.9 – 18.10.1974. *Report* Geneva, ICRC, 1975, para. 34, p. 11.

10. United Nations Conference on Prohibitions or Restrictions of Use of Certain Conventional Weapons Which May Be Deemed to be Excessively Injurious or to Have Indiscriminate Effects, Geneva 10 – 28 September 1979, 15 September – 10 October 1980, *Final report of the Conference to the General Assembly*, A/CONF.95/15, 27 October 1980, Annex I; *The Laws of Armed Conflicts. A Collection of Conventions. Resolutions and Other Documents*, Edited by D. Schindler and J. Toman, 3rd edition, Dordrecht, Martinus Nijhoff Publishers, Geneva, Henry Dunant Institute, 1988, pp. 179–196.

11. Sandoz, Yves, A new step forward in international law: Prohibition and restriction on the use of certain conventional weapons. *International Review of the Red Cross*, No. 220, January–February 1981, p. 11.

12. See Report of Committee III of the Geneva Diplomatic Conference on the Reaffirmation and Development of International Humanitarian Law Applicable in Armed Conflicts of 1977, Doc. CDDH/50, 28 March 1974, par. 21, CDDH/III/SR. 4, 13 March 1974 and CDDH/III/SR. 11, 21 March 1974.

13. See 1974 Report of Committee III of the Geneva Diplomatic Conference on the Reaffirmation and Development of International Humanitarian Law Applicable in Armed Conflicts of 1977, CDDH/50 rev.1, par. 46, 2 September 1974. 1974 discussions in Committee III, Doc. CDDH/III/SR.1–12, 1975, Report of Committee III, Doc. CDDH/215/Rev. 1, par. 51.

14. Mudge, G.A., 'Starvation as a Means of Warfare', *The International Lawyer* (Chicago), Vol. 4, 1970, pp. 228–268; Rosenblad Esbjörn, 'Starvation as a Method of Warfare. Conditions for Regulation by Convention', *The International Lawyer* (Chicago) Vol. 7, No. 2, 1973, pp. 252–270, Mayer Jean, 'Starvation as a Weapon', *in* CBW: *Chemical and Biological Warfare, London Conference on CBW*, Ed. by Steven Rose, London, 1968, pp. 76–84.

15. See p. 149–150.

16. See Report to the Third Committee on the work of the working group submitted by the Rapporteur, *Doc.* CDDH/III/264/rev.1, 18 March 1975, par. 3 and the Report of the Committee III, Second session, Doc. CDDH/215/rev.1, 15 December 1975, par. 21.

17. *Ibid.*

18. See the statements of the representatives of Canada, the Federal Republic of Germany, Italy and the United Kingdom explaining their votes in the plenary meeting, Doc. CDDH/SR.41 paras. 119 and 122, p. 179 and p. 187.

19. International Committee of the Red Cross, Draft Additional Protocols to the Geneva Conventions of August 12, 1949, Commentary, Doc. CDDH/3, Geneva, ICRC, October 1973, p. 2.

20. See Report to the Third Committee on the work of the working group submitted by the rapporteur (Diplomatic Conference on the Reaffirmation and Development of International Humanitarian Law Applicable in Armed Conflicts, Geneva, 1974–1977), Doc. CDDH/III/264/rev.1 of 18 March 1975 and CDDH/III/224 of 24 February 1975.

21. Doc. CDDH/SR.41, annex par. 7.

22. BMVg. ZDv 15/10 – Kriegsvölkerrecht – Leitfaden für den Unterricht (Teil 7): Allegemeine Bestimmungen des Kriegsführungsrechts und Landkriegsrecht (Lehrschrift), 1961, par. 68.

23. Brazil, Canada, Federal Republic of Germany and Nicaragua, Doc. CDDH/III/27.

24. Australia, Doc. CDDH/III/43, rev.1.

25. United Kingdom representative at the plenary meeting of 26 May 1977, Doc. CDDH/SR/41.

26. See Report of the Third Committee (Diplomatic Conference), Doc. CDDH/215/rev. 1 of the 15 December 1975, para. 98.

27. *Ibid.*

28. Doc. CDDH/III/GT/35, 11th March 1975.

CHAPTER X

PROTECTION OF THE VICTIMS OF ARMED
CONFLICTS

I – WOUNDED, SICK AND SHIPWRECKED PERSONS

JOSÉ FRANCISCO REZEK

A. General Elementary Principles

The state of war justifies the recourse to violence against an active adversary, with the aim of destroying or weakening his military potential. On this basis, it can be said that reason, cold and amoral, leads to the respect of those unable to do any harm. The motive for protecting wounded, sick and shipwrecked persons is however to be found in the feeling of humanity. While reason is the basis of a passive attitude as demonstrated in the respect shown to these persons, the active protection which modern law grants them, has its origin in pity, an emotion which, more than a century ago, overwhelmed the solitary witness of the suffering at Soliferino.

A definition of the three categories of protected persons we have mentioned did not appear in the 1949 Conventions, but in the First Additional Protocol of 1977. It has long been recognized that the wounded, sick and shipwrecked are not necessarily the same as persons *hors de combat*. For, on the one hand, a combatant may give up fighting without suffering from wounds or disease, while on the other hand a wounded or sick person may maintain a hostile attitude, in which case he will act at his own risk. Under the Protocol, wounded and sick persons are those who, "because of trauma, disease or other physical or mental disorder or disability, are in need of medical assistance or care and who refrain from any act of hostility". Refraining from hostile acts should also characterize the behaviour of shipwrecked persons, defined as those "who are in peril at sea or in other waters" and who continue to hold this ephemeral status during rescue operations.

While the First and Second Geneva Conventions of 1949 referred to the wounded, sick and shipwrecked belonging to the combatant forces in the strict sense or to a fairly limited number of other categories (Article 13), Protocol I includes both military and civilian persons among victims.[1] The official (quadripartite) distinction made thirty years ago was not established on any scientific or practical basis, and was not considered suitable for reinclusion. The new set of rules now applies to "all those affected by a situation" resulting from the ever-widening field of international armed conflicts.

Naturally enough, the texts relating to protection appear to be concerned chiefly with wounded, sick and shipwrecked persons belonging to the adverse Party. The form of language, however, should not obscure the principle that the fundamental duty of the State[2] which is a party to the conflict is also concerned with its own nationals, and particularly with those in a condition of dependence on the said State.

The question of the protection of victims of armed conflicts has gained through international humanitarian law a significance marked by two salient characteristics: the prohibition of reprisals, and the legitimation of assistance provided by neutral States. On the one hand, breaches of the provisions of this law may not be justified by the fact that they are made in response to illicit acts of an identical nature. On the other hand, the neutrality of States not parties to the conflict is in no way compromised by such relief actions as they may undertake. This is in fact no more than logical since the victims should be protected by the enemy as well as by the State on which they depend, and no reasonable argument can stem from a neutrality which could be invoked to compel neutral States to abstain from such protection.

The analytical study of the texts relating to the protection of wounded, sick and shipwrecked persons should be preceded by a succinct scrutiny of the principles that determine their general structure, as follows:

a) Suffering has the effect of peremptorily conferring equality. No distinction, apart from that based on strictly medical criteria, may be admitted, whether based on race, sex, nationality, religion, political opinions or any other criteria. It should be remembered that, even if his behaviour has been unlawful, a wounded person may not be the object of unfavourable distinction. Physical distress confers the right to protection on the irregular combatant as well as on the mercenary, to whom the First Additional Protocol of 1977 refused only the status of prisoner of war.

b) The protection due to the wounded, sick and shipwrecked is extended generally to the persons caring for them and to the property necessary to do so. It is obvious that such protection only applies to such persons and property when devoted exclusively to their humanitarian role. They lose their immunity if they take part in active military efforts, or if used to render military objectives immune from attack. In the former instance, loss of protection is not immediate but is subject to rejection of a request to cease action, and thus proven refusal to comply with such a demand is necessary.

c) The rights of wounded, sick and shipwrecked persons are inalienable, as are those of medical and religious personnel. Voluntary renunciation is inadmissible, mainly owing to the doubts that the condition of the protected persons would raise in view of the possible subjective authenticity of such a gesture. Moreover, as laid down in the texts of the Conventions, these rights reflect a minimum which can however be extended through special agreements between parties to the conflict. Such agreements may have no restricting effect on the application of general treaty law. On the contrary, inasmuch as they contain more favourable provisions on the humanitarian plane, they are not subject to renunciation.

d) At the outbreak of a given armed conflict, any State that is a party to it becomes responsible for the protection provided by law. In this respect its status differs from that of neutral States and international humanitarian organizations, whose individual decision to go to the aid of the victims is the sole source of such responsibility. The clarity of the texts should be noted: whenever they refer to persons in the power of a party to a conflict, these texts specify that such persons should not be at the mercy of groups of combatants or of military commanders. Furthermore, a voluntary response by the population in answer to an appeal to tend the wounded and sick in no way absolves the State of its responsibilities. With regard to respect pure and simple for persons in distress however, this responsibility applies both to the individual as well as to the State; the State nevertheless, has a duty to supervise that cannot be imposed on individuals.

e) A distinctive characteristic of the protection granted to wounded and sick persons is stability. For instance, to change the purpose of the medical units, equipment and transport that have passed into the hands of the adverse party under the law of war is inadmissible. Whether detained or interned, medical personnel must be permitted to continue their mission. The deliberate destruction of property protected in the interests of wounded and sick persons is forbidden not only to the adversary but also to the belligerent to whom the property belongs and who might contemplate destruction to prevent such property falling into enemy hands.

f) Finally, identification is closely linked with the safety of the protected persons and their property. Obviously, the three categories of victims under discussion can be recognized by the objective evidence of the injuries or ordeals they have undergone (wounds, disease, distress at sea), and which usually affect them unexpectedly. Identification as prescribed by the Conventions, the distinctive emblem of which is the red cross (red crescent, red lion and sun), is reserved for medical and religious personnel and for mobile and fixed property assigned to the protective function.

B. General Protection of Wounded, Sick and Shipwrecked Persons

Wounded, sick and shipwrecked persons should be cared for as their condition demands, on the basis of equality. This privileged status applicable to all victims of armed conflict is comparable to that of prisoner of war. Murder, torture, biological experiment, deliberate abandonment and intentional exposure to the risks of contagion or infection are grave breaches of the 1949 Conventions. The

1977 Protocol refers to them explicitly as war crimes, and has added to the list of prohibited acts, physical mutilation and the removal of tissue or organs, while laying down strict rules for any amputation, skin grafts or blood transfusions carried out in the interests of the patients, consistent with generally recognized medical standards.

It is generally necessary to collect the wounded, sick and shipwrecked persons after military engagements, and for this reason arrangements should be made whenever possible for a cease-fire. The military authorities can appeal for help to civilians and grant them the necessary facilities. If this does not occur, spontaneous charitable action should be allowed and must not be followed by adverse consequences, whatever the circumstances and whoever the beneficiaries.[3]

C. Medical Units

Entrusted as they are with the collection, evacuation, transport, diagnosis and treatment of wounded, sick and shipwrecked persons and with the prevention of disease, medical units are inviolable, whether stationary or mobile, permanent or temporary.[4] In this context, the 1977 Protocol does not confine itself to standardizing the terminology or supplying exact definitions: it has in the main extended to civilian medical units the wide protection granted to the medical services of the armed forces under the 1949 Conventions.[5]

The Protection enjoyed by these units ceases the moment they are used to commit acts harmful to the enemy. This basic rule makes it evident that the protection due to these units does not cease even if, for example, they include personnel and equipment of the veterinary service or, in the case of hospital ships, if the medical personnel on board is more numerous than needed at the time. The Conventions, moreover, make clarifications such as these, as well as others which appear to be more justified: immunity is not compromised if the personnel of the medical unit carry small arms for defence purpose, if there are sentries or groups of guards, if the units have in their possession portable arms and ammunition which have been taken from the persons under treatment but which the unit has not yet been able to turn over to the competent authorities. The First Convention adds in dealing with the medical units of the armed forces, that they do not lose their inviolability if they provide care for civilians in distress.

The 1977 Additional Protocol I has introduced a reciprocal rule for civilian medical units caring for combatants.

As with the medical units of armed forces the equipment at their disposal for performing their duties must remain reserved for the treatment of wounded and sick persons according to their needs, even though it may become the property of the Detaining Power, in accordance with the law of war. This however is not true of both mobile or fixed property belonging to the relief societies whose action is covered by the Conventions: these goods, regarded as private property, may not be requisitioned except in the case of urgent necessity and only then if requisitioning does not prejudice the welfare of the wounded and sick benefiting from their use.

D. Hospital Zones and Localities

Rules for hospital zones and localities appear only in the First Geneva Convention of 1949 and are optional. Such zones and localities are intended to provide better protection for medical services by placing them far from the theatre of war operations. They may be established by any State, even in peacetime. It is however the outbreak of armed conflict that should give rise to agreements for mutual recognition of such zones and localities, possibly through the good offices of the ICRC or of the Protecting Powers. In inviting the States to adopt these rules, the Diplomatic Conference appended to the First Convention a draft agreement relating to hospital zones and localities (Annex I) thus making it easier to understand their nature. These zones should comprise only a small part of the territory governed by the Power which has established them, and should not give the least support to any military operations, or be defended by military means. Without prejudice to the rights of the persons residing within these zones, such areas should be thinly populated in relation to accommodation availibility, and should be reserved for wounded and sick persons and for the personnel entrusted with administration and medical care. Control by special commissions is included in the provisions to ensure permanent observance of the conditions laid down by the Convention and by the relevant agreement.

E. Medical and Religious Personnel

The 1949 Conventions make it obligatory, in all circumstances, to respect and protect the personnel responsible for the collection, evacuation, transport or treatment of wounded, sick and shipwrecked persons and for the prevention of disease. The same applies to persons assigned to the administration of medical units and to chaplains attached to the armed forces. Identical status is bestowed on the personnel of national relief societies duly authorized by their government, provided that they are subject to military laws and regulations and that their actual relief work has been notified to the other parties. Such notification may be made during peacetime.

If they fall into the hands of the adverse Power, the members of such personnel may be subjected only to retention. They are not considered as prisoners of war, but should benefit at least from the rights granted to prisoners of war under the Third Geneva Convention. It should be noted that retention does not represent the rule but an exceptional measure, authorized when the medical situation, the spiritual needs and the number of prisoners of war require it. When retained, these persons should preferably be employed in the service of prisoners of the armed forces to which they themselves belong. In any case, they should never be obliged to perform work outside their medical or religious duties. The discipline of the camp, to which they are subject, should nevertheless not hamper their mobility to the extent required for the regular performance of their duties of assistance and for access to the competent authorities.

As soon as it is feasible, retention of such persons should cease and they should be returned to the party to the conflict to which they belong. They shall be allowed to take with them their personal possessions, valuables and instruments. Any arms belonging to these persons, and their means of transport, on the other hand, may remain in the hands of the Detaining Power. If circumstances permit the return of only part of the medical and religious personnel, selection of those to be returned to their own country should preferably be based on chronological order of capture and state of health; in any case, religious or political criteria are prohibited.

A special and somewhat precarious form of protection is stipulated for a second category of persons, temporary medical personnel, that is, soldiers trained to be employed, if need be, in auxiliary medical duties. Once captured, they become prisoners of war; the rules applied to them are not the same as those applied to permanent medical personnel, which lead to repatriation. But auxiliary personnel must be respected and protected if they are performing medical duties at the time of their engagement or at the time of their capture, and may be employed subsequently in medical activities where their help proves to be necessary.

The 1977 Additional Protocol I, in contrast to the Convention, requires temporary personnel to be employed exclusively in medical duties throughout the period of their engagement. In return, it gives this personnel the same rights, in the event of capture, as enjoyed by permanent medical personnel.

It should, moreover, be pointed out that the Detaining Power always remains responsible for the fate of prisoners of war: the employment of retained medical and religious personnel and of these specially trained prisoners of war does not exempt the Detaining Power from its obligations under international law.

The 1977 Additional Protocol I extends the protective provisions to civilian medical and religious personnel. They will be frequently employed under the authority of the adverse party in the event of territorial occupation. This considerably widens the possible field of voluntary action by neutral States and international humanitarian organizations, as will be seen below. The Protocol also establishes significant rules aimed at protecting the medical mission. No person performing or having performed activities of a medical nature, whether or not a member of the medical personnel

a) may be compelled to perform acts contrary to the rules of medical ethics or to the rules protecting the wounded and sick or to refrain from any action conforming to the said rules;

b) may be punished for performing such an act, regardless of the circumstances and the beneficiaries;

c) may be compelled to give information concerning patients if, in his or her opinion, such information could prove harmful to them or to their families.

This last rule, however, does not prevent the compulsory notification of communicable disease, and may be set aside, moreover, by the State to which the person performing medical duties belongs, but solely in cases required by law. Thus while the rule may be waived legitimately by a State that has specific laws on the subject, this is not the case where such internal law does not exist: it would be illicit to require information based only on administrative instructions, whether military or civilian.

F. Medical Transport

This expression covers the transportation by land, sea or air of wounded, sick and shipwrecked persons and of medical personnel and supplies. In addition, under one of the provisions of Additional Protocol I of 1977, it is extended to the transport of religious personnel.

Whether military or civilian, permanent or temporary, the means of medical transport (road vehicles, ships and small craft, or aircraft) must be respected and protected in the same way as mobile medical units. Because of the special conditions attaching to their use, hospital ships and medical aircraft are the subject of a more complex set of legal provisions.

a. Hospital Ships

Primarily, the fact that hospital ships may be used in the double role of means of transport and floating centres of treatment, has no legal significance. While the double nature of such ships makes them different from medical aircraft, which are not usually equipped to accommodate wounded and sick persons for long periods, it does not make them distinct from mobile medical units, the protection of which is taken as the model for all means of medical transport and which can themselves fulfil both functions.

The inviolability of hospital ships, nevertheless, presupposes that the State using them communicates the fact to the other parties to the conflict at least ten days before putting them into commission, specifying the characteristics of the vessel, including tonnage, length and the number of masts and funnels. Such ships may carry navigation and communications equipment but not use secret code. The Second Geneva Convention urges States to use, over long distances and far out at sea, only hospital ships of more than two thousand gross registered tons, but does not make this a condition for protection.

Apart from the hospital ships of international humanitarian organizations, of neutral States and of their relief societies, or even of private individuals, which will be mentioned later, the hospital ships of the relief societies belonging to a State party to a conflict enjoy the same protection as that granted to hospital ships of the armed forces, provided that they are acting on official commission and that the use of them has been notified to the other parties ten days in advance.

Since hospital ships must collect and care for wounded, sick and shipwrecked persons without any distinction, including that of nationality, it follows that they have the right to give aid to civilians. However, contrary to the case of combatants, civilians may not be captured at sea nor handed over to a party other than that to which they belong, even if such action does not threaten their health or prevent the treatment they are in need of. In the Additional Protocol I, medical ships and small craft not falling within the categories described in the Conventions also enjoy a certain protection. The Protocol, however, has not modified the terms of the restrictions set for the action of hospital ships in general; they remain subject to the right of control and inspection, may have their course prescribed, and may even be retained for a maximum of seven days for grave reasons. The rules of protection apply also to warships infirmaries and to coastal rescue craft.

b. Medical Aircraft

The legal regulations for medical aircraft have been largely redrafted and developed by the 1977 Additional Protocol I, but without challenging the basic principles.

First, *three zones* must be distinguished, on land or sea, each of them to include the airspace above it:

1. The zones not controlled by the enemy are those land or sea areas controlled by friendly forces and uncontrolled areas of the sea. Within these zones, whether in flight, on the ground or on the water, the medical aircraft is entitled to respect and protection, whether or not there has been any prior agreement with the adverse party. The State responsible for its use nevertheless possesses the option of notifying[6] the adverse party, a precautionary measure to be recommended, especially if the aircraft is intended to be flown within the range of enemy ground-to-air weapons.

2. Contact zones or their equivalent are the areas on land where the opposing forces confront each other, especially where they are exposed to direct fire from the ground. In the parts of these zones which are physically controlled by friendly forces and in land areas where control has not been clearly established, the safety of medical aircraft can be guaranteed only by prior agreement[7] between the military authorities of the opposing parties. Without such an agreement the aircraft operate at their own risk, though they are not officially deprived of immunity; once their character has been recognized by the adverse party they must be respected.

3. The overflying of land or sea areas physically controlled by an enemy always presupposes prior agreement by the competent authority of the latter. However, if a navigational error or an emergency affecting the safety of the flight causes the medical aircraft to fly into such areas without or in breach of an agreement, the aircraft must make every effort to identify itself. If it succeeds in doing so, the adverse party shall refrain as far as possible from attempting an attack, either

by ordering the aircraft to land or to alight on water, or by taking other measures and allowing time for compliance with the orders given.

Like the other vehicles and medical units, medical aircraft may not be used to gain military advantage or to render military objectives immune from attack. The general rule concerning weapons and ammunition which may be found in protected vessels or other form of transport[8] is fully applicable to medical aircraft. The use of medical aircraft to collect or transmit military intelligence data or to carry equipment for this purpose is also forbidden. Finally, only the prior consent of the enemy can permit them to search for the wounded, sick and shipwrecked in the two last-named types of zone.

In overflying a zone controlled by the enemy or a zone not clearly controlled by any force, medical aircraft must comply with any order to land or to alight on water for the purposes of inspection. This operation must be carried out rapidly, without aggravating the state of the wounded and sick, removal of whom from the aircraft shall not be ordered unless unavoidable.

The purpose of the inspection is strictly limited to verifying that the aircraft:
a) is in fact used exclusively for medical transport and under the authority of a party to the conflict, even if it does not belong to military aviation, or if its use as such is temporary;
b) is not in violation of the general and special restrictions to be observed;[9]
c) has not flown without or in breach of a prior agreement where such agreement is required.[10]

If the inspection shows that the conditions have been fulfilled, the aircraft may resume its flight without delay; the only passengers permitted to be retained are those belonging to the party that made the inspection or to its allies. If, on the other hand, the inspection brings to light a breach of any of the relevant rules, the aircraft may be seized by the adverse party. However, it may be used only as a medical aircraft if that was its permanent assignment. The occupants must be treated in conformity with the provisions of the Conventions and the Protocol, in particular those relating to wounded persons, prisoners of war, civilians and medical personnel.

G. Missing and Dead Persons

In the sections of the 1949 Geneva Conventions relating to wounded, sick and shipwrecked, provisions are included concerning dead persons, fundamentally inspired by the respect shown to them in certain civilizations and legal systems. They should always be searched for, especially after a combat, protected against pillage, and buried, as far as possible individually and according to the rites of their religion. As for the wounded and sick, the Information Bureau which each party is obliged to set up under the Conventions, shall record all information concerning the dead and forward it to the Power on which those persons depended, through the Protecting Power and the ICRC. Such information, intended chiefly for identification of the dead, should certainly include the location of the graves.

The 1977 Additional Protocol I devotes a whole section to missing and dead persons, as a supplement to the rules established in 1949. Without denying the moral value of respect for the dead, the Protocol had in view primarily "the right of families to know the fate of their relatives". Special attention, therefore, has been given to persons reported missing: as soon as feasible, and at the latest by the end of active hostilities, these persons must be searched for and the information relating to them transmitted to their State of origin, either directly or through the intermediary of the Protecting Power, the National Red Cross Society or the Central Tracing Agency of the ICRC, the latter body being informed in any case.

For the purpose of searching for, identifying and recovering the dead, the parties to the conflict are urged to create teams, accompanied, if appropriate, by personnel of the adverse party. Personnel of such teams shall be respected and protected while exclusively carrying out these duties.

The parties shall ensure that the graves of persons buried in their territory as a result of the conflict shall be respected and maintained. As soon as possible agreements should be concluded between them for the better observation of this rule and to facilitate access to the graves by relatives of the deceased and the return of the remains and personal effects of the dead to the home country. Exhumation is permitted only for this purpose or for "overriding public necessity". If the offer of facilities for return of the remains of the deceased to the home country has not been accepted within five years, then the State in which the graves are located may apply its own legislation relating to cemeteries and graves.

H. Identification

a) The *protective emblem*, the red cross or, in some countries, the red crescent or red lion and sun,[11] always on a white ground, serves to identify medical personnel, units, equipment and means of transport. The emblem should be as clearly visible as possible in order to be effective. The distinctive emblem in the form of a flag may be flown by stationary or mobile medical units and by hospital ships; it may be accompanied by the national flag of the party to the conflict to which the unit or the ship belongs. If such a unit or ship falls into the hands of the adverse party, the latter shall take down the national flag and continue to fly that of the distinctive emblem. The emblem may be painted or otherwise fixed on the roofs and other surfaces of protected buildings and on medical equipment, small craft, ships, aircraft and other vehicles. In the case of hospital ships, the white ground is provided by the ship itself, which must be white in colour. The protective emblem as worn by medical and religious personnel is carried on an armband issued and stamped by the military authority. Such personnel must also carry identity cards and discs as specified in the Conventions. The emblem should also appear, in reduced size, on the armband worn by temporary medical personnel, that is, by combatants trained to perform auxiliary duties in the medical service should the need arise,[12] while they are performing such duties. Protocol I, however, drops this distinction in favour of maximum visibility to limit the risks run by any protected person.

b) The red cross and its variants may be used permanently as an indicative symbol by the National Red Cross Societies. In time of war, however, care must be taken not to confuse this indicative symbol with the protective emblem. For this reason, the first must be of reduced size and must not be used on roofs and armbands. With the express consent of the National Red Cross Society and under the terms of their legislation, States may allow the indicative symbol to be used in peacetime to identify ambulances and first-aid posts provided exclusively for the treatment without charge of injured and sick persons. In this context, the most frequent misuse of the symbol arises from a misunderstanding of the significance of the red cross: it is taken by some to be the symbol of medicine in general and used, for example, to indicate pharmacies or private clinics.[13]

In addition to the distinctive emblem, the Additional Protocol I provides the option of using distinctive signals for the better identification of medical units and means of transport. Temporary medical aircraft, indeed, may use only the distinctive signals in an emergency if lack of time or the characteristics of the aircraft prevent its being marked with the distinctive emblem.

The new forms of identification governed by the Protocol are:

a) the light signal consisting of a flashing blue light, and intended, so far as air transport is concerned, for the exclusive use of medical aircraft, but freely used by all sorts of vehicles, including waterborne transport. This is however not the case if a special agreement has been concluded by the parties to the conflict with a view to reserving its use also for medical transport, on land and on sea.

b) the radio signal consisting of a detailed informative message in English, preceded by a distinctive priority signal to be designated and approved by International Telecommunications Union conference and restricted exclusively to medical units and transport *in general*;

c) an SSR (Secondary Surveillance Radar) code, restricted exclusively to *medical aircraft*, to be established by the parties concerned in accordance with procedures to be recommended by the International Civil Aviation Organisation. The parties to a conflict may also conclude special agreements on the adoption of a similar electronic system to facilitate identification of medical vehicles and medical ships and small craft.

I. Neutral States and Humanitarian Organizations

The legal obligations resulting from neutrality do not, as stated, require abstention from care for victims of war. Without violating the status to which it is committed to adhere, the neutral State[14]

a) is required to apply, by analogy, the protective rules to wounded, sick and shipwrecked persons and to medical and religious personnel[15] who may be located in no matter what circumstances, in the spatial areas of its sovereignty;

b) is authorized, in certain conditions, to provide relief to the victims of armed conflict on the territory of the parties to a conflict.

Certain provisions require explanation: provided that they are not transporting combatants or war materials, convoys of wounded and sick persons may be authorized to pass through neutral territory, under Article 14 of the Hague Convention No. V of 1907. However, wounded and sick persons thus transported and belonging to the party adverse to that which transports them lose their status as prisoners of war; they must be retained by the neutral Power and interned in such a way that they no longer take part in the hostilities. Internment is also the rule for wounded and sick persons of the transporting party if for some reason that party entrusts them to the neutral State.[16]

Concerning the overflying of neutral territory by medical aircraft, the rules of the 1949 Geneva Conventions have been redrafted following the 1977 Additional Protocol I. The Conventions insist on the possible overflight without prior agreement, but in conditions so strict and complex that the supposed liberality of the provisions are nullified. Hence forth neutral territory overflown by medical aircraft is treated in the same way as territory controlled by the adverse party or as areas the control of which has not been clearly established.[17]

The principle, therefore, is the prohibition of overflight without prior agreement; in any case there exists at all times a possible order to land or to alight on water for inspection. However, if the aircraft is seized, it is obvious that the persons on board do not become prisoners of war: they must be retained and interned by the neutral State, when international law so requires,[18] so that they may not take part again in hostilities.

The facilities that a neutral State decides to grant for the transport of wounded and sick persons in its territory must be *equal* for all parties to the conflict. The same applies to the restrictions. This equality of treatment, however, is not required when the neutral State is helping to care for victims on the territory of the parties to the conflict. The Conventions describe the aid which the relief societies of neutral Powers may supply to one party, provided that these societies have the consent both of their own State and of the party benefiting from their action, and when the adverse party has been duly notified. The 1977 Protocol goes further: it provides that the neutral State itself may place at the disposal of one of the parties to the conflict permanent medical units and means of transport with the appropriate personnel. The security provided under the protective emblem to the personnel and goods thus placed at the service of the humanitarian cause has not been changed in essentials: personnel falling into the power of the party adverse to the one being helped may not be retained. Such persons must be freed as soon as possible and returned, either to the neutral State to which they belong or to the territory in which they were serving; they may not be deprived of their property, including, unless this is completely impossible, their means of transport.

As in the case of neutral States, and under similar conditions, international humanitarian organizations are authorized by the Additional Protocol I to bring aid to the victims of war in the field of operations, by sending medical units, personnel and transport.[19]

Notes

* The French use the word "réserves" but this does not seem appropriate in this context.
1. The provisions of the Fourth Geneva Convention of 1949 are somewhat lacking in this respect, referring almost exclusively to civilian hospitals and medical transport (Articles 16 to 22).
2. It should be pointed out that, since the adoption of the 1977 Additional Protocol I, a party to a conflict does not need to be a State, as international armed conflicts now include struggles against colonial domination, foreign occupation and racist regimes (Additional Protocol I, Article 1, para. 4).
3. In the context of war at sea, this type of appeal may be made to neutral civilian craft, which may also act on their own initiative, being covered, in either case, by the same guarantee.
4. The temporary assignment of units, personnel and means of transport of medical purposes confers, throughout the duration of such assignment, status identical to that of permanent medical units, personnel and means of transport, provided that the temporary assignment is exclusively for medical purposes.
5. Civilian medical units, and the property belonging to the relief societies covered by the Conventions, may be *requisitioned* by any Occupying Power, but only in specific cases and according to strictly defined methods (see at the end of page 156).
6. The notification shall indicate the number, the flight plans and the means of identification of the medical aircraft in operation. Acknowledgement must be made without delay.
7. The request for agreement, containing the same particulars as laid down for notification, must be given a rapid reply, whether it accepts, rejects or modifies the terms of the agreement; in the latter case there will be a further communication. Once agreement has been reached, the parties shall at once communicate its content to the military forces concerned.
8. Cf. *supra*, p. 156.
9. Cf. *supra*, p. 160–161.
10. Prior agreement is *required* only for the overflight of areas physically controlled by the adverse party. For contact zones and land areas where control is not clearly established, prior agreement is merely strongly recommended, by reason of the risks otherwise entailed for the medical aircraft.
11. Iran, which alone used this emblem, renounced recently its use and replaced it by a red crescent.
12. Cf. *supra*, p. 158.
13. The distinctive emblem may be used at any time by the international bodies of the Red Cross and by their personnel. In such a case it is difficult to make a clear differentiation between the use of the protective emblem and that of the distinctive emblem.
14. The expression "neutral Power", used in the Conventions, has been replaced in the Protocol by that of "neutral and other States not parties to the conflict". This was done to distinguish the States having permanent neutral status from those which are not implicated in the conflict.
15. Since the adoption of the 1977 Additional Protocol I, civilian wounded, sick and shipwrecked persons and medical personnel are also covered.
16. According to the 1949 Conventions, this internment is obligatory for wounded, sick and shipwrecked persons belonging to the fighting forces of a party to the conflict who have been disembarked in the ports of a neutral State or collected in its military aircraft or warships. The Protocol states that the *costs* of internment or hospitalization will in all cases be chargeable to the State to which the interned persons belong.

17. Cf. *supra*, p. 160 ff.

18. This form of words, found in several places in the Conventions and the Additional Protocol I, is explained by the fact that certain persons who become prisoners of war if they fall into the power of the enemy may not be retained by neutral countries. This is the case, for instance, for the crew members of civilian aircraft and merchant ships belonging to as party to the conflict.

19. Although not a masterpiece of composition, the 1977 Additional Protocol I is a definite advance in several points on the 1949 Conventions. Nevertheless, it may be asked whether such progress was on a par with the efforts undertaken by the ICRC and the duration of the Diplomatic Conference.

It should be recalled that the said Conference was intended to reaffirm as well as to develop international humanitarian law. Strict legal logic would deny the need to reaffirm provisions of law actually in force, but minds aware of modern conditions would not be satisfied with such an argument.

Concluded after the traumatic experiences of the Second World War, when there was general agreement on the importance of guarantees at international and internal level, for the rule of law and respect of human beings, the Conventions have been subject in recent years to a process of erosion, since the States, faced with threats to their security, tended to lose sight of fundamental humanitarian values.

The work accomplished in 1977 should therefore be hailed as admirably successful, not only because it developed humanitarian law but also because it made sure that neglect and ill-will did not obscure the gains of 1949.

CHAPTER XI

PROTECTION OF THE VICTIMS OF ARMED CONFLICTS

II – PRISONERS OF WAR

CLAUDE PILLOUD

A. Introduction

Respect for prisoners of war – for their person, honour, physical and mental health – is a relatively recent notion.

In ancient times, warriors who fell into the power of their enemies were almost invariably exterminated. But it did not take long for the victorious forces to discover that prisoners constituted a useful and very cheap supply of manpower. That is how the custom gradually grew, in Egypt, Athens, and later Rome, of reducing the captured enemy combatants to slavery, although from time to time it did happen that prisoners of war were butchered.

With the rise of chivalry of Europe, in the early medieval period, the practice of releasing a prisoner of war on payment of a ransom was introduced, a practice that found additional favour when, in the eleventh century, the Church forbade the enslavement of people of the Christian faith. Islam, too, had adopted a generous attitude towards captured combatants. Nevertheless, the wars between Muslims and Christians were marked by wholesale massacres or by the cruel and inhumane treatment of prisoners of war. Some generous gestures towards captured combatants, however, did take place, as also occurred within the areas of other civilizations, for instance in India.

From the 16th century onwards the situation improved considerably in Europe and the exchange of prisoners of war at the close of hostilities became a rule as from the 18th century. Under the influence of the philosophers and publicists, it was felt that the captured enemy combatant was not, in principle, responsible for acts committed by his government; consequently he should not be the victim of revenge and should be treated humanely for the duration of his captivity. Conventions drawn up between States during the 18th century provided for humane treatment of POWs, and during the French Revolution unilateral decrees stipulated that no act of violence should be committed against POWs.

This liberal tendency continued during the 19th century and in 1899 the Hague Regulations Concerning the Laws and Customs of War on Land were adopted; the second chapter of these regulations deals with prisoners of war and is the first international ruling in this field. Revised in 1907, the Convention covered treatment of POWs until 1929 when a special Convention concerning their treatment was drawn up in Geneva. Revised in 1949 and completed in 1977 by an Additional Protocol, this Convention constitutes a charter or, as it is sometimes called, the POW Code. Considerable service has been rendered by this Convention in the course of innumerable conflicts: it has become an essential safeguard for millions of individuals subjected to trying and often painful conditions of captivity.

B. Definition

Taken generally, combatants who fall into enemy hands become prisoners of war.[1] The idea of what constitutes a combatant is described in Chapter VIII so that reference should be made to this chapter for further detail.[2]

Likewise, when they fall into enemy hands, persons not directly belonging to the armed forces but who nonetheless are attached thereto are considered as POWs, i.e., civilian members of airforce crews, war journalists, caterers, members of welfare services attached to the armed forces; these persons should be supplied with a special identity card.[3] The same applies to members of the merchant navy not benefitting from more favourable treatment.[4] Finally, the population of non-occupied territory who spontaneously take up arms at the approach of the enemy without having had the time to set up a regular armed force, but openly carry arms and respect the law and customs of war, should also be considered, if captured, as prisoners of war.[5]

Members of the armed forces who have returned to civilian life and who, for security reasons, have been interned by the occupying power in occupied territory, should be granted POW status. Furthermore, a Neutral Power which interns military personnel who have sought refuge on its territory, should grant them POW if not more favourable treatment.[6]

C. Capture

Captivity starts on the combatant falling into enemy hands. Capture can take different forms., i.e., the combatant can give himself up to the adverse force by throwing away his weapons, hoisting the white flag or raising his hands. Surrender can be collective or the result of local or general capitulation. Capture can also take place if the combatant is wounded and prostrate, showing no resistance, on territory captured by the enemy. Persons giving themselves up or who are *hors de combat* as the result of wounds or illness, should not be attacked; they should, however, abstain from any hostile act and not attempt to escape.[7]

Where an army contingent has taken POWs and cannot evacuate or handle them in accordance with international rules, they should be liberated with all due precautions to ensure their safety, and after their being disarmed where necessary.[8]

Certain forms of warfare make it very difficult for the individual to show his intention to surrender. Where, however, the individual is in obvious danger, he should not be attacked. No drowning persons should be attacked.[9] Occupants of an aircraft in difficulty, who have abandoned the aircraft by parachute, should not be shot down, and once they land should be given the opportunity to surrender before being attacked; nor should they counter-attack. This ruling evidently does not apply to troops transported by air.[10]

Anyone taking part in hostilities who falls into the hands of the adverse Party can be considered as a POW. Should there by any doubt as to an individual having the right to the status of POW, such a person will continue to be protected by the Convention and the Protocol whilst clarification of his status by a competent tribunal is awaited.[11]

D. Basic Protection

a. Basic Notions of Protection

As seen from the above, progress over the years has been slow in its effort to show that the captured enemy combatant should not be held responsible for the war and the manner in which it is carried out. For this reason captivity as a result of war should not be considered as of a punitive or infamous character;[12] its sole objective is to make the combatant incapable of doing harm and to prevent him from re-engaging in hostilities.

During their captivity POWs remain members of their armed forces but are subject to the laws, regulations and general orders in force within the armed forces of the Detaining Power,[13] without, however, being in duty bound to the latter (Detaining Power).[14]

b. Humane Treatment

Prisoners of war must at all times be humanely treated.[15] They are entitled to respect for their person, both physical and moral. The following acts, for example, are contrary to respect for the physical person: any unlawful act or omission causing death or seriously endangering the health of a prisoner of war, not to mention physical mutilations, medical or scientific experiments which are not justified by the patient's treatment, removal of tissue or organs for transplantation;[16] acts of violence on the part of civilians or military persons;[17] prolonged questioning, whether or not accompanied by acts of brutality, with the aim of

extracting information;[18] continual harassment; omission of medical care to the
wounded and sick;[19] prolonged deprivation of sanitary facilities[20] or of physical,
intellectual and recreational pursuits;[21] inadequate conditions of food,[22] quarters[23] and clothing[24] extended over any length of time; keeping prisoners in a
danger zone;[25] making them do labour of a dangerous nature or one which does
not take into account the prisoners' physical aptitude or their professional
qualifications.[26]

Respect for prisoners means respect for their person and honour[27] and
protection against public curiosity.[28] Humiliating and degrading treatment is
therefore banned, as is the internment of prisoners in penitentiaries,[29] degrading
and humiliating labour or labour directly connected with war operations,[30] lack
of separate quarters for women and men,[31] insults uttered against a prisoner's
person, flag, country, religion or beliefs,[32] forcing prisoners to wear their enemy's
uniform, the prohibition of wearing badges of rank and decorations and the
confiscation of such insignia,[33] refusal to reply to prisoners' salutes.[34]

c. Reprisals

Measures of reprisal against prisoners of war are prohibited.[35] Reprisals are
unlawful measures resorted to by a belligerent to counter and eliminate unlawful
acts committed by an adversary. No reprisals may be made against persons
protected by the 1949 Geneva Conventions and the 1977 Additional Protocol or
against cultural property. Reprisals may be resorted to only if understood in the
manner of conducting hostilities.[36]

d. Responsibility

The Detaining Power is responsible for the treatment given by its agents to
prisoners of war, irrespective of the individual responsibilities that may exist.[37]
Any breaches of the provisions of the Convention involve the responsibility of
the violators of those provisions and must be repressed. Persons having committed breaches may be brought before the courts of the High Contracting Party
holding such persons, or it may hand them over for trial to another High
Contracting Party concerned.[38] Grave breaches against prisoners of war shall be
those involving any of the following acts: wilful killing, torture or inhumane
treatment, including biological experiments, wilfully causing great suffering or
serious injury to body or health, compelling a prisoner of war to serve in the
forces of the hostile Power, or wilfully depriving a prisoner of war of the rights
of fair and regular trial prescribed in the Convention, unjustified delay in the
repatriation of prisoners of war, practices of apartheid and other inhuman and
degrading practices involving outrages upon personal dignity, based on racial
discrimination.[39]

Prisoners of war may only be transferred to a Power which is bound by the
Geneva Convention of 1949 and is willing and able to apply the Convention.[40]

This latter Power is then responsible for the treatment given to the transferred prisoners of war.

e. Maintenance

The Power detaining prisoners of war shall be bound to maintain them free of charge – their quarters, clothing, food and medical attention.[41] The upkeep provided must be sufficient to maintain the prisoners in good health.

f. Equality of Treatment

Taking into consideration rank and sex, all prisoners shall be treated alike. Any adverse distinction based upon race, colour, language or belief, political or other opinion, national or social origin, wealth, birth or other status, or on any other similar criteria shall be prohibited.[42] For example, it is unlawful to give privileges to those prisoners who accept to take part in ideological or political propaganda courses, or who agree to sign statements in favour of or against other prisoners, to reveal military information, to encourage minorities who might militate in favour of separatist activities, to keep apart on racial or colour grounds men belonging to the same unit and to treat them differently. On the other hand, should there be amongst prisoners tensions which might imperil the lives or physical integrity of some prisoners, it would not be unlawful to put the opposing groups in separate camps or in separate sections of a camp.

The Convention itself provides for privileged treatment for officers: exemption from work,[43] higher pay;[44] for sick prisoners: appropriate diet,[45] isolation wards,[46] early repatriation;[47] for women, separate dormitories and conveniences.[48] The prisoners' age and professional qualifications may also be taken into consideration for any privileged treatment.[49]

g. Discipline

Under the reservation of guarantees in the IIIrd Geneva Convention, prisoners of war shall be subject to the discipline in force in the armed forces of the Detaining Power.[50] Orders must be given in a language which they understand.[51] The use of weapons against prisoners of war, especially against those who are escaping or attempting to escape, shall constitute an extreme measure, which shall always be preceded by appropriate warnings.[52]

h. Disciplinary Punishments

The only disciplinary punishments applicable to prisoners of war are: a fine which shall not exceed 50 per cent of the advances of pay and working pay, discontinuance of privileges, fatigue duties not exceeding two hours daily, and confinement. The duration of any disciplinary punishment shall not exceed thirty days.[53] Fatigue duties shall not be applied to officers.[54] A period of at least three days shall elapse between two successive punishments.[55] A prisoner of war undergoing confinement shall continue to enjoy the benefits of the Convention.[56]

i. Judicial Proceedings

A prisoner of war shall be tried only by a military court offering guarantees of independence and impartiality and affording the accused the rights and means of defence provided for by the Convention.[57] He shall, in particular, be entitled to choose counsel for his defence, to call witnesses and to obtain the services of a competent interpreter; the representatives of the Protecting Power shall be entitled to attend the trial and give assistance to the accused,[58] who shall have, in the same manner as the members of the armed forces of the Detaining Power, the right of appeal or petition.[59] If the death penalty is pronounced on a prisoner of war the sentence shall not be executed before the expiration of a period of six months.[60]

Prisoners prosecuted and convicted for acts committed prior to capture shall retain the benefits of the Convention;[61] they may not be punished more than once for the same act and may not be sentenced to any penalties except those provided for in respect of members of the armed forces of the Detaining Power.[62] No coercion may be exerted on a prisoner of war in order to induce him to admit himself guilty of the act of which he is accused.[63]

E. Protecting Powers – International Committee of the Red Cross

The Convention shall be applied with the co-operation and under the scrutiny of the Protecting Powers whose duty it is to safeguard the interests of the Parties to the conflict. For this purpose, the delegates of the Protecting Powers may go to all places where prisoners of war may be and freely interview prisoners, without witnesses. The delegates of the International Committee of the Red Cross shall enjoy the same prerogatives. Prisoners may at all times lodge complaints with the Protecting Power and send appeals to any of the benevolent organizations which might extend them their aid and, in particular, to the International Committee of the Red Cross.[64]

F. Non-Renunciation of Rights

Prisoners of war may not renounce the rights secured to them by the 1949 Convention and the 1977 Additional Protocol. Any renunciation of such rights, even if made voluntarily by a prisoner, shall be void and no special agreement concluded by the Detaining Power may deprive him of his rights.[65]

The intention here is to protect the prisoners against any action they themselves might take and any agreements which their Power of origin might be compelled under duress to conclude with the Detaining Power. A prisoner, for example, must not accept certain privileges in exchange for his consent to work in an armaments factory; he would be liable, after his repatriation at the end of hostilities, to be prosecuted in his own country. Similarly, prisoners of war may not renounce their status and become civilian workers.

Furthermore, a prisoner may accept his release on parole only if the law of the Power to which he belongs allows him to do so.

G. Beginning of Captivity

a. Questioning

When questioned, a prisoner of war is bound to give only four items of information: his surname and first names, rank, date of birth and army or equivalent number. These indications are given on the identity card normally carried by the prisoner; the card should not be taken away from him. If he refuses to give this information he may render himself liable to restriction of the privileges accorded to his rank, even should the Detaining Power get to know of it later.

Prisoners who refuse to answer may not be threatened, insulted, or exposed to any unpleasant or disadvantageous treatment.[66]

b. Personal Property

Prisoners may keep effects and articles of personal use, such as those serving as clothing and protection, and for eating. Examples of articles of clothing are: all garments, underwear, footwear (shoes and boots), belt, overcoat, knapsack; for eating: billycan, water-bottle, eating utensils, rations and haversack; for personal protection: helmet, gas-mask, groundsheet, packet of dressings, identity disc; other personal objects: toilet articles, watch, wallet, keys, prayer-book, pencil, fountain-pen, pocket torch, eye-glasses, badges of rank, decorations.[67] Sums of money and articles of value may be taken away but a receipt must be given for them, and such objects and sums of money must be returned at the termination of captivity. Objects of a personal and sentimental value, but of small commercial value – such as photographs, wedding rings, medals – may not be taken from prisoners of war.

On the other hand, arms, munitions, means of transport (horses, vehicles, motors), portable wireless equipment, optical instruments and military documents, such as maps, plans, written orders, etc. may be confiscated.[68]

c. Evacuation

Prisoners captured in a fighting zone shall be evacuated as soon as possible to camps situated in an area far enough for them to be out of danger.[69] The evacuation shall always be effected humanely and the prisoners shall be provided with potable water, food and, if necessary, clothing and medical attention. A list of the prisoners who are evacuated shall be established as soon as possible.[70]

d. Capture Cards

As soon as possible after capture, and not more than one week after arrival at a camp, every prisoner shall be given the possibility of sending a card to his family and also one to the Central Agency (see below), informing them of his capture, state of health and, if possible, his address.[71]

e. Official Information Bureaux

The Parties to the conflict and the neutral States who may have accepted to take in members of the belligerent armies shall institute, upon the outbreak of the conflict, an official Information Bureau for prisoners of war who are in their power[72] and in respect of dead combatants whose remains have been collected.[73]

The official bureaux shall receive full information on the identity of the prisoners, on any changes in the conditions of captivity or in their status (transfers, releases, repatriations, admissions to hospital, escapes, deaths) and on their state of health.

In the case of prisoners who have died in captivity and also as regards the bodies of combatants collected by the adverse party, the information will refer to the place of internment in order that graves may always be found.

Such information shall be immediately forwarded to the enemy Power concerned through the intermediary of the Protecting Powers, and likewise to the Central Agency mentioned below. The same provisions shall apply to personal valuables, sums of money and documents left by the deceased.[74]

The Bureau shall also be responsible for replying to enquiries sent to it; it will make any enquiries necessary to obtain the information asked for if it is not in its possession.[75]

The organization of the Bureau may be entrusted to the military services or to a civilian administration; in some countries, the work is done by their National Red Cross (Red Crescent) Society. Prisoners of war may be employed in such a Bureau.[76]

f. Central Agency

Under the Convention, a Central Prisoners of War Information Agency shall be created in a neutral country by the International Committee of the Red Cross.[77] The Agency, which is known as the Central Tracing Agency, is in Geneva and operates whenever there is a conflict.

The functions of the Agency are to collect all the information it may obtain through official or private channels respecting prisoners of war, and to transmit it as rapidly as possible to the country of origin.[78] It endeavours to reply to enquiries sent it by the families of missing combatants.

g. Relief Organizations

All facilities shall be granted to religious organizations and relief societies wishing to assist prisoners. The number of such societies may be limited. The special position of the International Committee of the Red Cross in this field shall be respected. Both material and spiritual relief may be offered.[79]

H. Internment of Prisoners of War

The provisions in respect of internment are laid down in the 1949 Convention in considerable detail, no doubt as a result of the excesses noted during the second world war. It must not be forgotten, moreover, that the monotony of life in captivity is relieved by details which assume great importance for the prisoners.

a. Places of Internment

Prisoners of war may be interned in camps which are fenced in, or they may be placed in other camps or establishments with an obligation not to go beyond certain bounds. They may be interned only in premises located on land, in a place where there are no extremes of climate and in reasonable conditions of safety.[80]

It is therefore prohibited to put prisoners on board vessels or in establishments located in the fighting zone. They shall have shelters against air bombardment, to the same extent as the civilian population.[81] The camps shall be indicated by the letters PW or PG, and the Detaining Powers shall communicate to each other the geographical location of prisoner of war camps.[82]

b. Quarters

Prisoners shall be quartered under conditions as favourable as those under which the forces of the Detaining Power are billeted in the area; the said conditions shall make allowance for the habits and customs of the prisoners and shall in no case be prejudicial to their health.[83]

Provision should be made for adequate surface and cubic space,[84] as well as for heating, lighting, precautions against fire hazard and protection from dampness.[85]

c. Food

Food rations shall be sufficient in quantity, quality and variety to keep prisoners in good health; account shall be taken of their habitual diet; prisoners who work shall be issued with appropriate rations.

Prisoners shall be associated with the preparation of their meals. Collective disciplinary measures affecting food are prohibited.[86] Canteens shall be installed in camps where prisoners may procure foodstuffs, soap and tobacco, and ordinary articles in daily use. The tariff shall not be in excess of local market prices.[87]

d. Clothing

Clothes, underwear and footwear shall be supplied in sufficient quantities by the Detaining Power, who shall make allowance for the climate and for the type of work the prisoners may be made to do.[88]

e. Hygiene and Medical Attention

All sanitary measures shall be taken to ensure the cleanliness and healthfulness of camps. Prisoners shall have for their use conveniences maintained in good and clean condition and suitable premises where they can wash themselves, take showers and do their personal laundry.[89] Every camp shall have an infirmary where prisoners may receive medical attention. Isolation wards shall be set aside for cases of contagious disease. Prisoners shall have the attention, preferably of medical personnel of their own nationality.[90] Medical inspections shall be made at least once a month; their purpose shall be, in particular, to supervise the general state of health, nutrition and cleanliness of prisoners and to detect contagious diseases.[91] Prisoners may not be prevented from presenting themselves to the medical authorities for examination.[92]

f. Medical Personnel and Chaplains

Members of the medical personnel and chaplains, while retained by the Detaining Power with a view to assisting prisoners of war, shall not be considered as prisoners of war, but shall receive the benefits of the Convention. They shall be granted all facilities necessary for the performance of their functions which they shall exercise with the agreement of and in liaison with the detaining authorities.[93] For example, they shall be granted a significant amount of liberty and shall have at their disposal the necessary means of transport for visiting prisoners,[94] they shall be allowed special facilities for correspondence[95] and shall not be compelled to carry out work.[96]

g. Religious Duties

Prisoners shall enjoy complete latitude in the exercise of their religious duties, on condition that they comply with the disciplinary routine prescribed by the detaining authorities. Premises shall be provided for religious services.[97] Chaplains who are retained with a view to assisting prisoners, and prisoners of war who are ministers of religion shall be at liberty to minister freely to the members of their community, and shall receive all necessary facilities to do so.[98] When no chaplains are retained and no minister of a particular faith is to be found among the prisoners, a minister of religion belonging to the Detaining Power, of the same faith as that of the prisoners or, if none is available, of a similar faith, shall be provided.[99]

h. Recreation, Study, Sports and Games

While respecting the individual preferences of every prisoner, the Detaining Power shall encourage the practice of intellectual, educational and recreative pursuits and sports and games amongst prisoners. Adequate premises and equipment shall be provided (library, sports equipment, reading rooms, playing fields, etc.).[100]

This provision does not authorize the Detaining Power to organize, for the purpose of imparting political or ideological instruction, lectures or meetings which prisoners would be compelled to attend to obtain or retain certain privileges.

i. Administration

Every camp shall be put under the immediate authority of a responsible commissioned officer belonging to the regular armed forces. Such officer shall have in his possession a copy of the Convention and of the Protocol and shall ensure that their provisions are applied. In every camp the text of the Convention and of the Additional Protocol shall be posted in the prisoners' own language. Similarly, regulations, orders, notices and publications of every kind concerning the prisoners shall be posted and issued to them in a language which they understand.[101]

Prisoners must show to all officers of the Detaining Power the external marks of respect provided for by the regulations applying to their own forces. Officer prisoners of war are bound to salute only officers of a higher rank. All prisoners must salute the camp commander regardless of his rank.[102]

j. Transfers

The transfer of prisoners from one camp to another shall always be effected humanely and in conditions not less favourable than those under which the forces of the Detaining Power are transferred. The prisoners shall be allowed to take with them their personal effects. The transfer shall not be prejudicial to their health, nor shall it be such as to increase the difficulty of their repatriation.[103] If the fighting draws closer to a camp, its prisoners shall not be transferred unless their transfer can be carried out in adequate conditions of safety, or if they are exposed to greater risks by remaining on the spot than by being transferred.[104]

k. Labour

The Detaining Power may utilize the labour of prisoners, taking into account their age, sex, physical aptitude and professional qualifications.[105] Non-commissioned officers shall only be required to do supervisory work, i.e. to be in charge of administrative and other tasks performed by other ranks; they shall in no way be made to do any manual labour.[106] Officers shall not be compelled to work, but they may ask for suitable work to be given them.[107]

l. Unauthorized Work

Labour imposed upon prisoners shall not be directly related to military operations. Furthermore, no prisoner may be employed on tasks which he is physically incapable of carrying out, or on humiliating labour or, unless he be a volunteer, on labour which is of an unhealthy or dangerous nature.[108]

m. Working Conditions

Prisoners must be granted suitable working conditions, especially as regards accommodation, food, clothing and equipment; they shall be given all the advantages granted to the workers of the Detaining Power and shall receive adequate working pay.[109] The duration of the daily labour of prisoners shall never be excessive. Conditions of labour shall not be rendered more arduous by disciplinary measures. National legislation concerning the protection of labour and the safety of workers shall be applied.[110] Prisoners who sustain accidents in connection with work shall receive all necessary care and a medical certificate shall be issued to them.[111] If any prisoner considers himself incapable of working, he shall be permitted to appear before the medical authorities of his camp, who may recommend that the prisoner be exempted from work.[112]

n. Financial Resources

Prisoners may be authorized to have in their possession a sum of money in cash, but the authorities may set a limit to the maximum amount each one may hold. Any amount in excess may be taken from a prisoner against delivery of a receipt but must be returned to him in the same currency at the end of captivity. A monthly advance of pay shall be paid to the prisoners.[113] These various amounts are often paid to prisoners as camp money, with which they can make purchases at the canteen.

o. Relations with the Exterior

Prisoners shall be allowed to send and receive mail. Correspondence may be limited to two letters and four cards monthly sent by each prisoner, should such a restriction be required by circumstances (e.g. if the means of transport or censorship services cannot cope with a big volume of correspondence).[114] Prisoners may be permitted to send telegrams should they be for a long time without news, or should they be unable to receive or to give news because they are at a great distance from their homes.[115] As a general rule, correspondence of prisoners shall be in their native language.[116] Facilities shall be provided to prisoners, such as permission to consult a lawyer, for the preparation, execution and transmission of legal documents, for example, powers of attorney and wills.[117] The censoring of correspondence and documents shall be done as quickly as possible, once only by each of the despatching State and the receiving State.[118]

p. Relief

Prisoners shall be permitted to receive individual and collective relief parcels. Relief consignments, which have at times been very substantial, in no way relieve the Detaining Power of its obligation to provide for prisoner maintenance free of charge.[119] Relief may consist of food, clothing, medical supplies, articles of religious, educational or recreational character, books, musical instruments, sports gear, and so forth.[120] The receipt, distribution or disposal of collective relief consignments shall be assigned to the prisoners' representatives.[121] The amount of relief may be limited only as proposed by the Protecting Power or the International Committee of the Red Cross in the interest of the prisoners themselves on account of exceptional strain on transport or communications.[122]

q. Exemption from Postal and Transport Charges

Mail and parcels to prisoners of war shall be exempt from postal charges. This exemption applies to letters and "declared value" parcels weighing up to 5 kg. It also applies to postal money orders to or from prisoners.[123] All relief shipments shall be exempt from import, customs and other dues.[124]

r. Censorship and Examination

Relief consignments to prisoners of war may be examined, but this shall not expose the goods contained in the parcels to deterioration; the examination shall be done in the presence of the addressee and delivery to him shall not be unduly delayed.[125]

s. Prohibition of Correspondence

Any prohibition of correspondence ordered by parties to the conflict, either for military or political reasons, shall be only temporary and its duration shall be as short as possible.

t. Complaints and Requests

Prisoners of war shall have the right to make known to the military authorities in whose power they are and to the Protecting Power's representatives their requests and complaints concerning conditions of captivity to which they are subjected. Such complaints and requests may be submitted in writing or by word of mouth to the officer in charge of the camp or to his superiors. They may be entrusted to the prisoners' representative for submission; they may not give rise to any punishment, even if they are unfounded.[126]

u. Prisoner of War Representatives

In all places where there are prisoners of war, the prisoners freely elect by secret ballot, every six months, representatives of their own nationality, language and customs. Every representative elected must be approved by the Detaining Power. In camps for officers, the senior officer among the prisoners shall be recognized as the prisoners' representative.[127]

Prisoners' representatives shall further the physical, spiritual and intellectual well-being of prisoners of war and shall represent the prisoners in dealing with the military authorities, the Protecting Powers, the International Committee of the Red Cross and any other organization providing them with assistance. In particular they shall deal with administrative questions such as requests for family news, the drawing up and forwarding of official documents, the forwarding of wills, complaints and requests,[128] management of the canteen,[129] taking possession, storage and distribution of collective relief,[130] transport of prisoners' community property in the event of transfer,[131] checking of prisoners' accounts,[132] taking charge of parcels and money remittances intended for prisoners of war undergoing confinement as a disciplinary punishment,[133] receipt of notification of judicial proceedings against prisoners of war,[134] proposal of wounded and sick prisoners of war for examination by mixed medical commissions.[135]

Prisoners' representatives shall be exempt from work if their duties take up all their time,[136] and they shall be granted all material facilities, particularly a certain freedom of movement and correspondence, for the discharge of their duties; they may appoint assistants.[137]

I. End of Captivity

a. Escape

It can happen that captivity is brought to an end by successful escape. Escape is considered as successful if a prisoner has rejoined his own army or that of an allied power, when he has left the territory under control of the Detaining Power or of its allies, or has joined a ship flying the flag of his own country or of an allied power in the territorial waters of the Detaining Power or its allies.[138]

Prisoners who have made good their escape in any of these ways and who are captured again shall not be liable to any punishment for their previous escape.[139] A prisoner of war who attempts to escape and is recaptured before making good his escape shall be liable only to disciplinary punishment. However he may be subjected to special surveillance, provided the guarantees laid down in the Convention are respected.[140]

b. Repatriation During Hostilities

Seriously wounded and sick prisoners shall be repatriated as soon as they are fit to travel. Other wounded and sick prisoners may be hospitalized in a neutral country.[141] Mixed medical commissions shall be set up to examine prisoners whose state of health may justify repatriation or hospitalization in a neutral country. No sick or injured prisoner of war may be repatriated against his will during hostilities, nor may he be employed on active military service after repatriations.[142]

c. Release and Repatriation at the Close of Hostilities

Prisoners of war shall be released and repatriated without delay after the cessation of active hostilities.[143] Any unwarranted delay in repatriation shall be deemed a grave breach of the Convention and the Protocol.[144] If parties to a conflict omit arrangements for repatriation from the agreement concluded on the cessation of hostilities the Detaining Power shall itself establish and execute without delay a plan of repatriation.[145] Conditions of repatriation shall be identical to those laid down for the transfer of prisoners of war.[146] Articles of value and any cash impounded from prisoners shall be restored to them[147] and they shall be allowed to take with them their personal effects and correspondence.

The plan for repatriation may set an order of priorities, giving preference to wounded and sick, followed by those who have been a long time in captivity, and finally to the older prisoners.

Prisoners undergoing punishment or awaiting trial for an indictable offence may be detained until the end of the proceedings or until punishment has been completed; their names shall be communicated to the prisoners' own governments.[148]

d. Deaths

In the event of the death of a prisoner of war, the body shall be medically examined to confirm death and enable a report to be made on the cause of death and, where necessary, establish identity.[149] A death certificate shall be drawn up with all required information for identification of the deceased, and showing the date and place of death, the cause of death, the date and place of burial and all particulars necessary to identify the grave.[150] Death certificates and wills shall be forwarded without delay to official information offices.

Dead prisoners of war shall be decently buried in individual graves which shall be suitably tended and marked. Bodies may be cremated only for imperative reasons of hygiene, on account of the religion of the deceased, or in accordance with his expressed wish.[151] Every death or serious injury of a prisoner caused by a sentry, another prisoner or any other person shall be immediately followed by an official inquiry.[152]

Notes

1. Additional Protocol I, art. 44, § 2.
2. Cf. Chapter VIII, p. 104 ff.
3. IIIrd Geneva Convention, art. 4 A, § 4.
4. IIIrd Geneva Convention, art. 4 A, § 5.
5. IIIrd Geneva Convention, art. 4 A, § 6.
6. IIIrd Geneva Convention, art. 4 B, § 1 and 2.
7. Additional Protocol I, art. 4, § 1 and 2.
8. Additional Protocol I, art. 41, § 13.
9. IInd Geneva Convention of 1949, art. 12.
10. Additional Protocol I, art. 42.
11. IIIrd Geneva Convention, art. 5, § 2; Additional Protocol I, art. 45.
12. In certain countries the fact of being taken prisoner is or was prejudicial to the person in question: in Japan, for instance, this was the case up to the 2nd World War. Even now military instructions forbid members of the armed forces to give themselves up to the enemy without having exhausted all means in their own defence.
13. IIIrd Geneva Convention, art. 82, § 1.
14. *Ibid.*, art. 87, § 2.
15. IIIrd Geneva Convention, art. 13, § 1.
16. IIIrd Geneva Convention, art. 13, § 1; Additional Protocol I, art. 11, § 1 and 4.
17. IIIrd Geneva Convention, art. 13, § 2.
18. *Ibid.*, art. 17, § 4.
19. *Ibid.*, art. 15 and 30.
20. *Ibid.*, art. 29.
21. *Ibid.*, art. 38.
22. *Ibid.*, art. 15 and 26.
23. *Ibid.*, art. 15 and 25.
24. *Ibid.*, art. 15 and 27.

25. *Ibid.*, art. 19, § 1.
26. *Ibid.*, art. 52 and 49.
27. *Ibid.*, art. 14, § 1.
28. *Ibid.*, art. 13, § 2.
29. *Ibid.*, art. 22, § 1.
30. *Ibid.*, art. 50 and 52.
31. *Ibid.*, art. 25, § 4.
32. *Ibid.*, art. 13, § 2.
33. *Ibid.*, art. 18, § 3 and 40.
34. *Ibid.*, art. 39, § 2 and 3.
35. *Ibid.*, art. 13, § 3.
36. Cf. p. 77 ff.
37. IIIrd Geneva Convention, art. 12, § 1.
38. IIIrd Geneva Convention, art. 129; Additional Protocol I, art. 86–89.
39. IIIrd Geneva Convention, art. 130; Additional Protocol I, art. 11 and 85.
40. IIIrd Geneva Convention, art. 12, § 2 and 3.
41. IIIrd Geneva Convention, art. 15.
42. IIIrd Geneva Convention, art. 16; Additional Protocol I, art. 75.
43. IIIrd Geneva Convention, art. 49.
44. *Ibid.*, art. 60.
45. *Ibid.*, art. 30.
46. *Ibid.*, art. 30.
47. *Ibid.*, art. 109.
48. *Ibid.*, art. 25 and 29.
49. *Ibid.*, art. 16.
50. *Ibid.*, art. 82.
51. *Ibid.*, art. 41.
52. *Ibid.*, art. 42.
53. *Ibid.*, art. 90.
54. *Ibid.*, art. 89.
55. *Ibid.*, art. 90.
56. *Ibid.*, art. 98.
57. *Ibid.*, art. 84 and 99.
58. *Ibid.*, art. 105.
59. *Ibid.*, art. 106.
60. *Ibid.*, art. 101.
61. *Ibid.*, art. 85.
62. *Ibid.*, art. 87, § 1.
63. *Ibid.*, art. 99, § 2.
64. *Ibid.*, art. 82. Cf. also the chapter XVI: Implementing international humanitarian law.
65. *Ibid.*, art. 6, § 7.
66. *Ibid.*, art. 17.
67. *Ibid.*, art. 18, § 1 and 3.
68. *Ibid.*, art. 18, § 3 and 4.
69. *Ibid.*, art. 19, § 1.
70. *Ibid.*, art. 20.
71. *Ibid.*, art. 70.
72. *Ibid.*, art. 122.
73. IIIrd Geneva Convention, art. 122; Additional Protocol I, art. 33.
74. IIIrd Geneva Convention, art. 122, § 3 and 9.
75. *Ibid.*, art. 122, § 7.
76. *Ibid.*, art. 122, § 1.

77. *Ibid.*, art. 123.
78. *Ibid.*, art. 123.
79. *Ibid.*, art. 125.
80. *Ibid.*, art. 21, 22 and 23.
81. *Ibid.*, art. 23, § 2.
82. *Ibid.*, art. 23, § 4.
83. *Ibid.*, art. 25, § 1.
84. *Ibid.*, art. 25, § 2.
85. *Ibid.*, art. 25, § 3.
86. *Ibid.*, art. 26, § 6.
87. *Ibid.*, art. 28.
88. *Ibid.*, art. 27.
89. *Ibid.*, art. 29.
90. *Ibid.*, art. 30.
91. *Ibid.*, art. 31.
92. *Ibid.*, art. 30, § 4.
93. *Ibid.*, art. 33, § 1.
94. *Ibid.*, art. 33, § 2 a.
95. *Ibid.*, art. 35.
96. *Ibid.*, art. 33, § 2 c.
97. *Ibid.*, art. 34.
98. *Ibid.*, art. 35 and 36.
99. *Ibid.*, art. 37.
100. *Ibid.*, art. 38.
101. *Ibid.*, art. 41.
102. *Ibid.*, art. 39, § 2 and 3.
103. *Ibid.*, art. 46 and 48.
104. *Ibid.*, art., 47.
105. *Ibid.*, art. 49.
106. *Ibid.*, art. 49, § 2.
107. *Ibid.*, art. 49, § 3.
108. *Ibid.*, art. 50, 52 and 55.
109. *Ibid.*, art. 51, 53 and 54.
110. *Ibid.*, art. 51 and 53.
111. *Ibid.*, art. 54.
112. *Ibid.*, art. 55.
113. *Ibid.*, art. 60.
114. *Ibid.*, art. 71, § 1.
115. *Ibid.*, art. 71, § 2.
116. *Ibid.*, art. 71, § 3.
117. *Ibid.*, art. 77.
118. *Ibid.*, art. 76.
119. *Ibid.*, art. 72, § 2.
120. *Ibid.*, art. 72.
121. *Ibid.*, art. 73.
122. *Ibid.*, art. 72, § 3.
123. *Ibid.*, art. 74, § 2.
124. *Ibid.*, art. 74, § 1.
125. *Ibid.*, art. 76, § 2.
126. *Ibid.*, art. 78.
127. *Ibid.*, art. 79.
128. *Ibid.*, art. 78, § 2 and 4.

129. *Ibid.*, art. 28, § 2.
130. *Ibid.*, art. 73, § 2.
131. *Ibid.*, art. 48, § 3.
132. *Ibid.*, art. 65, § 1.
133. *Ibid.*, art. 98, § 5.
134. *Ibid.*, art. 104, § 2.
135. *Ibid.*, art. 113, § 2 and 3.
136. *Ibid.*, art. 81, § 1.
137. *Ibid.*, art. 81, § 2.
138. *Ibid.*, art. 91, § 1.
139. *Ibid.*, art. 91, g 2.
140. *Ibid.*, art. 92.
141. *Ibid.*, art. 109 and 110.
142. *Ibid.*, art. 109 and 117.
143. *Ibid.*, art. 118.
144. Additional Protocol I, art. 85, § 4 b.
145. IIIrd Geneva Convention, art. 118, § 2.
146. *Ibid.*, art. 119, § 1.
147. *Ibid.*, art. 119, § 2.
148. *Ibid.*, art. 119, § 5 and 6.
149. *Ibid.*, art. 120, § 3.
150. *Ibid.*, art. 120, § 2.
151. *Ibid.*, art. 120, § 4 and 5.
152. *Ibid.*, art. 121.

CHAPTER XII

PROTECTION OF THE VICTIMS OF ARMED CONFLICTS

III – CIVILIAN POPULATION

OJI UMOZURIKE

A. Introduction

The involvement of civilian populations in armed conflicts has been intensified by two historical developments. The first is the idea of popular sovereignty whereby major acts of state, such as the declaration of war and the protection of territorial integrity and independence, are no longer the exclusive concerns of absolute rulers but of the people whose views are expressed through their accredited representatives. Armies are no longer the instruments sovereigns use to satisfy their lust for power and conquest; they are no longer cannon fodder manipulated by sovereigns. The army has become much closer to the people from whom the soldiers are recruited. The dangers to which the army is exposed are not now as remote from civilians as they used to be. The importance of foreign mercenaries in national defence or in other aspects of national policy has correspondingly decreased. In wars of national liberation against colonial powers or against occupying or racist regimes, civilians are exposed to reprisals because of the proximity of zones of military operations to the places where civilians live.

The second development is the improvement in military technology – in weaponry, delivery and mobility. The intensification of warfare from the days of bows and arrows, swords, cannons, muskets and breech-loading guns, to today's machine-guns, warships, submarines, aircraft, intercontinental ballistic missiles, and even artificial satellites, has eroded the protection of civilians. It is now hardly necessary for armies to be ranged against each other in pre-determined battle-fields within sight of each other, as warfare can now be carried on simultaneously over wider areas – villages, towns, cities and regions in which civilians are invariably present.

The need to devise and maintain safeguards for civilians becomes urgent, both as a humanitarian imperative and as an economic measure. The aim of warfare is to institute peace in the manner envisaged by the belligerent. Lack of humanitarian considerations in the conduct of war against combatants, and especially for civilians, who are always in the majority, jeopardizes the return to peace and concord in both internal and international relations. It is necessary to economize on military resources which, far from being unlimited, are often scarce. To obtain maximum effect, war implements should be used against combatants rather than against civilians.[1]

B. Definition of Civilians and Civilian Populations

Who is a civilian and what constitutes a civilian population? The Geneva Convention Relative to the Protection of Civilian Persons in Time of War of 12 August 1949[2] refers to two categories of civilians. One, designated "protected persons", consists of persons who find themselves, in the event of a conflict or occupation, in the hands of a party to the conflict or Occupying Power of which they are not nationals. This excludes nationals of a state not bound to the Convention, nationals of a neutral state, and nationals of a co-belligerent state having normal diplomatic representation in the state. Special safeguards for this category are laid down in Part III of the Convention. The second category, which includes the first, comprises the entire populations of countries in conflict, regardless of nationality, race, religion or political opinion, and is protected under Part II.

Article 50 of the 1977 Protocol to the Geneva Conventions of 12 August 1949 and Relating to the Protection of Victims of International Armed Conflicts (hereafter referred to as Protocol I) defines a civilian population:

> "1. A civilian is any person who does not belong to one of the categories of persons referred to in Article 4 A (1), (2), (3) and (b) of the Third Convention and in Article 43 of this Protocol." [These consist of members of the armed forces, militias, volunteer corps, including those of organized resistance movements fulfilling certain conditions, and inhabitants who spontaneously take up arms to resist an invader]. "In case of doubt whether a person is a civilian, that person shall be considered to be a civilian.
> 2. The civilian population comprises all persons who are civilians.
> 3. The presence within the civilian population of individuals who do not come within the definition of civilians does not deprive the population of its civilian character."

It may be said in brief that a civilian is a person who is not a member of the armed forces and does not belong to the militia, volunteer corps or organized resistance movement whether or not such movement is recognized by the adverse party. The term excludes an inhabitant of a non-occupied territory who spontaneously takes up arms to resist an invader. A civilian is thus a person not directly involved in hostilities and a civilian population consists of such persons. The basic rule is that the parties to a conflict should distinguish between civilians and civilian objects on the one hand and combatants and military objects on the other, and should direct their operations against the latter. The safeguards for the former are operative whether the conflict is of an international character or not, and in whatever territory they may be, whether the war is specifically declared or not, and whether or not a party to the conflict is recognized by the adversary.[3]

C. Pre–1949 Safeguards for Civilians

The protection of civilians in multilateral conventions dates back to the Geneva Convention for the Amelioration of the Condition of the Wounded in Armies in the Field of 22 August 1864.[4] At that time, civilians were usually at risk if they ventured near the battle-fields or if combatants took shelter in their homes after a battle. The Convention therefore provided that inhabitants who brought help to the wounded "shall be respected and shall remain free".[5] In addition, generals of belligerent powers were to appeal to their humanity and inform them of the immunity which humane conduct conferred upon them. A civilian giving shelter to a wounded combatant was protected and exempted from billeting or from paying war contributions. The aim was to encourage humanitarian involvement of civilians in support of wounded and sick combatants.

The Regulations Respecting the Laws and Customs of War on Land[6] annexed to the Hague Convention of 1907 (Convention IV), prohibit the attack or bombardment of undefended towns, villages, dwellings or building. They give protection to inhabitants of occupied territories, who are not to be compelled to give information about the other belligerent nor to swear allegiance to the occupying power. Property rights, religious convictions and family honour and rights are to be respected. Pillaging is prohibited. Collective punishment for the acts of individuals is also prohibited unless the persons involved are jointly and severally responsible. There are to be no requisitions in kind or services except for the needs of the army of occupation, and taxes and tolls can only be collected if they are for the needs of the state. While Convention IV of the Hague introduced new rules, it was not an exhaustive codification of existing rules. Cases not specifically dealt with were to be considered under customary rules.[7]

D. The Geneva Convention Relative to the Protection of Civilian Persons in Time of War of 12 August 1949

Developments in the law of war have always followed experiences gained in conflicts. The wars of the 19th century and the Russo-Japanese war (1904–5) preceded the Hague Convention of 1907. The Treaty of Versailles concluded the First World War and embodied the Covenant of the League of Nations.[8] Article 25 required members to encourage and promote the establishment and cooperation of National Red Cross Societies with a view, *inter alia*, to mitigating suffering. The horrors of the Second World War led to yet more detailed provisions for the protection of persons affected by conflicts and the Geneva Convention Relative to the Protection of Civilians in Time of War (hereinafter called the Fourth Convention) contains 159 articles for the safeguard of civilians.

Article 27 provides general safeguards for protected persons. Their persons, honour, family rights, religious convictions and customs should be respected. They shall be humanely treated and protected against violence, threats, insults and public curiosity.

Women shall be protected, especially against rape, enforced prostitution and indecent assault. Protected persons shall be treated with consideration without adverse distinction based on race, religion or political conviction, but without prejudice to any measures of control and security necessitated by the state of emergency.

No physical or moral coercion is permissible against protected persons, even to obtain information. Under Article 32, the parties "specifically agree that each of them is prohibited from taking any measure of such a character as to cause the physical suffering or extermination of protected persons in their hands". The prohibition applies "not only to murder, torture, corporal punishment, mutilation and medical or scientific experiments not necessitated by the medical treatment of a protected person, but also to any other measures of brutality whether applied by civilian or military agents".

A protected person may not be punished for an offence he has not personally committed, and collective penalties, reprisals, pillaging and the taking of hostages are prohibited. Protected persons shall be given the facility for making application to the Protecting Power or to humanitarian organizations, such as the International Committee of the Red Cross, whose agents, and those of other organizations giving spiritual succour, should be granted access to them.

Articles 35 to 46 deal with the treatment of aliens in the territory of a party to a conflict. They are entitled to leave unless the Detaining Power has good cause to refuse for reasons based on national interest. Repatriation shall be carried out in hygienic conditions and in a safe manner. Non-repatriated persons are entitled to certain benefits – they shall be allowed to receive relief and necessary medical attention and to practice their religion without hindrance. Children, pregnant women and mothers of young children shall receive preferential treatment to the same extent as nationals of the state. Protected persons may be compelled to work only under the same conditions as nationals. They shall not be transferred to a Power which is not party to the Convention. This is to ensure that the guarantees contained in the Convention are not evaded. Nor may a protected person be transferred to a state where he fears persecution. The right of extradition for criminal offences under pre-existing treaties is not impaired. Refugees who do not enjoy the protection of any government are also protected even if they otherwise belong to the enemy state.

However, civilians can be interned, if the security of the Detaining Power makes it "absolutely necessary". The detaining authority may have recourse to this measure – it being the most severe one it can use against protected persons – if it has serious reasons to believe that the activities of these persons pose a threat to its security (for example, subversive activities such as espionage or sabotage). Just being a national of the enemy state is not sufficient reason justifying internment. Moreover, according to Article 43, any person interned shall be entitled to have an appropriate court reconsider his case at least twice a year.

Section III of Part III deals with civilians in occupied territories. This is a particularly sensitive area that is difficult to control. The transfer or deportation of protected persons from occupied territory to the territory of the Occupying Power is strictly prohibited. The Nazis did just this during the Second World War and used such persons in manning their war machines. Nor should the Occupying Power transfer its own population to the occupied territory.

There is special protection for mothers of young children, for expectant mothers and for children whose identification marks and parentage should be documented. Their continued education, if possible by persons of their own language and religion, should be ensured.

Protected persons shall not be compelled to serve in the armed forces or auxiliary forces of the Occupying Power, or be compelled to work except in categories of jobs necessary for the occupying army, for the public utility services or for the feeding, sheltering, clothing, transportation or health of the population. The right of a worker to apply to the representative of a Protecting Power for intervention is preserved.

The destruction of property – public, private or collectively owned – is prohibited. The Occupying Power should ensure that food and medical supplies are available for the civilian population. Such necessities may not be requisitioned except in compelling circumstances for the use of the occupation forces and the administration personnel and with compensation, and provided civilian requirements are already satisfied. Civilian hospitals may be temporarily requisitioned for the use of military personnel. The Occupying Power shall allow ministers of religion to cater for the needs of detainees.

To obviate the abuses that occurred during the Second World War, Article 54 provides that the Occupying Power may not alter the status of public officials or judges in the occupied territories, or in any way apply sanctions to them, should they resign for reasons of conscience. In other words, they should retain the status they held before the occupation and maintain their independence. However, the Occupying Power may requisition public officials for public services or remove them from their posts for as long as the occupation lasts.

According to Article 64, the Occupying Power shall respect the penal laws in force, except for reasons affecting its security. It should also maintain the national tribunals.

The death penalty shall be applicable only to persons at least 18 years old who are found guilty of espionage, voluntary homicide or serious acts of sabotage and provided that such offences are punishable by death under the law of the occupied country.

The Occupying Power shall not prosecute protected persons for acts committed before the occupation, with the exception of breaches of the laws and customs of war.

Concerning legal guarantees, accused persons shall have the right of defence, a proper trial, the right of appeal, assistance by the Protecting Power and proper treatment in prison.

There are provisions to allow relief organizations to carry out their work for the needy. The passage of relief shall be facilitated, allowed exemption from tax or customs duties, except in exceptional circumstances. Relief supplies may not be requisitioned except in cases of urgent necessity. Elaborate provisions are made for trials and sentencing, the right of appeal and the right to apply for pardon by those accused by the Occupying Power of committing crimes.

An important innovation brought by the Fourth Convention is that all civilians deprived of their freedom, for any reason whatever, henceforth enjoy a status similar to that of prisoners of war. Section IV of Part III is entirely devoted to the treatment of internees.

Regulations on the treatment of interned persons provide for the retention of their civil status, for their maintenance in clean and healthy surroundings, for grouping of nationals or of families, for the supply of adequate food and clothing, and for adequate religious, intellectual and physical activities. Their personal belongings, including monies, may be retained and they may even receive allowances to purchase necessities.

Detention administration should be the responsibility of an officer of the military or civil administration of the Detaining Power. The text of the Convention, including agreements concluded under it, shall be posted inside the internment camp in the detainees' own language. There is no provision for detainees whose language does not exist in written form or into whose language the Convention and the regulations have to be translated. Presumably the language of the former colonial power of such territory will suffice. Dangerous physical exertion, physical or moral victimization, tattooing or imprinting markings on the bodies of internees, and similar inhumane acts are prohibited. Internees are encouraged to channel their grievances, if possible, through committees elected by them to the detaining authorities.

Chapter VIII of Section IV guarantees certain minimum relations with the outside world through the receipt of parcels and visits. Under Chapter X, if detainees have to be transferred, the operation must be carried out humanely, bearing in mind their health, general condition of safety and availability of transport.

The wills of detainees shall be put in an appropriate place for safe-keeping and a doctor's certificate issued for every death. The dead shall be entitled to decent burial or cremation in accordance with the religion of the deceased, if that is possible. Single and marked graves are preferred to collective graves, depending on the circumstances.

Internment shall cease as soon as hostilities are over. But those against whom penal proceedings are pending, or who have been sentenced to be deprived of their liberty may be detained until the determination of their case or the completion of their sentence. The parties shall then ensure the repatriation of the detainees to their last place of residence or facilitate such repatriation. The parties are required to set up national bureaux through which information can be obtained or given about detainees subject to security arrangements, and a Central Information Agency shall be created in a neutral country, its duty being to collect and collate information obtained from private or official sources and transmit it to the countries of origin or to relations of the persons affected, provided such information is not detrimental to the persons concerned.

The Convention also provides for the protection of civilian populations in general, regardless of nationality, race, religion or political belief. The Contracting Parties shall, in time of conflict or peace, establish hospitals and possibly safety zones and localities for the protection of the wounded, sick, aged, young persons, expectant mothers and mothers of young children. Such hospitals and zones or localities shall not be the object of attack. There are also safeguards for hospital staff and for land, sea and air transports and conveying wounded and sick civilians, and provisions for the free passage of consignments of medical and hospital stores, essential food-stuffs and clothing, and objects necessary for religious worship intended for civilian populations. There are measures relating to children's welfare – their maintenance, education and religious upbringing, if possible, under the supervision of persons of a similar cultural tradition.

All persons are entitled to exchange news of a personal nature with their families and such correspondence shall be transmitted speedily. Should it be necessary, family correspondence may be limited in frequency and restricted to standard message forms. In particular, each party shall facilitate enquiries by members of dispersed families with a view to renewing contact, subject to security regulations.

The provisions discussed above relate to conflicts of an international character. Article 3 which is common to all the Conventions relates to armed conflicts not of an international character i.e., internal armed conflicts such as civil wars and insurrections. Persons not taking part in hostilities, including civilians, are in all circumstances to be treated humanely without any adverse discrimination based on race, colour, creed, sex or social status. Violence to life and person, outrages upon personal dignity, the taking of hostages and conviction without proper trial are prohibited. The wounded and the sick shall be collected and cared for and impartial humanitarian organization shall be allowed to render their services. The parties to the conflict should, as much as possible, adopt the more detailed provisions relating to international conflicts. The observance of these rules in no way affects the legal status of the parties so that an incumbent government, for instance, need not fear that its observance of the Conventions in its dealings with insurgents would amount to recognition.[9]

As already pointed out, the Geneva Red Cross Conventions were considerably expanded after the experience of the Second World War of which Europe was the main theatre. The experience of European civilians in occupied territories was therefore uppermost in the minds of the legislators laying down the rules.

E. Protocols Additional to the Geneva Conventions of 12 August 1949, and Relating to the Protection of Victims of International Armed Conflicts (Protocol I)

The outbreak of wars in certain regions of the world revealed the inadequacy of the four Geneva Conventions of 1949. More experience was gained from international wars, especially the Vietnam war and the recurrent Arab-Israeli conflicts in the Middle East. The liberation wars in Southern Africa had their impact, for the leaders of liberation movements were for the first time invited to take part in conferences. Experience was also gained from civil wars. The provision of relief for civilians affected by the Nigerian Civil War encountered new difficulties. Resolutions had come from International Red Cross Conferences and from the General Assembly of the United Nations urging the updating of humanitarian law and its more effective application.[10] The Geneva Conference on the Reaffirmation and Development of International Humanitarian Law commenced discussions in 1974 on a negotiating text that was produced by the International Committee of the Red Cross. The two Protocols were approved on 10 June 1977.

Protocol I deals with conflicts of an international character (these now include liberation wars fought by people against colonialist regimes in the exercise of their right to self-determination or against alien occupation). Part IV of Protocol I deals specifically with the civilian population. Protocol II deals with conflicts of a non-international character.

The provisions relating to the protection of civilian populations against the consequences of war – a vitally important body of law – are covered in other chapters of this book.

The Protocol supplements the relief provisions of the Fourth Convention. The basic requirements are that an Occupying Power should ensure, to the fullest extent and without adverse distinction, the provision of food, clothing and other essentials for the civilian populations. Relief operations may be conducted with the consent of the parties and offers of such relief are not to be considered as interference or as unfriendly acts. Parties to a conflict "shall allow and facilitate rapid and unimpeded passage of all relief consignments, equipment and personnel provided in accordance with this Section, even if such assistance is destined for the civilians of the adverse Party". The duty to allow the passage of relief is accompanied by the right to prescribe technical arrangements, including search, and the right to make distribution conditional on local supervision. Relief consignments shall, however, in no case be diverted to other ends except in cases of great urgency and in the interest of the civilian population concerned. The parties shall facilitate effective international co-ordination and collaboration in relief matters. While relief personnel are to be protected, they must refrain from activities that compromise the security of their area of operation.

The operation of relief for enemy-occupied territory is provided for in the Protocol and in the Fourth Convention. For relief to qualify for immunity and protection, it is necessary that it should go to civilians and not to combatants. There are enormous problems in ensuring this. If the whole population were involved in the war effort, it is arguable that the adversary could, if it were in its power to do so, deny the passage of relief to that population. An army could become merged with the population from which it constantly draws strength to such an extent that relief to the civilian population would constitute delayed relief to the army as well. The provision of relief to the civilian population of the weaker adversary, especially if such relief were crucial, might be a mere palliative that would prolong the fighting capacity of the side that was anyway doomed to lose the conflict. There might be a point where the decision to continue relief operations becomes inseparable from the choice by the relief operator as to whether the party receiving relief could be expected to win or lose. Humanitarian relief could become inextricably involved with power politics. In such situations, the relief operator would invariably be exposed to suspicion and criticism by one or the other party. Since relief has to be conducted with the consent of the parties, it follows that the civilian population would stand to suffer if agreement were unreasonably withheld by one or both sides.

The question may then be asked: is starvation a legitimate instrument of warfare? The old rules seemed to allow it and belligerents did not hesitate to impose a blockade to promote their military objective. One eminent writer in 1945 stated: "If the (non-combatant) lives in a besieged locality he may legally be starved or bombed. If he lives in a country which does not grow enough food to support its population, a blockade can legally starve him to death".[11] We are now a long way from 1945, especially with 1949 and 1977 as landmarks. The present situation is that starvation may be used as an instrument of warfare against combatants, but not against civilians or combatants who have surrendered or have been rendered *hors de combat*. The starvation of the last two groups would constitute a grave breach of the Conventions and of the Protocols. It also falls within the prohibitions of the Genocide Convention of 1948,[12] Article II (c) of which outlaws acts "deliberately inflicting on a group conditions of life calculated to bring about its physical destruction in whole or in part ".[13]

Section III of Part IV of Protocol I provides additional safeguards for civilians of specified categories. It deals with the protection of refugees and the reunion of dispersed families. Fundamental guarantees for persons not otherwise specifically protected, like mercenaries, include humane treatment, non-discrimination on the basis of race, sex, creed, political opinion, social status or other criteria. In particular, the following grave acts against civilians are prohibited: acts of violence to life, health, physical or mental well-being, such as murder, torture, corporal punishment and mutilation. Outrages upon personal dignity, collective punishments, the taking of hostages or threats to commit such acts are also prohibited. The right to fair trial is guaranteed without prejudice to any more favourable rules that may be provided by international law. International law prescribes minimum standards of treatment for foreigners; such treatment must not fall below the minimum standards of civilized nations.[14]

Women are protected from indecent assault such as rape and forced prostitution, and no sentences of death may be passed on pregnant women. Children also are entitled to special protection. No child under 15 years of age may be recruited into the army and no death sentence may be passed on a youth less than 18 years of age. The mass evacuation of children to a foreign country is prohibited except as a temporary measure by the state of which they are nationals. If they have to be evacuated, their education and moral and spiritual well-being must be adequately catered for, and appropriate precautions taken, such as the provision of information and identification marks, to facilitate their repatriation.

Article 79 provides safeguards for journalists to whom identity cards should normally be issued. When engaged in dangerous professional missions in areas of armed conflict, they should be treated as civilians and protected as such. For their part, they must take no action that would adversely affect their status as civilians.

Article 85 of Protocol I, dealing with repression of breaches of the Conventions and of the Protocol, enumerates a list of grave breaches which are considered to be war crimes and therefore strictly prohibited. Article 85 (4) (c) provides that "practices of *apartheid* and other inhuman and degrading practices involving outrages upon personal dignity, based on racial discrimination", when committed wilfully and in violation of the Conventions or the Protocol, also constitute a grave breach. The practice of apartheid has been generally condemned by the international community as a flagrant breach of fundamental human rights.

F. Protocols Additional to the Geneva Conventions of 12 August 1949, and Relative to the Protection of Victims of Non-international Armed Conflicts (Protocol II)

Protocol II of 1977 containing 28 articles is devoted to conflicts of a non-international character, like Article 3 common to all four of the 1949 Geneva Conventions. It offers civilians the most essential guarantees in international conflicts; these include the prohibition of inhumanity, violence to life, health and physical or mental well-being, collective punishments, taking of hostages, terrorism, outrages on personal dignity, pillage or threats to commit such acts. Curiously, slavery and the slave trade in all its forms are also prohibited. These provisions are relevant to countries where these practices still continue. Certain aspects of labour practices in colonial or apartheid regimes are proximate to slavery and the slave trade and would appear to be prohibited by the Protocol in the event of internal conflict.[15]

Part IV of the Protocol lays down further guarantees for civilian populations. For as long as they take no direct part in hostilities, they shall not be the object of attacks or threats of violence. It is prohibited to starve civilians as a method of combat. The destruction, attack, removal or immobilization of objects indispensable to the survival of the civilian population such as foodstuffs, agricultural areas, crops, livestock, drinking water, installations and supplies and irrigation works are prohibited (Article 14 Protocol II). Works and installation containing dangerous forces, cultural objects and places of worship are also protected. The displacement of civilians for reasons connected with the conflict is not allowed except if required by extreme necessity. Article 18 safeguards the operation of relief societies. If the civilian population suffers undue hardship from a lack of essential supplies, relief action of an exclusively humanitarian and impartial character shall be undertaken with the consent of the parties.[16]

G. Some Observations on the Protection of Civilians

The first remark to be made is that with conventional weapons it is easier to draw distinctions between civilians and civilian objects on the one hand, and combatants and military objects on the other. With weapons of mass destruction it becomes extremely difficult to make the distinction. Article 55 of Protocol I provides as follows:

> "1. Care shall be taken in warfare to protect the natural environment against widespread, long-term and severe damage. This protection includes a prohibition of the use of methods or means of warfare which are intended or may be expected to cause such damage to the natural environment and thereby to prejudice the health or survival of the population.
>
> 2. Attacks against the natural environment by way of reprisals are prohibited."

The use of weapons of mass destruction at present possessed by only a few Powers, will invariably be a breach of these provisions. It has been argued that the question of control of such arms should be left to the Powers that possess them. The better view seems to be that the ability to cause mass destruction is a matter of international concern and the destruction or control of such weapons should be internationally conducted. The real solution is the complete destruction of these weapons and an absolute ban on their production. The long-term interests of all nations demand this direct approach but the Powers possessing them or those that have acquired the scientific know-how are quite likely to reject the suggestion.

It is now possible to shoot war-heads from great distances and it is almost impossible for continental ballistic missiles released from high flying objects, from submarines or from underground platforms to make any distinction in favour of civilians. The greater the distance from which war-heads are released, the greater the difficulty of protecting civilians and civilian objects in the vicinity of the target areas.

Objects indispensable to the survival of the civilian population are protected under Article 54 of Protocol I, but derogations from this are permissible if dictated by imperative military necessity. Obviously the military commander will have to make an assessment and take the crucial decision. His objectiveness may be impaired under the stress of the conflict. Similarly, the provision that civilian populations could be moved if necessitated by the military situation, might be subjectively interpreted by the military commander.

The special relationship between liberation movements and the civilian population in guerrilla warfare presents special difficulties. Without civilian cover it is almost impossible for guerrillas to operate. The temptation is therefore great to punish the civilian population as a deterrent, much like emptying the water in order to catch the fish. Colonial powers frequently resorted to this strategy in colonial or anti-liberation wars. The distinction of colonizers and colonized along racial lines has exposed white civilians in isolated communities to attacks by liberation movements in the dependent territories of Southern Africa. It is imperative that liberation movements, even if they cannot become parties to the Conventions, should respect them in order to benefit from the provisions favourable to them and enhance their respectability as alternative governments. That their leaders have already proclaimed their adherence to the Conventions and the Protocols raises hopes for the greater security of white civilian populations.[17]

There has tended to be insufficient international concern in conflicts of a non-international character where the economic interests of outside Powers are not affected. Apart from economic interests, States have tended to show concern where they have an affinity or, in some cases, a common religious belief, with a party embroiled in civil conflict. According to present rules of international law, international conflict endangering world peace and security should be the concern of the international community. Civil conflicts arising from a breach of international norms are also matters of international concern. These principles reinforce the provisions for the observance of the Conventions and the Protocols. The narrow interpretation given to 'special interests' as ground for the right to enforce the provisions of the mandate system in Namibia by the International Court of Justice is now generally discredited.[18]

The Protocols are a radical step forward in the humanitarian protection of civilians caught up in armed conflicts. The humanitarian march towards fuller protection must continue with the active participation of States, liberation movements and humanitarian organizations.

Notes

1. See, further, Almond Jr., H.H., 'Law and Armed Conflict: Some of the Shared Policies'. *Case Western Reserve Journal of International Law* (Cleveland), Vol. 9, No. 2, 1977, pp. 175–203; Schwarzenberger, G., 'From the Laws of War to the Law of Armed Conflict' (Chapt. 10) in Schwarzenberger, G., *International Law and Order*, New York, Washington, Praeger, 1971, pp. 169–184.

2. *United Nations Treaty Series*, Vol. 75, pp. 287–417. *The Laws of Armed Conflicts, A Collection of Conventions, Resolutions and Other Documents*, Edited by D. Schindler and J. Toman, 3rd edition, Dordrecht, Martinus Nijhoff Publishers, Geneva, Henry Dunant Institute, 1988, pp. 495–556. *International Red Cross Handbook*, 12th edition, Geneva, ICRC, League of Red Cross Societies, 1983, pp. 136–194.

3. See also Mallison, W.T., The Humanitarian Law of Armed Conflict Concerning the Protection of Civilians, in a panel discussion on Humanitarian Law of Armed Conflict, *The International Lawyer*, (Chicago), Vol. XI, No. 1, 1977, pp. 102–105.

4. For full text see *The Laws of Armed Conflicts, A Collection of Conventions, Resolutions and Other Documents*, Edited by D. Schindler and J. Toman, 3rd edition, Dordrecht, Martinus Nijhoff Publishers, Geneva, Henry Dunant Institute, 1987, pp. 279–283. *International Red Cross Handbook*, 12th edition, Geneva, ICRC, League of Red Cross Societies, 1983, pp. 19–20.

5. Article 5 of the Geneva Convention of 22 August 1864, for the Amelioration of the Condition of the Wounded in Armies in the field.

6. For full text see *International Red Cross Handbook*, 12th edition, Geneva, ICRC, League of Red Cross Societies, 1983, pp.323–332; *The Laws of Armed Conflicts, A Collection of Conventions, Resolutions and Other Documents*, Edited by D. Schindler and J. Toman, 3rd edition, Dordrecht, Martinus Nijhoff Publishers, Geneva, Henry Dunant Institute, 1988, pp. 75–98.

7. On the declaratory nature of the Hague Conventions, see the cases of L.v.K. (Bulgarian Occupation of Greece); Greece, Court of Alleap of Thrace, Judgment No. 21 of 1947. *Annual Digest and Reports of Public International Law Cases*, Vol. 14, London, Butterworth, 1947, pp. 242–245; V.v.O. (Italy in Corfu Case), Greece, Court of First Instance of Corfu; Judgment No. 163 of 1947; *Annual Digest and Reports of Public International Law Cases*, Vol. 14, (London, Butterworth) 1947, pp. 264–265.

8. *The Consolidated Treaty Series*, Vol. 225, 1919, pp. 189–394; T.S. 4 (1919), Cmd. 153.

9. See also Lauterpacht, H., 'The Problem of the Revision of the Law of War', *British Yearbook of International Law*, (London) Vol. XXIX, 1952, pp. 360–382; Yingling, R.T. and Ginnane, R.W., 'The Geneva Conventions of 1949', *American Journal of International Law* (Washington), Vol. 46, 1952, pp. 393–427; Gutteridge, J.A.C., 'The Geneva Conventions of 1949', *British Yearbook of International Law*, (London), Vol. XXVI, 1949, pp. 294–326; Krafft, A., 'The Present Position of the Red Cross Geneva Conventions' *Transactions of the Grotius Society* (London), Vol. 37, 1951, pp. 134–147; Schwarzenberger, G., 'Neo-Barbarism and International Law', *Yearbook of World Affairs* (London), Vol. 22, 1968, pp. 191–213; Umozurike, U.O., 'The 1949 Geneva Conventions and Africa', *Indian Journal of International Law* (New Delhi), Vol. XI, 1971, pp. 205–218.

10. See resolutions of the XXth and XXIst International Red Cross Conferences held in Vienna 1965 *(International Red Cross Handbook*, 12th edition, Geneva, ICRC, League of Red Cross Societies, 1983, pp. 625–627, *The Laws of Armed Conflict, A Collection of Conventions, Resolutions and Other Documents*, Edited by D. Schindler and J. Toman, 3rd edition, Dordrecht, Martinus Nijhoff Publishers, Geneva, Henry Dunant Institute, 1988, pp. 259–260) and Istanbul 1969 (*International Red Cross Handbook*, 12th edition, Geneva, ICRC, League of Red Cross Societies, 1983, p. 627) and also the United Nations General Assembly Resolutions 2444 (XXIII) of 19 December 1968 and 2675 (XXV) of 9 December 1970. *The Laws of Armed Conflicts. A Collection of Conventions, Resolutions and Other Documents*, Edited by D. Schindler and J. Toman, 3rd edition, Dordrecht, Martinus Nijhoff Publishers, Geneva, Henry Dunant Institute, 1988, pp. 263–264, 267–268.

11. Nurrick, L., 'The Distinction Between Combatant and Non-combatant in the Law of War'. *American Journal of International Law* (Washington, D.C.), Vol. 39, 1945, p. 696.

12. For the full text see U.N.T.S., Vol. 78, p. 277; *The Laws of Armed Conflicts. A Collection of Conventions, Resolutions and Other Documents* Edited by D. Schindler and J. Toman, 3rd edition, Dordrecht, Martinus Nijhoff Publishers, Geneva, Henry Dunant Institute, 1988, pp. 231–235.

13. See also Rosenblad, E., 'Starvation as a method of Warfare: Conditions for regulations by Convention', *International Lawyer* (Chicago), Vol. 7 No. 2, 1973, pp. 252–270.

14. For these minimum standards, see e.g., Roy, G., 'Is the Law of Responsibility of States for Injuries to Aliens a Part of Universal International Law?'. *American Journal of International Law*, (Washington) Vol. 55, 1961, p. 863; L.F.H. Neer and Pauline Neer v. United Mexican States, 15 October 1926, in: *Report of International Arbitral Awards*, New York, United Nations, 1951, Vol. IV, p. 60–66; Thomas H. Youmans (U.S.A.) v. United Mexican States, 23 November 1926, *Ibid.*, pp. 110–117; Harry Roberts (U.S.A.) v. United Mexican States, 2 November 1926, *Ibid.*, pp. 77–81.

15. The policy of paying lower wages to non-whites in South Africa and in Namibia under South African rule is reminiscent of the exploitation of slave labour.

16. For articles on the preparatory conferences see Suter, Keith D., 'An enquiry into the meaning of the phrase 'Human Rights in Armed Conflicts", *Revue de Droit Pénal Militaire et de Droit de la Guerre* (Bruxelles), Vol. XV, No. 3–4, 1976, pp. 393–439; Aldrich, G.H., 'Establishing Legal Norms through Multinational Negotiations: The Laws of War', *Case Western Reserve Journal of International Law* (Cleveland), Vol. 9, No. 1, 1977, pp. 9–16; Reed, Walter, 'Laws of War: The Developing Law of Armed Conflict – Some Current Problems'. *Case Western Reserve Journal of International Law* (Cleveland), Vol. 9, No. 1, 1977, pp. 17–38, 175–251; Forsythe D.P. 'The 1974 Diplomatic Conference on Humanitarian Law: Some observations'. *AJIL*, Vol. 69, No. 1, 1975, pp. 77–91; Forsythe, D.P., 'Support for a Humanitarian *Jus in Bello*', *International Lawyer* (Chicago) Vol. XI, No. 4, 1977, pp. 723–728; Pictet, J.S., 'Fresh Aspect of International Humanitarian Law', *International Review of the Red Cross* (Geneva), No. 199, 1977, pp. 339–401; Malisson, W.T., 'The Humanitarian Law of Armed Conflict Concerning the Protection of Civilians', *International Lawyer* (Chicago), Vol. XI, No. 1, 1977, pp. 102–106; Forsythe, D.P., 'Three Sessions of Legislating Humanitarian Law: Forward March, Retreat, or Parade Rest?', *International Lawyer* (Chicago), Vol. XI, No. 1, 1977, pp. 131–142: Prugh, C.S., 'Current Initiatives to Reaffirm and Develop International Humanitarian Law Applicable in Armed Conflict', *International Lawyer* (Chicago), Vol.VIII, No. 2, 1974, pp. 262–267.

17. On the liberation movements and the Geneva Conventions see Abi-Saab, G., 'Wars of National liberation and the Development of Humanitarian Law' in: *Declarations on Principles – A Quest for Universal Peace*, R.J. Akherman, P.J. Van Kricken and Ch.O. Pannenborg (eds.), Leyden, A.W. Sijhoff, 1977, pp. 143–170; Chimango, L.J., 'The Relevance of Humanitarian International Law to the Liberation Struggles in Southern Africa – the Cases for Mozambique in Retrospect', in *The Comparative and International Law Journal of Southern Africa* (Cape Town), Vol. VIII, Nov. 1975, pp. 287–317; Rubin, A.P., 'The Status of Rebels under the Geneva Conventions of 1949', *International and Comparative Law Quarterly* (London), Vol. 21, No. 3, 1972, pp. 472–496; Abi-Saab, G., 'Wars of National Liberation and the Laws of War', *Annals of International Studies* (Geneva), Vol. 3, 1972, pp. 93–117; Schwarzenberger, G., 'Privileged Belligerency in Guerrilla Warfare: An Implied Test of Legitimacy?', *Human Rights Journal* (Strasbourg), Vol. 4, 1971, pp. 535–553; Draper, G.I.A.D., 'The Status of Combatants and the Question of Guerrilla Warfare', *British Yearbook of International Law* (London), Vol. 45, 1971, pp. 173–218; Kahn, R., 'Guerrilla Warfare and International Law', *International Studies* (New Delhi), Vol. 9, No. 2, 1967, pp. 103–127; Ford, W.J., 'Resistance Movements and International Law', *International Review of the Red Cross* (Geneva), 7th year, October–November–December 1967, pp. 515–531, 579–587, 627–639, and 8th year, January 1968, pp. 7–15.

18. South-West Africa, Second Phase, Judgements, I.C.J. Reports 1966, pp. 6–505; Gross, E.A., 'The South-West Africa Case: What Happened?' *Foreign Affairs* (New-York), Vol. 45, No. 1, October 1966, pp. 36–48; Falks, R.A., 'The South-West Africa Cases: An Appraisal', *International Organizations* (Boston, Mass.), Vol. XXI, No. 1, 1967, pp. 7–23; Rao, P.C., 'South-West Africa Cases: Inconsistent Judgements from the International Court of Justice', *Indian Journal of International Law* (New Delhi),

Vol. 6, No. 3, 1966, pp. 383–394; Higgins, R., 'The International Court and South-West Africa: The Implications of the Judgement', *International Affairs* (London), Vol. 42, No. 4, October 1966, pp. 573–599; Umozurike, U.O., 'The Namibia (South-West Africa) Cases 1950–1971', *Africa Quarterly* (London), 1973, pp. 41–58.

CHAPTER XIII

PROTECTION OF CULTURAL PROPERTY[1]

STANISLAW-EDWARD NAHLIK

A. Historical Summary

The idea of protecting cultural property[2] in the event of war is not a very old one. Pillage and destruction have been a part of war throughout the centuries. Certain property was sometimes spared, but this was due only to its sacred character. Medieval Christianity considered especially the question of whether the cause for which it fought was a just one, and gave little thought to the manner in which hostilities were conducted.

Appreciable progress was made during the Renaissance, due primarily to the recognition that a work of art has qualities surpassing those embodied in the works of ordinary craftsmanship, a unique character, marking the individual genius of its creator. The budding science of international law gradually began to draw conclusions from this new perception. A Polish jurist, Jacob Przyluski (Jacobus Prilusius), was perhaps the first to express the idea of the respect which all belligerents should accord to works of art, not only for the religious character they might have.[3] Those regarded as the classic authors in the field of international-al law all made their separate, and in the beginning fragmentary, contributions to the development of concrete legal rules in this area. Reacting to ravages wrought by the troops of Louis XIV in the Palatinate, Justin Gentilis, a German jurist of Italian origin, wrote eloquently about this subject in his *Dissertatio de eo quod in bello licet*.[4] Among the authors of the age of the enlightenment, with Emer de Vattel in the lead, the idea spread more and more that in time of war every belligerent should spare the buildings which do honour to humanity and in no way serve to render the enemy more powerful.[5]

This ideal did not remain a merely theoretical one, as we can see from the evidence of many wars of the 18th Century, which were generally more moderate than those which had ravaged Europe during the previous century. Even in the peace treaties, beginning with the Peace of Westphalia, we find more and more clauses providing for the restoration of things to their places of origin, first of archives alone and then of works of art, displaced in the course of the fighting.

There were striking examples of this change of attitude at the beginning of the following century. In 1812, a British court annulled the capture of a collection of works of art which were destined for the Academy of Fine Arts in Philadelphia on the grounds that, "the arts and sciences are admitted amongst all civilized nations to form an exception to the severe rights of war and to be entitled to favour and protection".[6] In 1815, the allies provided for the restitution of works of art taken from different countries by Napoleon because, in the words of a memorandum circulated by Lord Castlereagh, the removal of works of art was "contrary to every principle of justice and to the usages of modern warfare".[7]

It is not at all surprising then, during the second half of the 19th century, to find people undertaking to codify the laws of war and to make sure that these laws would have something to say about the fate, in wartime, of works of art, historic monuments and other objects of cultural value.

B. Incidental Regulations

We know the many efforts made during the latter decades of the 19th century to control and regulate, by means of conventions, this or that problem of the law of war and finally the law of war as a whole.[8]

This process reached its climax on 18 October 1907 with the signing at The Hague of no fewer than thirteen conventions, of which twelve dealt with the law of war.

Starting from the assumption that only members of the armed forces and the objects used for military purposes are exposed to the hazards of war, there was no idea in the beginning of devoting a special convention to objects which do not have a military character. So it was that in the otherwise impressive work accomplished at The Hague we find hardly anything but rules dealing only incidentally with the protection of cultural property. These can be divided into two categories: those which contribute to the protection of such property only in an indirect way and those which refer to such property specifically. Both are found in the Regulations annexed to the Fourth Hague Convention of 1907 concerning the laws and customs of war on land.

In the first category, we may include all the rules aiming at the protection of civilian property in general: the prohibition of pillage, a rule stating that it is forbidden to destroy or seize the enemy's property, a rule stating that it is forbidden to attack or bombard "by whatever means" towns, villages, dwellings or building which are undefended, and one stating that "the pillage of a town or place, even when taken by assault, is prohibited".[9] Each of these rules, in an indirect manner, protects cultural property.

But there are also some rules which expressly refer to groups of objects which, in the language used today, would be included in the definition of "cultural property". These include the following:

"In sieges and bombardments all necessary steps must be taken to spare, as far as possible, buildings devoted to religion, art, science or charitable purposes, historic monuments... provided they are not being used at the time for military purposes".[10]

"The property of municipalities, that of institutions dedicated to religion, charity and education, the arts and sciences, even when State property, shall be treated as private property".[11]

"All seizure of, destruction or wilful damage done to institutions of this character, historic monuments, works of art and science, is forbidden, and should be made the subject of legal proceedings".[12]

The criteria under which an object enjoys the protection accorded by this convention are therefore of three kinds: certain objects are protected by virtue of their intrinsic qualities, others by virtue of the institution to which they belong and still others by virtue of the purpose they are intended to serve. Bringing these three criteria together would seem to provide a sufficiently solid basis for protection, but it nevertheless still leaves loopholes, or at least doubts, of which an interpreter acting in bad faith could take advantage.

We may also note that the efficacy of these rules, in specific cases, may be undermined by one or another of the reservations found in the text of the convention or of the regulations: the conduct of the adversary (use of an object for a military purpose), reference to protective steps being taken "as far as possible", reference to military necessity (mentioned in the preamble to the Convention), the *si omnes* clause (under which the Convention applies in principle only in the event that all the parties in a war are parties to it)[13] and its application only in case of "war" and not taking into account such conflicts as do not meet the definition of "war".

C. Towards Specialized Regulation

In the peace treaties concluded after the First World War, in both the West and the East, there were interesting clauses providing for the restitution of cultural property.[14] Some of these clauses were not restricted to settling the disposition of objects removed during that war itself, but went far back into the past to repair injustices committed in previous centuries. In the event that major objects had since been destroyed, a highly ingenious innovation was provided, that of restitution by replacement, whereby the guilty party had to supply the injured party with other objects having the same value and of the same kind.

Some wartime events showed the inadequacy, with regard to the protection of cultural property, of the rules formulated at The Hague in 1899 and 1907. A number of proposals were therefore put forward, suggesting that a special convention be devoted to this problem, inspired by the Geneva Conventions providing protection for the wounded and sick and for prisoners of war. There was discussion for example of establishing a "Golden Cross" as a distinctive sign for the protection of the world's historic and artistic heritage. In the Americas, the Roerich Pact signed in Washington on 15 April 1935 provided for the "neutralization" of artistic and scientific institutions and of historic monuments in the event of war.[15] In general terms, the most interesting initiative was that of the *Office international des musées*. A committee of experts under the chairmanship of the eminent Belgian jurist, Charles de Visscher, prepared for the Office a draft for a convention on the protection of monuments and works of art in the event of armed conflicts.[16] Only the outbreak of the Second World War prevented the submission of this project to an international diplomatic conference.

The pillage and destruction during that war surpassed anything known before, and conclusions were reached as a result. Clauses concerning restitution, some times providing once more for restitution by replacement, were included in the peace treaties,[17] and commissions of experts, sent by countries which had suffered particularly heavy losses, travelled throughout Europe and brought back to their homelands such objects as they were able to locate. In the trials of war criminals, a great many defendants were found guilty, among other things, of criminal actions against the cultural patrimony of the occupied countries.[18]

Experience during the war produced an acceleration thereafter of efforts to draft a "monographic" convention which would govern the destiny of the cultural heritage of nations in the event of armed conflict. Preparatory work, begun on the initiative of the Italian Government, was turned over to a new intergovernmental organization, Unesco. When the initial work was finished, a diplomatic conference was convened in 1954 at The Hague.[19] Here, on 14 May of the same year, several documents were signed which, taken together, amounted to a veritable code for the protection of cultural property in the event of war.[20] They consisted of: the Convention for the Protection of Cultural Property in the Event of Armed Conflict, Regulations for the execution of that Convention and a Protocol for the Protection of Cultural Property in the Event of Armed Conflict. The latter one of the three constituted a separate document which countries could sign or not sign, independently of the Convention. The Regulations, on the other hand constituted an annex to the Convention and were an integral part of it.

D. A Code for the Protection of Cultural Property

The great advantage of the codification of 1954 rests in the fact that it introduces a uniform concept covering all objects which should enjoy protection, objects which had previously been defined in quite different ways,[21] that is, the concept of "cultural property".

This term covers three groups of objects: (a) those which have, in themselves, artistic, historic or archeological value; (b) those which, while they do not themselves have such value, serve to exhibit or shelter objects belonging to the first group; (c) those which include a substantial number of the objects of the kind specified under (a) and (b) and are known as "centres containing monuments". (Such centres usually consist of sections of cities or even entire cities or towns).[22]

To complete the list of objects enjoying protection under the Convention, we may mention: (d) means of transport used to move cultural property, either inside a country or to another country in order to protect it from the effects of hostilities[23] and (e) personnel assigned to the protection of cultural property.[24]

Any object (and any person) enjoying such protection must be identified by a special sign, in the way that the Red Cross sign serves to protect human beings, but this sign is not quite as simple as the red cross. It is described as "a shield, pointed below, per saltire blue and white (a shield consisting of a royal blue square, one of the angles of which forms the point of the shield, and of a royal blue triangle above the square, the space on either side being taken up by a white triangle)".[25] This sign, even though it is not as complicated as it sounds when you look at it, is nevertheless not easy to describe in words – but it seems that all the simpler signs were already being used for other purposes such as traffic regulations!

1. The Protection May Be of Either a "General" or a "Special" Character

A) Objects automatically entitled to "general" protection include all objects which meet the definition of "cultural property" in the Convention.

Such protection comprises two aspects: "safeguarding" and "respect". It is interesting to note the extent to which the Convention divided the responsibility for protection between the parties to a conflict. "Safeguarding" refers in particular, under the terms of the Convention, to preparing in time of peace such measures which, in the event of armed conflict, would protect the objects "against the foreseeable effects of an armed conflict". It is obvious that measures of this character can only be taken by the States holding the objects. It is a different matter when we consider "respect". Here, the responsibility is divided. One of the parties is required to abstain from using the protected property for purposes which "are likely to expose it to destruction or damage in the event of armed conflict", meaning, above all, for any military purpose. The other party is obliged to refrain "from any act of hostility directed against such property".[26] This is followed by reference to more specific prohibitions,[27] of which the ban against "any act directed by way of reprisals"[28] seems to be the most important.

B) Property placed under "special" protection enjoys immunity. It means that the country possessing the property undertakes to refrain from using it for any military purpose and that the adverse party must abstain from any act of hostility directed against it.[29] The granting of this kind of protection is subject however to very rigorous conditions, with regard both to substances and procedure. As concerns substance,[30] the property in question must not only be "of very great importance", and not be used for military purposes, but it must also be "situated at an adequate distance from any large industrial centre or from any important military objective constituting a vulnerable point". The meaning of "an adequate distance" can only be judged in each individual case, since neither the Convention nor the Regulations attached to it have any precise indication on this point. With regard to procedural requirements, any country desiring to have one of its possessions enjoy "special" protection must, in time of peace, request its inclusion in the "International Register of Cultural Property under Special Protection"[31] maintained by Unesco. The relatively complicated procedures for such registration are set forth in detail in the Regulations.[32] Once an object has been inscribed in the Register, the country owning it must mark it with three of the distinctive signs.[33] Properly organized transports for cultural property are also entitled to special protection.

2. Two Important Reservations May Limit the Efficacy of Any Measure of Protection

If one of the Parties to the Convention violates its obligations under the Convention, in particular if it uses an object of cultural property for a military purpose, the adverse Party is released from its obligation to ensure the immunity of the property concerned.[34] This release is only temporary, since it is justified only as long as the violation causing it persists, but it does nevertheless constitute a substantial limitation on the privileges enjoyed by an object of cultural property. The Convention provides for this limitation only on property which is under special protection. The reason for this restriction is not as surprising as one might think at first. The objects which enjoy only general protection may be too numerous to make it possible to abstain from using each and every one of them for any military purpose whatsoever. On the other hand, objects under special protection are relatively few in number and hence are generally well known. Furthermore, in asking that they be placed on the Unesco Register, the State to which they belong undertakes a solemn commitment not to make any military use of them and is certainly guilty if this promise is violated. Nevertheless, despite the sound logic of this reasoning, there is reason to recognize that a kind of reprisal may often be involved in such cases, even if the word reprisal is not used.

The other reservation is even more serious: the clause concerning military necessity. This clause, introduced into the Hague Conventions of 1899 and 1907 under the pressure of the German delegation and disputed by the majority of the other delegations, led by those from the Anglo-Saxon countries, and omitted from the Geneva Conventions of 1949, was not included in the draft of the Convention submitted to the Conference in 1954. On this occasion however, it was the military delegate from the United States, supported by the British delegate, who insisted that it be inserted in the text. A substantial number of States[35] were opposed to the idea of its inclusion. It was nevertheless accepted, since the delegates from the Anglo-Saxon countries made it a *conditio sine qua non* for their acceptance of the Convention. All that its adversaries could obtain was the inclusion of various qualifications in the clause. With regard to objects enjoying only general protection, the obligations may be waived only in cases where military necessity "imperatively requires" such a waiver.[36] Concerning an object enjoying special protection, the qualifications are more numerous. It must be an "exceptional" case and the necessity must be "unavoidable"; the withdrawal of immunity can only be temporary and the adversary must be notified in advance if circumstances permit. Finally, it can only be a high-ranking officer ("the officer commanding a force the equivalent of a division in size or larger") who can decide upon the necessity for withdrawing immunity.[37] There are thus apparently many precautions. It is nonetheless true that there is no cultural object, of even the greatest value, which is totally protected from a "military necessity", however transient it may be, which in a particular case may justify its destruction, in the opinion of a military commander.

3. The Execution of the Obligations Under the Convention is the Responsibility of the Contracting Parties

It is consequently up to each of them to take the appropriate measures to this effect.[38] A resolution voted on the same day that the Convention was signed recommended that all Parties constitute consultative national committees to prepare such measures and oversee their observation.

The initial idea had been to create a permanent international body which, in the field of the protection of cultural property, would exercise functions analogous to those of the International Committee of the Red Cross with regard to the protection of human beings. It was finally decided to abandon this idea so as to avoid adding to the multiplicity of international organizations and instead to entrust certain functions to an organization already in existence, Unesco. This institution, depository of the Convention, was designated to serve as an intermediary between the Parties, in particular by calling meetings, as the occasions arise,[39] in which the Parties can share their experiences and, if need be, undertake a revision of the Convention. Unesco can, in addition, give assistance to the Parties, especially with regard to the technical aspects of the protection of cultural property.[40]

In case of war the parties to the conflict may have the benefit of assistance by Protecting Powers.[41] Certain control functions may be carried out on the territory of each of the parties to the conflict by a "Commissioner-General for Cultural Property" chosen by agreement (or in the absence of an agreement, by the President of the International Court of Justice) from an international list of persons, nominated by the Parties and kept up to date by the Director-General of Unesco.[42]

The Conference renounced the idea of drawing up a list of possible violations of the Convention,[43] limiting itself to a single article of a general character, whereby:

"The High Contracting Parties undertake to take, within the framework of their ordinary criminal jurisdiction, all necessary steps to prosecute and impose penal or disciplinary sanctions upon those persons, of whatever nationality, who commit or order to be committed a breach of the present Convention."[44]

While not assuring any uniformity of interpretation in evaluating the seriousness of violations, and thereby the concrete sanctions that should be imposed, the foregoing article does at least state the general principle that one cannot violate with impunity the obligations set forth in the Convention.

The original draft of the Convention devoted an entire chapter to the restitution of cultural property taken to another country in the course of a conflict. The principle of such restitution had been recognized so many times in international practice, particularly in peace treaties, that one could already see in it a principle of customary law. On the eve of the 1954 Conference, however, objections were made to its inclusion on the grounds that systems of civil law were not the same with respect to matters of ownership and possessions and that, as a result, the inclusion of precise rules concerning the restitution of objects which might have undergone changes in ownership could present great difficulties and dissuade certain States from acceding to the Convention.[45] These rules were therefore removed from the Convention and became the subject of a separate Protocol.

Under the terms of this Protocol, the Parties agreed to prevent the exportation of cultural property from occupied territories, to take into official custody any such property imported into their territory and to return it after the end of hostilities to the authorities of the territory it came from.[46] A comparable obligation was assumed by countries not involved in the conflict.[47] Holders in good faith of such property were to be paid indemnities by the State whose obligation it was to prevent its exportation.[48]

E. After 1954

1) The Convention entered into force after a very brief time, since the number of ratifications required to give it effect was unusually low, only five being needed.[49] As of 31 July 1988, there were 75 States formally bound by the Convention, either by ratification or accession.[50] In analyzing the list of Parties to the Convention, we note that it includes nearly all the countries of continental Europe as well as most of those in the Near East and Middle East. On the other hand, there are quite a few countries missing, notably among those of the Third World. It is also to be regretted that, with the only exception of Australia which ratified the Convention in 1984, all the other Anglo-Saxon countries have thus far abstained from adherence to the Convention – all the more so since the 1954 Conference made so many concessions, of which we need mention only one: the insertion of the clause concerning military necessity, even with regard to objects

placed under special protection. It is to be observed that very few of the countries which became Parties to the Convention failed at the same time to adopt the Protocol providing for restitution.

With regard to the institutional innovations introduced by the Convention, it is noteworthy that Commissioners-General for Cultural Property, provided for in the Regulations, have been appointed, at least for the Israelo-Arab conflict. On the other hand, the International Register of Cultural Property, for objects enjoying special protection, has very few such objects listed. Most of the States, probably, could not decide to make the formal promise to renounce any possible utilization of this or that object for military purposes. However, even the few items that are listed are quite significant. The example of Austria illustrates the fact that a country can begin by inscribing only one object (a refuge in which, in the event of an armed conflict, works of art of the greatest value would be sheltered), without waiting for the drawing up of a more complete list of objects. Another interesting example is that of the Vatican City, the whole territory of which is inscribed. Before this was done, the Italian Government had stated that it would renounce all military use of only one street (the Via Aurelia) in the vicinity of the Vatican. This shows that there has not been any excess rigour applied to the idea of the "adequate distance" which, under the terms of the Convention, must separate an object under special protection from "any important objective constituting a vulnerable point".

The Director-General of Unesco has so far convened only one meeting of the Parties to the Convention, in 1962 in Paris. The exchanges of views and experiences by those who participated in this meeting were extremely interesting. There was no follow up however to the suggestion of the Polish delegate[51] that preparatory work be undertaken with a view to revising certain clauses of the Convention, nor to the unanimous resolution by the participants asking that appropriate Unesco bodies constitute a committee of experts which, in the absence of a permanent specialized body, would oversee the application of the Convention.[52]

2) The problem of the effective protection of the cultural heritage of the nations, indeed of all humanity, reappeared in an incidental manner in the Diplomatic Conference on Humanitarian Law at Geneva, from 1974 to 1977. On the initiative of the Greek delegation, the following provision was included in Protocol I:

> "Without prejudice to the provisions of the Hague Convention for the Protection of Cultural Property in the Event of Armed Conflict of 14 May 1954 and of other relevant international instruments, it is prohibited:
> a) to commit any acts of hostility directed against the historic monuments, works of art or places of worship which constitute the cultural or spiritual heritage of peoples;
> b) to use such objects in support of the military effort;

c) to make such objects the object of reprisals."[53]

Despite the shortening undergone by Additional Protocol II during the last session of the Diplomatic Conference, this also included a similar provision (omitting only the substance of paragraph c above), with regard to conflicts of a non-international character.[54]

The Diplomatic Conference also adopted a resolution urging States which had not yet done so t₃ become Parties to the 1954 Convention.[55]

The importance of these gestures, with regard to a problem which was marginal to the principal subject of the Diplomatic Conference of 1974–1977, is that they highlight the unity and indivisibility of international humanitarian law. Civilized man is not satisfied with material values alone. He cherishes and respects the cultural and spiritual values, represented in monuments, works of art and places of worship, which constitute the visible evidence of human genius, and hence the common heritage of all mankind. Each generation must defend this heritage, with vigour and determination, against all dangers so that it may be handed down intact to the generations to come.

Notes

1. In view of limitations on the length of this chapter, it has also been necessary to impose corresponding limits on the reference notes. Readers interested in the problem can find further details in our work *Protection internationale des biens culturels en cas de conflit armé*, published in the *Recueil des cours de l'Académie de droit international de La Haye*, Vol. 120, 1967 –I, pp. 61–163, referred to below in the abbreviated form: Nahlik, *Protection internationale des biens culturels*.
2. To simplify this discussion, we are using this term from the outset, although it was not introduced into international legal terminology until 1954.
3. *Leges seu statuta ac privilegia Regni Poloniae...*, Cracow, 1553, f. 875.
4. Argentorati, 1690, Cf. especially p. 21 et seq.
5. *Le droit des gens, ou principes de la loi naturelle*. London (in fact: Neuchâtel), 1758, Book III, Chapter IX, par. 168. Cf. also last reprint of the edition in the collection of the Classics of the International Law, published by the Carnegie Institution of Washington, Washington D.C., 1916: Geneva, Slatkine Reprints – Henry Dunant Institute, 1983. French text: Vol. II, p. 139; English text: Vol. III, p. 293.
6. Quoted in J.B. Moore, *A Digest of International Law*, Vol. VII, Washington, Government Printing Office, 1906, p. 460.
7. Quoted by G.F. Martens, *Nouveau Recueil de traités*, Vol. II, p. 632 et seq.
8. Since other chapters of this manual analyze other aspects of the law of war in detail, we believe it is unnecessary to enumerate the different stages in this process and refer only to the treaties resulting from the Second Hague Conference of 1907.
9. Regulations Respecting the Laws and Customs of War on Land, annexed to the Fourth Convention, having the same title, signed at The Hague on 18 October 1907, published *inter alia* in F.G. Martens, *Nouveau Recueil Général de traités*, 3ème série, Vol. III, p. 461 et seq., *International Red Cross Handbook*, 12th edition, Geneva, ICRC, League, 1983, p. 323 et seq.; *The Laws of Armed Conflicts. A Collection of Conventions, Regulations and Other Documents*. Edited by D. Schindler and J. Toman, 3rd edition, Dordrecht, Martinus Nijhoff Publishers, Geneva, Henry Dunant Institute, 1988, pp. 75–93. Rules referred to (in order of quotation) are in Articles 47, 23 (g), 25 and 28. With regard to undefended towns and other localities, a comparable prohibition is to be found in Article 1, paragraph 1 of the IXth Hague Convention concerning Bombardment by Naval Forces in Time of War, published *inter alia* in F.G. Martens, *Nouveau Recueil Général de traités*, 3ème série, Vol. III, p. 604

et seq., *International Red Cross Handbook*, 12th edition, Geneva, ICRC, League, 1983, p. 336–337; *The Laws of Armed Conflicts. A Collection of Conventions, Regulations and Other Documents.* Edited by D. Schindler and J. Toman, 3rd edition, Dordrecht, Martinus Nijhoff Publishers, Geneva, Henry Dunant Institute, 1988, pp. 811–817.

10. The Hague Regulations Respecting the Laws and Customs of War on Land of 1907, Article 27, paragraph 1 (for an analogous rule, see IXth Hague Convention concerning Bombardment by Naval Forces in Time of War, Article 5, paragraph 1). It goes without saying that the difference between this and Article 25 is in the fact that this reference, in principle, is to attack against towns and other localities which are defended.

11. The Hague Regulations Respecting the Laws and Customs of War on Land of 1907, Article 56, paragraph 1.

12. *Ibid.*, paragraph 2.

13. This clause has nevertheless lost its original importance. Under rulings of the International Military Tribunal at Nuremberg, 30 September and 1 October 1946, The Hague Regulations Respecting the Laws and Customs of War on Land of 1907 constituted a reflection of rules recognized by all civilized nations and could be regarded as declaratory in international law. Cf., for example, the text published in the *American Journal of International Law* (Washington D.C.), Vol. 41, 1947, pp. 248–249.

14. In the West, especially in the peace treaties signed by the Allies with Germany at Versailles on 28 June 1919, Articles 245–247, and with Austria at Saint-Germain-en-Laye on 10 September 1919, Articles 191–196, and, in the East, the Peace treaty between Poland and Russia and Ukraine, signed at Riga on 18 March 1921, Article XI. Texts are published in F.G. Martens, *Nouveau Recueil Général de traités*, 3ème série, Vol. XI, p. 323 et seq. (Treaty of Versailles) and 691 et seq. (Treaty of Saint-Germain). For the Treaty of Riga, Cf. *League of Nations, Treaty Series*, Vol. VI, p. 52 et seq.

15. Text: The Department of State Information Bulletin (Washington D.C.), 1936, No. 67. *The Laws of Armed Conflicts. A Collection of Conventions, Regulations and Other Documents.* Edited by D. Schindler and J. Toman. 3rd edition, Dordrecht, Martinus Nijhoff Publishers, Geneva, Henry Dunant Institute, 1988, pp. 737–740.

16. Text: *Art et archéologie, Recueil de législation comparée et de droit international.* Office international de musées, Paris, 1940, No. 2, p. 60 et seq.

17. In particular that between the Allies and Italy, signed at Paris on 10 February 1947, Article 75. Text: *United Nations Treaty Series*, Vol. 3, p. 135 et seq.

18. For details, Cf. Nahlik, *Protection internationale des biens culturels*, p. 105 et seq.

19. Cf. publication of the Government of the Netherlands: *Intergovernmental Conference on the Protection of Cultural Property in the Event of Armed Conflicts – The Hague, 1954. Records of the Conference.* The Hague, Staatsdruckkerij – en uitgeverijbedrijf, 1961, 452 p.

20. Texts: *Intergovernmental Conference on the Protection of Cultural Property in the Event of Armed Conflicts – The Hague, 1954. Records of the Conference.* The Hague, Staatstdruckkerij – en uitgeverijbedrijf, 1961, p. 2–81; United Nations Treaty Series, Vol. 249, pp. 215–386; International Red Cross Handbook, 12th edition, Geneva, ICRC, League, 1983, pp. 339–369; *The Laws of Armed Conflicts. A Collection of Conventions, Regulations and Other Documents.* Edited by D. Schindler and J. Toman, 3rd edition, Dordrecht, Martinus Nijhoff Publishers, Geneva, Henry Dunant Institute, 1988, pp. 745–784.[Referred to below as the Convention of 1954, Regulations of 1954 and Protocol of 1954, respectively.]

21. On this subject, cf. earlier paragraphs of this chapter, in particular the articles quoted from the Regulations of 1907.

22. The full text of the definition (Convention of 1954, Article 1) is as follows:

For the purposes of the present Convention, the term "cultural property" shall cover, irrespective of origin or ownership:

a) movable and immovable property of great importance to the cultural heritage of every people, such as monuments or architecture, art or history, whether religious or secular; archeological sites; groups of buildings which as a whole, are of historical or artistic interest; works of art; manuscripts, books and other objects of artistic, historical or archeological interest; as well as scientific collections and important collections of books or archives of reproductions of the property defined above;

b) buildings whose main and effective purpose is to preserve or exhibit the movable cultural property defined in sub-paragraph (a) such as museums, large libraries and depositories of archives, and refuges intended to shelter, in the event of armed conflict, the movable cultural property defined in subparagraph (a);

c) centres containing a large amount of cultural property as defined in sub-paragraphs (a) and (b), to be known as "centres containing monuments".

23. Articles 12 and 13 of the Convention of 1954.
24. Article 15 of the Convention of 1954.
25. Article 16, paragraph 1 of the Convention of 1954.
26. Articles 2, 3 and 4, paragraph 1 of the Convention of 1954.
27. Article 4, paragraphs 5 and 7 of the Convention of 1954.
28. Article 4, paragraph 4 of the Convention of 1954.
29. Article 9 of the Convention of 1954.
30. Article 8, paragraph 1 of the Convention of 1954.
31. Article 8, paragraph 6 of the Convention of 1954.
32. Articles 11–16 of the Regulations of 1954.
33. Article 17, paragraph 1 of the Convention of 1954.
34. Article 11, paragraph 1 of the Convention of 1954.
35. All the States of the socialist group and, in the West, notably Spain, France, Greece, Ecuador and San Marino. The States of the Third World were relatively few in number at that time and did not play an important role in the Conference.
36. Article 4, paragraph 2 of the Convention of 1954.
37. Article 11, paragraph 2 of the Convention of 1954.
38. Cf. in particular Article 25 of the Convention of 1954, and elsewhere (for example Article 7).
39. Article 27 of the Convention of 1954.
40. Article 23 of the Convention of 1954.
41. Articles 21–22 of the Convention of 1954.
42. Articles 1–10 of the Regulations of 1954.
43. In an article "Des crimes contre les biens culturels", *Annuaire de l'A.A.A.* (The Hague), Vol. 29, 1969, p. 14 et seq., and in Nahlik, *Protection internationale des biens culturels*, p. 149 et seq., the author has attempted to make such a list of violations and arrived at a total of thirty.
44. Article 28 of the Convention of 1954.
45. It was in particular l'Institut international pour l'unification du droit privé, which on 29 January 1954, expressed such an objection. Cf. *Intergovernmental Conference on the Protection of Cultural Property in the Event of Armed Conflicts – The Hague, 1954. Records of the Conference.* The Hague, Staatsdruckkerij – en uitgeverijbedrijf, 1961, p. 351 et seq.
46. Protocol of 1954, paragraphs 1–3.
47. Protocol of 1954, paragraph 5.
48. Protocol of 1954, paragraph 4.
49. Article 33 of the Convention of 1954. The Convention and Protocol entered into force on 7 August 1956.
50. Communication from Unesco of 15 August 1988.
51. The author of this chapter.
52. Report on this meeting. Unesco document CUA/120 of 3 September 1962.
53. Protocol Additional to the Geneva Conventions of 12 August 1949 Relative to the Protection of Victims of International Armed Conflicts (Protocol I) of 8 June 1977, Article 53.
54. Protocol Additional to the Geneva Conventions of 12 August 1949 Relative to the Protection of Victims of Non-International Armed Conflicts (Protocol II) of 8 June 1977, Article 16.

55. Resolution 20 (IV), adopted at the fifty-fifth plenary meeting of 7 June 1977 by 53 votes in favour, 0 against and 33 abstentions.

SECTION 2

CONFLICTS OF A NON-INTERNATIONAL CHARACTER

CHAPTER XIV

NON-INTERNATIONAL ARMED CONFLICTS

GEORGES ABI-SAAB

Armed strife within human communities is probably the earliest known form of war. On historic and statistical record, such conflicts have been no less frequent, brutal or devastating than intercommunal (or, to use contemporary legal idiom, interstate) wars.

Important as it has always been, this type of armed conflict was totally ignored up to 1949 in the successive international legal efforts at codifying and developing the rules of the law of war; though paradoxically enough the first modern endeavour in this field which inspired the international action that followed – the Lieber Code[1] – was elaborated in the context of the American Civil War. This omission was not an oversight but a natural consequence of the sovereignty reflex of States, which explains their resistance to any attempt at extending to these conflicts the application of the laws of war.

I. The Traditional Approach

Until the adoption of the Geneva Conventions of 1949, the prevailing view was that internal conflicts were not subject to international legal regulation, but that they fell within the domestic jurisdiction of the State on whose territory they take place – which really means of "the established government" of that State – and are therefore exclusively governed by its municipal law. Any dealings by third parties with "the rebels" was considered an act of intervention in the internal affairs of that State.

This legally radical separation of internal wars from the international level, was not, however, as rigorously observed in practice as it sounded in theory. One can cite numerous instances, both before, and particularly after the Napoleonic wars, of intervention by major European powers against democratic uprisings in Europe, not to speak of their increasing interest in conflicts arising in different parts of the Ottoman Empire, and in their extra-european spheres of influence as a prelude to their formal colonization; or of the intervention of the United States in the frequent internal upheavals in Latin America.

However, a changing international context characterized by a greater degree of stability in the global balance of power, and the rise of the positivist doctrines of the State both in municipal and international law, led, by the end of the nineteenth century, to the crystallization and hardening of the traditional approach described above.

Even according to this traditional approach, the legal status of internal conflicts could be radically altered by resorting to the institution of "recognition of belligerency". If such a recognition emanated from the established government, it entailed the application of the *jus in bello* in its entirety to its relations with the rebels; if it emanated from third parties it enabled them to require to be treated as neutrals by both belligerent parties.

But as the recognition of belligerency is a purely discretionary act, it has been of a very rare occurrence, especially in the twentieth century. And even in the few instances when it did take place, it intervened at an advanced stage of the conflict – usually after the rebels had secured control over a part of the national territory and the parties started to assert belligerent rights on the high seas, i.e. when the armed conflict in its material aspects became similar to an interstate war. For it is only then that reciprocity could come into play and the institution of recognition of belligerency would offer some advantage to the established government or to third parties with a view to protecting their interests in the areas held by the rebels as well as their maritime commerce behind the shield of neutrality.

Indeed, when the Institute of International Law adopted in 1900 a resolution on the rights and duties of foreign powers in case of insurrection,[2] it considered control by the insurgents of part of the national territory a necessary precondition for "recognition of belligerency" by third parties. In its absence, recognition would be considered "premature", and would constitute an act of intervention in the internal affairs of the State concerned. In any case, recognition of belligerency by third parties did not bind the government of that State. Its effects were limited to the relations of the belligerents with the recognizing third parties, i.e. to the "external" aspects of the armed conflict, but did not affect the relations between the belligerents themselves. In other words, it had no direct incidence on the conduct of hostilities or on the protection of their potential victims – questions which are the main concerns of humanitarian law.

Apart from this purely consensual institution, States resisted any attempt at mandatory international regulation of internal conflict. It is true that a few progressive voices advocated, also around the turn of the century, a theory of an "obligatory recognition of belligerency", which would have extended *ipso jure* the application of the *jus in bello* to the relations between the belligerents, once the conditions of recognition of belligerency by third parties were met. But these voices were in advance on their time, and remained without echo.[3]

This does not mean that efforts were not made to help the victims of internal conflicts on purely humanitarian and "operational" – rather than legal – grounds. Indeed, already in the late nineteenth century and the early twentieth, opinions were expressed from time to time within the ICRC and by representatives of National Societies in the International Red Cross Conferences in favour of extending their activities to cases of internal armed conflict. But it was not until 1921, following the practical activities of the National Societies and the ICRC in the internal upheavals which took place in several European countries, particularly in Russia and Hungary at the end and after the First World War, and a series of reports by National Societies on their role in such upheavals, that the International Red Cross Conference adopted a series of resolutions asserting the right and even the duty of the National Societies as well as the ICRC to provide relief to the victims of civil wars.[4]

When the Statutes of the ICRC were revised in 1928, a new paragraph was added to Article IV enumerating the aims and objects of the ICRC, still unchanged in the current version, which read:

> "d) to be a neutral intermediary, whose intervention is recognized to be necessary, especially in case of war, civil war or civil strife;..."

That was, however, an internal legal mandate which laid down the line of action to be pursued by the Red Cross organisms including the ICRC in such situations, but which imposed no legal obligation on governments to accept or allow such activities on their territories or to apply all or part of the laws of war or the Geneva Conventions in case of internal armed conflict.

The upheavals of the interwar period, and particularly the Spanish Civil War, brought out clearly the limits of this extra-legal or "on sufferance" humanitarian approach to internal conflicts; and preparations were in process for a revision conference in 1940 to deal with this as well as other defects in the existing conventions when the Second World War broke out.

II. Common Article 3

1. The Elaboration of Common Article 3

After the War, and as a result of its traumatic impact, the drive for the revision of the Geneva Conventions regained and even gathered momentum. In this respect, the approach to internal conflicts was greatly influenced, apart from the lessons of the Spanish Civil War, by the massive atrocities committed against minority groups during the war and the surge of the movement for the international protection of human rights within the United Nations. It was strongly felt that a minimum of humanitarian legal regulations should apply in all armed conflicts, regardless of their internal or international character.

Thus the *Draft Conventions for the Protection of War Victims*, prepared by the ICRC and submitted to the XVII International Red Cross Conference at Stockholm in 1948, contained a fourth paragraph of Common Article 2, which reads:

> "In all cases of armed conflict which are not of an international character, especially cases of civil war, colonial conflicts, or wars of religion, which may occur in the territory of one or more of the High Contracting Parties, the implementing of the principles of the present Convention shall be obligatory on each of the adversaries. The application of the Convention in these circumstances shall in no way depend on the legal status of the Parties to the conflict and shall have no effect on that status."[5]

This draft, while maintaining the distinction in legal status between international conflicts and conflicts not of an international character would have led to the integral application of the Conventions to the latter. This maximalist approach met with heavy resistance both in Stockholm and later at the Diplomatic Conference of 1949 in Geneva. One of the main concerns of its opponents was that in spite of the express formal denial of any effect of such an integral application on the legal status of the parties to the conflict, the possibility such a solution opens to "rebels" to appoint another State as "Protecting Power" would inexorably internationalize the conflict. It would amount to an *ipso jure*, i.e. mandatory and automatic, recognition of belligerency.

In these circumstances, even according to the proponents of this solution, the integral application of the Conventions would have had to be limited to characterized civil wars, which were materially identical to interstate conflicts, such as the Spanish Civil War. In other words, the internal armed conflict had to be strictly and restrictively defined. But the elaboration of such a definition proved to be a highly controversial and an almost impossible task.

The alternative minimal solution, which finally prevailed, was to apply to internal armed conflicts not the Conventions as such but only the basic principles of these Conventions; a solution which can be workable even with a loose definition or in the absence of any definition of the internal armed conflict. At one stage of the negotiations an attempt was made to enumerate these basic principles in a draft preamble to the Conventions. But as later on, the idea of an elaborate substantive preamble was abandoned, these principles were included in a separate article specifically addressing itself to internal armed conflicts.[6]

Thus Article 3, Common to the four Conventions, reads:

> "In the case of armed conflict not of an international character occurring in the territory of one of the High Contracting Parties, each Party to the conflict shall be bound to apply, as a minimum, the following provisions:
> (1) Persons taking no active part in the hostilities, including members of armed forces, who have laid down their arms and those placed *hors*

de combat by sickness, wounds, detention, or any other cause, shall in all circumstances be treated humanely, without any adverse distinction founded on race, colour, religion or faith, sex, birth or wealth, or any similar criteria.

To this end, the following acts are and shall remain prohibited at any time and in any place whatsoever with respect to the above-mentioned persons:

a. violence to life and person, in particular murder of all kinds, mutilation, cruel treatment and torture;
b. taking of hostages;
c. outrages upon personal dignity, in particular humiliating and degrading treatment;
d. the passing of sentences and the carrying out of executions without previous judgement pronounced by a regularly constituted court, affording all the judicial guarantees which are recognized as indispensable by civilized peoples.

(2) The wounded and sick shall be collected and cared for. An impartial humanitarian body, such as the International Committee of the Red Cross, may offer its services to the Parties to the conflict. The Parties to the conflict should further endeavour to bring into force, by means of special agreements, all or part of the other provisions of the present Convention. The application of the preceding provisions shall not affect the legal status of the Parties to the conflict."

2. *Common Article 3 in Practice*

This article – which was described as a "Convention within the Conventions" and "a Convention in miniature" – though falling short of the maximalist solution, constituted a great step forward in relation to pre-existing law. Its mere existence made a big dent in the wall of State sovereignty by establishing the principle of the applicability of a minimum of humanitarian regulation whenever an internal armed conflict materializes on the territory of a State, as a matter of legal obligation and independently of any act of will on the part of the "established government". But in spite of this breakthrough at the level of principle, the article suffers from technical deficiencies which were progressively revealed by the difficulties that have surrounded its application since 1949.

A) In the first place, when the application of humanitarian law depended on "recognition" (of belligerency or, alternatively, of insurgency) there was no problem identifying the conflicts to which they apply or determining the moment from which this application became operative. But the "automatic" character of common article 3, i.e. its *ipso jure* operation in all conflicts not of an international character, combined with its very condensed and vague formulation, gave rise to such problems.

Indeed, the article defines only negatively the armed conflicts to which it should apply, by stating what they are not, but without providing any substantive or procedural criteria for their identification. The absence of a substantive definition of these conflicts raises the problem of their *threshold*, i.e. what are the minimum (necessary and sufficient) conditions which make it possible to ascertain the existence of an "armed conflict not of an international character", and how to distinguish such conflict from lesser forms of violence and breakdown of the civil order which do not reach that threshold (and which are referred to in ICRC language as "internal disturbances and tensions")?

And the silence of the article as to the procedure (i.e. the competent authority) for determining the existence of such a conflict – a procedure which could have mitigated the inconveniences of the absence of a substantive definition – raises the problem of the *moment* from which the existence of such a conflict cannot be denied, particularly by the "established government".

B) At the other end of the spectrum, the absence of a substantive definition raised also the problem of the *ceiling* of this category of conflicts, i.e. their distinction from international armed conflicts. This problem proved to be particularly acute in view of the nature of the strategic and political configurations of post-war international relations which favoured certain types of armed conflicts difficult to classify along the international/non-international spectrum.

For while the world was quickly divided into two antagonistic blocks by the cold war and the policy of containment was followed, the nuclear balance of terror prevented degenerating into a generalized conflagration. The pent up pressures found their outlets in that vast zone of competition between the two blocks – the Third World – which was in the process of decolonization and nation building.

Thus, while the Third World War did not materialize, the post-war world witnessed the proliferation of "limited wars" which though often taking place on the territory of one State, are in reality "wars by proxy" with the encouragement and the covert and sometimes overt intervention of the contending blocks. Many of these "limited wars" thus reflect certain characteristics of both international and non-international armed conflicts, which makes it difficult to determine with certainty their legal status in relation to the Conventions. Examples of these ambiguous conflicts are those between divided States, territories or zones of occupation, civil wars with foreign intervention (either on the side of the "established government" or on the side of the "rebels"), and wars of national liberation.

C) Even if the preceding difficulties were resolved, or in cases where they do not arise, there remains the problem of determining the scope of protection provided in common article 3. As was mentioned above, this article contains, in a highly condensed form, the principles of the Conventions, respect for which is considered essential in all armed conflicts. Its compact and general language makes it highly non "self-executing" (or self-sufficient) as a legal regulation, and leaves a wide margin for interpretation, hence controversy, as to the scope of protection it affords.

Given the conditions in which humanitarian law is called upon to apply, what is most needed is a clear regulation of specific hypotheses and situations. This is done in large measure in the almost 500 articles of the Conventions in relation to international armed conflicts; but obviously not in common article 3 alone in relation to non-international armed conflicts. Thus numerous crucial issues which proved to be of frequent recurrence and great practical consequence (such as the treatment, protection and access to captured combatants and civilian detainees, and the protection of civilian populations against indiscriminate attacks) are not, or only obliquely, addressed by this article.

D) Yet another source of inextricable practical difficulties relate to the nature of conflicts to which common article 3 is called upon to apply. Indeed, the great majority of non-international (as well as some international) armed conflicts constitute at least in their early stages what strategists call "asymmetrical conflicts". In such situations, the large disparity in strength – especially in air and fire power – between the parties, leaves no choice to the weaker one, usually the "rebels", but to carry on a "poor man's war", by resorting to non-conventional or guerrilla warfare, based on mobility, surprise and camouflage. But the Geneva Conventions (and The Hague Regulations before them) are modelled after conventional warfare where regular armies – composed of military personnel clearly distinguishable from civilian populations – confront each other along an equally distinguishable front line. This poses in an acute manner the question of their adequacy and their practical applicability to guerrilla warfare. To the extent that common article 3 draws on the principles and underlying approach of the Conventions, it suffers from the same defects as regards guerrilla warfare.

E) Finally, the elaborate mechanisms of implementation and scrutiny established by the Conventions are not referred to, except in a very diluted form, in common article 3. This limitative approach was a condition *sine qua non* for acceptance of the solution of common article 3 by governments; it was essential for them as a protection against such political dangers as the appointment by "rebels" of a Protecting Power, which would in fact, if not in law, confer on them an international status.

It is precisely to avert this objection that common article 3, paragraph 4, expressly provides that "the application of the preceding provisions shall not affect the legal status of the Parties to the conflict". In spite of this disclaimer, however, common article 3 does confer certain objective legal status on "rebels" in conflicts not of an international character. This status is more limited in its legal effects than the one deriving from the "recognition of belligerency" as it does not entail the application of the *jus in bello* as a whole (but only those principles enumerated in common article 3). On the other hand, it is an objective status emanating from the Conventions themselves and thus transcending the discretionary and relative character of the "recognition of belligerency". Its effect is to have a minimum legal standard apply, independently of the will of the established government, as soon as violence attains a certain threshold.

These legal and political consequences of the application of common article 3 explain the reluctance of governments to admit the applicability of the article in concrete situations involving them. But even when they admit it, they do not have an obligation to submit to any "scrutiny". Common article 3, paragraph 2, merely stipulates:

> "An impartial humanitarian body, such as the ICRC, may offer its services to the Parties to the conflict".

Neither the tender of the offer of services nor its acceptance are obligatory. Both remain optional for the humanitarian body and for the government in question.

This guarded approach, in deference no doubt to the traditional considerations of sovereignty under conditions of stress, rendered the application of common article 3 even more problematic. The ICRC offer of services was not always accepted by the "established government", especially when it denied the existence of the conflict, and in any case rarely at the very beginning of the conflict. But even when it was accepted, the text left much room for controversy as to what the role of the ICRC is and what it is supposed to do. Thus even the acceptance of the ICRC offer did not necessarily ensure the strict adherence to the letter and spirit of common article 3, as witnessed in many recent conflicts.

* * *

In the face of such difficulties, the consistent strategy of the ICRC was to strive to extend its activities to all situations of internal conflict, disturbances or tension; in other words, to use the ambiguities of the text in order to push the threshold as far down as possible, and to establish its *locus standi* to act even in situations falling below it. In particular, the ICRC strove to have access in all such situations to prisoners and detainees with a view to ensuring their humane treatment, an activity which is highly prized by the ICRC and in which it feels particularly confident.

As part of this strategy, commissions of experts were established from time to time to help clarify the law and consolidate humanitarian initiatives and action. Thus a "Commission of experts for the examination of the question of assistance to political detainees" was convened in 1953, and another "for the study of the question of the application of humanitarian principles in the event of internal disturbances" in 1955. In both cases, humanitarian standards (especially for the treatment of prisoners and detainees) were found to exist, on the basis of the 1949 Conventions, common article 3 (in spite of the fact that the situations envisaged did not fall formally within their ambit) and the international legal instruments for the protection of human rights.[7] Moreover, the role of the ICRC was asserted, particularly as an exercise of its "right of initiative" (which was considered as morally binding on governments, as long as the ICRC made a clear distinction between the humanitarian on the one hand, and the legal and political aspects of the case on the other). But the most important from the point of view of common article 3 was the "Commission of experts for the study of the question of aid to the victims of internal conflicts" which met in 1962 and which found that "the existence of an armed conflict, within the meaning of article 3, cannot be denied if the hostile action, directed against the legal government is of a collective character and consists of a minimum amount of organization".[8]

But these were mere expert opinions which could not by themselves bind governments, and which were in any case, and in spite of their usefulness, too brief and general to serve as an effective complement to common article 3.

The increasing awareness of the shortcomings of article 3 on the one hand and the proliferation of internal conflicts which – far from being a peripheral appendage to international conflicts – proved to be the most typical and endemic form of armed conflict of present-day international relations on the other, were at the basis of the feeling of dissatisfaction with the state of the law, and explain in large part the efforts starting in the late sixties for updating humanitarian law; efforts which culminated in the adoption of the two Protocols Additional to the Geneva Conventions in 1977.

III. Protocol II

I. The Groundwork

Prompted by the newly found interest of the UN General Assembly, following the Teheran International Conference on Human Rights of 1968, in the "respect of human rights in armed conflicts",[9] i.e. in the development of humanitarian law, and capitalizing on the revival of political interest in the subject, the ICRC started to prepare for a new effort in that direction. It presented a substantial report on the subject to the XXIst International Red Cross Conference held at Istanbul in 1969,[10] then convened a Conference of Government Experts which met in Geneva in 1971 and 1972. In the light of the deliberations of this Conference, the ICRC prepared two draft Protocols Additional to the Geneva Conventions – one dealing with international conflicts, the other exclusively devoted to non-international armed conflicts – to serve as bases for discussions of the Diplomatic Conference which was convened by the Swiss Federal Government in Geneva in 1974 and which adopted the two Protocols at the end of its fourth session in 1977.

At the first session of the Government Experts Conference in 1971, the Norwegian experts put forward the idea of a single additional protocol to the Third (Prisoners of War) and the Fourth (Civilians) Geneva Conventions; a protocol which would apply to all armed conflicts, whether internal or international.[11] But this maximalist solution was too idealistic to attract wide political support, and was quickly abandoned in favour of a Canadian proposal of a separate "Draft Protocol to the Geneva Conventions of 1949 relative to conflicts not of an international character".[12]

At the second session of the Government Experts Conference in 1972, the ICRC submitted two preliminary draft Protocols. As far as non-international armed conflicts are concerned, the ICRC followed a three-pronged strategy with a view to achieving maximum feasible extension of humanitarian protection. Apart from a complete draft Protocol of 48 articles which aimed at elaborating in much greater detail the substantive protection provided in common article 3 and at clarifying its ambit, it endeavoured to deal with the problems of ceiling and threshold. In relation to the former, an annex to the draft Protocol provided for the integral application of the Geneva Conventions to internal conflicts in which the "rebels" possess a high degree of organization and exercise effective control over part of the national territory, as well as (though with some qualifications) to cases of internal armed conflict with operational military intervention by a foreign power.[13] But this attempt at internationalizing high intensity internal armed conflicts was strongly resisted, and the ICRC dropped the idea in the draft Protocol it submitted to the Diplomatic Conference.

As far as wars of national liberation are concerned, "most of the experts... who spoke on the subject [during the first session of the Government Experts Conference] considered that wars of liberation were international armed conflicts".[14] As a result, the ICRC prepared a preliminary draft declaration which was submitted to the second session which provided two alternative versions: the application of a) at least common article 3 and its projected additional Protocol, or b) a list of rules to be appended to the declaration.[15] But this proposal was rejected by the overwhelming majority as being either too little (by the proponents of the international status of wars of national liberation, who were the large majority) or too much (by their opponents).[16] As a result, the ICRC all but ignored the issue in the draft Protocols it submitted to the Diplomatic Conference.

As concerns the threshold, the ICRC had put forward in the background documents it submitted to the Government Experts Conference, the idea of a "Declaration of fundamental rights of the individual in time of internal disturbances or public emergency".[17] But this draft declaration – which was patterned after international humanitarian law and the International Covenant on Civil and Political Rights – reproduced common article 3 almost entirely while adding new elements to it. No wonder that when it came up for discussion during the second session of the Conference in 1972, it was strongly resisted.[18] As a result, the ICRC did not refer to the matter at all in the draft Protocol submitted to the Diplomatic Conference.

In the light of the deliberations of the Government Experts Conference, the ICRC concentrated its efforts, in the draft Protocol submitted to the Diplomatic Conference, on the clarification of the concept and ambit of non-international armed conflicts and on elaborating at great length the substantive protection.

Draft Protocol II was not examined so to speak during the first session of the Diplomatic Conference in 1974, a session which was practically wholly devoted to the controversy over wars of national liberation, and which ended up by the adoption in committee of an amendment to article 1 of draft Protocol I, recognizing the international character of such wars.[19]

However, even in the opening general debate, both in plenary and in the first committee during the first session, but particularly after the adoption of the above-mentioned amendment, strong doubts were expressed towards the very idea of a Protocol wholly devoted to non-international armed conflicts. The two most populous states of the world, China and India, in addition to Indonesia, the Philippines, Iran, several Latin American and African countries criticized the idea either in its principle, or, more frequently, in a roundabout manner, by suggesting very limitative conditions for its application or drastic reductions in its content.

Though basically reflecting a concern by many (but not all[20]) Third World countries lest the projected Protocol would in fact serve as an instrument of internationalizing their internal problems and as a basis for foreign intervention in such situations, a more limitative approach to certain aspects of the Protocol was also adopted both by the socialist states and by some Western countries, particularly Canada. To start with, this approach took the form of restrictive amendments to draft article 1, defining the material field of application of the Protocol.

2. The Ambit of Protocol II

Article 1 of the ICRC draft Protocol II provided:

> "1.– The present Protocol shall apply to all armed conflicts not covered by Article 2 common to the Geneva Conventions of August 12, 1949 taking place between armed forces or other organized armed groups under responsible command.
> 2.– The present Protocol shall not apply to situations of internal disturbances and tensions, *inter alia* riots, isolated and sporadic acts of violence and other acts of similar nature.
> 3.– The foregoing provisions do not modify the conditions governing the application of Article 3 common to the Geneva Conventions of August 12, 1949."

The restrictive amendments to this draft article crystalized around two ideas. The first was to introduce a requirement of recognition by the government of the territorial state of the applicability of the Protocol to a situation arising on its territory.[21] This requirement, which is reminiscent of the institution of recognition of belligerency, would have completely defeated the purpose of the Protocol. This is why, in spite of the insistence of its proponents, and the sympathy with the aim of the amendment which was shared by many others, it had no chance of success.

The other restrictive idea was to introduce a high intensity requirement, particularly territorial control, as a condition for the applicability of the Protocol. A Pakistani amendment was introduced in this sense;[22] and it was this limitation that was finally adopted, once it became clear that the ICRC draft as it stood had no chance of securing the necessary majority.

Article I of Protocol II, in its final version, reads:

> "1. This Protocol, which develops and supplements Article 3 common to the Geneva Convention of 12 August 1949 without modifying its existing conditions of application, shall apply to all armed conflicts which are not covered by Article 1 of the Protocol Additional to the Geneva Conventions of 12 August 1949, and relating to the Protection of Victims of International Armed Conflicts (Protocol I) and which take place in the territory of a High Contracting Party between its armed forces or other organized armed groups which, under responsible command, exercise such control over a part of its territory as to enable them to carry out sustained and concerted military operations and to implement this Protocol.
> 2. This Protocol shall not apply to situations of internal disturbances and tensions, such as riots, isolated and sporadic acts of violence and other acts of a similar nature, as not being armed conflicts."

This text differs from the ICRC draft in several respects:

1) The ICRC draft provided a positive definition of non-international armed conflict which was clearly inspired by the formula of the 1962 Commission of Experts, based upon the collective character of the hostilities (i.e. armed conflict) and the organization of the parties to the conflict. To these requirements, the final version adds that of territorial control by the rebels, which must be substantial enough to "enable them to carry out sustained and concerted military operations...". This last phrase could be constructed as not only requiring a high intensity armed conflict, but even as implying that the territorial control should be such as to allow the rebels to resort to conventional warfare, though such a construction, it is submitted, would be exaggerated.

All the same, the requirement of territorial control excludes from the ambit of the Protocol, many, if not most, current forms of internal armed conflicts, in particular, all the low intensity asymmetric conflicts, urban guerilla and other highly mobile forms of guerilla warfare. It also makes it more difficult to argue in favour of the application of the Protocol to situations, frequently met in recent conflicts, in which territorial control shifts or rotates (sometimes following sunset or sunrise) between governmental and rebel forces.

2) *Ratione personae:* unlike the ICRC draft which applies to all conflicts between any "armed forces or other organized armed groups under responsible command", the Protocol applies only to armed conflicts between the armed

forces of a High Contracting Party and "dissident armed forces or other organized armed groups". In other words, while the ICRC draft would have applied to any armed conflict between organized armed groups, whether one of them is governmental or not, the final version applies only to armed conflicts between governmental and dissident or rebel forces. Thus an armed conflict between two or more non-governmental groups, as was the case in the Lebanese civil war, would not be covered by this article, if it is interpreted literally.

3) While the definition provided in the ICRC draft coincided with the concept of non-international armed conflict as it was then understood, the draft did safeguard, *ex abundante cautela*, the autonomy of common article 3 in relation to the field of application of the new Protocol, with a view to preserving the possibilities of future evolution through application and interpretation of this article, particularly by extending its ambit through lowering its threshold.

With the restrictive conditions inserted into article 1, the safeguard of the autonomy of common article 3 became a matter not of precaution but of necessity, as it became clear that the Protocol would cover only one species, the most characterized and intense one, of the armed conflicts governed by common article 3.

But the reverse is not true in the sense that all armed conflicts which are covered by article 1 of the Protocol are *a fortiori*, and remain, governed by common article 3. It is only in this sense that the opening phrase of article 1 can be understood: "This Protocol, which develops and supplements Article 3... without modifying its existing conditions of application...". The Protocol supplements, but does not replace or displace common article 3 in relation to one species only of the armed conflicts governed by the latter, and does not limit the application of common article 3 to this species (and it is in this sense that it does not modify its conditions of application).

4) Paragraph 2 of the adopted article, the same as the ICRC draft, excludes from the field of application of the Protocol "situations of internal disturbances and tensions, such as riots, isolated and sporadic acts of violence and other acts of similar nature...". This is a logical conclusion of the introduction of a positive definition in the ICRC draft, and *a fortiori* of the much more restrictive definition of the adopted article. But the adopted article, unlike the ICRC draft, goes on to characterize the excluded situations "as not being armed conflicts". This characterization was strongly defended by the East German delegation[23] and reflects the restrictive attitude of the socialist group as to the threshold of internal conflicts. Its purpose was to seal this threshold once and for all, in order to ward off the dangers of humanitarian concern and intervention in situations falling below it, and more particularly to foreclose any possibility of future evolution of common article 3 in the direction of a lowering of threshold and embracing one or more of the excluded situations.

In other words, the added phrase was intended more for common article 3 than for the conflicts covered by the Protocol and which are far removed from the situations it deals with. But if this characterization is harmless in the context of the Protocol (and was, in consequence easily acceptable in order to reach consensus), it is obviously very dangerous if transposed to common article 3. This is why the transposition was quickly refuted by certain delegates on the ground of the autonomy of common article 3 in relation to the Protocol;[24] an autonomy which it safeguards in its article 1, as was explained above.

3. The Contents of Protocol II

The ICRC draft Protocol II contained 47 articles divided into eight parts. Both in its structure and contents, it strikes by its parallelism with draft Protocol I, with the notable exception of the absence of prisoner of war status for captured combatants (and the consequences thereof).

The reticence encountered as regards the very idea of the Protocol, and the restrictive amendments and obstructionist tactics of several very active delegations should have sufficed to make it clear that a "law of war" approach (along the lines of the inter-state armed conflict model) would be very hard to get through, and that only a "human rights" approach, (based on the government-subject model) stood some chance of commanding general acceptance. But the adoption in committee in 1975 of the revised version of article 1, which limits the application of the Protocol to characterized high intensity armed conflicts materially identical to inter-state wars, encouraged well-intentioned and maximalist delegations to push for an even greater parallelism between the two Protocols through an almost literal transposition of provisions adopted for Protocol I into Protocol II. In the meantime, the active opponents of the Protocol continued their guerilla warfare against it, while a majority of delegations, particularly from the Third World, adopted a rather reserved position, holding their judgment until they could gauge the final result.

As it emerged from the committees during the last session of the Conference in 1977, the Protocol (whose articles were adopted by very weak majorities and large numbers of abstentions) was even more elaborate and analogous to Protocol I than the ICRC draft. It was clear that such a Protocol stood very little chance of commanding the two thirds majority necessary for its final adoption in plenary. At that stage, the acute realization by the ICRC and the proponents of the Protocol (as well as by its opponents) that there was a serious risk of failure, led to a last–minute salvage operation, which went quite a way towards appeasing the opponents of the Protocol, in the form of a Pakistani "simplified" draft (prepared with the active participation of the Iraqi and the Canadian delegations). The reason for their resigned acceptance of this rather truncated version is very well expressed in a phrase by a Dutch delegate that "half an egg is better than an empty shell". The simplified version was discussed and adopted in plenary with minor modifications. By comparison to the ICRC draft it has 28 articles (instead of 47), of which 10 are mere final clauses. Only 15 articles deal with substantive protection (instead of 33), as the first three define the scope of application of the Protocol.

The Omissions: Substantively, what differentiates the simplified version from its predecessor is that it was radically expurgated of three elements which figured in the ICRC draft (and whose omission is also significant in revealing the motivations of the governments which were lukewarm towards the Protocol).

1) The term "parties to the conflicts", though used in common article 3, was systematically removed and the articles were either reformulated or, where reformulation was impossible, dropped. Thus, draft article 3 (reiterating the final paragraph of common article 3) which provided that: "The application of the Protocol or any eventual special agreements shall have no effect on the status of the parties to the conflict...", and which was included for the sole benefit of governments, was dropped because it obviously could not stand without the use of the expurgated term.

The resulting Protocol reads like a series of injunctions addressed exclusively to governments, or rather of unilateral undertakings subscribed to only by them. But of course this cosmetic reformulation cannot alter the legal basis and structure of the Protocol. After all, common article 3 continues to apply to these conflicts, together with Protocol II which is supposed to supplement it, and the "parties to the conflict" figure prominently in common article 3. Moreover, even a superficial analysis of the contents of the Protocol reveals that its prescriptions are addressed to all those who take part in the armed conflict. It follows that to the extent that "rebels" are directly attributed rights and obligations under common article 3 and Protocol II, they are the addressees of their provisions and thus have an objective legal status under these legal instruments, whether they are mentioned expressly therein or not. This status is much more limited than the one emanating from a "recognition of belligerency", but it is an *ipso jure* status which, at least in theory, is both objective (i.e. independent from the will of the government) and automatic (i.e. arising directly from the legal instrument, as soon as the situation provided for comes into being).

Once it is established that the Protocol is addressed and applies to both parties, another related question arises: whether and on what basis it is legally binding on "rebels". It is true that as a matter of practical consideration, the rebels are the weaker party and thus have an interest in the application of humanitarian law and can thus be deemed to have accepted its legal instruments. But this would bring us back to the consensual solutions which are clearly incompatible with the *ipso jure* effect of these instruments. A more acceptable legal explanation is that once the Protocol is internationally accepted in the name of the State by its government, it becomes part of the law of the land, and thus binds both individuals and government, including any actual or future government, as well as any counter movement which disputes the representativity or the authority of such government.

2) Part IV on Methods and Means of Combat, which dealt with part of the "Law of the Hague", and which constitutes, at least symbolically, the hard-core of a "law of war" approach, was completely dropped (though draft article 22 on "quarter" was included in article 1, paragraph 1, as will be described below). But

this Part did not exhaust the "Law of the Hague", and indeed substantial aspects of it, much more important than the rules provided in Part IV, survive in Part VI on "Civilian Population".

In any case, the applicability of the discarded rules to non-international armed conflicts (including those governed by Protocol II) as part of the "Law of the Hague" on the basis of customary law, is not affected by this deletion, though of course this remains subject to controversy both as to the principle itself and as to the scope of its application.

3) In the third place, Part VII of the ICRC draft, on the "Execution of the Protocol" was also dropped, particularly draft article 39, which under the title "Co-operation in the Observance of the Present Protocol" provided:

> "The parties to the conflict may call upon a body offering all guar-
> antees of impartiality and efficacy, such as the ICRC, to co-operate
> in the observance of the provisions of the present Protocol. Such a
> body may also offer its services to the parties to the conflict."

But even this provision – which did no more than reiterate, perhaps in a more explicit manner, the voluntary system of scrutiny provided in the second paragraph of common article 3 – ran into heavy resistence and had to be reduced to its simplest expression ("The ICRC may offer its services to the parties to the conflict") in order to secure its adoption in Committee, before it was completely dropped in the final simplified version.

Likewise, the only article which survived from Part VI on Relief (article 18 in the final Protocol) refers ambiguously only to "relief societies located in the territory of the High Contracting Party, such as Red Cross (Red Crescent...) organizations" (which "may offer their services for the performance of their traditional functions in relation to the victims of the armed conflict"), without any express mention of the ICRC or other international humanitarian organisms. But clearly this provision can be interpreted as including, in addition to national societies, the ICRC delegations present in the territory of the State concerned.

In any case, here again this omission cannot change the legalities of the situation. For, as was observed by several delegates, as the Protocol "develops and supplements", common article 3 "without modifying its existing conditions of application", this article – and in particular its second paragraph concerning the offer of services by humanitarian organizations – continues to apply to all non-international armed conflicts, including those covered by Protocol II.[25] Paradoxically, it can thus be said that in this respect it is common article 3 which "develops and supplements" the Protocol rather than vice versa.

The great reluctance to recognize a role, be it on a consensual basis, for third parties, even humanitarian ones, in non-international armed conflicts reflects the great wariness of most Third World governments about the possibility of opening a wedge for foreign intervention in their internal troubles under a humanitarian guise. The ICRC draft included an article 4 entitled "Non-Intervention" which was aimed at meeting this concern, and which read: "Nothing in the present

Protocol shall be interpreted as affecting the sovereignty of States or as authorizing third States to intervene in the armed conflict".

The final adopted version (article 3) reads:

"1. Nothing in this Protocol shall be invoked for the purpose of affecting the sovereignty of a State or the responsibility of the government, by all legitimate means, to maintain or re-establish law and order in the State or to defend the national unity and territorial integrity of the State.

2. Nothing in this Protocol shall be invoked as a justification for intervening, directly or indirectly, for any reason whatever, in the armed conflict or in the internal or external affairs of the High Contracting Party in the territory of which that conflict occurs."

Not only is this version much more elaborate and stronger in tone and content but it also does not limit the interfering subjects to "third States", in order to cover also non-state entities including humanitarian and relief organizations. The same concern also explains the deletion from article 18 on relief, of the last sentence of paragraph 1 of the corresponding article in the ICRC draft (article 33) which provided that "relief actions fulfilling the above conditions shall not be regarded as interference in the armed conflict".

The extent of the fear of intervention is well illustrated by an Indian amendment which would have suspended the application of the Protocol in case of foreign intervention.[26] Though this extreme proposal was not pushed through, it was symptomatic of the general state of mind and atmosphere which prevailed at the Conference on the subject.

In conclusion, the three categories of omission, despite appearances, do not change the legalities of the situation, as the expurged elements continue to produce their legal effects in the armed conflicts governed by the Protocol, on the basis either of common article 3 or of customary law. But appearances are important for governments, and the omissions leave them with much room for manœuver through interpretation.

If in what it was made not to say the Protocol falls short of common article 3, it remains to be seen how much, if at all, it has added to it in what it does say.

The Additions: The contribution of the Protocol to common article 3 has to be sought in the substantive protection it provides for the potential victims of the armed conflicts it governs. These are described in article 2 ("Personal field of application") as "all persons affected by an armed conflict as defined in Article 1".

Three Parts of the Protocol (II, III and IV) are devoted to substantive protection:

A) Part III "Wounded, Sick and Shipwrecked", elaborates in two articles (article 7 "Protection and care", art. 8 "Search") the general proposition of common article 3, para. 1 (2), that: "The wounded and sick shall be collected and cared for". But the great addition, which has been almost transposed from

Protocol I is the detailed protection provided for medical and religious personnel (article 9), medical duties (article 10), medical units and transports (article 11), as well as for the distinctive emblem (article 12).

B) Part II "Humane Treatment" is composed of three very long articles (4 to 6). They correspond to common article 3 par. 1 (1) which, it may be useful to recall, uses the same terms in the general formulation of the principle of humane treatment, without any adverse distinction, to all persons who are in the power of a party to the conflict and who are not taking an active part in hostilities, before enumerating more specifically four injunctions, the first three dealing with the physical and moral integrity of the protected persons while the fourth deals with the problem of "due process of law" in penal prosecutions.

Article 4 of the Protocol on "Fundamental guarantees" covers materially the same ground as the general principle and the first three specific injunctions of common article 3 para. 1 (1), but it adds much in terms of elaboration and concrete application. It is very close to the corresponding parts of article 75 of Protocol I (which bears the same title, but covers as well the scope of articles 5 and particularly 6 of Protocol II); and both have drawn their inspiration from the International Covenant on Civil and Political Rights (e.g. articles 6, 7 and 8) as well as from the Fourth Geneva Convention (article 33). In addition, the provision concerning "quarter" was inserted at the end of its first paragraph (after the deletion of the Part on "Methods and Means of Combat") and those on the special protection of children were added to it as paragraph 3.

Article 5 deals more particularly with the treatment of persons whose liberty is restricted and who, as a result, need in addition to the fundamental guarantees of article 4, special protection relating to the conditions of their detention or restriction of freedom. Many of the standards set therein find their sources in the Third and Fourth Geneva Conventions, as well as in the International Covenant on Civil and Political Rights (e.g. article 10). But as they apply to all persons whose liberty is restricted and not only to those who have participated in hostilities, they cannot be said to constitute a special *treatment* similar to that of prisoners of war.

Article 6 deals with the "due process of law" and corresponds to the fourth specific injunction of common article 3 para 1 (1), which it elaborates to a great extent. It finds its sources both in the Third and Fourth Geneva Conventions and the International Covenant on Civil and Political Rights (e.g. articles 14, 15) as well as in article 75 of Protocol I. Article 6 does not prohibit criminal prosecution of persons for their mere participation in the hostilities, for such immunity can only derive from the granting of prisoner of war status to captured combatants. The only element in the ICRC draft which pointed in that direction, namely the reprieve from executing capital punishment until the cessation of hostilities, met with heavy resistance and failed to be adopted (though the exhortation to the authorities to grant as wide an amnesty as possible at the end of hostilities, which was intended more particularly for this hypothesis, was maintained).

Though these three lengthy articles are heavily inspired by the International Covenant on Civil and Political Rights, they are not superfluous in relation to it, for two reasons at least. In the first place, they are more detailed and more geared to factual situations likely to arise in armed conflicts. Secondly, they cannot be waived, whereas certain corresponding provisions of the Covenant, under its article 4, can in case of emergency (which obviously includes an internal armed conflict). Thus, in these respects, the Protocol sets a higher threshold. At the same time, the Covenant provides for many contingencies which are not covered by the Protocol. The two instruments are thus complementary where there is an identity of parties, but can be applied independently where there is no such identity.

C) If Part II clearly follows a "human rights" approach, Part IV on "Civilian Population" is by contrast strongly influenced by a "law of war" approach. The difference is particularly clear when it comes to determining the protected persons. Part II prescribes "humane treatment" of all persons in their power by the parties to the conflict, without distinguishing between those who had taken part in hostilities and those who had not (the same as Part III on "Wounded, Sick and Shipwrecked"). Part IV, on the other hand, necessarily distinguishes *civilians*, defined in article 13 para. 3, as those who (and "for such time as they") do not "take a direct part in hostilities", and who are consequently entitled to "general protection against the dangers arising from military operations" (article 13 para. 1), from those who do take part in hostilities (i.e. combatants, though the Protocol was systematically expurgated of that term to avoid any semblance of status attaching to it), and who obviously are not entitled to such protection. This distinction derives inexorably from the legal structure of the prescribed rules. For with the exception of the last two articles of Part IV (art. 17 "Prohibition of forced movement of civilians", and art. 18 "Relief societies and relief action") which, like those of Part II, are clearly addressed to the party to the conflict which controls the protected persons, the core articles of Part IV are addressed simultaneously to all parties to the conflict and perhaps more particularly to the one which does not control the protected civilian population; a structure which places them squarely within the "Law of the Hague" i.e. the law governing the conduct of hostilities and combat.

Though heavily pruned in the final version of the Protocol, these articles still include the fundamental rule of "general protection of the civilian population against the dangers arising from military operations" (article 13 para. 1) which imposes an obligation of due diligence and discrimination on the parties to the conflict in all circumstances; the prohibition of taking civilians for a target (including indiscriminate attacks and threats or attacks aiming at terrorizing the civilian population) (article 13 para. 2); the protection of objects indispensable to the survival of the civilian population i.e. the prohibition of starvation as a method of combat (article 14); the protection of works and installations containing dangerous forces (article 15); and the protection of cultural objects and places of worship (article 16). These provisions have been taken almost literally from Protocol I and constitute even in the context of that Protocol, and *a fortiori* in Protocol II, an innovation and a great step forward in the protection of civilians.

* * *

It is too early to evaluate Protocol II in the light of practice. On the basis of its legislative history, it is clear that the great wariness and sensitivity of a large number of states, particularly of the Third World, as regards all possible sources of foreign intervention in their internal affairs, has led to a very high threshold for the application of the Protocol, and has thus excluded from its ambit all but the most intense and characterized civil wars, which constitute a very small proportion of contemporary internal conflicts. And while it thus resolves, albeit restrictively, the problem of the substantive definition of the conflict, it leaves open the other problem of the procedural determination of its existence. At the same time, and this is its other fundamental shortcoming, the role of humanitarian organisms both in terms of relief and of co-operation in the implementation of the Protocol, is drastically reduced. On both these points, the Protocol has to be supplemented by common article 3.

Where Protocol II comes into its own is in the substantive protection, it provides through its much greater, and greatly needed, elaboration of the elliptic declarations of principle of common article 3, and through introducing new fundamental rules concerning the protection of civilians against the effects of hostilities, as well as the protection of medical personnel and transports.[27]

The legislative history clearly indicates that Protocol II represents the most of what was realistically possible to achieve in the international community of 1977.

IV. Some Concluding Remarks

Only time can tell whether Protocol II was worth the effort and whether what was really needed was a detailed regulation for cases in the upper reaches of the category of non-international armed conflicts rather than around its threshold or, for that matter, for the category as a whole.

In the meantime, three types of cases can be distinguished:

1) At the apex there are the intense and characterized internal armed conflicts covered by Protocol II, which constitute only one part of the non-international armed conflicts governed by common article 3, and for which the Protocol provides detailed regulation which elaborates and adds to the prescriptions of common article 3. This means that common article 3 continues to apply to all the armed conflicts governed by Protocol II, and can thus fill the gaps left open in the Protocol, such as the one relating to the role of the ICRC. Moreover, for states parties to the International Covenant on Civil and Political Rights, the

Covenant continues to apply and where the guaranteed rights coincide, the higher standard or stricter obligation prevails.

2) In cases falling below the very high threshold defined by article 1 of Protocol II, particularly where rebels do not exercise territorial control, only common article 3 applies (supplemented for those states which are parties to it, by the International Covenant on Civil and Political Rights). In relation to these conflicts, the direct contribution of the Diplomatic Conference and the ensuing Protocols in providing answers to the problems revealed in practice by the application of common article 3, is rather limited. The Protocols succeed simply in clarifying the status of, and the law applicable to, certain doubtful ceiling cases, such as wars of national liberation (recognized by Protocol I as international armed conflicts) and high intensity internal armed conflicts, which are now covered by Protocol II (though the third case in this category, i.e. non-international armed conflict with foreign operational military intervention, did not receive any clarification).

Indirectly, however, Protocol II can have a substantial impact in elucidating the material protection provided for in common article 3. Indeed, both Part II on "Humane Treatment" and Part III on "Sick, Wounded and Shipwrecked" elaborate in greater detail and more concrete terms the general principles enunciated in common article 3, and can legitimately be considered as an authoritative interpretation of these principles. Part III on the protection of "civilian population", though constituting an innovation, can also be taken into consideration in the interpretation of common article 3, which, being a part of a law-making multilateral treaty of humanitarian import, has to be interpreted in the light of its unfolding object and purpose, and according to the principle of inter-temporal law of its evolving legal environment of which the Protocol is a part.

The Protocol does not help, however, in providing either any guidance as to the definition of non-international armed conflicts, of which it covers only one species, or a procedure for the determination of the existence of such a conflict; and of course it remains silent on the role of international humanitarian organisms in securing the observance of humanitarian rules. On all these questions, it is the accumulated practice, particularly of the ICRC, which continues to provide whatever guidance there can be had both for conflicts covered by common article 3 as well as by Protocol II, but particularly for those covered only by common article 3.

3) Where no progress at all has been achieved and where there is even a semblance of regression is in defining the threshold of non-international armed conflicts, more particularly as it relates to internal disturbances and tensions which hover below it, and which have been expressly classified in article 1 para. 2 of the Protocol as "not being armed conflicts". But as was mentioned above, this classification which stands as far as Protocol II is concerned, does not automatically apply to common article 3, whose ambit and conditions of application have been kept separate from those of the Protocol.

This does not mean that these situations constitute non-international armed conflicts in the sense of common article 3. But the general policy of the ICRC has always tended towards assimilating them to non-international armed conflicts, but without classifying them legally as such. And there is no reason why, if practice follows suit, such an evolution cannot be hardened into law.

In the meantime, these situations remain subject to the existing international instruments of protection of human rights, such as the International Covenant on Civil and Political Rights for those States which are parties to it, as well as the Universal Declaration of Human Rights. But in addition we have the principles of the Geneva Conventions which are the irreducible hard-core applicable in all circumstances and which provide the ICRC with a *locus standi* (but not a right binding on the State concerned) to exercise its right of initiative in such situations. And it is through such initiatives that the ICRC sets the pattern for the development of humanitarian law.

Notes

1. Instructions for the Government of Armies of the United States in the Field. Prepared by Francis Lieber and promulgated as General Order No. 100 by President Lincoln on 24 April 1863. These Instructions are reproduced *in: The Laws of Armed Conflicts. A Collection of Conventions, Resolutions and Other Documents*, Edited by D. Schindler and J. Toman, 3rd edition, Dordrecht, Martinus Nijhoff Publishers, Geneva, Henry Dunant Institute, 1988, pp. 3–23. Cf. in general, on the Lieber Code as well as on the subsequent developments up to and including Protocol II, Rosemary Abi-Saab, *Droit humanitaire et conflits internes. Origines et évolution de la réglementation internationale*. Genève/Paris, Institut Henry-Dunant/Editions A. Pedone, 1986, 280 p.

2. Institut de droit international. *Annuaire*, 1900, Vol. 18, p. 229. Institut de droit international. *Tableau général des résolutions (1873–1956)*, publié par Hans Wehberg. Bâle, Editions juridiques et sociologiques S.A., 1957, pp. 171–173.

3. Fiore, E.G. *Nouveau droit international public*, Paris, 1885, p. 285; Bluntschli, Jean-Gaspar. *Le droit international codifié*. Paris, Félix Alcan, 1895, para. 512.

4. *Dixième Conférence internationale de la Croix-Rouge, tenue à Genève du 30 mars au 7 avril 1921. Compte-rendu*, pp. 217–218.

5. Pictet, Jean (ed.). *Commentary of the Geneva Conventions of 12 August 1949*, Vol. III – Geneva Convention Relative to the Treatment of Prisoners of War. Geneva, ICRC, 1960, p. 31.

6. *Ibid.*

7. ICRC. *Commission of Experts for the Examination of the Question of Assistance to Political Detainees (Geneva, June 9–11, 1953)*. Geneva, ICRC, 1953, 8 p. – ICRC. *Commission of Experts for the Study of he Question of the Application of Humanitarian Principles in the Event of Internal Disturbances (Geneva, October 3–8, 1955)*, Geneva, ICRC, 1953, 8 p.

8. ICRC. *Commission of Experts for the Study of the Question of Aid to the Victims of Internal Conflicts (Geneva, October 25–30, 1962)*, Geneva, ICRC, 1962, p. 3.

9. See the stream of resolutions starting with the United Nations General Assembly resolution 2444 (XXVIII) of 19 December 1968 and the series of Secretary-General reports, the first submitted in 1969, all under the title mentioned in the text.

10. XXIst International Conference of the Red Cross, Istanbul, 1969. *Reaffirmation and Development of the Laws and Customs Applicable in Armed Conflicts*. Report submitted by the ICRC, Geneva, ICRC; May 1969.

11. ICRC. Conference of Government Experts on the Reaffirmation and Development of International Humanitarian Law Applicable in Armed Conflicts (Geneva, 24 May–12 June 1971): *Report on the Work of the Conference*. Geneva, 1971. (Doc. CE/Com. II/1–3), p. 61.

12. *Ibid.* (Doc. CE/Plen. 2 bis), pp. 57–61.

13. ICRC. Conference of Government Experts on the Reaffirmation and Development of International Humanitarian Law Applicable in Armed Conflicts (Second session 3 May–3 June 1972): *Report on the Work of the Conference*. Vol. 2 Geneva, ICRC, 1972, p. 22.

14. XXIst International Conference of the Red Cross, Istanbul, 1969. *Reaffirmation and Development of the Laws and Customs Applicable in Armed Conflicts*. Reports submitted by the ICRC, Geneva, ICRC; May 1969, p. 54 (para. 321).

15. ICRC. Conference of Government Experts on the Reaffirmation and Development of International Humanitarian Law Applicable in Armed Conflicts (Second session 3 May–3 June 1972): *Report on the Work of the Conference*. Vol. 2. Geneva, ICRC, 1972, p. 23.

16. *Ibid.*, Vol. 1, p. 201 (para. 4.217–4.224).

17. ICRC. Conference of Government Experts on the Reaffirmation and Development of International Humanitarian Law Applicable in Armed Conflicts (Geneva, 24 May–12 June 1971): Vol. V – *Protection of Victims of Non-International Armed Conflicts* (Doc. CE/56). Geneva, 1971, pp. 85–88.

18. ICRC. Conference of Government Experts on the Reaffirmation and Development of International Humanitarian Law Applicable in Armed Conflicts (Second session 3 May–3 June 1972): *Report on the Work of the Conference*. Vol. 1. Geneva, ICRC, 1972, pp. 124–125 (para. 2.564–2.570).

19. On this question, see Abi-Saab G., Wars of National Liberation in the Geneva Conventions and Protocols. *Recueil des cours*, Vol. 165, 1979–IV, pp. 353–446.

20. E.g. Egypt CDDH/I/SR. 24.

21. E.g. the amendments of Romania CDDH/I/30.

22. CDDH/I/26; also in the same vain Indonesia CDDH/I/32, and Brasil CDDH/I/79.

23. CDDH/I/SR. 28; CDDH/I/SR. 29, para. 30.

24. E.g. Italy CDDG/I/SR. 29, para. 25; Federal Republic of Germany, CDDH/I/SR. 29, para. 5; CDDH/SR. 49, para. 58.

25. E.g. Egypt CDDH/SR. 56, Annex, p. 6.

26. CDDH/I/240.

27. It is to be regretted however that the only draft provision which provided specific protection to captured combatants and which aimed at avoiding the commitment of the irreversible in the heat of the battle (the reprieve of capital punishment executions for offences related to the conflict until hostility has ceased), failed to be adopted.

CHAPTER XV

INTERNAL DISTURBANCES AND TENSIONS

ASBJÖRN EIDE

Introduction: The Role of International Law in Internal Conflicts

Like the preceeding article, the present contribution deals with international law applicable in internal conflicts, resuming discussions where the previous one ends. We are here concerned with those situations which are not covered by Protocol II, and therefore we have to examine the scope of application of Protocol II to determine what falls outside its provisions. Furthermore, we have to determine what law is applicable when Protocol II does not directly apply.

We are concerned with international law. It is not our purpose, therefore, to examine domestic law, either within any given state, or on a comparative basis. The questions discussed in this article mainly centre around government conduct towards its opponents within the state. All domestic legal systems have provisions dealing with such questions in many different branches of domestic law – in constitutional law, in penal law, in administrative law, in regulations for the police, for the military, for the prison administration, and in various other rules. This wide spectrum will not be examined here even though a detailed examination of the problems in this article would have to include also a comparative study of domestic law relating to such questions.

Why is there a distinction between international and internal conflicts? The most frequent answer is that international law should be restricted to questions which are international in nature and which cannot therefore be regulated easily by domestic law. On the other hand, internal affairs, according to this view, should be regulated by domestic law.

This argument is too facile. Even in regard to international conflicts, domestic law is applicable. The provisions contained in the Geneva Conventions will in many legal systems not be directly binding on individuals (military personnel, administrators and so on) unless they have been incorporated into domestic law. Consequently, even during international conflicts the regulation of behaviour does to a large extent come within the purview of domestic law.

When conflicts take place within a country, however, the government is more concerned with its capacity to deter dissident or opposition groups from carrying out actions against it than with measures to restrain its own security forces. Thus, the predisposition to exert control tends to overshadow the concern to exercise humanitarian constraint. Naturally, this varies with different governments, depending in part on the degree of democratic participation in governmental authority.

Where there is a responsible government, it will seek to restrain the violence exercised by its own security forces, partly in order not to exacerbate the conflict and partly because the government, in principle, should be the representative of the whole of the people including those who are in opposition. But in polarized and emotionally enflamed situations, there will be strong pressure on the government to take extreme measures. International law prohibiting the use of such measures will in such cases make it possible to resist such pressure.

A. Applicable International Law

The Four Legal Categories of Conflicts

Protocol II, which was adopted in 1977, deals with non-international armed conflicts, but is limited in its application by Article 1. According to paragraph 1 of that article, the Protocol shall apply to all armed conflicts which are not covered by Article 1 of Protocol I,

> "and which take place in the territory of a High Contracting Party between its armed forces and dissident armed forces or other organized armed groups which, under responsible command, exercise such control over a part of its territory as to enable them to carry out sustained concerted military operations and to implement this Protocol".

There are two aspects to the dividing line between conflicts which fall within the scope of Protocol II and those which do not. One is the magnitude of the conflict. The dissident forces have to exercise control over a part of the territory so as to enable them to carry out sustained and concerted operations. The other aspect is the relationship between the parties. According to the provision just quoted, the Protocol covers only conflicts between the armed forces of a "High Contracting Party" – i.e., the government of the state – and dissident forces.

An interesting situation arises when a government has been ousted by a military coup, followed by civil strife. In such an event the former government may well be on the side of those who are fighting against the regular armed forces. Does this situation fall under Protocol II or not?

This raises a fundamental problem. What constitutes a government (and hence a "High Contracting Party")? In recent international law this has been determined largely on the basis of who has actual control over the territory. It follows from this that whoever gains control may be said to be the government. The situation becomes particularly complicated if the pre-existing government, possibly even a democratically elected government, is able to maintain control over a peripheral part of the country only, whereas the military architects of the coup obtain control over the central areas. In such a situation, it may be doubtful who is the government but there should be no doubt that this situation falls within Protocol II.

In Article 3 common to the Geneva Conventions, which also deals with internal conflicts, there is a different approach.

> "In the case of an armed conflict not of an international character occurring in the territory of one of the High Contracting Parties, each Party to the conflict shall be bound to apply as a minimum,..." (the article goes on to describe what provisions shall apply in this situation).

Article 3 requires neither that the conflict be between the government and dissident forces nor that one party have control over a part of the territory. But it does require that the conflict be an armed conflict. Clearly, therefore, Article 3 has a wider scope than Protocol II, but, in practice Protocol II may well be interpreted in such a way that it coincides with the scope of Article 3.[1]

According to Protocol II, Article 1, Paragraph 2, certain situations are expressly excluded:

> "This Protocol shall not apply to situations of internal disturbances and tensions, such as riots, isolated and sporadic acts of violence and other acts of a similar nature, as not being armed conflicts".

We are therefore faced with at least the following legal categories:[2]

(1) International conflicts (now including wars of national liberation);
(2) Armed conflicts falling under Protocol II;
(3) Armed conflicts falling under Article 3 common to the Geneva Conventions of 1949 but not falling under Protocol II, either because of lack of magnitude or because of party relationship as discussed above;
(4) Conflicts and events which are not armed conflicts, as indicated in paragraph 2 of Article 1 as quoted above.

B. Survey of Relevant Human Right Provisions

a) Entrenched provisions and conditions for derogation

When neither Protocol II nor Article 3 of the Geneva Conventions applies, what international law does apply?

In fact, there is an increasingly wide set of rules which apply in all circumstances, whether the domestic situation is calm or is troubled by riots, disorders, or even armed strife. The United Nations has stated in several resolutions that human rights continue to apply in armed conflicts.[3] There is even less doubt that they apply under disturbances and tensions.

Account must be taken of instruments with global range and some with regional range. The most relevant human rights provisions are the following:
- the Universal Declaration of Human Rights;
- the Convention on the Prevention and Punishment of the Crime of Genocide;
- the Convention on the Elimination of All Forms of Racial Discrimination;
- the International Covenant on Civil and Political Rights;
- the International Covenant on Economic, Social and Cultural Rights;
- the Convention on the Prevention and Suppression of the Crime of Apartheid;
- the European Convention on Human Rights;
- the American Convention on Human Rights;
- the African Charter on Human and Peoples' Rights.

The Universal Declaration of Human Rights must now be considered part of general international law. Its norms are largely peremptory.[4] The conventions, on the other hand, are binding only on those states which have ratified them. The Geneva Conventions have rallied most ratifications; while fewer states have ratified the human rights conventions.[5] There are many more states that have ratified the International Covenant on Civil and Political Rights than the 1977 Protocols. It may be a question of time until the number of ratifications of Protocol I exceeds those of the International Covenant on Civil and Political Rights, but it is doubtful whether the number of ratifications of Protocol II will ever surpass those of the Covenant.[6]

When dealing with international law applicable in regions of disturbances and tension, reference must be made to the so-called "escape clauses" in the human rights instruments. They are found in Article 4 of the International Covenant on Civil and Political Rights, in Article 15 of the European Convention, and in Article 27 of the American Convention. They are more or less similar in nature.

In accordance with such escape clauses, states may take measures derogating from their obligations under certain circumstances. The first condition is that there should exist a public emergency which threatens the life of the nation.

State authorities are not entitled to use escape clauses in order to protect the interests of a class or group and hence to protect the existing political and economic structure, when the disorders or riots are due to demands for a general participation in the conduct of public affairs. Only when the life of the nation as a whole, including all its different opponents, is threatened can the escape clause be invoked.

Secondly, the public emergency must be officially proclaimed.

When this is done, the government may take measures which derogate from its obligations under the human rights instruments, but only to the extent strictly required by the exigencies of the situation. Thus, derogations cannot be made beyond what is required to solve the particular problem at hand. For example: if the unrest is motivated by a demand for political participation – a right which is expressly recognized in the International Covenant on Civil and Political Rights (Article 25) – any derogation must be accompanied by efforts to create political conditions which allow for general participation.

A further requirement is that the derogations do not involve discrimination on grounds of race, colour, sex, language, religion or social origin.

Even when there is a public emergency, there are some rights and prohibitions from which no derogation can be made, even if it is felt that the "exigencies of the situation" render it necessary e.g., the right to life, the prohibition of torture and maltreatment, the prohibition of slavery, the prohibition of imprisonment merely on grounds of inability to fulfil a contractual obligation, the prohibition of arbitrary or retroactive penalties, the right for everybody to be recognized as a person before the law, and the right to freedom of thought, conscience and religion.[7]

In the Universal Declaration of Human Rights, which in essence is binding on all states as part of general international law and has acquired the character of a peremptory set of international norms, there is no reference to an escape clause. However, the Declaration must be interpreted in the light of the escape clauses in the conventions. In other words, states which have not ratified the conventions and are therefore bound only by general international law – including the Universal Declaration – do not have wider obligations than states which have ratified the conventions.

It should be kept in mind that not every situation in which disorders and riots occur will qualify as a "public emergency". If the situation does not so qualify, the whole set of human rights – as contained in the Universal Declaration and in the various conventions, provided the state concerned is a party to them – apply.

b) Comparison between the different norms applicable in the several kinds of conflict

We have pointed out that there are several categories of conflicts to which different legal instruments are applicable. The next question is: how different are the relevant legal instruments? The differences can be seen by juxtaposing the substantive provisions of Protocol II, Article 3 common to the Geneva Conventions of 1949, and the relevant provisions of the human rights instruments. This has been done in the Table below. For the human rights instruments, the International Covenant on Civil and Political Rights has been chosen, and only those provisions have been included from which no derogation can be made, for the reasons given above.

Two observations should be made here. On the one hand, the general law of human rights is more comprehensive than the provisions contained either in Article 3 of the Geneva Conventions or in Protocol II. On the other hand, when we are faced with situations of public emergency, Article 3 and, in particular, Protocol II, may provide somewhat more comprehensive protection than these provisions of the Covenant on Civil and Political Rights from which no derogation can be made.

To clarify this, some areas of special importance will be investigated in the next section. It should also be noted that in the above comparison, provisions on implementation have not been discussed. To these we will return below (p. 250).

C. Special Problems in Times of Internal Disturbances and Tension

a) Use of analogies from the law applicable in armed conflict

Where there are internal disturbances and tension, there is neither a full-fledged armed conflict nor the normal tranquility of a society. For the purpose of this article, I have found it useful to draw analogies from certain aspects of humanitarian law applicable in armed conflict, to investigate what relevance these may have.

In passing it should be remembered that the occurrence of turbulence, riots and other disturbances demonstrates that the government is unable to maintain full control, though the reasons for this may vary.

The cause may be found in the ethnic or social base of the government itself. When it is seen to impose on a majority policies which reflect the interests of a dominant minority, the government itself in its general policies is violating human rights. Sometimes the disturbances may have their cause in policies of racial discrimination, such as in South Africa. The situation at Sharpeville in 1950 can be used to illustrate a context in which there were non-violent protests (against the pass laws of which the main purpose was the maintenance of control of a majority of the population) and where violent repressive action was taken by the government forces.

But if the government has the backing of a majority for policies of a discriminatory nature against disaffected minorities, do such policies constitute violation of human rights – in particular of the Convention on the Elimination of All Forms of Racial Discrimination?

The prohibition of genocide must also be taken into account here. The measures prohibited in the Genocide Convention of 1948 can conceivably occur even if the situation does not fall within Protocol II. Disturbances and riots may be reactions to such policies of genocide, and actions carried out in order to bring the riots to an end may constitute violations of Article III of the Genocide Convention of 1948.

Note should also be taken of situations in which the government does nothing to prevent – and even encourages – the pursuance of violence by some civilian groups against other civilian groups. This is a kind of state-tolerated terrorism which does occur in some societies today, and which occurred extensively in the early stages of the evolution of fascism in the inter-war years in Europe. In such cases the party relationship becomes ambiguous. When the government is not directly involved in the conflicts between the different groups, but clearly sides by acts of omission with one of the groups in its action against the other, this must be considered equivalent to direct state violation of human rights.

It is a general feature of disturbances and tensions that the party relationship is not very clear. In most cases, there is no clear, well-organized party on what can be loosely called the "dissident" side, but there is one on the side of the government. Under such circumstances, humanitarian law and human rights apply directly only to the government side, not to the others – though everyone is under a general obligation to respect the human rights of others.

The constraints on the government (its organized armed forces, paramilitary forces, or police) will be manifest particularly in the following circumstances:
– during actions to maintain or restore control (breaking up riots, enforcing compliance with curfews, etc.);
– the treatment of detained persons;
– the treatment of the civilian population in areas where there is strong resistance to governmental directives.

We shall briefly examine the substance of the applicable law of human rights under the following headings:
– "combat" law – i.e., the law concerning the means and methods to be used prior to restoring control or apprehending persons;
– prisoner-of-war status and treatment of detained persons;
– provisions for implementation.

D. "Combat" Law

Is there anything similar to "combat law" in cases of disturbances and tension below the level of armed conflicts? The main general principle in humanitarian law is that military action should be limited to the weakening of the armed forces of the enemy.[8] In internal conflicts below the threshold referred to in Protocol II, there is no direct equivalent to this. But even below the threshold, there can be cases of guerrilla forces which carry out sporadic action against the government side, even though they do not control any part of the territory. There can be such cases as the taking of hostages by terrorists. There can also be general unrest, with street demonstrations and opposition to curfews.

What are the limits to the means and methods that can be used by the government agencies in these cases? Are the security forces and the police limited, under international law, in their choice of action?

Special dangers arise when the local population sympathizes with or even supports those who are carrying out sporadic violence. This may make the government side more callous in their action against the population. Under such circumstances, the tension may be simmering on the threshold of full-fledged guerrilla warfare.

The human rights instruments do not contain provisions specifically related to these situations. But taking as a basis that human rights apply in all situations, also during armed conflict, it seems not illogical to reason as follows.

Humanitarian law applicable in armed conflict consists mainly of the Geneva Conventions and of the 1977 Protocols, which provide some protection in armed conflict. From another angle, humanitarian law can be looked upon as a subdivision of human rights. Since armed conflicts create special problems, special regulations have been made to supplement the general provisions on human rights. This is the function of humanitarian law. To the extent, therefore, that situations occur which present the same type of risks as do armed conflicts, humanitarian law should apply to such situations.

Admittedly, in Protocol II, there is much less reference to combat situations than in Protocol I. But this is mainly due to the fact that there was a strong reluctance, when negotiating Protocol II, to use the word "parties to the conflict" in that Protocol. The reason for this reluctance was that governments taking part in the negotiations did not want to formulate provisions which implied that more than one authority could exist within a state.

Certain provisions in Protocol II do concern combat, i.e. Articles 7, 15, 16 and 17. While these are much shortened versions of provisions in Protocol I, this should not be understood to mean that the governments should not respect the same constraints as in international conflicts; but it may be explained by the reason just mentioned above.

The fact that analogies may be drawn to justify application of Protocol I and Protocol II to situations of disturbances and tension would imply that the security forces and the police cannot carry out indiscriminate action, that they cannot, for instance, use gas in contravention of the Geneva Protocol of 1925 for the Prohibition of the Use in War of Gases, and they may not order the forced movement of civilians in contravention of Article 17 of Protocol II.

In other words, when the conflict has not reached the level of armed combat, the government security forces and police must obviously not be entitled to go beyond what they are permitted to do in cases where there is an armed conflict.

Nevertheless, the situation in regard to this question is not at all clear under international law. Further international legislation is needed to settle the many doubtful questions that arise.

E. Prisoner-of-War Status and the Treatment of Detainees and Others whose Liberty has been Restricted.

The Third Geneva Convention of 1949 – the Convention relative to the Treatment of Prisoners of War – contains detailed minimum rules for the protection of prisoners of war. The most significant element for our purpose is the principle that they cannot be punished by the detaining power for having participated in the war, though they may be punished for having committed war crimes. This immunity from punishment for participation in the war is the cornerstone of the system of prisoner-of-war protection. It applies only when the prisoner fulfils certain requirements.[9]

This immunity – and the whole of the Third Convention – applies only in international conflicts which now also include wars of national liberation as defined in Article 1, paragraph 4, of Protocol I. In non-international conflicts it does not apply, nor, therefore, to situations falling within the scope of the present chapter.[10]

Participation in armed action or any other action directed against the government is therefore punishable only in accordance with the domestic law of the country concerned. But this does not mean that there can be arbitrary action against detained persons and prisoners. The ordinary human rights provisions continue to apply, and these afford a minimum of protection of which no prisoner may be deprived.

The right to life continues to apply. While the death penalty has not yet been abolished by international law, executions may only take place under the very restrictive conditions established by Article 6 of the International Covenant on Civil and Political Rights.

Torture is also prohibited under all circumstances. This is stated in all the relevant documents, not only those relating to human rights, but also those relating to humanitarian law applicable in armed conflict, including Article 3 common to the Geneva Conventions, and Protocol II, Article 4. Similarly, slavery and servitude are also prohibited under all circumstances. The same applies to the principle of non-retroactivity in criminal law.

Further protection for persons detained or otherwise deprived of their liberty is provided by Articles 4, 5 and 6 of Protocol II. It goes further than that contained in those provisions of the International Covenant on Civil and Political Rights from which no derogation may be made even in times of public emergency. On this particular question, Protocol II represents an advance over earlier instruments on human rights, and it should be remembered that, since Protocol II deals with armed conflicts of a certain magnitude, it will undoubtedly be applied in cases which can be described as "public emergency". When, nevertheless, advanced provisions are adopted concerning treatment of detained persons under Protocol II, they are likely to become the general minimum of protection for persons whose liberty has been restricted.

F. Implementation

"Implementation", as used here means the series of procedures and mechanisms by which action can be taken to obtain compliance with the law. This is a wide concept implying a number of aims.

One of these aims is to ensure that the relevant international law penetrates the domestic normative system of all states. One major activity to achieve this is the dissemination of knowledge of the relevant rules of international law. The wider the knowledge about such rules, the more likely they are to be applied. This is partly because those in a position of authority will become aware of their duties, and also because potential victims will get to know of their rights.

More thorough implementation consists in the incorporation of the relevant parts of international law into domestic law. This will include domestic procedural law, penal law, administrative law, as well as regulations for the police and for the military.

Another dimension of implementation is international supervision of compliance with humanitarian law or with the law of human rights. Ultimately, implementation could also include international procedures for the repression of breaches.

Protocol II contains in Article 19 an obligation to disseminate the Protocol as widely as possible. There is, however, no obligation to include the provisions of the Protocol in domestic legislation. The same applies to Article 3 common to the Geneva Conventions of 1949. The various human rights instruments provide a more complex picture. The Convention on the Prevention and Punishment of the Crime of Genocide, of 1948, includes in Article V an obligation to give effect to the provisions of the Convention, and in particular to provide effective penalties for persons guilty of genocide. Similar obligations are undertaken by those states which have ratified the International Convention on the Suppression and Punishment of the Crime of Apartheid (Article IV).

No mechanism has been established by Protocol II for international supervision of compliance. By virtue of paragraph 2 of Article 3 common to the Geneva Conventions of 1949, an impartial humanitarian body, such as the International Committee of the Red Cross, may offer its services to the parties to the conflict. This could include supervision of compliance with Article 3, based on the consent of the parties.

The various human rights instruments also present a complex picture in regard to international supervision. In principle, compliance by all states may be supervised by the United Nations, a procedure which has evolved in accordance with resolution 1503 (XLVIII) of the Economic and Social Council. States which have ratified the International Covenant on Civil and Political Rights are subject to the supervision of the Human Rights Committee. These procedures are still being evolved, but it must be admitted that supervision so far is ineffectual.

With regard to international repression of breaches, international law is weak. Proposals to establish international criminal tribunals have failed, but with the development of human rights, they might be put into effect in the future; but alas, that future seems far distant.

Notes

1. This can go both ways: either by restricting the scope of Article 3 or by expanding in practice the scope of Protocol II. The international community would be best served by the second alternative, and while governments may be somewhat cautious in accepting it, they will also stand to gain by the wider interpretation. In any case, the growing application of general human rights instruments also to armed conflicts (see below) will reduce the significance of the distinction. See also note 2 below.
2. It is the first category which traditionally has belonged to "*jus in bello*". In our time, also categories 2 and 3 below fall into that branch of international law. But the extended concept "humanitarian law applicable in armed conflict" embraces also category 4, where relevant provisions are found in the

international human rights instruments. While these are general in nature and apply also in "peaceful" circumstances, there is no doubt that they are also applicable in armed conflict.

3. The General Assembly of the United Nations made this clear in resolution A/2675 (XXV), 1970, and in subsequent resolutions.

4. That the central provisions contained in the Universal Declaration and the International Covenants of Human Rights are binding irrespective of consent, is an opinion widely shared. See, e.g., the discussion of this issue by Theodore C. Van Boven, Survey of the Positive International Law of Human Rights, in: *The International Dimensions of Human Rights*, (Karel Vasak, ed.), Vol. 1, Paris/Westport, Unesco / Greenwood Press, 1982, p. 106.

5. On 30 June 1988, 165 States were parties to the Geneva Conventions for the Protection of War Victims of 12 August 1949. On the same date, 87 States were parties to the International Covenant on Civil and Political Rights. For other human rights instruments, see *Human Rights: Status of International instruments*. New York, United Nations, 1987. For treaties and conventions relative to International Humanitarian Law, Cf. *The Laws of Armed Conflicts. A Collection of Conventions, Resolutions and Other Documents*. Edited by D. Schindler and J. Toman, 3rd edition, Dordrecht, Martinus Nijhoff Publishers, Geneva, Henry Dunant Institute, 1988.

6. On 30 June 1988, 76 States have ratified Protocol I (as compared to 87 ratifications and accessions to the International Covenant on Civil and Political Rights) and 67 States are parties to Protocol II.

7. The discussion of the "escape clauses" in the human rights conventions is based on the provisions found in art. 4 of the International Covenant on Civil and Political Rights. The provisions found in other instruments are very similar to that one.

8. The conditions for prisoner – of – war status are now contained in Article 43 and 44 of Protocol I.

9. At the Diplomatic Conference negotiating the Geneva Conventions in 1949, a proposal was circulated (by Norway) providing for treatment similar to that of prisoner of war, for combatants in internal conflicts. The reaction was negative, and it was withdrawn. A similar proposal (but more restricted, i.e. only to cases where one or both sides in the internal conflict received support from the outside) was circulated by the ICRC at the Expert Conference in 1972, but again the reaction was negative and it was not included in the draft presented by the ICRC to the Diplomatic Conference in 1974. For details on this question, see Allan Rosas, *The Legal Status of Prisoners of War. A study in international humanitarian law applicable in armed conflicts*. Helsinki, Suomalainen Tiedeakatemia, 1976, p. 288 ff., Rosemary Abi-Saab, *Droit humanitaire et conflits internes*, Genève/Paris, IHD/Ed. Pédone, 1986, 280 p.

10. Article 4 of Protocol II applies also to persons not having their liberty restricted. Some of its provisions will therefore apply also in regard to combat, as discussed above.

Article 3 common to the Geneva Conventions	International Covenant on Civil and Political Rights (Entrenched clauses)	Protocol II
(1) Persons taking no active part in the hostilities, including members of armed forces who have laid down their arms and those placed *hors de combat* by sickness, wounds, detention, or any other cause, shall in all circumstances be treated humanely, without any adverse distinction founded on race, colour, religion or faith, sex, birth or wealth, or any other similar criteria. To this end, the following acts are and shall remain prohibited at any time and in any place whatsoever with respect to the above-mentioned persons:	*No corresponding provision*	*Article 4* – FUNDAMENTAL GUARANTEES 1. All persons who do not take a direct part or who have ceased to take part in hostilities, whether or not their liberty has been restricted, are entitled to respect for their person, honour and convictions and religious practices. They shall in all circumstances be treated humanely, without any adverse distinction. It is prohibited to order that there shall be no survivors. 2. Without prejudice to the generality of the foregoing, the following acts against the persons referred to in paragraph 1 are and shall remain prohibited at any time and in any palce whatsoever:
(a) violence to life and person, in particular murder of all kinds, mutilation, cruel treatment and torture; (c) outrages upon personal dignity, in particular humiliating and degrading treatment;	*Article 6* 1. Every human being has the inherent right to life. This right shall be protected by law. No one shall be arbitrarily deprived of his life. 2. In countries which have not abolished the death penalty, sentence of death may be imposed only for the most serious crimes in accordance with the law in force at the time of the commission of the crime and not contrary to the provisions of the present Covenant and to the Convention on the Prevention and Punishment of the Crime of Genocide. This penalty can only by carried out pursuant to a final judgement rendered by a competent court.	(a) violence to the life, health and physical or mental well-being of persons, in particular murder as well as cruel treatment such as torture, mutilation or any form of corporal punishment; (e) outrages upon personal dignity, in particular humiliating and degrading treatment, rape, enforced prostitution and any form of indecent assault;

Article 3 common to the Geneva Conventions	International Covenant on Civil and Political Rights (Entrenched clauses)	Protocol II
	Article 6 (continued) 3. When deprivation of life constitutes the crime of genocide, it is understood that nothing in this article shall authorize any State Party to the present Covenant to derogate in any way from any obligation assumed under the provisions of the Convention on the Prevention and Punishment of the Crime of Genocide. 4. Anyone sentenced to death shall have the right to seek pardon or commutation of the sentence. Amnesty, pardon or commutation of the sentence of death may be granted in all cases. 5. Sentence of death shall not be imposed for crimes committed by persons below eighteen years of age and shall not be carried out on pregnant women. 6. Nothing in this article shall be invoked to delay or to prevent the abolition of capital punishment by any State Party to the present Covenant. *Article 7* No one shall be subjected to torture or to cruel, inhuman or degrading treatment or punishment. In particular, no one shall be subjected without his free consent to medical or scientific experimentation.	*Article 6¹* – PENAL PROSECUTIONS 4. The death penalty shall not be pronounced on persons who were under the age of eighteen years at the time of the offence and shall not be carried out on pregnant women or mothers of young children.

Article 3 common to the Geneva Conventions	International Covenant on Civil and Political Rights (Entrenched clauses)	Protocol II
(b) taking of hostages;		*Article 4* – FUNDAMENTAL GUARANTEES *Acts prohibited:* ... (*b*) collective punishments; (*c*) taking of hostages; (*d*) acts of terrorism; ... (*g*) pillage; (*h*) threats to commit any of the foregoing acts.
	Article 8 1. No one shall be held in slavery; slavery and the slave-trade in all their forms shall be prohibited. 2. No one shall be held in servitude.	... (*f*) slavery and the slave trade in all their forms; ...
	No provision which is entrenched from derogation. The equivalent is found in Art. 9 and 14. But Art. 16 is relevant: *Article 16* Everyone shall have the right to recognition everywhere as a person before the law.	*Article 6¹* – PENAL PROSECUTIONS 1. This Article applies to the prosecution and punishment of criminal offences related to the armed conflict.

Article 3 common to the Geneva Conventions	International Covenant on Civil and Political Rights (Entrenched clauses)	Protocol II
(d) the passing of sentences and the carrying out of executions without previous judgment pronounced by a regularly constituted court, affording all the judicial guarantees which are recognized as indispensable by civilized peoples.		*Article 6* 2. No sentence shall be passed and no penalty shall be executed on a person found guilty of an offence except pursuant to a conviction pronounced by a court offering the essential guarantees of independence and impartiality. In particular: (*a*) the procedure shall provide for an accused to be informed without delay of the particulars of the offence alleged against him and shall afford the accused before and during his trial all necessary rights and means of defence; ... (*e*) anyone charged with an offence shall have the right to be tried in his presence; *f*) no one shall be compelled to testify against himself of to confess guilt.
Nothing corresponding	*Article 15* 1. No one shall be held guilty of any criminal offence on account of any act or omission which did not constitute a criminal offence, under national or international law, at the time when it was committed. Nor shall a heavier penalty be imposed than the one that was applicable at the time when the criminal offence was committed. If, subsequent to the commission of the offence, provision is made by law for the imposition of the lighter penalty, the offender shall benefit thereby.	*Article 6* ... (*b*) no one shall be convicted of an offence except on the basis of individual penal responsibility; (*c*) no one shall be held guilty of any criminal offence on account of any act or omission which did not constitute a criminal offence, under the law, at the time when it was committed; nor shall a heavier penalty be imposed than that which was applicable at the time when the criminal

Article 3 common to the Geneva Conventions	International Covenant on Civil and Political Rights (Entrenched clauses)	Protocol II
		Article 6 2(c) (continued) offence was committed; if, after the commission of the offence, provision is made by law for the imposition of a lighter penalty, the offender shall benefit thereby;
		(*d*) anyone charged with an offence is presumed innocent until proven guilty according to law;
	Article 15 2. Nothing in this article shall prejudice the trial and punishment of any person for any act or omission which, at the time when it was committed, was criminal according to the general principles of law recognized by the community of nations.	... 3. A convicted person shall be advised on conviction of his judicial and other remedies and of the time-limits within which they may be exercised.
		... 5. At the end of hostilities, the authorities in power shall endeavour to grant the broadest possible amnesty to persons who have participated in the armed conflict, or those deprived of their liberty for reasons related to the armed conflict, whether they are interned or detained.
Nothing corresponding		
No corresponding provision	*No corresponding provision*	*In addition, Protocol II contains in Art. 4 rules to protect children and to reunite families, and in Art. 5 detailed rules on minimum standards of treatment of detained persons.*

PART IV

APPLICATION OF INTERNATIONAL
HUMANITARIAN LAW

CHAPTER XVI

IMPLEMENTING INTERNATIONAL HUMANITARIAN LAW

YVES SANDOZ

A. Presentation

After an introduction situating the relative importance of implementing international humanitarian law in the context of current law and international systems, this article reviews the legal means of putting it into effect.

We think these means come under the following three headings:

First, *means of prevention*, to be used before the provisions of humanitarian law on behalf of victims are to apply, and intended to ensure that these provisions are correctly applied when the time comes to apply them.

Secondly, *means of control*, that is, of constant supervision to ensure that when the provisions on behalf of victims are being applied, they are properly observed.

Finally, *means of repression*, important because penalties are an integral part of any sound legal system, and mainly because they should be a valuable deterrent.

We have added a fourth category under the heading "*Other means*", which deals with means which cannot be classified under the previous headings, or at least under only one of them.

For instance, this applies to the international enquiry into allegations of reprehensible acts which is intended to repress any such acts and to provide permanent scouting. Similarly we felt that the role of the United Nations and of the media in general ought to be looked at under this fourth heading.

This article concludes with a short chapter on the special problem of implementing international humanitarian law in non-international armed conflicts. The system as a whole has been devised for international conflicts; it cannot simply be switched over to non-international conflicts, whose basic data are completely different.

B. Introduction

There can be no talk of implementing international humanitarian law without placing it within the framework of international law and, in a more general way, against the background of the modern world.

From the very beginning, international humanitarian law has sought to limit the suffering due to armed conflicts, by protecting and assisting victims of such conflicts in so far as possible. That aim has not changed. But whilst international humanitarian law did have an indisputable place in an international system which, to quote Clausewitzs famous aphorism, regards war as "politics continued by other means', it is less easily assimilated, from a purely logical stance, into the present system now that the UN Charter unequivocally outlaws international war.[1] Humanitarian law in general therefore applies only where there has already been a breach of international law. That being so, does it still have a meaning? The International Law Commission thought not when it refused to place it on the agenda at the beginning of its work in 1948.

Nevertheless, States decided otherwise when, in 1949, they adopted the four Geneva Conventions which are now the basis of international humanitarian law and, later on, when most of them ratified these instruments.

Why, it might be asked, did they come to this unreasonable decision? Quite simply to look the facts in the face. It very soon became clear that States could not agree among themselves to give the UN the means of enforcing the rules they had adopted as part of its mandate. The UN could not prevent international armed conflicts, and States realized that they would have to depend upon themselves, or on alliances with other States, for their own security. The UN had shown it was incapable of preventing the very many armed conflicts which broke out after it was founded.

However, another question arises as to the actual meaning of international humanitarian law. If a State deliberately violates international law by engaging in an international armed conflict, why should it show any greater respect for international humanitarian law? This is a pertinent question and deserves consideration. One can hardly imagine any State enacting a code of good behaviour for the use of individual lawbreakers on its territory – a code that would, in effect, say to them: "Thou shalt not steal; but if you do, do it decently".

If such apparently unusual language can be used to States, the reason is that there is no system of implementing international law even remotely comparable to State systems. There are no real courts and no real police. Hence the importance of having rules at different levels in the hope that, at each level, they will be observed at least in part. The UN Charter will prevent some conflicts, while in those it fails to prevent, international humanitarian law will prevent some excesses. Clearly this is a pessimistic view of the world and of the role of international law; but it is a realistic one even though, let us hope, respect for the law is a principle to which most States and individuals are still attached, irrespective of any threat of penalty.

Moreover, this approach at different levels is particularly suitable for armed conflicts. It is often hard to say which State is guilty of infringing the Charter in an international armed conflict. This is generally an issue for political discussion leading to resolutions being adopted by a majority at the General Assembly and in the Security Council of the United Nations, but the accused Party's "guilt" is nevertheless still denied by a perhaps considerable, minority and especially by the interested Party.

International humanitarian law offers a totally independent system, and in this it is effective at least to some extent. If it had ruled that it was applicable only after one of the Parties had been found "guilty", or even if it had adjusted the extent of its application, in function of the belligerent's guilt (as at times some people have wished) international humanitarian law would undoubtedly have remained a dead letter. Applying it, or applying it in a certain way, would have been tantamount to pleading guilty; it would have meant surrender in the prior debate. Obviously, then, a multi-level system is meaningless unless the levels – in this case, *jus ad bellum* and *jus in bello* – are completely independent of each other.

The fact remains that the mere existence of international humanitarian law reveals the weak point of international law – its implementation. Of course, implementation at each level also has to be looked at independently. Certainly at each level it only needs imagination to find out the best answers; indeed, the aim of the present article is to examine what means international humanitarian law proposes. But it has to be borne in mind that a perfectly applicable system of international humanitarian law is inconceivable without a change in relations between States so profound as to be able to prevent conflicts from breaking out in the first place. Paradoxically, the comparative inability to implement international humanitarian law is essential to its existence.

C. Implementation During International Armed Conflicts

(a) Means of Prevention

1. Respect for the Law by the States Concerned

Pacta sunt servanda: The best guarantee that international humanitarian law will be applied clearly lies in the respect shown by States for this basic maxim. By formally accepting the Geneva Conventions and, in the case of some, by acceding to their Additional Protocols, States have undertaken to ensure that these instruments are respected by everyone under their authority, irrespective of any express ruling on the subject in the Conventions themselves. From a general standpoint, the defence of international law and of the idea that its concomitant legal obligations are as binding on States as the law of the land on an individual is perhaps one of the most decisive factors today – though apparently very abstract in the intended context – making for the strict application of international humanitarian law.

When adopting the Geneva Conventions, States saw fit to emphasize still further the obligation to abide by treaties, even though this is an integral part of any international treaty. It is mentioned in the Article 1, common to all four Conventions, which reads: "The High Contracting Parties undertake to respect and ensure respect for the present Convention in all circumstances". The significance of the phrase "to ensure respect" will be considered later.[2] It is interesting to note the wealth of precautions in the Geneva Conventions and their Additional Protocols concerning the obligation of respect. As we have pointed out, it is not essential to quote Article 1, referred to above; nor should it be necessary to quote the provisions examined below concerning the means we have described as "preventive". For each individual concerned to respect humanitarian law, preventive means are essential and ought to be looked upon as implicitly contained in treaty obligations directly concerning victims. Their express mention shows that States deemed it necessary not only to confine themselves to obligations regarding results, but also to stipulate express obligations as regards means.

Furthermore, the 1977 Protocol I accentuates this tendency. Before the specific article on that subject, Article 80 states in a general way:

> "*Measures for execution*
> 1. The High Contracting Parties and the Parties to the conflict shall without delay take all necessary measures for the execution of the obligations under the Conventions and this Protocol. 2. The High Contracting Parties and the Parties to the conflict shall give orders and instructions to ensure observance of the Conventions and this Protocol, and shall supervise their execution."

The wording goes so far as to tell the State how it must assume a responsibility, already made clear beyond doubt by the text. Such a strict approach to hard facts is welcome: despite the express obligations as regards means, means are usually still very inadequate.

2. General Dissemination of the Conventions and Protocol I.

There is an essentially identical article in each of the four Conventions (respectively Articles 47–48–127–144) stipulating that the High Contracting Parties have an obligation to "undertake, in time of peace as in time of war, to disseminate the text of the present Convention as widely as possible in their respective countries, and, in particular, to include the study thereof in their programmes of military and, if possible, civil instructions, so that the principles thereof may become known to the entire population, in particular to the armed fighting forces, medical personnel and the chaplains".

Protocol I takes up the same idea in Article 83, para. 1, which states:

> "The High Contracting Parties undertake, in time of peace as in time

of armed conflict, to disseminate the Conventions and this Protocol as widely as possible in their respective countries and, in particular, to include the study thereof in their programmes of military instruction and to encourage the study thereof by the civilian population, so that these instruments may become known to the armed forces and to the civilian population".

This obligation of general dissemination is evidently essential. International humanitarian law imposes obligations on every individual belonging to a Party to the conflict and therefore each person must be trained to act in accordance with this law if confronted with events which call for it to be applied. Combatants and the general public need to know only the specific provisions which might directly concern them, not the entire body of the law. It must also be stressed that both the Conventions and the Protocols mention that the task of dissemination must already be carried out in peace-time. It must be part of everyone's preparation for time of war. One does not wait for armed conflict to break out before giving military training or building shelters. The same must also hold true of disseminating international humanitarian law and this can be done thoroughly only in peace-time. Most States still have a long way to go in this direction.

3. Special instruction for the Authorities Directly Concerned.

The third and fourth Conventions stipulate that civilian or military authorities who in time of war assume responsibilities for persons protected by these Conventions "must possess the text of the Convention and be specially instructed as to its provisions" (Article 127, para. 2 and Article 144, para. 2, respectively).

Protocol 1 reasserts this provision and even amplifies it slightly. Article 83, para. 2, states:

"Any military or civilian authorities who, in time of armed conflict, assume responsibilities in respect of the application of the Conventions and this Protocol shall be fully acquainted with the text thereof."

It is not simply a matter of giving instruction; these people must actually "be fully acquainted with the text thereof". Likewise, it is perfectly logical that those who are directly involved should be given special training. For instance, a future POW camp commander would be expected to be more fully instructed in this subject than a private soldier.

4. Duties of Commanders

Military commanders' obligations are not restricted solely to monitoring the application of the law and repressing breaches thereof (aspects which we shall return to later); according to the terms of Protocol I they are also in duty bound to disseminate knowledge of the law. In fact, the High Contracting Parties and Parties to the conflict are expressly called upon to require "that, commensurate with their level of responsibility, commanders ensure that members of the armed forces... are aware of their obligations under the Conventions and this Protocol" (Article 87, para. 2). Hence, when through pure ignorance subordinates act in breach of the law, their commanding officers' responsibility will definitely be involved.[3]

5. Training Qualified Personnel

Protocol I, Article 6, para. 1, calls on the Contracting Parties to endeavour in peacetime "to train qualified personnel to facilitate the application of the Conventions and of this Protocol, and in particular the activities of the Protecting Powers".

In spite of this emphasis on the value of qualified personnel in helping the protecting Powers to carry out their duties [4], their potential usefulness in ensuring that international humanitarian law is applied in their own countries should not be overlooked: they can advise and instruct the authorities directly concerned and actively participate in general dissemination activities.

6. Legal Advisers in the Armed Forces

Such advisers are expressly provided for in Protocol I (Article 82). Their role is "to advise military commanders at the appropriate level on the application of the Conventions and this Protocol and on the appropriate instruction to be given to the armed forces on this subject". The obligation is not set out in a very binding manner – such advisers must be available "when necessary" – but here again the tendency to impose obligations in terms of means and not only in terms of results is reinforced in Protocol I.

7. Communication of Translations of the Conventions and Protocols and Laws of Application.

The official versions of the Geneva Conventions are in French and English. The depositary was also responsible for having official translations made into Russian and Spanish. The official versions of the Protocols are in Arabic, Chinese, English, French, Russian and Spanish. States bound by these Conventions and whose national languages are other than the ones above must obviously have the texts translated so that they can be applied by their population and be disseminated. It is a sensible preventive measure to communicate these translations to the other Contracting Parties in peacetime as required by the Conventions (Articles 48, 49, 128 and 145 respectively) and Protocol I (Article 84); in time of armed conflict this should prevent differences of interpretation which might have unfortunate consequences.

The same holds true of transmission of any laws and regulations for their application, which although undoubtedly desirable [5] are not obligatory: a Contracting Party may simply incorporate the treaty text into its national legislation.

(b) Means of Control

1. – Obligation on Parties to the Conflict to Put an End to All Breaches

General obligation

Since the Contracting Parties have a permanent obligation to respect the Conventions to which they have subscribed, it is obviously essential, that they exercise sufficient supervision especially in case of conflict, to ensure that the law is respected. Given the present world order, any system of supervision has to rely on the good faith of signatory States and their willingness to apply the law. But no one can be expected to do the impossible; the chance of individual violations can never be ruled out, however efficient the training and dissemination. In such cases the obligation on the Contracting Parties to put an end to such violations, although obviously contained in the general obligation to respect the Conventions and Protocols, is expressly repeated in addition to the obligations concerning their repression. [6] (See Articles 49 para. 3, 50 para. 3, 129 para. 3 and 146 para. 3 of the Conventions and Article 85 para. 1 of Protocol I).

Obligations on Military Commanders

Protocol I, Article 87, paras. 1 and 3 clearly define an obligation in terms of means:
"1. The High Contracting Parties and the Parties to the conflict shall require military commanders, with respect to members of the armed forces under their command and other persons under their control, to prevent and, where necessary, to suppress and to report to competent authorities breaches of the Conventions and of this Protocol.
3. The High Contracting Parties and Parties to the conflict shall require any commander who is aware that subordinates or other persons under his control are going to commit or have committed a breach in the Conventions or of this Protocol, to initiate such steps as are necessary to prevent such violations of the Conventions or this Protocol, and, where appropriate, to initiate disciplinary or penal action against violators thereof".
Under Protocol I therefore, military commanders are the mainstay of the supervisory system to be set up by Contracting Parties and Parties to the conflict. This seems justified as Protocol I adds to the Geneva Conventions many rules directly linked to the conduct of hostilities. The role of commanders in repression will be considered below. [7]

Obligation on the High Contracting Parties to Ensure Respect for International Humanitarian Law.

This obligation is mentioned in Article 1 of each Convention and in Article 1, Protocol I. Its meaning is not obvious and has been the subject of lengthy discussions. It was one of the main subjects of an enquiry by the *Centre d'études de droit international médical* in Liège and the *Committee on International Medical an Humanitarian Law* of the International Law Association [8].

Some people feel that this obligation should be seen merely as clarification of the obligation to respect international humanitarian law and is consequently for domestic application. However, prevailing opinion favours a more comprehensive interpretation to the effect that the High Contracting Parties have an obligation to ensure that other States respect the Conventions. The Commentary published under the general editorship of Jean Pictet states that this expression must be interpreted both as strengthening the obligation within the body of national law [9] and as implying an obligation towards other States. [10]

The idea of an obligation towards other States parties to the Conventions was further confirmed at the International Conference on Human Rights (Teheran, 1968), which adopted a resolution wherein the Conference noted "that States parties to the Red Cross Geneva Conventions (sic) sometimes failed to appreciate their responsibility to take steps to ensure respect of these humanitarian rules in all circumstances by other States, even if they are not themselves directly involved in an armed conflict..." The existence of such an obligation will therefore be conceded. What it actually means still has to be defined. This question too was discussed at length during the inquiry referred to above [11]. As the findings of this inquiry have confirmed, it seems clear that on this basis the most that can be done is to take diplomatic measures or publicly denonce violations. It would be improper, and probably dangerous, to impose non-military sanctions (and still more obviously, to impose military sanctions or any form of intervention).

Therefore, one must not interpret this as merely an obligation in terms of means without any attendant obligation as regards effects.

In practice, States parties to the Geneva Conventions have not really implemented this provision, at any rate publicly, and do not really try to monitor the extent to which it is observed.

2. – *Protecting Powers*

Definition

A "Protecting Power" is a "State instructed by another State (known as the Power of origin) to safeguard its interests and those of its nationals in relation to a third State (known as State of residence)" [12]

History

We cannot give here a lengthy historical description of this institution, which dates back to the 16th century [13], although Protecting Powers are not specifically mentioned in the Hague Conventions. It will be recalled, however, that the Protecting Powers played an important part in applying these Conventions during the First World War by virtue of an international custom recognized to varying extents. Their task was by no means always easy, and States wanted to see it mentioned in a Convention.

This was done in 1929, in Article 86 of the Convention Relative to the Treatment of Prisoners of War. Nevertheless, such an article could not go very far, for it is not possible to dictate to a Protecting Power "duties which were carried out solely at the behest of the appointing Power". [14] A legal basis for the activities of Protecting Powers had to be established and defined, and the Detaining Power had to be made subject to an obligation to support and facilitate the Protecting Power's activities; but as was only logical, the choice of delegates of the Protecting Power was subject to the consent of the Detaining Power.

This article states:

> "The High Contracting Parties recognize that a guarantee of the regular application of the present Convention will be found in the possibility of collaboration between the Protecting Powers charged with the protection of the interests of the belligerents; in this connection, the Protecting Powers may, apart from their diplomatic personnel, appoint delegates from among their own nationals or the nationals of other neutral Powers. The appointment of these delegates shall be subject to the approval of the belligerent with whom they are to carry out their mission."

> "The representatives of the Protecting Power or their recognized delegates shall be authorized to proceed to any place, without exception, where prisoners of war are interned. They shall have access to all premises occupied by prisoners and may hold conversation with prisoners, as a general rule without witnesses, either personally or through the intermediary of interpreters."

> "Belligerents shall facilitate as much as possible the task of the representatives or recognised delegates of the Protecting Power. The military authorities shall be informed of their visits."

> "Belligerents may mutually agree to allow persons of the prisoners' own nationality to participate in the tours of inspection."

This article was widely applied during the Second World War but proved imperfect in several respects.

As the conflict spread the few States remaining neutral had to agree to act as Protecting Power for more than one country. It came to the point where they were representing adverse Parties and so tended to become a kind of arbitrator in humanitarian affairs who could use reciprocity as a bargaining counter:

While these initial observations are not critical, the following are:

– since their State of origin was not recognized by the Detaining Power, several million prisoners of war had no Protecting Power;

– the lack of a Protecting Power was cruelly felt by civilians in enemy hands, for whom nobody had thought of providing any such protection;

– lastly;

"The outrageous nature of some of the violations committed where there had been no control modified the conception of what that control should be. It was no longer merely a question of recognizing a belligerent's right to supervise the application of the Convention by his enemy and of facilitating his task in so doing. The idea of the private interest of each of the belligerents was replaced by the conception of the overriding general interest of humanity, which demanded such control, no longer as a right, but as a duty." [15]

Bearing all these considerations in mind, the ICRC directed its attention after the war to three points:
– the extension to all the Conventions of the principle of supervision by the Protecting Power.
– arrangements for the replacement of Protecting Powers no longer able to act:
– making supervision obligatory. [16]

The Law in Force

– The 1949 Geneva Conventions

The common Article 8, 8, 8 and 9 of the Geneva Conventions of 12 August 1949, now in force, states:

"The present Convention shall be applied with the co-operation and under the scrutiny of the Protecting Powers whose duty it is to safeguard the interests of the Parties to the conflict. For this purpose, the Protecting Powers may appoint, apart from their diplomatic or consular staff, delegates from amongst their own nationals or the nationals of other neutral Powers. The said delegates shall be subject to the approval of the Power with which they are to carry out their duties."

"The Parties to the conflict shall facilitate, to the greatest extent possible, the task of the representatives or delegates of the Protecting Powers."

"The representatives or delegates of the Protecting Powers shall not in any case exceed their mission under the present Convention. They shall, in particular, take account of the imperative necessities of security of the State wherein they carry out their duties. Their activities shall only be restricted as an exceptional and temporary measure when this is rendered necessary by imperative military necessities." (The last sentence appears only in the first and second Conventions).

It can be seen therefore that most States adopted the ICRC's point of view; thus –

– the establishment of Protecting Powers is provided for in the four 1949 Conventions;
– an article, also common to the four Conventions, makes provision for designating substitutes for Protecting Powers in cases where it has proved impossible to designate such Protecting Powers. Another common article concentrates on the work of the ICRC. [17];
– in theory the system is obligatory (the Convention "*shall be* applied with the co-operation.."), the only reservation being that delegates of the Protecting Powers "shall be subject to the approval of the Power with which they are to carry out their duties" and the impossibility of agreement on this point cannot be ruled out.

Furthermore, it will be noted that the Protecting Power's terms of reference are very vaguely defined here. They are however specified in other articles, namely two other general provisions common to the four Conventions, including the important one of the offer of good offices in case of disagreement as to the interpretation of the application of the Conventions (Articles 11, 11, 11 and 12); they are also mentioned in three provisions of the First Convention, one of the second Convention, twenty-seven of the Third Convention and thirty-three of the Fourth Convention. [18]

However, it is important to note that the role of the Protecting Power is not confined to the missions laid down in those articles where one Protecting Power is specifically mentioned. The principle of co-operation in application and scrutiny assign to the Protecting Power "a general mission.. giving it the right – and the power – to intervene in cases other than these particular ones." [19]

The only restrictions that can be imposed on the activities of the Protecting Powers stem from "imperative military necessities" and such restrictions can only be "exceptional and temporary". Furthermore, this provision for restricting the activities of the Protecting Power is made only in the First and Second Conventions, where its role is much less important than in the Third Convention (activities to help prisoners of war) and the Fourth Convention (activities to help civilians). This distinction is made because, unlike the other two Conventions, the first two Conventions "are mainly intended to be applied on the battlefield". [20]

– 1977 Additional Protocol I

Article 5 of Protocol I was adopted to strengthen the system laid down by the Conventions.

It states:

Article 5–Appointment of Protecting Powers and of their substitute.

"1. It is the duty of the Parties to a conflict from the beginning of that conflict to secure the supervision and implementation of the Conventions and of this Protocol by the application of the system of Protecting Powers, including *inter alia* the designation and acceptance of those Powers, in accordance with the following paragraphs. Protecting Powers shall have the duty of safeguarding the interests of the Parties to the conflict.

"2. From the beginning of a situation referred to in Article 1, each Party to the conflict shall without delay designate a Protecting Power for the purpose of applying the Conventions and this Protocol and shall, likewise without delay and for the same purpose, permit the activities, of a Protecting Power which has been accepted by it as such after designation by the adverse Party.

"3. If a Protecting Power has not been designated or accepted from the beginning of a situation referred to in Article 1, the International Committee of the Red Cross, without prejudice to the right of any other impartial humanitarian organization to do likewise, shall offer its good offices to the Parties to the conflict with a view to the designation without delay of a Protecting Power to which the Parties to the conflict consent. For that purpose it may, *inter alia*, ask each Party to provide it with a list of at least five States which that Party considers acceptable to act as Protecting Power on its behalf in relation to an adverse Party, and ask each adverse Party to provide a list of at least five States which it would accept as the Protecting Power of the first Party; these lists shall be communicated to the Committee within two weeks after the receipt of the request; it shall compare them and seek the agreement of any proposed State named on both lists.

"4. If, despite the foregoing, there is no Protecting Power, the Parties to the conflict shall accept without delay an offer which may be made by the International Committee of the Red Cross or by any other organization which offers all guarantees of impartiality and efficacy, after due consultations with the said Parties and taking into account the result of these consultations, to act as a substitute. The functioning of such a substitute is subject to the consent of the Parties to the conflict; every effort shall be made by the Parties to the conflict to facilitate the operations of the substitute in the performance of its tasks under the Conventions and this Protocol.

"5. In accordance with Article 4, the designation and acceptance of Protecting Powers for the purpose of applying the Conventions and this Protocol shall not affect the legal status of the Parties to the conflict or of any territory, including occupied territory.

"6. The maintenance of diplomatic relations between Parties to the conflict or the entrusting of the protection of a Party's interests and those of its nationals to a third State in accordance with the rules of international law relating to diplomatic relations is no obstacle to the designation of Protecting Powers for the purpose of applying the Conventions and this Protocol.

"7. Any subsequent mention in this Protocol of a Protecting Power includes also a substitute."

With reference to the relevant articles of the Conventions, it is noteworthy that
– para. 3 lays down procedure for designation and confers a role on the ICRC within that procedure:
– para. 6 clarified the fact that neither the maintenance of diplomatic relations nor confiding the protection of a Party's interests and nationals to a third State in accordance with the rules of international law relating to diplomatic relations, shall be an obstacle to the designation of a Protecting Power for the purpose of applying the Geneva Conventions and Additional Protocol I;
– para. 5 expressly mentions that the designation and acceptance of Protecting Powers "shall not affect the legal status of the Parties to the conflict or of any territory, including occupied territory."
The Protecting Power's terms of reference are unchanged by the Protocol, but extend to it where it is applicable. Like the Conventions, Protocol I contains several direct references to Protecting Powers within the meaning of its Article 5.

Practical Application

The system of the Protecting Powers provided for in the 1949 Conventions has worked badly. Since 1949 there have been very few conflicts indeed in which Protecting Powers were designated (Suez, Goa, Bangladesh), and study of each shows that even there the system really never worked as expected. [21]
As Protocol I has not yet been put to the test in an armed conflict, it is too early to judge how efficient its additional provisions are.
The reasons why the system of Protecting Powers has worked badly have been examined. [22] Some of the main reasons are said to be
– the fear that the designation of a Protecting Power will be seen as recognition of the other Party (where it is not recognized);
– unwillingness to admit that an armed conflict exists or that there are differences of opinion as to the character of a conflict;
– the maintenance of diplomatic relations between belligerents;
– the pace of events in some wars;
– the difficulty of finding neutral States acceptable to both parties and able and willing to act in this capacity.
Protocol I to some extent rules out a few of these reasons, but it would be rash to predict that the system of Protecting Powers will certainly be revived.

3. Substitutes for the Protecting Powers

The Law in Force

– The Geneva Conventions of 1949

The legislator in 1949 was well aware of the practical difficulties that might arise in designating Protecting Powers. He therefore wisely provided an alternative, consisting in the designation of substitutes for the Protecting Powers, in the common Article 10-10-10-11 of the Conventions, reading as follows:

> "Article 10 – Substitutes for Protecting Powers
> The High Contracting Parties may at any time agree to entrust to an organization which offers all guarantees of impartiality and efficacy the duties incumbent on the Protecting Powers by virtue of the present Convention.
> When wounded and sick, or medical personnel and chaplains do not benefit or cease to benefit, no matter for what reason, by the activities of a Protecting Power or of an organization provided for in the first paragraph above, the Detaining Power shall request a neutral State, or such an organization, to undertake the functions performed under the present Convention by a Protecting Power designated by the Parties to a conflict.
> If protection cannot be arranged accordingly, the Detaining Power shall request or shall accept, subject to the provisions of this Article, the offer of the services of a humanitarian organization, such as the International Committee of the Red Cross, to assume the humanitarian functions performed by Protecting Powers under the present Convention.
> Any neutral Power, or any organization invited by the Power concerned or offering itself for these purposes, shall be required to act with a sense of responsibility towards the Party to the conflict on which persons protected by the present Convention depend, and shall be required to furnish sufficient assurances that it is in a position to undertake the appropriate functions and to discharge them impartially.
> No derogation from the preceding provisions shall be made by special agreements between Powers one of which is restricted, even temporarily, in its freedom to negotiate with the other Power or its allies by reason of military events, more particularly where the whole, or a substantial part, of the territory of the said Power is occupied.
> Whenever in the present Convention mention is made of a Protecting Power, such mention also applies to substitute organizations in the sense of the present Article."

This article in fact does not provide a single alternative, but a whole series of proposals.

The parties to the conflict may first of all designate a substitute organization (provided it "offers all guarantees of impartiality and efficacy") in preference to Protecting Powers (para. 1). This allows the Parties a choice, not merely a subsidiary possibility applicable only in the event of failure to find Protecting Powers.

Secondly, it imposes on the Powers detaining persons protected by the Conventions the duty of requesting a neutral State, or an organization as provided for in the above paragraph, if those persons do not already benefit from the activities of a Protecting Power or such an organization (para. 2). There is a twofold difference between this and the previous paragraph: first, the possibility referred to here is really a subsidiary one and may only be envisaged if Article 8-8-8-9 or the first paragraph of Article 10-10-10-11 has not been applied – a situation that should be exceptional: secondly, not only is protection provided at the express request of the adverse Party, but the choice of the State or organization need not be ratified by the adverse Party. This obviously weakens the scope of the protection, even if there is an express reference to the responsibility of the State or organization so designated towards the Party to the conflict on which protected persons depend (para. 4).

Lastly, this course is envisaged where none of the above-mentioned alternatives has been adopted; in other words where the detaining Power has not even found a neutral State or organization fulfilling the necessary conditions and prepared to undertake this responsibility.

In this case, the detaining Power "shall request" a humanitarian organization – or, if need be, "shall accept" the offer of such an organization – to assume the "humanitarian functions" provided for in the Geneva Conventions – not all the functions imcumbent upon protecting powers, but only those that are obviously humanitarian. It is difficult, however, to say where these end, and this has not been done so far. The Article gives no further definition of the organization than the word "humanitarian", but the International Committee of the Red Cross is mentioned as an example. The humanitarian institution referred to in this Article is sometimes called a "quasi-substitute" for the Protecting Powers. [23]

– The Additional Protocol of 1977

As regards the substitutes for the Protecting Powers, Article 5, paragraph 4 of Protocol I contains some modifications to the provisions of Article 10-10-10-11.

First of all, it no longer offers the possibility of designating a substitute for the Protecting Powers by joint agreement between the parties to a conflict. The designation of a substitute is nevertheless still possible under the Protocol although not expressly mentioned therein, for Protocol I is an expansion of the Conventions and does not formally exclude this possibility.

Article 5 goes on to require the Parties to a conflict to accept without delay an offer by an organization offering all guarantees of impartiality and efficacy to act as a substitute, where the procedure for the appointment of Protecting Powers has come to nothing.

Admittedly, this obligation is subject to certain restrictions. The parties must be consulted before the offer is made, and the substitute may not function without the consent of the Parties to the conflict. However, the principle that the Parties to the conflict are obliged to accept the offer of a substitute has two new features; first it rules out the rather unsatisfactory possibility of a Party designating a substitute of its own accord if it disagrees with the choice of a Protecting Power or substitute (according to Protocol I, all the Parties must agree on the same substitute); secondly, it places the obligation at the level of substitute and not at the level of humanitarian organization or "quasi-substitute". It therefore tends to drop the distinction between the humanitarian and other functions of the Protecting Powers.

Practical application

The rather complicated series of provisions contained in Article 10-10-10-11 of the Conventions has never been formally used. In practice, this role has been taken over by the ICRC, exactly on what grounds has not been clearly establish-ed. [24]

The Special Role of the ICRC

The ICRC can act by virtue of the system of Protecting Powers, as a substitute or "quasi-substitute", or outside the system in its own capacity.

In the context of the system provided for in Article 10-10-10-11 of the Conventions, one may ask whether the ICRC is entitled to act as substitute, i.e., whether it can claim to be the "organization which offers all guarantees of impartiality and efficacy" referred to in the Conventions. Literally interpreted, the Conventions appear to take the opposite view. Since the ICRC is cited as an example of a "humanitarian organization" suitable to act as "quasi-substitute" and since in the same article it is not mentioned as an example of the kind of organization referred to above, it might reasonably be concluded that States had not thought of using it for this purpose.

The fact that, since the Conventions were adopted, no organization has been appointed to act as substitute; that the ICRC has amply demonstrated its impartiality and efficacy; and that this time the legal drafters of Protocol I of 1977 quoted it as an example of an organization which "offers all guarantees of impartiality and efficacy" (Article 5, para. 4) – these facts amply demonstrate that the ICRC can claim to play such a role.

Has it really done so? *De facto*, certainly, in many circumstances, even though it has rarely been able to assume all the tasks incumbent upon a Protecting Power. But it cannot be said to have done so *de jure*, and as the ICRC is well aware it is largely responsible for this. At present, one of the main problems with any humanitarian work is the effect it might have on politics. States in conflict very often disagree in their definition of the conflict or even on whether it exists. The ICRC's strength lies in avoiding this pitfall. The Geneva Conventions, their Additional Protocols and the Statutes of the International Red Cross leave it every latitude to do so. The ICRC is empowered to offer its services under several headings; as a substitute or "quasi-substitute" within the system of Protecting

Powers as an impartial humanitarian organization outside that system (Articles 9-9-9 and 10 in international armed conflicts and Article 3 in non-international armed conflicts); and on the basis of its task, recognized by the Statutes of the International Red Cross, of "working for the faithful application" of the Geneva Conventions (Statutes, Article 6.4). The ICRC does not generally say on what grounds it offers its services, for if it did, this might be a major reason for rejecting them.

It is probably because of this necessary ambiguity, together with its recognized efficacy and impartiality, that *de facto* the ICRC does a great deal – although still far from enough – to monitor the application of the Geneva Conventions. Before the choices of justifying its actions in strict legal terms or of giving practical help to victims, it cannot but choose the latter.

Formation of a New Monitoring Body

The idea has been mooted on various occasions of setting up a body for the sole purpose of monitoring the application of international humanitarian law in time of armed conflicts [25] or of entrusting this task to an existing body [26] but nothing has ever come of it and it was rejected by the 1974–1977 Diplomatic Conference.

4. Synthesis

The trend of the entire monitoring system based on the system of Protecting Powers is towards simplicity. Conflicting Parties must normally agree among themselves to opt either for protecting powers or for a substitute, which may be the ICRC. If formal agreement is not reached on these points, and irrespective of any such agreement, the ICRC must or may undertake tasks within limits not yet clearly defined.

In practice only the ICRC has acted in this capacity to any important extent since 1949, generally without stating the exact legal basis of its activity. But indisputably that basis exists.

(c) Repression of Violations

1. General Observations

The Parties to the Geneva Conventions, although not under the obligation of putting an end to violations of the Conventions, are under the obligation of repressing those violations known as grave breaches and considered as war crimes.

To be more precise, in the case of a grave breach the application of the adage *aut judicare at dedere* is required, a Contracting Party having the choice of referring the authors of such breaches to its courts or handing them over "for trial to another High Contracting Party concerned, provided such High Contracting Party has made out a *prima facie* case" (common Articles 49-50-129-146).

Each of the Conventions lists grave breaches (in Articles 50-51-130-147). This list is supplemented by Article 11 paragraph 4, and Article 85 paragraphs 3 and 4, of Protocol I.

It is furthermore expressly mentioned that an omission can be a grave breach (Article 86, Protocol I).

It is the responsibility of the Contracting Parties to incorporate these currently valid provisions in their national legislation, either by means of laws for their application or by incorporating them as they stand.

The obligation to repress grave breaches is absolute and would be unaffected even by an agreement between the interested Parties (see the common Article 51-52-131-148).

2. Responsibility of Superiors and Duty of Commanders

Article 86, paragraph 2 of the Protocol provides as follows:

> "The fact that a breach of the Conventions or of this Protocol was committed by a subordinate does not absolve his superiors from penal or disciplinary responsibility, as the case may be, if they knew or had information which should have enabled them to conclude, in the circumstances at the time, that he was committing or was going to commit such a breach and if they did not take all feasible measures within their power to prevent or repress the breach."

This article is interesting because it raises the question of individual penal responsibility. It cannot however impose sanctions where only the Contracting Parties are competent to do so, that is, in cases of breaches, other than grave breaches, of the Conventions or Protocol I. In the case of grave breaches, those in which intention is an constituent factor should first be examined, and a superior cannot be found guilty of these unless that factor is proved.

Lastly, Article 87 paragraphs 1 and 3 of Protocol I requires the Contracting Parties to instruct military commanders to repress and report to the authorities breaches that they have been unable to prevent their subordinates from committing. Here too the legislator has gone far by imposing this obligation of means, but it can only be a source of satisfaction that emphasis is placed on this essential role of military commanders. It should however be clear that the role of military commanders in repression can only be disciplinary or preventive, and that penal sanctions are a matter for the competent authorities in accordance with national legislation.

Furthermore, for prisoners of war, civilian internees, or the population of occupied territories, humanitarian law does not of course stress repression but the legal and other guarantees to be given: the danger to be avoided in such cases is, indeed, excesses against unprotected persons and not laxity towards the authors of breaches.

3. Mutual Assistance in Criminal Matters

War crimes and grave breaches of the Conventions or Protocol I are impres-criptible and punishable everywhere. [27]

The principle of mutual assistance in any proceedings relating to such breaches was laid down by Protocol I (Article 88, para. 1). However this article does not state either the procedure or the scope of such mutual assistance, but only that it must be "the greatest measure of assistance".

Co-operation in the matter of extradition is given legal mention in Article 88, para. 2 of Protocol I, but with the important restriction provided by the phrase "when circumstances permit". States were unwilling to enter into a more restrictive formal engagement in the already wide area of breaches of the Conventions and Protocol I.

4. Practical Application

It is too early to assess the practical importance of the innovations made by Protocol I in respect of repression of breaches.

The provisions of the Conventions in this respect appear to have been comparatively limited. There may be three major reasons for that: the psychological difficulty, in a wartime atmosphere leading generally to hatred of the enemy, of condemning "excessive zeal" used against the enemy; the fact that in many cases the authorities themselves are responsible for breaches, of which they are guilty either intentionally or more often because their instruction in international humanitarian law has been neglected, and that the separation of legal and political powers is often seriously compromised in such situations; and lastly, let it be said once more, the lack of compulsory jurisdiction and supranational means of coercion whereby States can be forced to respect their engagements.

However, it should not be forgotten that on various occasions breaches have been repressed, and that the deterrent effect of these provisions, although impossible to assess, has certainly been considerable.

5. Other Means

– International Enquiry.

All criminal proceedings entail an enquiry. This type of enquiry is prescribed in national legislation and is not mentioned in the Conventions or in Protocol I.

Very often, however, one of the Parties to the conflict accuses another Party of violating the Conventions.

(d) The Enquiry Procedure Instituted by the Conventions of 1949.

In this case the common Article 52-53-132-145 of the Conventions provides that "an enquiry shall be instituted in a manner to be decided between the interested Parties". If the Parties do not agree on that manner, they must agree "on the choice of an umpire who will decide on the procedure to be followed".

This procedure does however require agreement at least on the umpire, which is probably one reason why it has never been successful. But another reason for its failure is the furious controversy surrounding widely publicized allegations of breaches. A State committing breaches can fairly often be persuaded to put an end to them provided the negotiations are completely confidential; but it will not usually tolerate aspersions on its humanitarian standards or good faith by an enquiry over which it has not full control.

1. The Fact-Finding Commission Instituted by Protocol I of 1977

Article 90 of Protocol I of 1977 instituted a Fact-Finding Commission. The procedure applied by this institution does not take the place of that provided for in the Conventions, but supplements it.

The major innovation made by the procedure to be followed by that Commission is that it has to enquire into any allegation of a grave breach or other serious violation [28] of the Conventions or of Protocol I, with or without the agreement of the accused Party.

However, the Parties to Protocol I are not bound to that procedure unless they make an express declaration recognizing the competence of the Commission to enquire into the allegations made by a Party that has made a similar declaration. Also the Commission (whose conclusions are not made public without the express agreement of the Parties concerned) makes a report and recommendations to the Parties but has no competence other than this. There is no real reason to regret that the Commission's powers are comparatively limited; they could be no wider in the present state of international order.

The Commission is composed of "fifteen members of high moral standing and acknowledged impartiality", elected for five years by the Parties who have declared that they accept its competence, pursuant to a clearly defined procedure. The enquiries are in principle made by a Chamber of seven members, five of whom are appointed by the President of the Commission and one by each of the Parties directly concerned.

It is too early to assess the value of this procedure, as it has not yet been put to the test; the Protocol prescribes that it cannot operate until 20 Parties to the Protocol have expressly declared that they accept the competence of the Commission. So far, nothing like that number of Parties have done so. [29]

2. The Role of the ICRC

The role of the ICRC is to ensure that the Conventions are applied. It reports direct to the Parties concerned, in principle confidentially, breaches of international humanitarian law that it has itself ascertained. It is however extremely wary if asked to take part in an enquiry into alleged breaches. The atmosphere of bitter recrimination often surrounding such allegations and the indignation natural at a time of armed conflict make the investigator's task extremely difficult. Logically, an enquiry should lead to conclusions that either condemn the accused Party or give the lie to the accusing Party. In either case one of the

Parties will find it very hard to accept the result. The ICRC realizes this. It realizes that by agreeing to be an investigator it agrees to be mixed up in polemics that can only harm its protection and assistance activities in at least one of the Parties; but as everyone understands, the ICRC cannot work really effectively unless it can act in each of the conflicting Parties.

It has therefore adopted the very rigorous principle that it will only agree, as a last resort, to take part in the constitution of a Commission of Enquiry outside its own organization if all the interested Parties so request.

This contingency has not arisen under the Conventions of 1949.

3. Procedure in Case of Disagreement Concerning the Application and Interpretation of the Provisions of the Conventions and of Protocol I.

– Procedure Prescribed by the Conventions.

Where they deem it advisable, particularly in cases of disagreement between the Parties concerning the "application or interpretation" of the provisions of the Conventions (see the common Article 11-11-11-12) the Protecting Powers may lend the Parties to the conflict their good offices with a view to settling the disagreement.

No such meeting has ever taken place, one reason being that the system of Protecting Powers has only very rarely been used. [30]

– Procedure Established by Protocol I of 1977

Article 7 of that Protocol reads:

> "The depositary of this Protocol shall convene a meeting of the High Contracting Parties, at the request of one or more of the said Parties and upon the approval of the majority of the said Parties, to consider general problems concerning the application of the Conventions and of the Protocol."

In this case the meeting does not concern only the Parties to the conflict, but all the Contracting Parties. So far the depositary has not received any request pursuant to this Article.

4. Co-operation With the Uinted Nations.

Article 89 of Protocol I reads:

> "In situations of serious violations of the Conventions or of this Protocol, the High Contracting Parties undertake to act, jointly or individually, in co-operation with the United Nations and in conformity with the United Nations Charter."

The scope of this Article is not very clear, especially as States have not yet had occasion to show how they proposed to apply it.

5. The Role of the Media.

The media have no legal function in international humanitarian law. Undeniably, however, they influence its implementation by showing an image of the conflicting Parties towards which those Parties are generally far from indifferent, and that depends largely on the way in which those Parties apply humanitarian law.

(e) The Application of International Humanitarian Law in Non-International Armed Conflicts. [31]

The means we have called preventive also concerned the international humanitarian law applicable in non-international armed conflicts: Article 3 of the Conventions of 1949 and Protocol II of 1977 are part of international humanitarian law and can in no wise be excluded from the efforts made to disseminate and teach that law. One very short Article of Protocol II mentions dissemination; it reads: "This Protocol shall be disseminated as widely as possible".

There is however no specific provision mentioning application. As violations of Article 3 of the Conventions, or of Protocol II, cannot be classed as grave breaches, in the strict sense of the term, of the Conventions and Protocol, there is only an obligation to put an end to them but no obligation to punish their author.

The system of Protecting Powers is not of course involved and only the ICRC is granted a brief mention, as being able to "offer its services to the Parties to the conflict" (see Article 3 of the Conventions), but the Parties are not obliged to accept them. No enquiry procedure is provided for. In practice, however, the ICRC has generally been able to take action in this kind of conflict on as large a scale as its action in international conflicts.

(f) Conclusions

Experience shows that the application of international humanitarian law is cramped by rigid procedure, and that its greatest successes appear to have been obtained with the least restrictive procedure. The growing influence of the ICRC over the years, especially in non-international armed conflicts, clearly shows this, just as it shows that "the moderating activities of a third party unconnected with the objectives of the struggle and the exigencies of combat" [32] are still essential.

It would however be wrong to conclude that strictly legal argument should be rejected; it must still have a place in such activities, because it situates them and places discussion at its true level; but experience shows that it is not sufficient. Nowhere in the world is there any real supranational court or force, and persuasion based on honesty, neutrality and efficacy is probably the essential weapon of those wishing to promote the rule of international humanitarian law.

This branch of international law owes its modest but undeniable success very largely to the fact that it is of use to everybody and keeps clear of political quarrels. Anybody who wants to promote its implementation must never forget this.

Notes

1. Undoubtedly, the right of legitimate defence is recognized by the United Nations Charter (Art. 1) and the United Nations may in theory engage in military action against an aggressor (Art. 42), but an international war may no longer take place unless at least one of the Parties to the conflict violates the United Nations Charter.

2. Cf. p. 265–266.

3. Cf. p. 275 ff.

4. Cf. p. 266 ff.

5. For the importance of national laws in implementing international humanitarian law, cf. Bothe, Michel, The role of national law in the implementation of international humanitarian law, in: *Festschrift Patrnogic*, to be published.

6. Cf. p. 275 ff.

7. Cf. p. 275–276.

8. Cf. *Annales de droit international médical*. Commission médico-juridique, Monaco, No 18, décembre 1968, pp. 29–51.

9. "The use of words "and to ensure respect" was, however, deliberate; they were intended to emphasize and strengthen the responsibility of the Contracting Parties. It would not, for example, be enough for a State to give orders or directives to a few civilian or military authorities, leaving it to them to arrange as they pleased for the details of their execution. It is for the State to supervise their execution". Pictet, Jean (Ed.), *Commentary to the Geneva Conventions of 12 August 1949*. Vol. I – Geneva Convention for the Amelioration of the Condition of the Wounded and Sick in Armed Forces in the Field. Geneva, ICRC, 1952, p. 26.

10. "It follows, therefore, that in the event of a Power failing to fulfil its obligations, the other Contracting Parties (neutral, allied or enemy) may, and should, endeavour to bring it back to an attitude of respect for the Convention" (*Ibid.*).

11. Cf. *Annales de droit international médical*. Commission médico-juridique, Monaco, No 18, décembre 1968, especially p. 41 ff.

12. Pictet, Jean (Ed.), *Commentary to the Geneva Conventions of 12 August 1949*. Vol. I – Geneva Convention for the Amelioration of the Condition of the Wounded and Sick in Armed Forces in the Field. Geneva, ICRC, 1952, p. 86.

13. For an historical description, cf. Pictet, Jean (Ed.), *Commentary to the Geneva Conventions of 12 August 1949*, Vol. I – Geneva Convention for the Amelioration of the Condition of the Wounded and Sick in Armed Forces in the Field. Geneva, ICRC, 1952, pp. 86–93.

14. *Ibid.*, p. 89.

15. *Ibid.*, p. 91.

16. *Ibid.*, pp. 91–92.

17. As regards these articles, cf. pp.... and...

18. Pictet, Jean (Ed.), *Commentary to the Geneva Conventions of 12 August 1949*. Vol. I – Geneva Convention for the Amelioration of the Condition of the Wounded and Sick in Armed Forces in the Field. Geneva, ICRC, 1952, p. 96.

19. *Ibid.*, p. 96.

20. *Ibid.*, p. 96.

21. For further information, cf. especially Forsythe, David P., Who are the guardians: third parties and the law of armed conflict. *American Journal of International Law* (Washington D.C.), Vol. 70, No 1, January 1976, p. 41 ff., especially pp. 46–48.

22. Cf. in particular Abi-Saab, Georges, Le renforcement du système d'application des règles du droit humanitaire, *Revue de droit pénal militaire et du droit de la guerre* (Bruxelles), Vol. XII – 2, 1973, p. 223 ff., especially pp. 227–228.

23. Although the wording is not perfectly suited to our purpose, it will be used below for simplicity's sake.

24. Cf. below.

25. Cf. especially Patrnogic, Jovica, Control of the application of humanitarian conventions, *Revue de droit pénal militaire et de droit de la guerre* (Bruxelles), No. V − 2, 1966, p. 405 ff.

26. Cf. especially de La Pradelle, Paul and Aureglia, Louis, Rapport sur le contrôle de l'application des Conventions humanitaires en cas de conflits armés. *Annales de droit international médical* (Monaco), No. 6, December 1960, p. 17 ff.

27. Cf. the Convention on the Non-Applicability of Statutory Limitations to War Crimes and Crimes Against Humanity (United Nations General Assembly Resolution 2391 (XXIII) of 26 November 1968), common Article 49 (I), 50 (II), 129 (III) and 146 (IV) of the Geneva Conventions for the Protection of War Victims of 12 August 1949, and Article 85 of Additional Protocol I of 1977. *The Laws of Armed Conflicts. A Collection of Conventions, Resolutions and Other Documents*, Edited by D. Schindler and J. Toman, 3rd edition, Dordrecht, Martinus Nijhoff Publishers, Geneva, Henry Dunant Institute, 1988, pp. 925−932, 391−392, 418, 475−476, 546−547, 671−672.

28. The phrase *grave breach* has a precise meaning and designates breaches that are listed, whereas the phrase *serious violation* is to be understood as having its usual meaning, which the Commission is left to determine.

29. On 30 June 1988 only 11 of the 76 States Parties to Protocol I had made that declaration.

30. Cf. p. 271.

31. No mention will be made here of applicability of customary international law in non-international armed conflicts, regarding which, cf., inter alia, Kalshoven, Frits, in *Current Problems of International Law*, A. Cassese (ed.), Milan, 1975, pp. 265−285.

32. Bugnion, Francis. Le droit humanitaire applicable aux conflits armés internationaux: le problème de contrôle. *Annales d'études internationales* (Genève), Vol. 8, 1977, p. 57.

CHAPTER XVII

RESPONSIBILITY IN BREACHES OF INTERNATIONAL HUMANITARIAN LAW

IGOR P. BLISHCHENKO

The 20th century has seen the introduction into international relations of responsibility of States and private persons for breaches of international humanitarian law and of the laws and customs of war.[1] Article 3 of the Hague Convention concerning the Laws and Customs of War of 1907 states that a belligerent which violates the provisions of the Regulations respecting the Laws and Customs of War on Land – annex to the IVth Hague Convention – shall, if the case demands, be liable to pay compensation, and shall be responsible for all acts committed by persons forming part of its armed forces.

The article seems to stress responsibility for material damage. Its second sentence might well be interpreted as absolving private persons from responsibility for unlawful actions and shifting the responsibility for such actions to States.

Article 227 of the Versailles Treaty may be considered a milestone in the development of the recognition of responsibility in international humanitarian law. Under this article the Allied States arraigned Wilhelm II, the former German Emperor, "for a supreme offence against international morality and the sanctity of treaties". They proposed establishing a special international tribunal to try William II, but Holland would not extradite him. The repercussions of the Leipzig trials against other German war criminals were slight.

The process by which the criminal responsibility of private persons for the violation of laws and customs of war was instituted deserves to be noted. Development of this institution was discernible in the period between the World Wars, and in this connection the draft Code for Air Warfare (1923), the 1929 Geneva Convention for the Amelioration of the Condition of the Wounded and Sick in Armed Forces in the Field and the 1929 Geneva Convention Relative to the Treatment of Prisoners of War should be mentioned.

Article 29 of the first of these two Geneva Conventions sets forth the duty of governments whose penal laws were inadequate in proposing to their legislative bodies the necessary measures for the repression in time of war of any act contrary to the provisions of the Convention.

The concept of responsibility for violation of laws and customs of war and for war crimes was finally shaped after World War II. The crimes committed by the Nazi and Fascist regimes during this war caused justified anger among all nations. Even the most inveterate opponents of the elaboration of a system of rules of responsibility in international law could not prevent the establishment and development of the institution of responsibility for the violation of the laws and customs of war and for the committing of war crimes.[2]

The Allied Powers first established on their territories committees to inquire into the heinous crimes and damage caused by the Nazis and their accomplices to individuals, public bodies and States. Then a special committee on military crimes was established within the framework of the United Nations. The United Nations published a number of notes and statements which informed the world about the flagrant violations of the laws and customs of war and the responsibility for these crimes.[3]

In 1943 in many Soviet cities, for example, Kharkov, Krasnodar, Kiev, Minsk Riga, Smolensk, Briansk, Leningrad and others, war criminals trials were held.

On 8 August 1945, the Agreement between the governments of the Allied powers to prosecute and punish the principal war criminals of the Axis Powers was signed in London. This agreement was based on the Moscow Declaration of 30 October 1943, which stated that the German officers, soldiers and members of the Nazi Party who had committed crimes on a voluntary basis or had been responsible for such crimes should be sent for trial and punishment to the countries where they had committed the crimes.

Under the agreement of 8 August 1945 the International Military Tribunal was set up to try the principal war criminals whose crimes did not relate to a particular geographic region. All the Allied Powers were to try criminals individually or as members of organizations or groups. The Charter of the International Military Tribunal, as part of the agreement, constituted the *corpus juris* of the international crimes involving individual responsibility, and introduced into international law the notions of: (a) crimes against peace, in particular, planning, preparation, initiation or conduct of aggressive war or of war violating international treaties, agreements or promises or participation in common plans or treason aimed at the accomplishment of any of the above-mentioned actions; (b) war crimes, i.e., violation of laws and customs of war, such as murder, torture or enslavement of the civilian population of the occupied territory, execution or torture of prisoners of war or shipwrecked persons, the execution of hostages, damage to public or private property, destruction of cities or villages that is not required by military necessity; (c) crimes against humanity, viz., murders, annihilation, enslavement, exile and other cruelties perpetrated on the civilian population before or during the war, and persecution on political, racial or religious grounds with the aim of committing, or in connection with, any crime falling under the jurisdiction of the Tribunal regardless of whether or not these actions violate the internal law of the country where they have been committed.

The last paragraph of Article 6 stresses that the leaders, organizers, instigators and accomplices who have participated in the elaboration or the consummation of a plan or plot to commit any of the above-mentioned crimes, bear responsibility for all the actions committed by any person with the purpose of implementing such a plan.

It is necessary to note that at that time there were opponents to the prosecution of war criminals. They claimed that the Nuremberg Trial was an occupation court, not an international one, and that it was a trial of victors over the vanquished, not the administration of real justice.[4]

As far as the first statement is concerned, it is sufficient to say that the Charter of the Nuremberg Tribunal was approved not only by the four Powers; nineteen other States also acceded to it. In addition, on 11 December 1946 the United Nations General Assembly adopted Resolution 95 (1), in which it confirmed as generally recognized the principles of international law contained in the Charter of the Nuremberg Tribunal and reflected by the judgement of the Tribunal.

The principal Prosecutor from the U.S.A. at the Nuremberg Trials, Robert Jackson, declared in his speech at the trial that one result of the vast scope of the aggressive actions waged by the people to be tried was that few neutral States remained in the world. He added that either the victors should try the vanquished, or that the vanquished should be tried by their own people, an alternative which experience after the First World War had shown to be useless.[5]

Finally, it should be noted that the Allied Powers administered justice not only with respect to the citizens of the States of the Axis, but also with respect to their own citizens. The peace treaties of 1947 had a special paragraph according to which citizens of the Allied States could be extradited for trial and punishment.

The second session of the General Assembly instructed the Commission of International Law to formulate the principles of international law that were embodied in the Charter of the Nuremberg Tribunal and in its judgement. It also instructed the Commission to draw up a draft code of laws concerning crimes against peace and security, paying due attention to the Nuremberg principles (Resolution 177 (II)).

In 1954 the Commission of International Law adopted a draft code but the General Assembly postponed its consideration until the definition of aggression was adopted (Resolution 877 (IX)). In other words, the United Nations considered the Nuremberg principles as generally adopted.

It is important to mention the fact that the Nuremberg principles enunciated in the judgement of the Tribunal stipulated a longer enumeration of crimes involving international criminal responsibility. The Tribunal also formulated some new rules of international law.

Article I of the Convention on the Prevention and Punishment of the Crime of Genocide (1948), for example, states that "...genocide, whether committed in time of peace or in time of war, is a crime under international law which they (the States parties to the Convention) undertake to prevent and to punish".

The principles embodied in the Charter of the Nuremberg Tribunal influenced considerably the development of the rules of international law concerning the extradition of war criminals, the non-applicability of statutory limitations to war crimes and the increase in the number of crimes that can be termed "crimes against humanity".

The Convention on the Non-Applicability of Statutory Limitations to War Crimes and Crimes against Humanity, adopted by the United Nations General Assembly in 1968, adds the following to the war crimes and crimes against humanity defined by the Charter of the Nuremberg Tribunal: "eviction by armed attack or occupation and inhuman acts resulting from the policy of apartheid, and the crime of genocide as defined in the 1948 Convention on the Prevention and Punishment of the Crime of Genocide, even if such acts do not constitute a violation of the domestic law of the country in which they were committed".

It is useful to recall that the resolutions of the General Assembly 3 (I) of 13 February 1948 (Extradition and Punishment of War Criminals) and 170 (II) of 31 October 1947 (Extradition of War Criminals and Traitors) deal with the obligatory extradition of persons who have committed crimes under article 6 of the Charter of the Nuremberg Tribunal. Article I (2) of the Declaration on Territorial Asylum adopted by the General Assembly at the twenty-second session in 1967 says that "the right to seek and enjoy asylum may not be invoked by any person with respect to whom there are serious reasons for considering that he has committed a crime against humanity..." (UN General Assembly resolution 2312 (XXII)).

According to article I of the Convention on the Non-Applicability of Statutory Limitations to War Crimes and Crimes against Humanity (1968), no statutory limitation can be applied to war crimes and crimes against humanity and under article IV, the States parties to the Convention undertake to adopt legislative and other measures to that effect.

The Geneva Conventions for the Protection of War Victims envisage international criminal responsibility for a number of acts which were proscribed as war crimes not by the IVth Hague Convention (1907) but by the Charter and Judgement of the Nuremberg Tribunal.

Each of the Geneva Conventions contains an article stating:

> "The High Contracting Parties undertake to enact any legislation necessary to provide effective penal sanctions for persons committing, or ordering to be committed, any of the grave breaches defined in the following Article.
>
> Each High Contracting Party shall be under the obligation to search for persons alleged to have committed, or have ordered to be committed, such grave breaches, and shall bring such persons, regardless of their nationality, before its own courts. It may also, if it prefers, and in accordance with the provisions of its own legislation, hand such persons over for trial to another High Contracting Party

concerned, provided such High Contracting Party has made out a *prima facie* case.

Each High Contracting Party shall take measures necessary for the suppression of all acts contrary to the provisions of the present Convention other than the grave breaches defined in the following Article."[6]

According to that "following Article",[7] "graves breaches shall be those involving any of the following acts, if committed against persons or property protected by the present Convention: wilful killing, torture or inhuman treatment, includ-
ing biological experiments, wilfully causing great suffering or serious injury to body or health, unlawful deportation or transfer or unlawful confinement of a protected person, compelling a protected person to serve in the forces of a hostile Power, or wilfully depriving a protected person of the rights of fair and regular trial prescribed in the present Convention, taking of hostages and extensive destruction and appropriation of property, not justified by military necessity and carried out unlawfully and wantonly."

The Geneva Conventions attempt to prevent States from eluding their responsibilities by stipulating: "No High Contracting Party shall be allowed to absolve itself or any other High Contracting Party of any liability incurred by itself or by another High Contracting Party in respect of breaches referred to in the preceding Article."[8]

The creation of a special international criminal court was considered during the United Nations discussion of punishment of those directly responsible for violation of laws and customs of war.[9] Even draft statutes of such a court were worked out.

Whilst they are no substitute for international legislation based on agreements among States following the Nuremberg principles and the draft statutes of the international criminal court, national legislation and institutions for prosecution of those who are accused of international crimes must not be underestimated.[10] It was the Convention on the Non-Applicability of Statutory Limitations to War Crimes and Crimes against Humanity (1968) which envisaged the prosecution and punishment of criminals by national means in the first place.

The majority of States ratified the Geneva Conventions for the Protection of War Victims and, by making them a part of national law, assumed responsibility to prosecute in the event of their violation.

A number of States included in their criminal legislation penalties for persons committing the offences mentioned in the Geneva Conventions. For instance, in the Soviet Union, articles 30–39 of the Law of responsibility for war crimes (25 December 1958), hold criminally responsible individuals guilty of looting, of coercion of civilians in the area of military operations, of bad treatment of prisoners of war, and of unlawful display of the red cross or red crescent. These same actions are punishable also under the RSFSR Criminal Code (articles

266–269 and corresponding articles of the Criminal Codes of other Soviet Republics).

The application of the Geneva Conventions in several armed conflicts showed the effectiveness of the system for attribution of responsibility in the event of their violation.

For instance, war crimes are offences also against the *U.S. Uniform Code of Military Justice*. As such they are investigated by the *Criminal Investigation Division* and, in fact, from 1965 to August 1973, thirty-six cases involving war crime allegations against Army personnel were tried by court-martial. Twenty of these resulted in convictions. The My Lai (Son My) incident, the most notorious of the offences committed by U.S. troops in Vietnam, was not the result of inadequate laws but of the failure of unit leaders to enforce regulations. At higher levels the U.S. and Allied Forces commanders were genuinely concerned to ensure that their forces conducted themselves in accordance with the laws of war.

Criminal proceedings were also instigated against fourteen high-ranking officers of the American Army, including General Coster, the Commander of the Division of which the detachment charged with the My Lai massacre was a part. They were accused of hiding their knowledge of the crime from the American Supreme Command.[11]

In 1976, in Angola, mercenaries who had been recruited by two of the three liberation movements were captured, tried and convicted of crimes against the population and of violations of the 1949 Geneva Conventions.[12]

On the other hand the system has a serious shortcoming, namely, that there is no means of enforcing a State to apply the Geneva Conventions. The Ministry of Foreign Affairs of the Democratic Republic of Vietnam, in a letter dated 31 August 1965, told the International Committee of the Red Cross that U.S. pilots "destroying property and massacring the population" would be treated if captured as criminals and tried under the laws of the Democratic Republic of Vietnam. The Democratic Republic of Vietnam had, in fact, acceded to the Geneva Conventions with the reservation that it would not grant the benefits of the Conventions to military captives accused of grave war crimes in accordance with the principles elaborated by the Nuremberg Tribunal. That reservation in the opinion of the Democratic Republic of Vietnam Government increased responsibility for observing the laws and customs of war and intensified the humanitarian nature of the Convention directed against such crimes.

The question of responsibility for violations of the provisions of the Geneva Conventions of 1949 arose also in connection with the Middle East conflict. The Special Committee of the United Nations[13] stated that the grave breaches of the Geneva Conventions of 1949 raised the question of criminal proceedings against persons accused of these crimes.

The development of methods and means of conducting hostilities, and experience in armed conflicts revealed the shortcomings of the 1949 Geneva Conventions – including gaps in the attribution of responsibility for breaches –

and highlighted the necessity for Protocols to supplement the Geneva Conventions of 1949 on the protection of victims of war.

The 1977 Protocol I contains a section – "Repression of Breaches of the Conventions and of this Protocol" – which is a codification of the principles, norms and procedures to establish responsibility for violation of international humanitarian law.

The Protocol has expanded the list of international crimes, and has more precisely defined some which were already prohibited by the Geneva and the Hague Conventions.

First, in accordance with international or municipal law, criminal proceedings may be instituted against members of the armed forces who commit crimes against persons protected under articles 44 and 45 – combatants and prisoners of war and persons who have taken part in hostilities – and article 73 – refugees and stateless persons.

Article 44 of Protocol I relaxes considerably the requirements of Article 4 of the Third 1949 Geneva Convention, but a captured combatant, to receive prisoner-of-war status, must nevertheless have carried his arms openly during each military engagement and while he is engaged in a military deployment preceding an attack.

Article 85, paragraph 2, regards as grave breaches of the Protocol acts "against persons in the power of an adverse Party protected by Articles 44, 45 and 73 of this Protocol, or against the wounded, sick and shipwrecked of the adverse Party who are protected by this Protocol, or against those medical or religious personnel, medical units or medical transports which are under the control of the adverse Party and are protected by this Protocol".

In this connection article 11, "Protection of persons", is of great importance. It enumerates some acts to be suppressed. First, it stipulates that "the physical or mental health and integrity of persons who are in the power of the adverse Party or who are interned, detained or otherwise deprived of liberty" as a result of an international armed conflict "shall not be endangered by any unjustified act or omission". Accordingly, it is prohibited to subject such persons to any medical procedure not indicated by their state of health and which is not consistent with generally accepted medical standards.

Paragraph 2 states that "it is, in particular, prohibited to carry out on such persons, even with their consent, physical mutilations, medical or scientific experiments, removal of tissues or organs for transplantation".

Article 11, paragraph 4, prohibits "any wilful act or omission which seriously endangers the physical or mental health or integrity of any person who is in the power of a Party other than the one on which he depends".

To guarantee the proper function of the provisions of the Protocol, paragraph 6 of Article 11 requires the recording of blood or skin donations by the persons mentioned above. The medical records shall be available at all times for inspection by the Protecting Power.

Under Article 85, the following are grave breaches of the Protocol:

"(*a*) making the civilian population or individual civilians the object of attack;

(*b*) launching an indiscriminate attack affecting the civilian population or civilian objects in the knowledge that such attack will cause excessive loss of life, injury to civilians or damage to civilian objects;

(*c*) launching an attack against works or installations containing dangerous forces in the knowledge that such attack will cause excessive loss of life, injury to civilians or damage to civilian objects;

(*d*) making non-defended localities and demilitarized zones the object of attack;

(*e*) making a person the object of attack in the knowledge that he is *hors de combat*;

(*f*) the perfidious use, in violation of Article 37, of the distinctive emblem of the red cross, red crescent or red lion and sun or of other protective signs recognized by the Conventions or this Protocol."

Article 85 also regards the following acts as "grave breaches of this Protocol when committed wilfully and in violation of the Conventions or the Protocol":

(*a*) the transfer by the Occupying Power of parts of its own civilian population into the territory it occupies, or the deportation or transfer of all or parts of the population of the occupied territory within or outside this territory, in violation of Article 49 of the Fourth Convention;

(*b*) unjustifiable delay in the repatriation of prisoners of war or civilians;

(*c*) practices of apartheid and other inhuman and degrading practices involving outrages upon personal dignity, based on racial discrimination;

(*d*) making the clearly-recognized historic monuments, works of art or places of worship which constitute the cultural or spiritual heritage of peoples and to which special protection has been given by special arrangement, for example, within the framework of a competent international organization, the object of attack, causing as a result extensive destruction thereof, where there is no evidence of the violation by the adverse Party of Article 53, sub-paragraph (*b*), and when such historic monuments, works of art and places of worship are not located in the immediate proximity of military objectives;

(*e*) depriving a person protected by the Conventions or referred to in paragraph 2 of this Article of the rights of fair and regular trial".[14]

The above-mentioned provisions reflect, on the one hand, the complexity and gravity of armed conflicts and, on the other, the way the international community, to protect human rights in armed conflicts, has sought to attribute responsibility to persons guilty of crimes qualified by the Protocol as grave breaches. Article

86 of Protocol I is of great importance, since it requires the parties to suppress or prevent the breach of the Conventions and the Protocol by omission.

According to paragraph 2 of article 86, "the fact that a breach of the Conventions or of this Protocol was committed by a subordinate does not absolve his superiors from penal or disciplinary responsibility, as the case may be, if they knew, or had information which should have enabled them to conclude in the circumstances at the time, that he was committing such a breach and if they did not take all feasible measures within their power to prevent or repress the breach".

Article 87 imposes as an international obligation upon parties to an armed conflict the duty to require military commanders to prevent and, if necessary, to suppress and to report to competent authorities breaches of the Conventions or of the Protocol.

Any commander who is aware that subordinates or other persons under his control are going to commit or have committed a breach of the Conventions or of the Protocol must initiate steps necessary to prevent such violations and, where appropriate, disciplinary or penal action against violators.

A commander must take measures commensurate with his level of responsibility to ensure that members of the armed forces under his command were aware of their obligations under the Conventions and the Protocol (Article 87, paragraph 2).

Thus, grave breaches of the Conventions and the Protocol in international armed conflicts entail the individual penal and disciplinary responsibility of persons directly guilty thereof and of persons who are able to prevent or suppress such breaches but failed to do so.

Article 89 dwells upon the duty of the parties to the Conventions and the Protocol to co-operate in situations of serious violations of the Conventions and the Protocol. To that end the parties undertake to act, jointly or individually, in co-operation with the United Nations and in conformity with the United Nations Charter.

This co-operation implies action based on existing international agreements dealing with armed conflicts, and the working out and adoption of new international instruments. The former includes such international agreements as the 1968 Convention on the Non-Applicability of Statutory Limitations to War Crimes and Crimes against Humanity, the 1948 Convention on the Prevention and Punishment of the Crime of Genocide, and the International Convention on the Suppression and Punishment of the Crime of Apartheid, of 1973. The latter comprises the working out of a convention on the extradition of persons who have committed war crimes and crimes against humanity; a convention on an international criminal court for the trial of persons accused of war crimes and crimes against humanity, similar to the Nuremberg Tribunal; harmonization of national legal norms laying down the responsibility for war crimes and crimes against humanity.

Article 88 of Protocol I requires the Parties to co-operate in criminal prosecutions and in the matter of extradition, and to give due consideration to the request of the State on whose territory the alleged offence has occurred.

Article 91 stipulates that a party to a conflict which violates the provisions of the Conventions or of the Protocol shall be able to pay compensation, and shall be responsible for all acts committed by persons forming part of its armed forces. In other words, in addition to the individual penal responsibility which it envisages, the Protocol confirms the responsibility of the subject of international law for perpetrations of crimes and breaches of the provisions of the Conventions and the Protocol.

This approach is in accordance with the demands of international law.

Protocol II, relating to the Protection of Victims of Non-International Armed Conflicts has its own peculiarities, the first being the fact that when it is ratified and has entered into force for a particular State, its territorial scope will be limited by the boundaries of the State, and it will have legal force on this territory along with the internal laws and, in the first place, with the criminal codes on responsibility for criminal acts.[15]

It should be noted that Protocol II qualifies as crimes a number of acts not recognized as such by the majority of criminal codes.

These crimes:

(1) violence to the life, health and physical or mental well-being of persons not directly involved in military operations or of those who have terminated their military activities, whether or not their liberty has been restricted – in particular, murder, cruel treatment such as torture, mutilation or any form of corporal punishment;

(2) collective punishments;

(3) taking of hostages;

(4) acts of terrorism;

(5) outrages upon personal dignity, in particular humiliating and degrading treatment, rape, enforced prostitution and any form of indecent assault;

(6) slavery or the slave trade in any form;

(7) pillage;

(8) threats to commit any of the foregoing acts. (Protocol II, Article 4.)

According to Article 13, the civilian population shall not be the object of attack. The article also prohibits acts or threats of violence the primary purpose of which is to spread terror among the civilian population.

Article 7 of Protocol II binds the parties to a conflict to treat the wounded, sick and shipwrecked humanely and to give them "to the fullest extent practicable and with the least possible delay, the medical care and attention required by their condition".

Medical and religious personnel shall be respected, protected and granted all available help for the performance of their duties. They shall not be compelled to carry out tasks which are not compatible with their humanitarian mission (art.9). Article 10 stipulates that "under no circumstances shall any person be punished for having carried out medical activities... regardless of the person benefiting therefrom".

Medical units and transports shall not be attacked unless they are used to commit hostile acts. Article 12 prohibits the improper use of the emblem of the red cross, red crescent or red lion and sun, and Article 16 prohibits acts of hostility against historic monuments, works of art or places of worship which constitute the cultural or spiritual heritage of peoples and forbids their use in support of the military effort.

Starvation of civilians as a method of combat is prohibited. It is therefore prohibited "to attack, destroy, remove or render useless, for that purpose, objects indispensable to the survival of the civilian population, such as foodstuffs, agricultural areas for the production of foodstuffs, crops, livestock, drinking water installations and supplies and irrigation works" (article 14).

No attack on works or installations containing dangerous forces, namely dams, dykes and nuclear electrical generating stations, is permitted, even when these objects are military objectives, if such attack may cause the release of dangerous forces and consequent severe losses among the civilian population (art. 15). Also prohibited is any displacement of the civilian population for reasons related to conflict, unless the safety of the civilians or imperative military reasons so demand. Deportation of the civilian population is also prohibited (art. 17).

The conclusion is that the above-mentioned actions should be considered as criminal offences calling for prosecution and punishment of offenders. Article 6 (2) provides compulsory safeguards in the event of the prosecution and punishment of criminal offences connected with armed conflict. No provision of the criminal law of a Party to the Protocol may contradict the Protocol relating to non-international armed conflicts once it has entered into force. It is evident that the provisions of the Protocol are binding on any person as well as on officials of the parties involved in a conflict of a non-international nature.[16] The 1977 Additional Protocols to the Geneva Conventions of 1949 on the Protection of Victims of War proceed from the assumption of inadmissibility of any "order of a criminal nature", that is, an order which is aimed at breaching provisions of the Convention and the Protocols. Any person who issues such an order should be considered as a person who has committed a war crime. The carrying out of such an order is also considered as a crime under the Convention and the Protocols. The Protocols embody the precepts of the Charter of the Nuremberg Tribunal, Article 8 of which provides that "the fact that the Defendant acted pursuant to order of his government or of a superior shall not free him from responsibility, but may be considered in mitigation of punishment..."

The International Military Tribunal in its judgement stated that the majority of the accused had pleaded that they obeyed the orders of Hitler and for that reason were not responsible for actions committed pursuant to such orders. The Tribunal went on to say that Article 8 of the Charter was in conformity with the laws of all nations. The fact that a soldier killed or tortured in obedience to an order and in violation of international laws of war was never considered as an argument against conviction for such action.

In connection with the Keitel Case, the Tribunal stated that orders, even to rank and file soldiers, should not be considered as a reason for lenient punishment if the crimes were committed intentionally, cruelly, without any necessity and on such a scale as in the case in point.

It is worth mentioning that the Nuremberg Tribunal did not merely reject the defence of superior orders. In each particular case, it considered as a major factor any discretion which a subordinate might have had in obeying or disobeying an order. One should underline that the draft of Protocol I contained an article – No. 77 – according to which nobody was to be punished for refusal to carry out an order of his government or superior if the execution of such order would be a serious violation of the Geneva Conventions or of the Protocol. The fact that a person acted pursuant to such an order would not have absolved him from penal responsibility if it were established that the person should have known that he was seriously violating the Conventions or the Protocol and could have refused to obey the order. The absence of this article in the adopted Protocol does not mean that such an international legal provision does not exist or is of limited application. Having approved the principles of the Charter of the Nuremberg Tribunal as universal principles of international law, the United Nations General Assembly confirmed the legal consequences of issuing and of carrying out a criminal order.

In the present stage of warfare developments, safeguards against the issue of a felonious order and the prevention and suppression of violations by servicemen of the rules of international law are of the utmost importance.

From this point of view a number of decisions of national courts are rather interesting, for example, the decisions of the US Military Tribunal, which, in its judgement of leaders of the SS and other punitive bodies, claimed that a subordinate must carry out only just orders of his commander and, if he obeys a criminal order knowing its felonious nature, he cannot invoke the order of his commander as a reason to reduce his responsibility. If the order is quite obviously *ultra vires*, a subordinate cannot plead ignorance of the criminal nature of the order.[17]

Professor G. Buchheim of Mainz University (Federal Republic of Germany), in his speeches delivered as an expert during trials of Nazi criminals in Western Germany gave another concept of a criminal order. He said that responsibility for having obeyed a criminal order depends on the normative nature of the order. If the order does not have a normative nature, loyalty is involved instead of legal responsibility. In other words, he tried to shift the question of responsibility from the field of law to the field of morals, calling, in this case, upon "moral postulates of society as extenuating circumstances". Such a concept of responsibility for the execution of a criminal order cannot be accepted from the point of view of international law, and the very essence of normative provisions of international law combine moral and legal responsibilities based on agreements between States.

But how is this question decided in the Protocol Additional to the Geneva Conventions of 1949 on international armed conflicts? Let us refer to the documentary materials of the Diplomatic Conference on Humanitarian Law.

As already mentioned, the draft of the Protocols contained provisions according to which no one would be punished for refusal to execute an order of his superior, if the execution of such order would be a grave breach of international conventions or of the Protocol. The fact that a person acted in accordance with the order of his superior does not absolve him from criminal responsibility if it is established that the person should have known that he was committing a grave breach of the Conventions or of the Protocol and could have refused to carry out the order (Article 77 of the draft).

During the discussions, this text was withdrawn, but the idea of the interdiction of issuing a criminal order and the responsibility for it is based on the Nuremberg Charter and as formulated in Article 86 of Protocol I on the failure of a commander to act and on his penal or disciplinary responsibility, as the case may be, if he knew or had information which should have enabled him to conclude in the circumstances at the time, that such a subordinate person was committing or was going to commit such a breach, and if he did not take all feasible measures to prevent or repress the breach. In other words, a criminal order is absolutely illegal, and responsibility for it cannot be disclaimed by the person who gave the order or by the person who carried it out.

Thus a solid system of responsibility for breaches of laws and customs of war is introduced into contemporary international law. It will unquestionably contribute to the prevention of crimes and the consolidation of protection of human rights. As far as the obligations of States to carry this system of responsibility into effect on their territories is concerned, practice follows two directions: first, direct implementation of the above-mentioned provisions and, if there are no analogous provisions in criminal codes, introduction of sanctions for these particular delicts; and second, to extend national criminal codes to cover such delicts and to define sanctions for them.

Which way is the most convenient depends upon social, national, historical and legal peculiarities of the development of the State concerned. In all situations the above-mentioned system of responsibility and inevitability of punishment – bearing in mind the necessity of all States acceding to the 1968 Convention on the Non-Applicability of Statutory Limitations to War Crimes and Crimes against Humanity – may create a strong barrier against tyranny and better protect human rights in conditions of armed conflict.

Notes

1. Kalshoven, Frits. *The Law of Warfare: A Summary of its Recent History and Trends in Development.* Leyden, A.W. Sijthoff and Geneva, Henry Dunant Institute, 1973, 143 p.; Cassese, Antonio. Current trends in the development of the law of armed conflict. *Rivista Trimestriale di Diritto Publico* (Milano), Vol. 24, No. 4, 1974, pp. 1407–1448; Herczegh, Géza. Recent problems in international humanitarian

296 IGOR P. BLISHCHENKO

law. In: *Questions of International Law*, ed. by György Haraszti, Budapest, Akadémiai, 1977, pp. 77–93; Herczegh, Géza, Problème de la réaffirmation et du développement du droit international humanitaire. *Acta Juridica Academia Scientiarum Hungaricae* (Budapest), Vol. XIX, No. 3–4, 1977, pp. 333–361.

2. Pokstefl, J., Bothe, M. Bericht über Entwicklungen und Tendenzen des Kriegsrechts seit den Nachkriegskodifikationen. *Zeitschrift für auslandisches öffentliches Recht und Völkerrecht* (Stuttgart), Vol. 35, No. 3, 1975, pp. 574–640.

3. *Vneshniaya politika Sovetskogo sayuza v period Otechestvennoi voiny* (Foreign Policy of the Soviet Union during the Patriotic War), Vol. 1, Moskva, Gospolitizdat, 1946.

4. Cf. Knieriem, A. *The Nuremberg Trials.* Chicago, H. Regnery Co., 1959, p. 101–102; Kelsen H., Will the Judgement in the Nuremberg Trial Constitute a Precedent in International Law? *International Law Quarterly*, No. 2, 1972, p. 153; Maugham, F.H.M., *U.N.O. and the War Crimes*, Westport, Greenwood Press, 1975, p. 27, 46, 105.

5. *Proceedings of the Trial of the Major War Criminals at the International Military Tribunal, Nuremberg, 14 November 1945–1 October 1946.* Nuremberg, 1947, Vol. 2, p. 110.

6. Articles common to the Geneva Conventions of 1949: 49/50/129/146.

7. Articles common to the Geneva Conventions of 1949: 50/51/130/147.

8. Articles common to the Geneva Conventions of 1949: 51/52/131/148.

9. *Report of the Committee on International Criminal Jurisdiction. 1 to 13 August 1951.* General Assembly Official Records: Seventh session. Supplement No. 11 (A/2136), 26 p. – *Report of the Committee on International Criminal Jurisdiction. 27 July–20 August 1953.* General Assembly Official Records: Nineth session. Supplement No. 12 (A/2645), 28 p.

10. Baxter, R.R., The municipal and international law basis of jurisdiction over war crimes. *British Yearbook of International Law* (London), Vol. 28, 1951, pp. 382–393.

11. Taylor, T., *Nuremberg and Vietnam: An American Tragedy.* Chicago, Quadrangle Books, 1970, pp. 123–153.

12. Burchett, W., Roebuck, D., The Whores of War: Mercenaries Today, *Review of Contemporary Law* (Bruxelles), Vol. 2, 1977, pp. 31–41. Dempster, Ch., Tomkins, D., *Fire Power.* London, Corgi, 1978, 491 p.

13. Report of the Special Committee to investigate Israeli practices affecting the human rights of the population of the occupied territories. United Nations document A/9148, 25 October 1973, 48 p.

14. Cf. also: Bothe M., Ipsen, K., Partsch, K.J., Die Genfer Konferenz über humanitäres Völkerrecht: Verlauf und Ergebnisse. *Zeitschrift für ausländisches Recht und Völkerrecht* (Stuttgart), Vol. 38, No. 1–2, 1978, pp. 59–60.

15. Blishchenko, I.P. Deistvie mezhdunarodnogo dogovora na territorii SSSR. (Application of international treaties on the USSR territory.) *Izdatel'stvo Vuzov, Pravovedenie* (Moskva), No. 6, 1968, pp. 105–113; Blishchenko, I.P., International treaties and their application on the territory of the USSR. *A.J.I.L.* (Washington, D.C.) Vol. 69, No. 4, October 1975, pp. 819–827. Radoinov, P., *S"glasuvane na v"treshnod"rashavnoto i mezhdunarodnoto pravo* (Relationship of internal and international law). Sofia, Nauka i iskusstvo, 1971, 176 p.; Butkevich, V., *Sovetskoe pravo i mezhdunarodnyi dogovor* (Soviet law and international treaties). Kiev, Izadtel'stvo Vishcha shkola, 1977, 259 p.; Seidl-Hohenveldern, I., Transformation or Adoption of International Law into Municipal Law. *The International and Comparative Law Quaterly* (London), Vol. 12, 1963, pp. 88–124. Salmon, J., Le conflit entre le traité international et la loi interne à la suite de l'arrêt rendu le 27 mai 1971 par La Cour de cassation. *Journal des Tribunaux* (Bruxelles), No. 4753, 25 septembre 1971.

16. M. Bothe, K. Ipsen, K.J. Partsch. Die Genfer Konferenz über humanitäres Völkerrecht. *Zeitschrift für ausländisches öffentliches Recht und Völkerrecht* (Stuttgart), Vol. 38, No. 1–2, 1978, pp. 75–77. Veuthey, M., *Guérilla et droit humanitaire.* Genève, Institut Henry-Dunant. 1976, 431 p. (2nd edition, Genève, CICR, 1983, xl + 451 p.).

17. *Trials of War Criminals before the Nuremberg Military Tribunals under Control Council Law*, Vol. IV, No. 10. Washington, D.C., U.S. Government Printing Office, pp. 470–471.

CONCLUSIONS

KAREL VASAK

1. As the refuge of suffering men and women, humanitarian law is the most human of laws; in this respect it belongs to every place and period. It is no surprise, therefore, that it is deeply rooted in all civilizations, traditions and religions or that its champions, providing partisan politics do not interfere, find no difficulty in working side by side to bring relief and assistance to victims. This is undoubtedly the secret of the often unexpected successes scored in its protection activities by the International Committee of the Red Cross, whose single-nation composition might, *a priori*, give rise to suspicion or reticence despite Switzerland's recognized and respected neutrality. Historical and philosophical works on the humanitarian movement thus constitute not only an indispensable contribution to our knowledge of humanitarian law, but also an essential means of strengthening it, since legal rules are not followed as standard practice until they become part of the collective consciousness of all peoples and nations.

2. Humanitarian law, the law of humanity, has in the course of its application found itself converging ever more frequently with another law which, although of equally ancient origin, was not adequately codified until after the Second World War: the international law of human rights. The two bodies of law, at first existing in splendid isolation one from the other, then pitted against each other or at least presented as rivals in the efforts made by the organized international community to protect individuals, gradually changed shape in the minds of their respective champions so that the image used to illustrate the relationship between them is today totally appropriate: the image of a man who, to ensure the physical and mental suffering inflicted on him, needs to lean simultaneously on two crutches each of which represents one type of law. Jean Pictet understood very early this interdependance imposed by the intrinsic logic of the two bodies of law and the obvious interests of their beneficiaries, although historical differences in their development, implementation and structures for enforcement would suggest, if not their separation, at least a parallel existence. The most

striking evidence of their now irreversible convergence is undoubtedly contained in the texts of the two 1977 Protocols Additional to the Geneva Conventions of 1949.

3. Humanitarian law is, like the law of human rights, a protective law, but above all it is a conciliatory law. While its rules have always been formulated with the utmost stringency and are without doubt the most detailed in contemporary international law, it is persuasion and conciliation that guide the steps of those who strive to ensure that it is applied and respected. In practice, its implementation has rarely given rise to international disputes requiring judicial settlements. International justice, in the institutional and procedural sense of the term, is in this respect synonymous with failure, since helping victims is so much more urgent than any appeal that might be envisaged in the interests of international jurisprudence. The exemplary discretion of the International Committee of the Red Cross and the proverbial modesty of its delegates are not only traditional "attitudes"; they are above all means of facilitating the search for solutions in an unwavering spirit of conciliation.

4. Humanitarian law departs, in its fundamental conception, from the principle of reciprocity so all-pervasive in international law in general. It is an objective law, containing rules applicable to all elements of society: states, individuals and public or private entities. Moreover, it constitutes the most complete expression of the joint and several responsibility of all to ensure that it is respected, since States must not only apply its rules but also and above all ensure their application. This law inspired by compassion therefore becomes, upon implementation, a very strict law of universal justice. "*Inter armas caritas, per armis justicia*": thus completed, the ICRC motto would probably better express the two faces of humanitarian law, provided that arms, as instruments of justice, are understood to be more than just material means for enforcing applicable rules.

5. The right of humanitarian initiative, recognized by the international community, allows action to be taken, by the ICRC in particular, even when the situation calling for relief and assistance is not specifically covered by the applicable rules of humanitarian law. However, since man does not live by bread alone and cultural property is a natural extension of his aspirations, it is widely acknowledged today – as reflected in this work – that conventions for the protection of cultural property, the foremost of which is the 1954 Convention of The Hague, constitute an integral part of humanitarian law. Since it is Unesco that acts as the "Red Cross of cultural property", and is given legal power to do so by the Convention of The Hague and its constitutive act, logically it should also have a right of cultural intercession corresponding to the ICRC's right of humanitarian initiative. The right of cultural intercession, which appears between the lines of existing legislation, and has never been contested in the course of Unesco's history, has become indispensable owing to the increased incidence of armed

conflicts of all types during which enemy forces are tempted to treat not only human beings but also their cultural heritage without mercy.

6. Although its codification has been substantially developed since the Second World War, humanitarian law suffers from a congenital weakness so far shown by all branches of international law, that is, the lack of a comprehensive and effective system of verifying that its provisions are being observed. It does, however, thanks to the constant presence of various components of the International Red Cross, have an effective mechanism to encourage the implementation of its rules. As the innumerable activities of the National Red Cross and Red Crescent Societies, the League and the ICRC clearly show, the humanitarian conventions, far from being "orphans", are carefully nurtured by a large, if not always close-knit family.

7. It remains, and this has often been demonstrated by the horror and tragedy of recent events – that true recognition should be given to the right to humanitarian assistance, both national and especially international, of the victims of armed conflict and of its direct or indirect consequences, particularly since these victims are the primary concern of humanitarian law. It must also be clearly acknowledged that such situations give rise, beyond dispute, to the application of humanitarian law. The new human right, like any other, would be able to resist all sources of power, whether public and governmental or private. Nothing could demonstrate more effectively the complementarity of the two bodies of law – humanitarian law and the law of human rights – than the recognition of the right of all men and women to appeal to their brothers and sisters for help. It is indeed tragic that this all too human right should require legal endorsement.

SELECT BIBLIOGRAPHY

The present select bibliography includes a few basic studies and documents, mostly in the English language, suggested as reading matter for those who, encouraged by the studies included in the present volume, wish to acquire more knowledge about the international humanitarian law. For those who want to go even further, we recommand them to consult the following bibliographies:

Basic Bibliography of International Humanitarian Law. Geneva: Henry Dunant Institute, 1985, 106 p.

Bibliography of International Humanitarian Law Applicable in Armed Conflicts. 2nd ed. rev. and updated. Geneva: International Committee of the Red Cross & Henry Dunant Institute, 1987, 606 p.

ERICKSON, Richard, Selected Bibliography concerning the Laws of War including the Law Applicable to Air Operations, *The Air Force Law Review* (Maxwell Air Force Base, Alabama), Vol. 16 (1974), pp. 75–95.

HINZ, Joachim, Kriegsvölkerrecht: Bibliographie des deutschsprachigen Schriftums, *Revue de Droit pénal militaire et de Droit de la Guerre* (Bruxelles), Vol. II, No. 2 (1963), pp. 404–439; Vol. VII, No. 2 (1968), pp. 347–362; Vol. XII, No. 1 (1973), pp. 211–230; Vol. XIX, Nos. 1–2 (1980), pp. 131–153; Vol. XXII, Nos. 1–2 (1983), pp. 165–184.

LEGUY-FEILLEUX, J.R. The Law of War: A Bibliography 1945–1958, *World Polity* (Washington D.C.), Vol. 2 (1960), pp. 319–413.

SEVERIS, Micheline. Bibliographia de estudios de derecho internacional humanitario escritos en espagnol o portuges, *Revista Juridica de la Universidad de Puerto Rico* (Rio Piedras), Vol. 51, No. 2 (1982), pp. 321–374.

I. DOCUMENTARY SOURCES

1. *Collections and Compilations of Treaties and International Conventions*

DELTENRE, Marcel, *Recueil général des lois et coutumes de la guerre terrestre, maritime, sous-marine et aérienne, d'après les actes élaborés par les Conférences internationales depuis 1856.* Bruxelles: Wellens-Pay, 1943, lxxvi + 888 p.

FRIEDMAN, Leon (ed.), *The Law of War. A Documentary History.* New York: Random House, 1972, 2 vols., 1764 p.

HINZ, Joachim and RAUCH, Elmar, *Kriegsvölkerrecht: Völkerrechtliche Verträge über die Kriegsführung, die Kriegmittel und den Schutz der Verwundeten, Kriegsgefangenen und Zivilpersonen im Krieg.* Textsammlung mit Erläuterungen, Ubersichten und Stichwortverzeichnis. 3. neubearbeitete Aufl. Köln: C. Heymanns, 1984, x + 610 p.

International Red Cross Handbook. 12th ed. Geneva: International Committee of the Red Cross & League of Red Cross Societies in collaboration with the Henry Dunant Institute, 1983, 744 p.

LEVIE, Howard S. (ed.), *The Code of International Armed Conflict.* London – Rome – New York: Oceana Publications, 1986, 2 vols., 1100 p.

MECHELYNCK, Albert, *La Convention de La Haye concernant les lois et coutumes de la guerre sur terre d'après les actes et documents des conférences de Bruxelles et de La Haye de 1899 et 1907.* Gand: A. Hoste, 1915, 466 p.

SCHINDLER, Dietrich and TOMAN, Jiri (eds.), *The Laws of Armed Conflicts. A Collection of Conventions, Resolutions and Other Documents.* Dordrecht: M. Nijhoff, 1988, 1034 p.

SCOTT, James Brown, *The Hague Conventions and Declarations of 1899 and 1907.* 2nd ed. New York: Oxford University Press, 1915, 304 p.

SOLF, Waldemar A. and ROACH, J. Ashley (eds.), *Index of International Humanitarian Law.* Revised and Extended Edition of Jiri Toman's Index of the Geneva Conventions for the Protection of War Victims of 12 August 1949, by The Washington College of Law, The American University. Geneva: ICRC 1987, 284 p.

2. Preparatory Works of International Conferences

Actes de la Conférence de Bruxelles (1874). Bruxelles: Société Belge de Librairie, 1899, 400 p.

Actes de la Conférence diplomatique convoquée par le Conseil Fédéral Suisse pour la révision de la Convention du 6 juillet 1906 pour l'amélioration du sort des blessés et malades dans les armées en campagne et pour l'élaboration d'une Convention relative au traitement des prisonniers de guerre et réunie à Genève du 1 au 27 juillet 1929. Genève: CICR, 1930, viii + 772 p.

CARNEGIE ENDOWMENT FOR INTERNATIONAL PEACE, *The Geneva Convention of 1906 for the Amelioration of the Condition of Wounded in Armies in the Field.* Washington D.C., Carnegie Endowment for International Peace, 1916.

CARNEGIE ENDOWMENT FOR INTERNATIONAL PEACE, *The Proceedings of the Hague Peace Conferences.* Translation of the official texts. New York: Oxford University Press, 1920–1921, 5 vols.

CARNEGIE ENDOWMENT FOR INTERNATIONAL PEACE, *The Proceedings of The Hague Peace Conferences.* The Conferences of 1899 and 1907, index volume. New York: Carnegie Endowment for International Peace, 1921, 272 p.

CARNEGIE ENDOWMENT FOR INTERNATIONAL PEACE, *The Proceedings of The Hague Peace Conferences.* Translation of the official texts: the Conferences of 1899 and 1907, index volume. New York: UNIFO Publishers Ltd., 1975, xxiv + 272 p.

CARNEGIE ENDOWMENT FOR INTERNATIONAL PEACE, *Reports to The Hague Conferences of 1899 and 1907.* Oxford: Clarendon Press, 1917, xxxii + 940 p.

Commission of Jurists to consider and report upon the revision of the rules of warfare, The Hague, December 11th, 1922–February 19th, 1923. La Haye: Imprimerie Nationale, 1923, 302 p.

Compte rendu de la Conférence internationale réunie à Genève les 26, 27, 28 et 29 octobre 1863 pour étudier les moyens de pourvoir à l'insuffisance du service sanitaire dans les armées en campagne. Genève: Impr. J.G. Frick, 1863, 150 p.

Conférence internationale de la paix, La Haye, 18 mai–29 juillet 1899. La Haye: M. Nijhoff, 1907, 620 p.

CONFERENCE of government experts on the reaffirmation and development of international humanitarian law applicable in armed conflicts (Geneva, 24 May–12 June 1971): *Report of the work of the Conference.* Geneva: ICRC, 1971, 122 p.

CONFERENCE of government experts on the reaffirmation and development of international humanitarian law applicable in armed conflicts (Second session, 3 May–3 June 1972): *Report of the work of the Conference.* Geneva: ICRC, 1972, 2 vols.

DEUXIEME Conférence internationale de la Paix, La Haye, 15 juin–18 octobre 1907: *Actes et documents* (tome I: Séances plénières de la Conférence; tome II: Première commission; tome III: Deuxième, troisième et quatrième commissions). La Haye: Ministère des affaires étrangères, 1907, 3 vols.

Draft additional protocols to the Geneva Conventions of 12 August 1949: commentary. Geneva: ICRC, 1973, 176 p.

Final record of the Diplomatic Conference of Geneva of 1949. Bern: Federal Political Department, 1950, 4 vols.

INTERGOVERNMENTAL Conference on the protection of cultural property in the event of armed conflict, The Hague, 1954: *Records of the Conference.* The Hague: Staatsdrukkerij en -uitgeverijbedrijf, 1961, iv + 470 p.

INTERNATIONAL COMMITTEE OF THE RED CROSS, Conference of government experts on the use of certain conventional weapons (Lucerne, 24.9–18.10.1974): *Report.* Geneva: ICRC, 1975, 106 p.

INTERNATIONAL COMMITTEE OF THE RED CROSS, Conference of government experts on the use of certain conventional weapons (Second session, Lugano, 28.1–26.2.1976): *Report.* Geneva: ICRC, 1976, 232 p.

INTERNATIONAL COMMITTEE OF THE RED CROSS, Weapons that may cause unnecessary suffering or have indiscriminate effects: *Report on the work of experts.* Geneva: ICRC, 1973, 72 p.

Official records of the Diplomatic Conference on the reaffirmation and development of international humanitarian law applicable in armed conflicts – Geneva (1974–1977). Bern: Federal Political Department, 1978, 17 vols.

II. GENERAL WORKS AND ARTICLES

ABI-SAAB, Georges, Les guerres de libération nationale et la Conférence diplomatique sur le droit humanitaire, *Annales d'Etudes internationales* (Genève), Vol. 8 (1977), pp. 63–78.

ABI-SAAB, Georges, The implementation of humanitarian law, in: *The New Humanitarian Law of Armed Conflict*, ed. by Antonio Cassese. Napoli: Giuffré, 1979, pp. 310–346.

ABI-SAAB, Georges, Les mécanismes de mise en œuvre du droit humanitaire, *Revue générale de droit international public* (Paris), Vol. 82, No. 1 (1978), pp. 103–129.

ABI-SAAB, Georges, Wars of national liberation and the laws of war, *Annales d'Etudes internationales* (Genève), Vol. 3 (1972), pp. 93–117.

ABI-SAAB, Rosemary, *Droit humanitaire et conflits internes: origines et évolution de la réglementation internationale.* Genève: Institute Henry-Dunant & Paris: A. Pedone, 1986, 280 p.

ACTAS del Seminario sobre el derecho internacional humanitario, *Revista Juridica de la Universidad de Puerto Rico* (Rio Piedras), Vol. 5, Numero especial (1982), pp. 189–379.

ADACHI, Sumio, *Modern Law of War* [in Japanese]. Tokyo: Keiseisha Co. Ltd., 1979, xii + 190 p.

ALDRICH, George H., Progressive development of the laws of war: A reply to criticisms of the 1977 Geneva Protocol I, *Virginia Journal of International Law* (Charlottesville, Va.), Vol. 27 (1986), pp. 693–720.

ALMOND, Harry Havens, Human Rights in armed conflict: Interaction of foreign policy and law in world public order, in: *World in Transition*, ed. by Henry H. Han. Washington D.C.: University Press of America, 1979, pp. 21–40.

ARRASSEN, Mohamed, *Conduite des hostilités, droit des conflits armés et désarmement.* Bruxelles: Bruylant, 1986, 606 p.

AUBERT, Maurice, La répression des crimes de guerre dans le cadre des Conventions de Genève et du Protocole additionnel I et l'entraide judiciaire accordée par la Suisse, *Schweizerische Juristen-Zeitung / Revue Suisse de Jurisprudence* (Zürich), Vol. 79, No. 23 (1983), pp. 368–374.

BAILEY, Sydney D., *How Wars End: The United Nations and the Termination of Armed Conflicts, 1946–1964.* Oxford: Clarendon Press, 1982, 2 vols.

BAILEY, Sydney D., *Prohibitions and Restraints in War.* London: Oxford University Press, 1972, 194 p.

BAILEY, Sydney D., *War and Conscience in the Nuclear Age.* London: The Macmillan Press, 1987, 210 p.

BASSIOUNI, Cherif, Repression of breaches of the Geneva Conventions under the draft additional protocol to the Geneva Conventions of 12 August 1949, *Rutgers Camden Law Journal* (Lincoln), Vol. 8, No. 2 (1977), pp. 185–218.

BAXTER, Q., Human rights and humanitarian law, *The Australian Yearbook of International Law* (Canberra), Vol. 9 (1985), pp. 94–105.

BAXTER, Richard R., Conventional weapons under legal prohibitions, *International Security* (Cambridge, Mass.), Vol. 1 (1977), pp. 42–61.

BAXTER, Richard R., Humanitarian law or humanitarian politics?, *The Harvard International Law Journal* (Cambridge, Mass.), Vol. 16, No. 1 (1975), pp. 1–26.

BAXTER, Richard R., '*Jus in bello interno*': The present and future law, in: *Law and Civil War in the Modern World*, ed. by John Norton Moore. Baltimore: John Hopkins University Press, 1974, pp. 518–536.

BAXTER, Richard R., The law of war, in: *The Present State of International Law and Other Essays*, ed. by Maarten Bos. Deventer: Kluwer, 1973, pp. 107–124.

BAXTER, Richard R., Modernizing the law of war, *Military Law Review* (Charlottesville), Vol. 78 (1977), pp. 165–183.

BAXTER, Richard R., So-called 'unprivileged belligerency': Spies, guerillas and saboteurs, *British Yearbook of International Law* (London), Vol. 28 (1951), pp. 323–345.

BELLO, Emmanuel, *African Customary Humanitarian Law.* Geneva: Oyez Publishing Ltd. & ICRC, 1980, 158 p.

BEST, Geoffrey, Civilians in contemporary wars: A problem in ethics, law and fact, *Air University Review* (Alabama), Vol. 35, March–April 1984, pp. 29–40.

BEST, Geoffrey (ed.), *Humanity in Warfare: The Modern History of the International Law of Armed Conflicts*. London: Weidenfeld and Nicolson, 1980, xii + 400 p.

BIERZANEK, Remigiusz, Reprisals as a means of enforcing the laws of warfare: The old and the new law, in: *The New Humanitarian Law of Armed Conflict*, ed. by Antonio Cassese. Naples: Giuffré, 1979, pp. 232–257.

BIERZANEK, Remigiusz, Le statut juridique des partisans et des mouvements de résistances armés: Evolution historique et aspects actuels, in: *Mélanges offerts à Juraj Andrassy*, ed. by V. Ibler. La Haye: Nijhoff, 1968, pp. 54–77.

BIERZANEK, Remigiusz, Towards more respect for human rights in armed conflicts, *Studies on International Relations* (Warsaw), Vol. 1 (1973), pp. 75–121.

BINDSCHEDLER, Robert D. and CAFLISH, L., *Conference on Contemporary Problems of the Law of Armed Conflicts, Geneva, 15–20 September 1969*. New York: Carnegie Endowment for International Peace, 1971, 120 p.

BLISHCHENKO, Igor P., The national liberation movements and international humanitarian law, *Revue de Droit pénal militaire et de Droit de la Guerre* (Bruxelles), Vol. XII, No. 2 (1973), pp. 308–314.

BLISHCHENKO, Igor P., *Obychnoe oruzhie i mezhdunarodnoe pravo* [Conventional Weapons and International Law]. Moskva: Mezhdunarodnye otnosheniya, 1984, 216 p.

BLISHCHENKO, Igor P., Le mercenariat et le droit international, *Revue de droit contemporain* (Bruxelles), 1980, No. 2, pp. 45–63.

BOISSIER, Pierre, *From Solferino to Tsushima: History of the International Committee of the Red Cross*. Geneva: Henry Dunant Institute, 1985, 392 p.

BOND, James E., *The Rules of Riot: Internal Conflicts and the Law of War*. Princeton, N.J.: Princeton University Press, 1979, 280 p.

BOTHE, M., IPSEN, K. and PARTSCH, K.J., Die Genfer Konferenz über humanitares Völkerrecht, *Zeitschrift für ausländisches öffentliches Recht und Völkerrecht* (Stuttgart), Vol. 38, Nos. 1–2 (1978), pp. 1–159.

BOTHE, Michael, Conflits armés internes et droit international humanitaire, *Revue générale de droit international public* (Paris), Vol. 82, No. 1 (1978), pp. 82–102.

BOTHE, M., PARTSCH, K.J. and SOLF, W., *New Rules for Victims of Armed Conflicts: Commentary on the two 1977 Protocols additional to the Geneva Conventions of 1949*. The Hague: Nijhoff, 1982, 746 p.

CARNAHAN, Burrus M., The law of land mine warfare: Protocol II to the United Nations Convention on Certain Conventional Weapons, *Military Law Review* (Charlottesville), Vol. 105, pp. 73–95.

CARNAHAN, Burrus M., The law of air bombardment in its historical context, *The Air Force Law Review* (Alabama), Vol. 17, No. 2 (1975), pp. 39–60.

CARNEGIE ENDOWMENT FOR INTERNATIONAL PEACE, *Chemical Weapons and Chemical Arms Control*. New York: Carnegie Endowment, 1978, xiv + 128 p.

CASSESE, Antonio, The Geneva Protocols of 1977 on the humanitarian law of armed conflict and customary international law, *UCLA Pacific Basin Law Journal* (Los Angeles), Vol. 3, Nos. 1–2 (1984), pp. 55–118.

CASSESE, Antonio, Mercenaries: Lawful combatants or war criminals?, *Zeitschrift für ausländisches öffentliches Recht und Völkerrecht* (Stuttgart), Vol. 40, No. 1 (1980), pp. 1–30.

CASSESE, Antonio (ed.), *The New Humanitarian Law of Armed Conflict*. Napoli: Ed. Giuffré, 1979, xxiv + 502 p.

CASTREN, Erik, *The Present Law of War and Neutrality*. Helsinki: Suomalaisen kirjallisuuden seuran kirjapainan oy, Tome 85, Ser.B, 1954, 630 p.

DAVID, Eric, *Mercenaires et volontaires internationaux en droit des gens*. Bruxelles: Centre de droit international de l'Institut de sociologie, 1978, vi + 460 p.

DEBBASCH, Odile, *L'occupation militaire: Pouvoirs reconnus aux forces armées hors de leur territoire national*. Paris: Librairie générale de droit et de jurisprudence, 1962, 424 p.

DIALLO, Yolande, African traditions and humanitarian law, *International Review of the Red Cross* (Geneva), Vol. 16 (1976), pp. 387–401.

DIALLO, Yolande, Humanitarian law and traditional African law, *International Review of the Red Cross* (Geneva), Vol. 16 (1976), pp. 57–63.

DINSTEIN, Yoram, *The Defence of Obedience to Superior Order in International Law*. Leyden: A.W. Sijthoff, 1965, 278 p.

DINSTEIN, Yoram, The laws of war in the air, *Israel Yearbook on Human Rights* (Tel Aviv), Vol. 11 (1981), pp. 41–64.

DINSTEIN, Yoram, The laws of war at sea, *Israel Yearbook on Human Rights* (Tel Aviv), Vol. 10 (1980), pp. 38–69.

DJUROVIC, Gradimir, *The Central Tracing Agency of the International Committee of the Red Cross: Activities of the ICRC for the Alleviation of the Mental Suffering of War Victims*. Geneva: Henry Dunant Institute, 1986, 260 p.

DOMINICE, Christian, La mise en œuvre du droit humanitaire, in: *The International Dimensions of Human Rights*, ed. by Karel Wasak. Westport: Greenwood Press & Paris: Unesco, 1982, pp. 422–447.

DRAPER, G.I.A.D., The ethical and juridical status of constraints in war, *Military Law Review* (Charlottesville), Vol. 55 (1972), pp. 169–185.

DRAPER, G.I.A.D., The Geneva Conventions of 1949, *Recueil des Cours de l'Académie de droit international de La Haye* (La Haye), Vol. 114 (1965), pp. 63–162.

DRAPER, G.I.A.D., Implementation and enforcement of the Geneva Conventions and of the two Additional Protocols of 1977, *Recueil des Cours de l'Académie de droit international* (La Haye), Vol. 164, No. 3 (1979), pp. 1–54.

DRAPER, G.I.A.D., The modern pattern of war criminality, *Israel Yearbook on Human Rights* (Tel Aviv), Vol. 6 (1976), pp. 9–48.

DRAPER, G.I.A.D., *The Red Cross Conventions: Commentary and Texts*. London: Stevens, 1958, x + 228 p.

DRAPER, G.I.A.D., The status of combatants and the question of guerilla warfare, *British Yearbook of Internatinal Law* (London), Vol. 45 (1971), pp. 173–218.

DUFOUR, A., HAGGENMACHER, P. and TOMAN, J., *Grotius et l'ordre juridique international: Travaux du Colloque Hugo Grotius, Genève, 10–11 novembre 1983*. Lausanne: Payot, 1985, 156 p.

DUNANT, Henry, *A Memory of Solferino*. Geneva: ICRC, 1986, 148 p. (Originally in French, *Un Souvenir de Solférino*, 1862; Translations a.o. in Arabic, Dutch, Esperanto, German, Italian, Portuguese, Russian, and Spanish.)

DURAND, André, *From Sarajevo to Hiroshima. History of the International Committee of the Red Cross*. Geneva: Henry Dunant Institute, 1984, 676 p.

EIDE, Asbjörn, The new humanitarian law in non-international armed conflict, in: *The New Humanitarian Law of Armed Conflict*, ed. by Antonio Cassese. Napoli: Giuffré, 1979, pp. 277–309.

ELIAS, T.O., Development of international humanitarian law, in: *New Horizons in International Law*, ed. by T.O. Elias. Alphen: Sijthoff & Noordhoff, 1979, pp. 181–197.

EUSTATHIADES, Constantin T., La protection des biens culturels en cas de conflit armé et la convention de La Haye du 14 mai 1954, in: *Etudes de droit international*. Athènes: Ed. Klissiounis, 1959, Tome 3, pp. 393–524.

FALK, R.A., KOLKO, G. and LIFTON, R.J., *Crimes of War*. A legal, political, documentary and psychological inquiry into the responsibility of leaders, citizens and soldiers for criminal acts in wars. New York, 1971, 590 p.

FARER, Tom J., The humanitarian laws of war in civil strife: Towards a definition of 'international armed conflicts', *Revue belge de droit international* (Bruxelles), Vol. 7, No. 1 (1971), pp. 20–55.

FERNANDEZ-FLORES, José-Luis, *Del derecho de la guerra*. Madrid: Ediciones Ejercito, 1982, 562 p.

FORSYTHE, David P., *Humanitarian Politics: The International Committee of the Red Cross*. Baltimore – London: Johns Hopkins University Press, 1977, xiv + 298 p.

FREYMOND, Jacques, Confronting total war: 'Global' humanitarian policy, *American Journal of International Law* (Washington D.C.), Vol. 67, No. 4 (1973), pp. 672–692.

FREYMOND, Jacques, *Guerres, révolutions, Croix-Rouge: Réflexions sur le rôle du Comité international de la Croix-Rouge*. Genève: Institut universitaire des hautes études internationales, 1976, 222 p.

GASSER, Hans-Peter, A measure of humanity in internal disturbances and tensions: proposal for a Code of Conduct, *International Review of the Red Cross* (Geneva), No. 262 (1988), pp. 38–58.

GASSER, Hans-Peter, Some reflections on the future of international humanitarian law, *International Review of the Red Cross* (Geneva), No. 238 (1984) pp. 18–25.

Geneva Conventions of 12 August 1949: Commentary published under the general editorship of Jean S. Pictet. Vol. I: Geneva Convention for the Amelioration of the Condition of the Wounded and Sick in Armed Forces in the Field; Vol. II: Geneva Convention for the Amelioration of the Condition of the Wounded, Sick and Shipwrecked members of Armed Forces at Sea; Vol. III: Geneva Convention relative to the Treatment of Prisoners of War; Vol. IV: Geneva Convention relative to the Protection of Civilian Persons in Time of War. Geneva: ICRC, 1952–1960. (Published also in French)

GOLDBLAD, J., The laws of armed conflict: An overview of the restrictions and limitations on the methods and means of warfare, *Bulletin of Peace Proposals* (Oslo), 1982, pp. 127–134.

GREEN, Leslie, Aerial considerations in the law of armed conflict, *Annals of Air and Space Law* (Toronto), Vol. 5 (1980), pp. 89–117.

GREEN, Leslie, *Superior Orders in National and International Law*. Leyden: A.W. Sijthoff, 1976, 374 p.

GREENWOOD, Christopher, The concept of war in modern international law, *International Comparative Law Quaterly* (London), Vol. 36, No. 2 (1987), pp. 283–306.

GREENWOOD, Christopher, The relationship between *ius ad bellum* and *ius in bello*, *Review of International Studies* (Borough Green, Sevenoaks, Kent), 1983, No. 4, pp. 221–234.

GREIG, D.W. (ed.), A Collection of papers on the Protection of the Human Being in Armed Conflicts, *Australian Yearbook of International Law* (Canberra), Vol. 9 (1985), 400 p.

GREIG, D.W., The underlying principles of international humanitarian law, *The Australian Yearbook of International Law* (Canberra), Vol. 9 (1985), pp. 46–85.

GUERLT, Louis, *Zur Geschichte der internationalen und freiwilligen Krankenpflege im Kriege*. Leipzig: F.C.W. Vogel, 1873, 866 p.

HERCZEGH, Géza, *The Development of International Humanitarian Law*. Budapest: Akadémiai Kiado, 1984, 240 p.

HIEBEL, Jean-Luc, *Assistance spirituelle et conflits armés*. Genève: Institut Henry-Dunant, 1980, 462 p.

HIGGINS, Alexander Pearce, *The Hague Peace Conferences and Other International Conferences concerning the L.ws and Usages of War: Texts of Conventions with Commentaries*. Cambrdige (Mass.): The Cambridge University Press, 1909, 632 p.

HIGGINS, Rosalyn, Internal war and international law, in: *The Future of the International Legal Order*, ed. by Rosalyn Higgins. Princeton, 1971, Vol. 3, pp. 81–121.

HINGORANI, Rupchandre C., *Prisoners of War*. 2nd ed. Dobbs Ferry (N.Y.): Oceana Publications, Inc., 1982, xviii + 316 p.

HOSOYA, C. (ed.), *The Tokyo War Crime Trial: An International Symposium*. Tokyo: Kodansha, 1986, 226 p.

INTERNATIONAL INSTITUTE FOR PEACE AND CONFLICT RESEARCH, *The Problem of Chemical and Biological Warfare*. New York: Humanities Press, 1971, 5 vols.

INTERNATIONAL MILITARY TRIBUNAL, *Trial of Major War Criminals before the International Military Tribunal, Nuremberg, 14 November 1945 – 1 October 1946*. Nuremberg: 1947–1949, 42 vols.

International humanitarian law and the law of armed conflict: Its relevance to the nuclear challenge, in: *Lawyers and the Nuclear Debate: Proceedings of the Canadian Conference on Nuclear Weapons and the Law*, ed. by Maxwell Cohen and Margaret E. Gouin. Ottawa: University of Ottawa Press, 1988, pp. 81–131.

JAKOVLJEVIC, Bosko, *New International Status of Civil Defence*. The Hague: M. Nijhoff & Geneva: Henry Dunant Institute, 1982, 142 p.

JOHNSON, James Turner, *Just War Tradition and the Restraint of War: A Moral and Historical Inquiry*. Princeton (N.J.): Princeton University Press, 1981, 380 p.

KALSHOVEN, Frits, Applicability of customary international law in non-international armed conflicts, in: *Current Problems of International Law: Essays on U.N. Law and the Law of Armed Conflict*, ed. by Antonio Cassese. Milano: Giuffré, 1975, pp. 267–285.

KALSHOVEN, Frits, *Belligerent Reprisals*. Leyden: A.W. Sijthoff & Geneva: Henry Dunant Institute, 1971, 390 p.

KALSHOVEN, Frits, *Constraints on the Waging of War*. Geneva: ICRC, 1987, 176 p.

KALSHOVEN, Frits, The position of guerilla fighters under the law of war, *Revue de Droit pénal militaire et de Droit de la Guerre* (Bruxelles), Vol. XI, No. 1 (1972), pp. 55–91.

KUNZ, Josef L., The chaotic status of the laws of war and the urgent necessity for their revision, *American Journal of International Law* (Washington D.C.), Vol. 14, No. 1 (1961), pp. 37–61.

KUSSBACH, Erich, Le développement du statut des combattants et le droit international humanitaire, *Revue de Droit pénal militaire et de Droit de la Guerre* (Bruxelles), Vol. XXII, No. 3–4 (1983), pp. 377–418.

KUSSBACH, Erich, Protocol I and neutral States, *International Review of the Red Cross* (Geneva), No. 218 (1980), pp. 231–249.

LACHS, Manfred, Responsibility for the development of humanitarian law, in: *Studies and Essays on International Humanitarian Law and Red Cross Principles in Honour of Jean Pictet*. Geneva: ICRC & The Hague: M. Nijhoff, 1984, pp. 395–400.

LEVIE, Howard S., *Document on Prisoners of War*. Newport (Rhode Island): US Naval War College, 1979, xxviii + 854 p. (International Law Studies, Vol. 60)

LEVIE, Howard S., Humanitarian restrictions on chemiocal and biological weapons, *University of Toledo Law Review* (Toledo), Vol. 13, No. 4 (1982), pp. 1192–1202.

LEVIE, Howard S., *The Law of Non-International Armed Conflict: Protocol II to the 1949 Geneva Conventions.* Dordrecht: M. Nijhoff, 1987, 636 p.

LEVIE, Howard S., *Prisoners of War in International Armed Conflict.* Newport (Rhode Island): US Naval War College, 1978, lxx + 530 p. (International Law Studies, Vol. 59)

LEWIS, John R., *Uncertain Judgement: A Bibliography of War Crimes Trials.* Santa Barbara (Calif.), ABC-Clio, 1979, xxxiv + 240 p.

LUARD, Evan (ed.), *The International Regulation of Civil Wars.* London: Thames and Hudson, 1972, 240 p.

MALLISON, W.T. and JABRI, R.A., The juridical characteristics of belligerent occupation and the resort to resistance by the civilian population: Doctrinal developments and continuity, *The George Washington Law Review* (Washington D.C.), Vol. 42, No. 2 (1974), pp. 185–221.

MALLISON, W.T. and MALLISON, S.V., The juridical status of irregular combatants under the international humanitarian law of armed conflict, *Case Western Reserve Journal of International Law* (Cleveland), Vol. 9, No. 1 (1977), pp. 38–78.

MALLISON, W.T. and MALLISON, S.V., The juridical status of privileged combatants under the Geneva Protocol of 1977 concerning international conflicts, *Law and Contemporary Problems* (Durham), Vol. 42, No. 2 (1978), pp. 4–35.

MARKS, Stephen P., Principles and norms of human rights applicable in emergency situations: Underdevelopment, catastrophes and armed conflicts, in: *The International Dimensions of Human Rights*, ed. by Karel Vasak. Paris: Unesco, 1982, Vol. 1, pp. 175–212.

McDOUGAL, Myres S. and FELICIANO, Florentiono P., *Law and Minimum World Public Order: The Legal Regulation of International Coercion.* New Haven – London: Yale University Press, 1961, xxvi + 872 p.

MELANDER, Göran, International humanitarian law and human rights, *Scandinavian Studies in Law* (Stockholm), Vol. 29 (1985), pp. 137–148.

MENCER, Gejza, *Mezinarodni humanitarni pravo* [International humanitarian law]. Praha: Academia, 1980, 280 p.

MERON, Theodor, Draft Model Declaration on Internal Strife, *International Review of the Red Cross* (Geneva), No. 262 (1988), pp. 59–76.

MERON, Theodor, The Geneva Conventions as customary law, *American Journal of International Law* (Washington D.C.), Vol. 81, No. 2 (1987), pp. 348–370.

MERON, Theodor, *Human Rights in Internal Strife: Their International Protection.* Cambridge: Grotius Publications Ltd., 1987, 172 p.

MERON, Theodor, On the inadequate reach of humanitarian and human rights law and the need for a new instrument, *American Journal of International Law* (Washington D.C.), Vol. 77, No. 3 (1983), pp. 589–606.

MERTENS, Pierre, *L'imprescriptibilité des crimes de guerre et contre l'humanité: Etude de droit international et de droit pénal comparé.* Bruxelles: Editions de l'Université de Bruxelles, 1974, 230 p.

MIYAZAKI, Shigeki, The application of the new humanitarian law, *International Review of the Red Cross* (Geneva), Vol. 20 (1980), pp. 184–192.

Modern Wars: The Humanitarian Challenge. A report for the Independent Commission on International Humanitarian Issues. London: Zed Books, 1986, 196 p.

MOORE, John Norton, *Law and Civil War in the Modern World*. Baltimore: The John Hopkins University Press, 1974, 648 p.

MOREILLON, Jacques, *Le Comité international de la Croix-Rouge et la protection des détenus politiques*. Lausanne: L'Age d'homme, 1973, 304 p.

MULINEN, Frederic de, *Handbook on the Law of War for Armed Forces*. Geneva: ICRC, 1987, 232 p.

MURPHY, Thomas J., Sanctions and enforcement of the humanitarian law of the four Geneva Conventions of 1949 and Geneva Protocol I of 1977, *Military Law Review* (Charlottesville), Vol. 103 (1984), pp. 3–77.

NAHLIK, Stanisław E., Belligerent reprisals as seen in the light of the diplomatic conference on humanitarian law, Geneva, 1974–1977, *Law and Contemporary Problems* (Durham), Vol. 42, No. 2, pp. 36–66.

NAHLIK, Stanisław E., A brief outline of international humanitarian law, *International Review of the Red Cross* (Geneva), July–August 1984, pp. 3–48.

NAHLIK, Stanisław E., La protection internationale des biens culturels en cas de conflit armé, *Recueil des Cours de l'Académie de droit international* (La Haye), Vol. 120, No. 1 (1967), pp. 61–163.

NWOGUGU, I.E., Recent developments in the law relating to mercenaries, *Revue de Droit pénal militaire et de Droit de la Guerre* (Bruxelles), Vol. XX, No. 1–2 (1981), pp. 9–34.

PARKS, Hays W., Conventional aerial bombing and the law of war, in: *US Naval Institute Proceedings* (Annapolis), Vol. 108, No. 951 (1982), pp. 98–117.

PARKS, William Hays, The law of war advisor, *Revue de Droit pénal militaire et de Droit de la Guerre* (Bruxelles), Vol. XVIII, No. 4 (1979), pp. 357–417.

PARTSCH, Karl Josef, Humanitarian law and armed conflict, in: *Encyclopedia of Public International Law*, ed. by Rudolf Bernhardt. Amsterdam: North-Holland Publishing Company, 1985, Vol. 3, pp. 215–219.

PICTET, Jean, *Le Comité international de la Croix-Rouge: Une institution unique en son genre*. Paris: A. Pedone & Genève: Institut Henry-Dunant, 1985, 110 p.

PICTET, Jean, *Development and Principles of International Humanitarian Law*. Dordrecht: M. Nijhoff & Geneva: Henry Dunant Institute, 1985, 100 p.

PICTET, Jean, The formation of international humanitarian law, *International Review of the Red Cross* (Geneva), No. 244 (1985), pp. 3–24.

PICTET, Jean, *The Fundamental Principles of the Red Cross: Commentary*. Geneva: Henry Dunant Institute, 1979, 94 p.

PICTET, Jean, *Humanitarian Law and the Protection of War Victims*. Geneva: Henry Dunant Institute, 1986, 104 p.

PICTET, Jean, *The Principles of International Humanitarian Law*. Geneva: ICRC, 1967, 62 p.

POLTORAK, A.I., Vojna i mirnoe naselenie [War and civilian population], *Trudy voenno - yuridicheskoi akademii* (Moskva), 1950, No. 11, pp. 84–138.

POLTORAK, A.I. and SAVINSKII, L.I., *Vooruzhennye konflikty i mezhdunarodnoe pravo* [Armed Conflicts and International Law]. Moskva: Nauka, 1976, 416 p.

PREUX, Jean de, The Geneva Conventions and Reciprocity, *International Review of the Red Cross* (Geneva), No. 244 (1985), pp. 25–29.

RAMCHARAN, B.G., The role of international bodies in the implementation and enforcement of humanitarian law and human rights law in non-international armed conflicts, *American University Law Review* (Washington D.C.), Vol. 33, No. 1 (1983), pp. 99–115.

RAUCH, Elmar, Le droit contemporain de la guerre maritime: Quelques problèmes créés par le Protocole additionnal de 1977, *Revue général de droit international public* (Paris), Vol. 89, No. 4 (1985), pp. 958–976.

RAUCH, Elmar, L'emploi d'armes nucléaires et la réaffirmation et le développement du droit international humanitaire applicable dans les conflits armés, *Revue hellénique de droit international* (Athènes), Vol. 33, No. 1–4 (1980), pp. 53–110.

RAUCH, Elmar, The protection of the civilian population in international armed conflict and the use of landmines, *German Yearbook of International Law* (Göttingen), Vol. 24 (1981), pp. 262–287.

RAUCH, Elmar, *The Protocol Additional to the Geneva Conventions for the protection of victims of international armed conflicts and the United Nations Convention on the law of the sea: Repercussions on the law of naval warfare.* Berlin: Duncker and Humblot, 1984, 166 p.

Report of the International Committee of the Red Cross on its Activities during the Second World War. Vol. I: General activities; Vol. II: The Central Agency for Prisoners of War; Vol. III: Relief activities. Geneva: ICRC, 1948.

ROACH, J. Ashley, Certain conventional weapons conventions: Arms control or humanitarian law?, *Military Law Review* (Charlottesville), Vol. 105 (1984), pp. 3–72.

ROBERTS, Adam, What is military occupation?, *British Yearbook of International Law* (London), Vol. 55 (1984), pp. 249–305.

ROLING, V.A., Aspects of criminal responsibility for violations of the laws of war, in: *The New Humanitarian Law of Armed Conflict*, ed. by Antonio Cassese. Napoli: Giuffré, 1979, pp. 199–231.

ROLING, V.A., Criminal responsibility for violations of the laws of war, *Revue belge de droit international* (Bruxelles), Vol. 22 (1976), pp. 8–26.

ROSAS, Allan, International law and the use of nuclear weapons, in: *Essays in Honour of Eric Castren.* Helsinki: Finnish Branch of the International Law Association, 1979, pp. 73–95.

ROSAS, Allan, *The Legal Status of Prisoners of War: A Study in International Humanitarian Law applicable in Armed Conflicts.* Helsinki: Suomalainen Tiedeakatemia, 1976, 524 p.

ROSENBLAD, Esbjörn, *International Humanitarian Law of Armed Conflicts: Some Aspects of the Principle of Distinction and Related Problems.* Geneva: Henry Dunant Institute, 1979, 200 p.

ROUSSEAU, Charles, *Le droit des conflits armés.* Paris: A. Pedone, 1983, 630 p.

SIPRI, *Anti-personnel Weapons.* London: Taylor and Francis Ltd., 1978, 200 p.

SIPRI, *Incendiary Weapons.* Stockholm: Almqvist and Wiksell, 1975, 256 p.

SIPRI, *The Law of War and Dubious Weapons.* Stockholm: Almqvist and Wiksell, 1976, viii + 78 p.

SIPRI, *The Problem of Chemical and Biological Warfare.* A study of the historical, technical, military, legal and political aspects of chemical and biological warfare, and possible disarmament measures. Stockholm: Almqvist and Wiksell, 1971–1975, 6 vols.

SANDOZ, Yves, The application of humanitarian law by the armed forces of the United Nations Organization, *International Review of the Red Cross* (Geneva), Vol. 60 (1978), pp. 274–284.

SANDOZ, Yves, *Des armes interdites en droit de la guerre.* Genève: Impr. Grounauer, 1975, 138 p.

SANDOZ, Yves, Penal aspects of international humanitarian law, in: *International Criminal Law: Crimes*, ed. Cherif Bassiouni. Dobbs Ferry (N.Y.): Transnational Publ., 1986, Vol. 1, pp. 209–232.

SANDOZ, Yves, *Prohibitions or Restrictions on the Use of Certain Conventional Weapons*. Geneva: ICRC, 1981, 34 p.

SAUSSURE, Hamilton de, Belligerent air operations and the 1977 Geneva Protocol I, *Annals of Air and Space Law* (Toronto), Vol. 4 (1979), pp. 459–481.

SAUSSURE, Hamilton de, Recent developments in the law of air warfare, *Annals of Air and Space Law* (Toronto), Vol. 1 (1976), pp. 33–47.

SCHINDLER, Dietrich, The different types of armed conflicts according to the Geneva Conventions and Protocols, *Recueil des Cours de l'Académie de droit international* (La Haye), Vol. 163, No. 2 (1979), pp. 117–164.

SCHINDLER, Dietrich, State of war, belligerency, armed conflict, in: *The New Humanitarian Law of Armed Conflict*, ed. by Antonio Cassese. Napoli: Giuffré, 1979, pp. 3–20.

SCHWARZENBERGER, Georg, *International Law as Applied by International Courts and Tribunals*. Vol. 2: *The Law of Armed Conflict*. London: Stevens, 1968, 882 p.

SCHWARZENBERGER, Georg, *The Legality of Nuclear Weapons*. London: Stevens and Sons, 70 p.

SCOTT, James Brown, *The Hague Peace Conferences of 1899 and 1907*. Baltimore: Johns Hopkins Press, 1909, 2 vols.

SHIELDS-DELESSERT, Christiane, *Release and Repatriation of Prisoners of War at the End of Active Hostilities*. A study of Article 118, paragraph 1, of the Third Geneva Convention relative to the treatment of prisoners of war. Zürich: Schulthess Polygraphischer Verlag, 1977, 226 p.

SOLF Waldemar A. and GRANDISON W.G., International humanitarian law applicable in armed conflict, *The Journal of International Law and Economics* (Washington D.C.), Vol. 10, pp. 567–598.

SOLF Waldemar A., Protection of Civilians against the effects of hostilities under customary international law and under Protocol I, *The American University Journal of International Law and Policy*, (Washington D.C.), Vol. I, pp. 117–135.

SOLF Waldemar A. and CUMMINGS E.R., A survey of penal sanctions under Protocol I to the Geneva Conventions of August 12, 1949, *Case Western Reserve Journal of International Law* (Cleveland), Vol. 9, No. 2, pp. 205–251.

SORIANO, Samuel, International humanitarian law applicable in armed conflicts, *Philippine Yearbook of International Law* (Manila), Vol. 9 (1983), pp. 83–102.

SUTER, Keith, *An International Law of Guerilla Warfare: The Global Politics of Lawmaking*. London: Frances Pinter, 1984. 192 p.

SWINIARSKI, Christophe (ed.), *Studies and Essays on International Humanitarian Law and Red Cross Principles in Honour of Jean Pictet*. Geneva: ICRC & The Hague: M. Nijhoff, 1984, 1144 p.

TAKEMOTO, Masayuki, The enquiry procedure under international humanitarian law, *University Review of Law and Politics* (Kansai, Osaka), 1980, No. 1, pp. 21–46.

TAKEMOTO, Masayuki, The scrutiny system under international humanitarian law: An analysis of recent attempts to reinforce the role of protecting powers in armed conflicts, *The Japanese Annual International Law* (Tokyo), Vol. 19 (1975), pp. 1–23.

Traditional Asian approaches to the protection of victims of armed conflict and their relationship to modern international humanitarian law. The Chinese view, by Zhu Li Sun; A Japanese view, by S. Adachi; An Indian view, by L. Penna; A Malaysian view, by A. Ibrahim; An overview, by M. Sornarajah, *The Australian Yearbook of International Law* (Canberra), Vol. 9 (1985), pp. 143–246.

TUCKER, Robert W., *The Law of War and Neutrality at Sea*. Washington D.C.: US Government Printing Office, 1957, 448 p.

TUNKIN, G.I., Nyurnberskie printsipy i sovremennoe mezhudunarodnoe pravo [Nuremberg principles and contemporary international law], *Sovetskii ezhegodnik mezhdunarodnogo prava* (Moskva), 1979, pp. 97–107.

UNITED NATIONS, General Assembly, *Comprehensive study on nuclear weapons*. United Nations document A/35/392, 178 p. New York: Reports of the Secretary-General, 1980.

UNITED NATIONS, General Assembly, *Incendiary and other specific conventional weapons which may be the subject of prohibitions or restrictions of use for humanitarian reasons*. United Nations documents A/31/146, 22 p.; A/32/124, 4 p. New York: Reports of the Secretary-General, 1976–1977.

UNITED NATIONS, General Assembly, *Napalm and other incendiary weapons and all aspects of their possible use*. United Nations documents A/8803/Rev.1, 70 p.; A/9207, 24 p. New York: Reports of the Secretary-General, 1973.

UNITED NATIONS, General Assembly, *Respect for human rights in armed conflicts: Existing rules of international law concerning the prohibition or restriction of use of specific weapons*. United Nations document A/9215. New York: Survey prepared by the Secretariat, 1973, 2 vols.

VASAK, Karel, *The International Dimensions of Human Rights*. Paris: Unesco & Westport: Greenwood Press, 1982, 2 vols., 756 p.

VERZIJL, J.H.W., *International Law in Historical Perspective*. Part IX-A: *The Laws of War*. Alphen aan den Rijn: Sijthoff and Noordhoff, 1978, 548 p.

VEUTHEY, Michel, *Guérilla et droit humanitaire*. Genève: CICR, 1983, 452 p.

WILSON, Heather A., Humanitarian protection in wars of national liberation, *Arms Control* (London), Vol. 8 (1987), pp. 36–48.

ZYS, Danuta, *Practical Guide on Dissemination for National Societies*. Geneva: Henry Dunant Institute, 1983.

INDEX